Hakumei & Mikochi 1
Tiny Little Life in the Woods

Takuto Kashiki

Contents

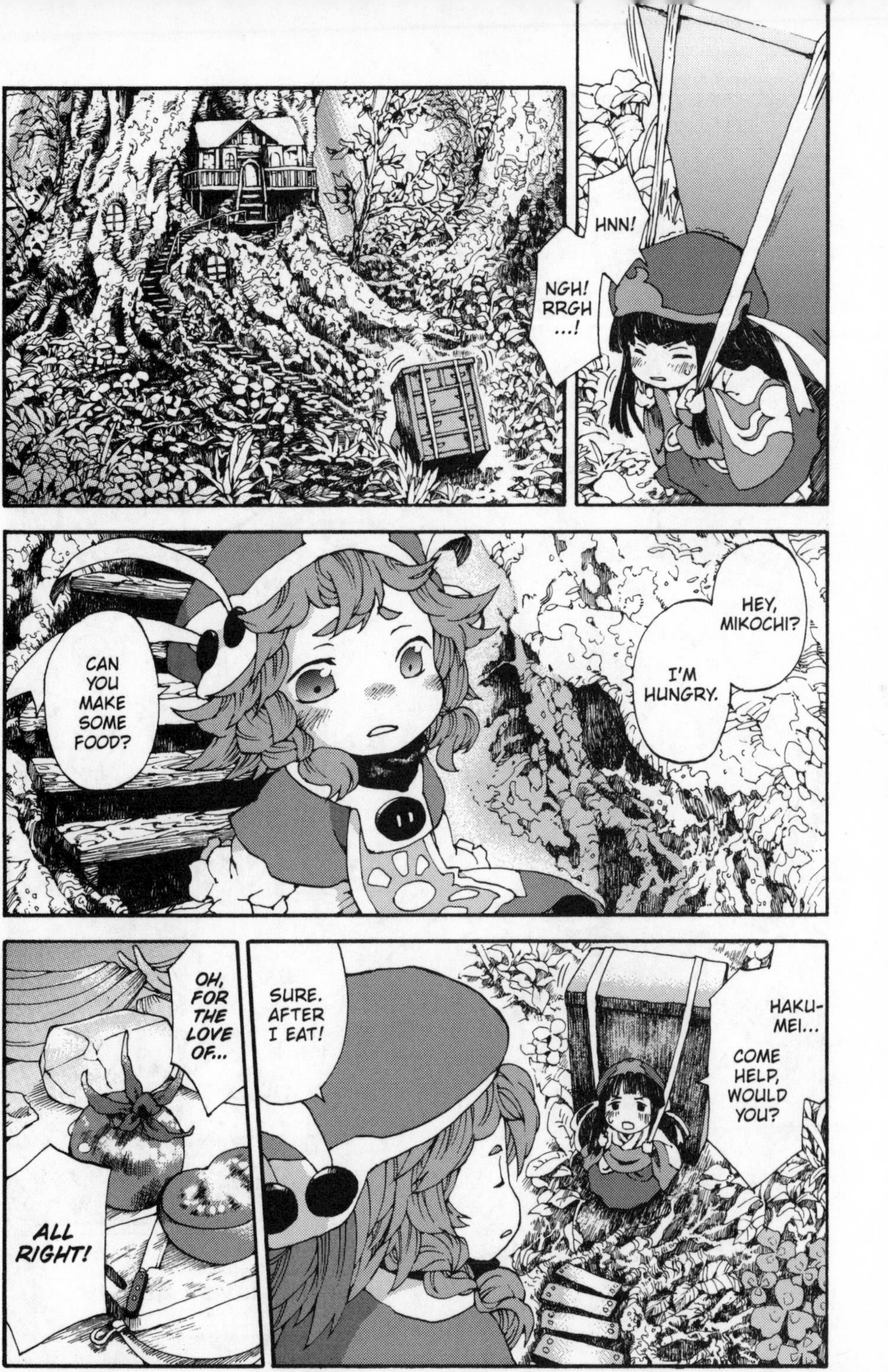
HNN!
NGH! RRGH ...!
HEY, MIKOCHI?
I'M HUNGRY.
CAN YOU MAKE SOME FOOD?
HAKU-MEI...
COME HELP, WOULD YOU?
SURE. AFTER I EAT!
OH, FOR THE LOVE OF...
ALL RIGHT!

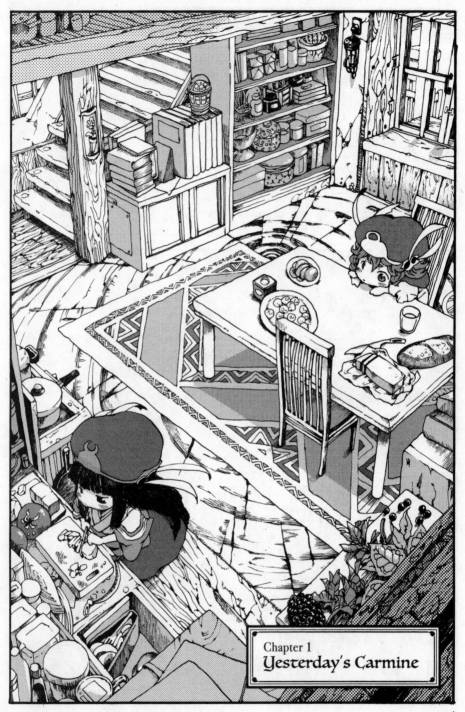

Chapter 1
Yesterday's Carmine

6

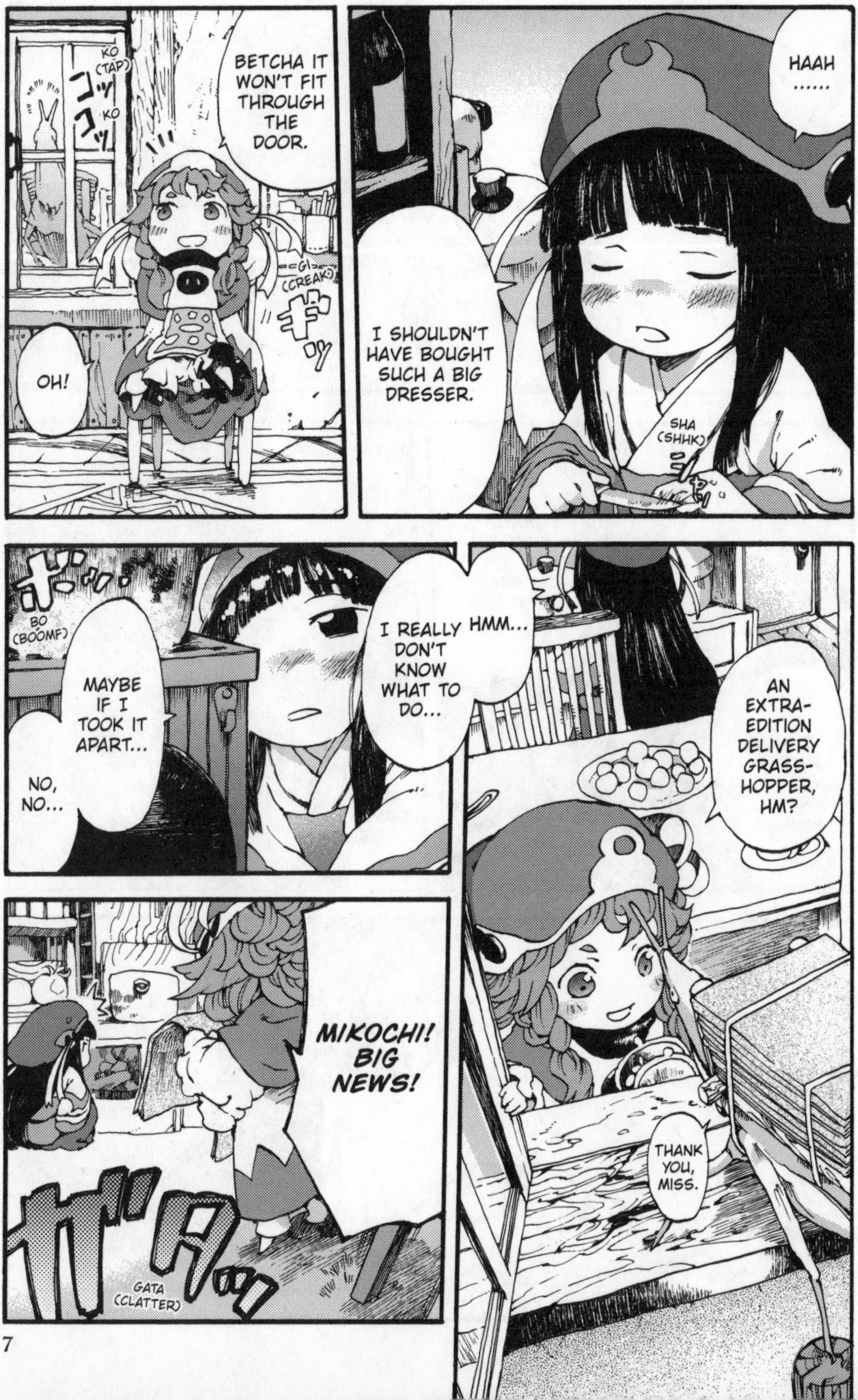
HAAH ......
I SHOULDN'T HAVE BOUGHT SUCH A BIG DRESSER.
SHA (SHHK)
KO (TAP) KO
BETCHA IT WON'T FIT THROUGH THE DOOR.
GI (CREAK)
OH!
BO (BOOMF)
MAYBE IF I TOOK IT APART...
NO, NO...
I REALLY DON'T KNOW WHAT TO DO...
HMM...
AN EXTRA-EDITION DELIVERY GRASS-HOPPER, HM?
THANK YOU, MISS.
MIKOCHI! BIG NEWS!
GATA (CLATTER)

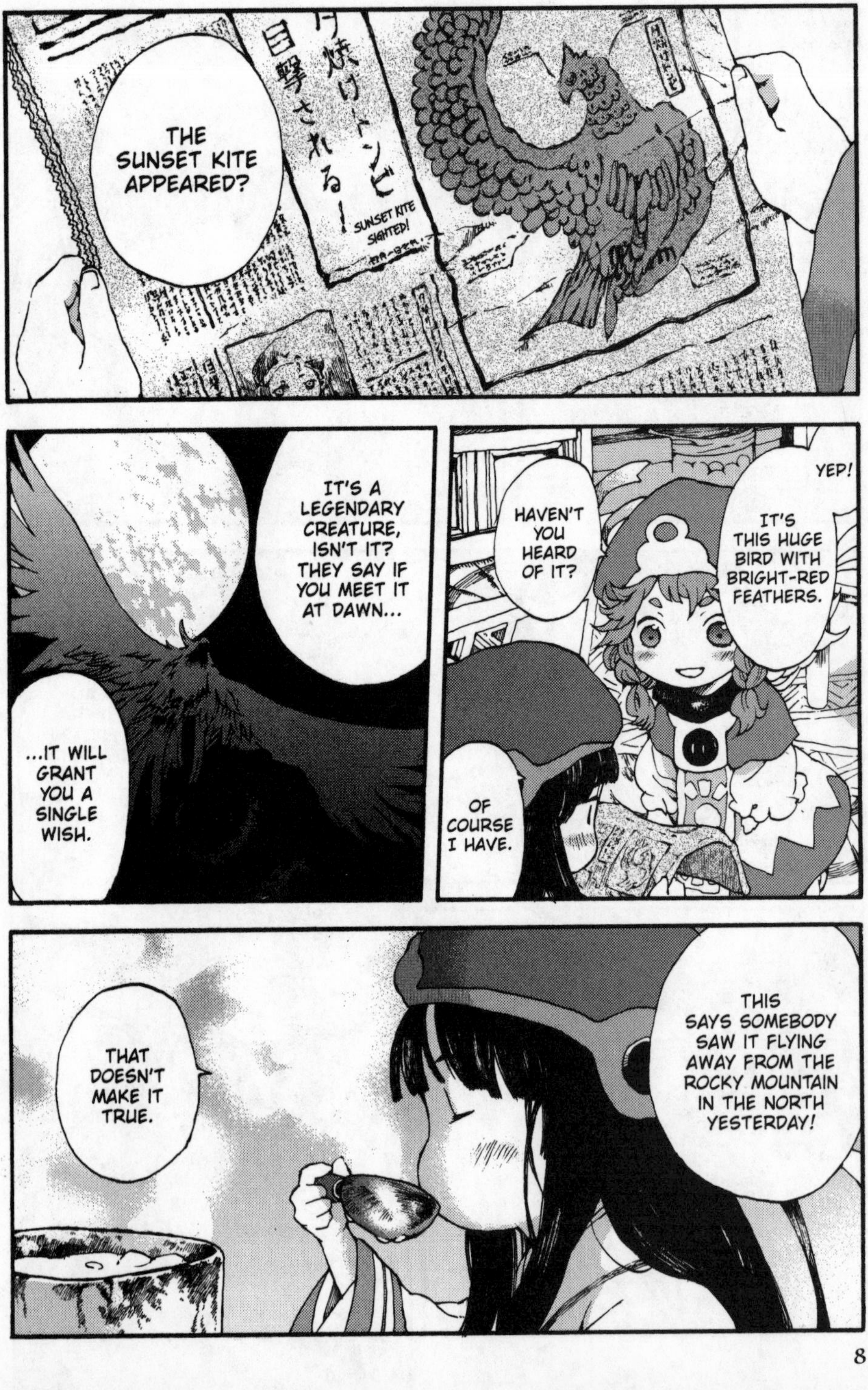
THE SUNSET KITE APPEARED?
SUNSET KITE SIGHTED!
YEP!
IT'S THIS HUGE BIRD WITH BRIGHT-RED FEATHERS.
HAVEN'T YOU HEARD OF IT?
OF COURSE I HAVE.
IT'S A LEGENDARY CREATURE, ISN'T IT? THEY SAY IF YOU MEET IT AT DAWN...
...IT WILL GRANT YOU A SINGLE WISH.
THIS SAYS SOMEBODY SAW IT FLYING AWAY FROM THE ROCKY MOUNTAIN IN THE NORTH YESTERDAY!
THAT DOESN'T MAKE IT TRUE.

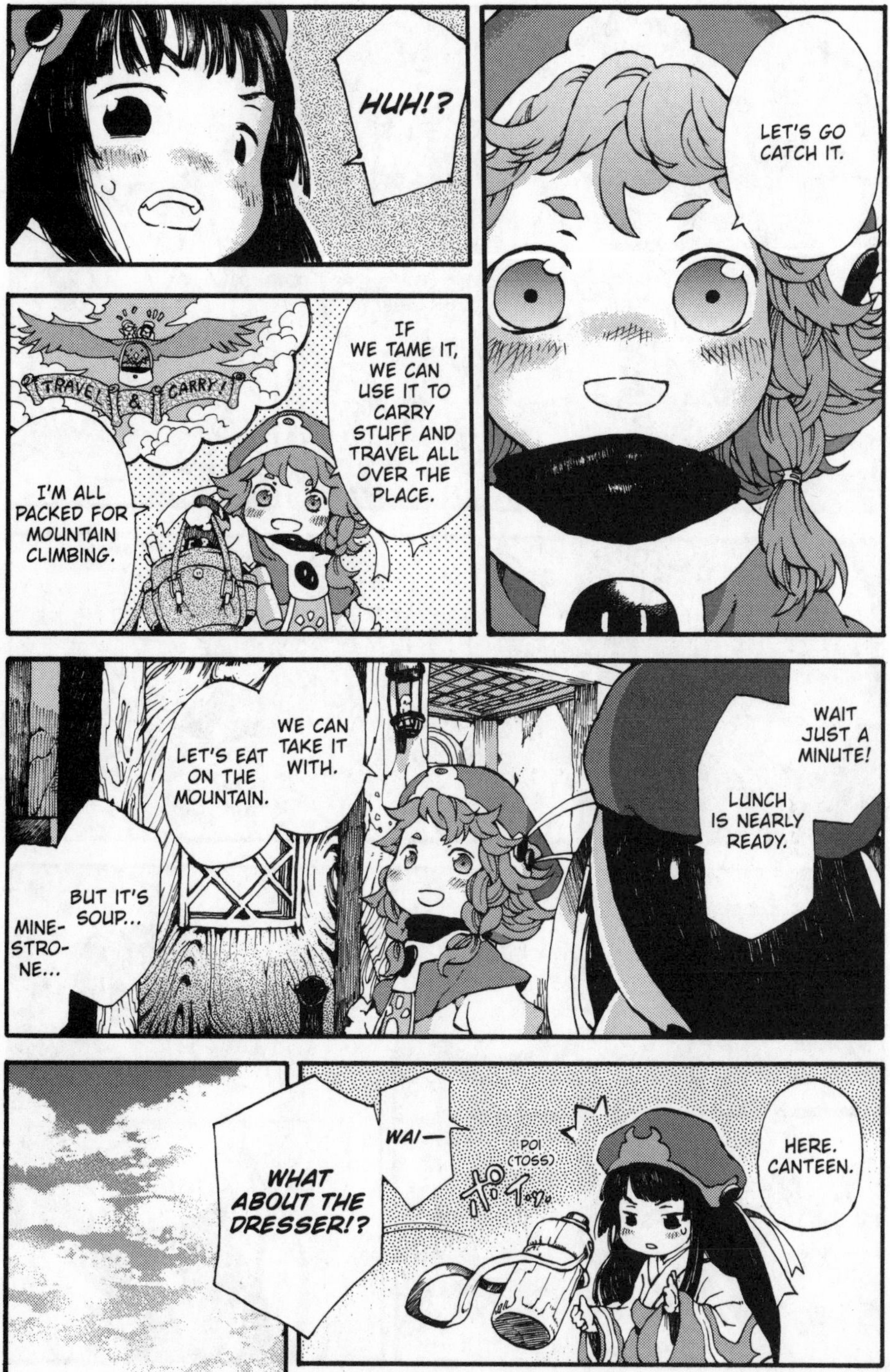

LET'S GO CATCH IT.
HUH!?
TRAVEL & CARRY!
IF WE TAME IT, WE CAN USE IT TO CARRY STUFF AND TRAVEL ALL OVER THE PLACE.
I'M ALL PACKED FOR MOUNTAIN CLIMBING.
WAIT JUST A MINUTE!
LUNCH IS NEARLY READY.
WE CAN TAKE IT WITH.
LET'S EAT ON THE MOUNTAIN.
BUT IT'S SOUP...
MINE-STRO-NE...
HERE. CANTEEN.
POI (TOSS)
WAI—
WHAT ABOUT THE DRESSER!?

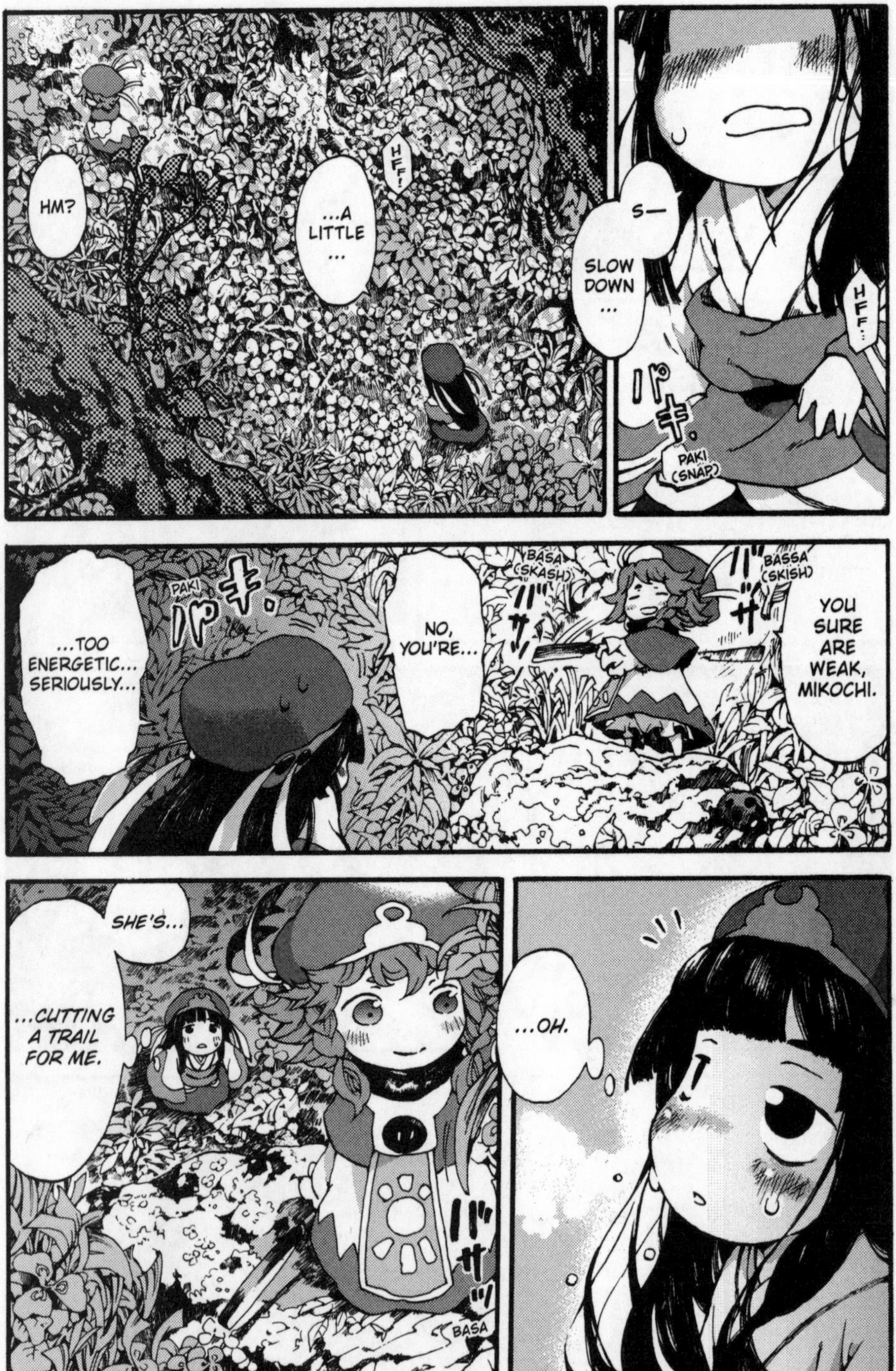
S—
SLOW DOWN ...
HFF...
PAKI (SNAP)
HFF!
...A LITTLE ...
HM?
YOU SURE ARE WEAK, MIKOCHI.
BASSA (SKISH)
BASA (SKASH)
NO, YOU'RE...
PAKI
...TOO ENERGETIC... SERIOUSLY...
...OH.
SHE'S...
...CUTTING A TRAIL FOR ME.
BASA

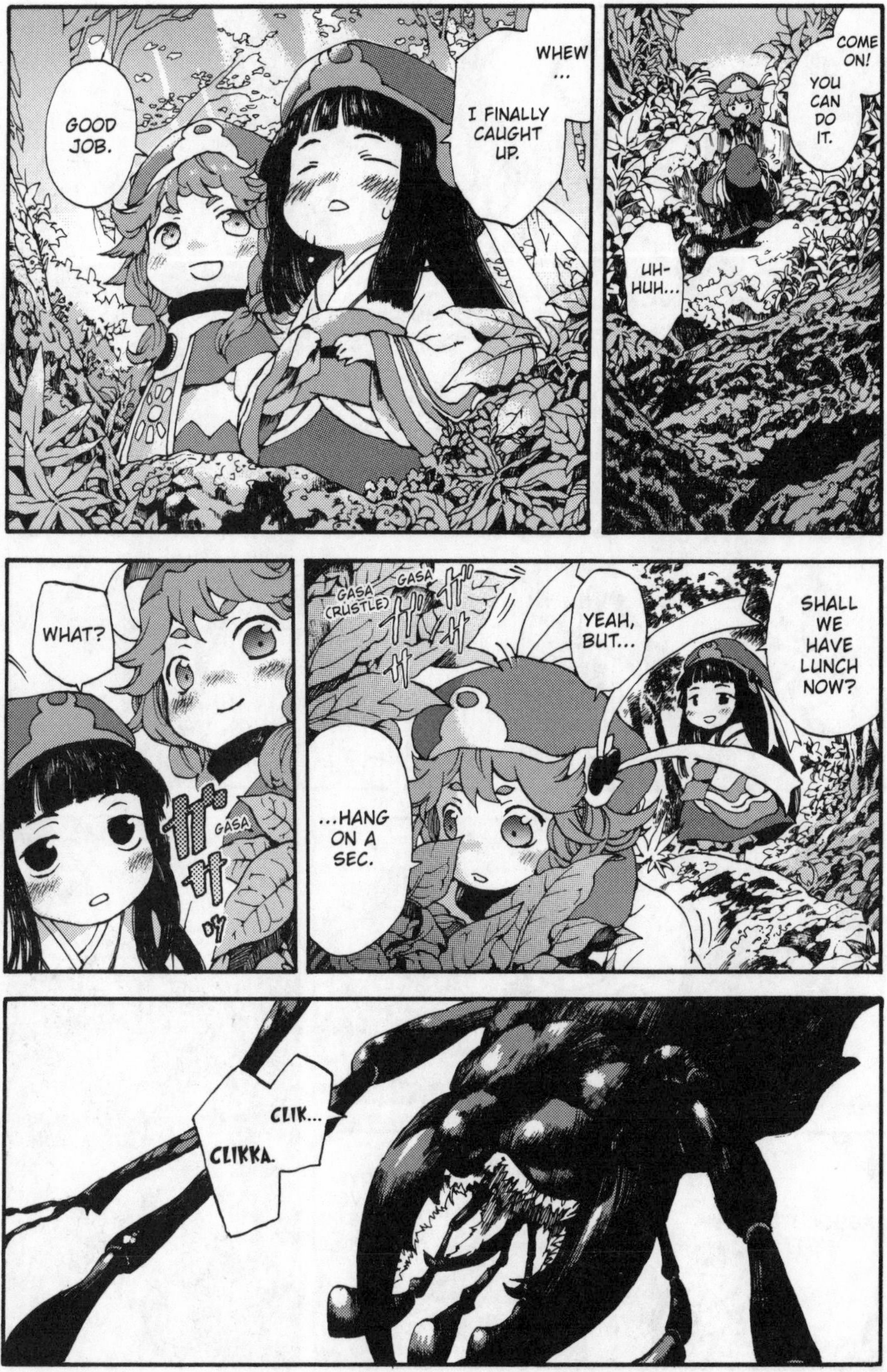
COME ON! YOU CAN DO IT.
UH-HUH...
WHEW... I FINALLY CAUGHT UP.
GOOD JOB.
SHALL WE HAVE LUNCH NOW?
YEAH, BUT...
GASA GASA (RUSTLE)
...HANG ON A SEC.
WHAT?
GASA
CLIK... CLIKKA.

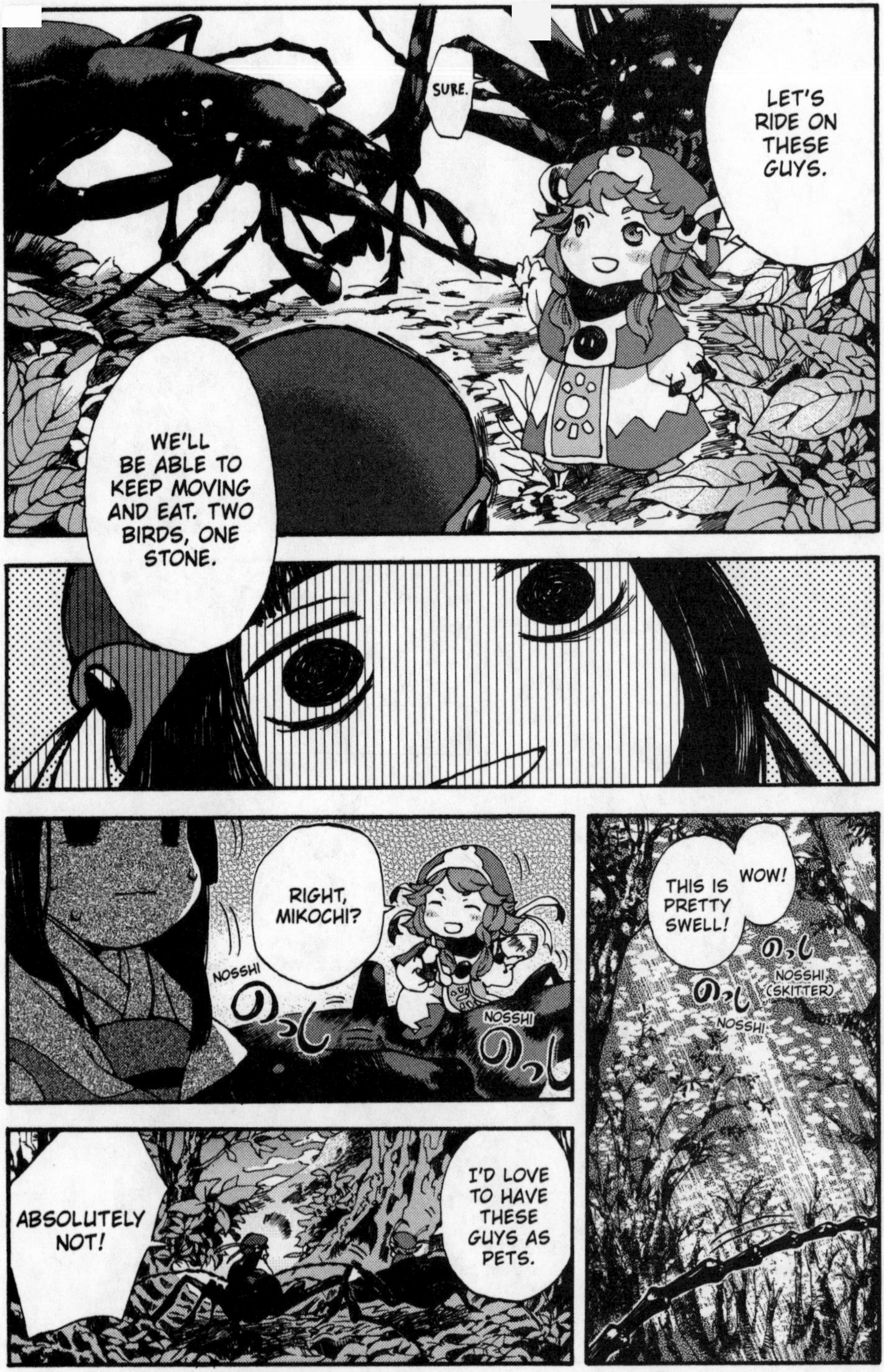
LET'S RIDE ON THESE GUYS.
SURE.
WE'LL BE ABLE TO KEEP MOVING AND EAT. TWO BIRDS, ONE STONE.
WOW!
THIS IS PRETTY SWELL!
のっし
NOSSHI (SKITTER)
のっし
NOSSHI
RIGHT, MIKOCHI?
NOSSHI
のっし
NOSSHI
のっし
I'D LOVE TO HAVE THESE GUYS AS PETS.
ABSOLUTELY NOT!

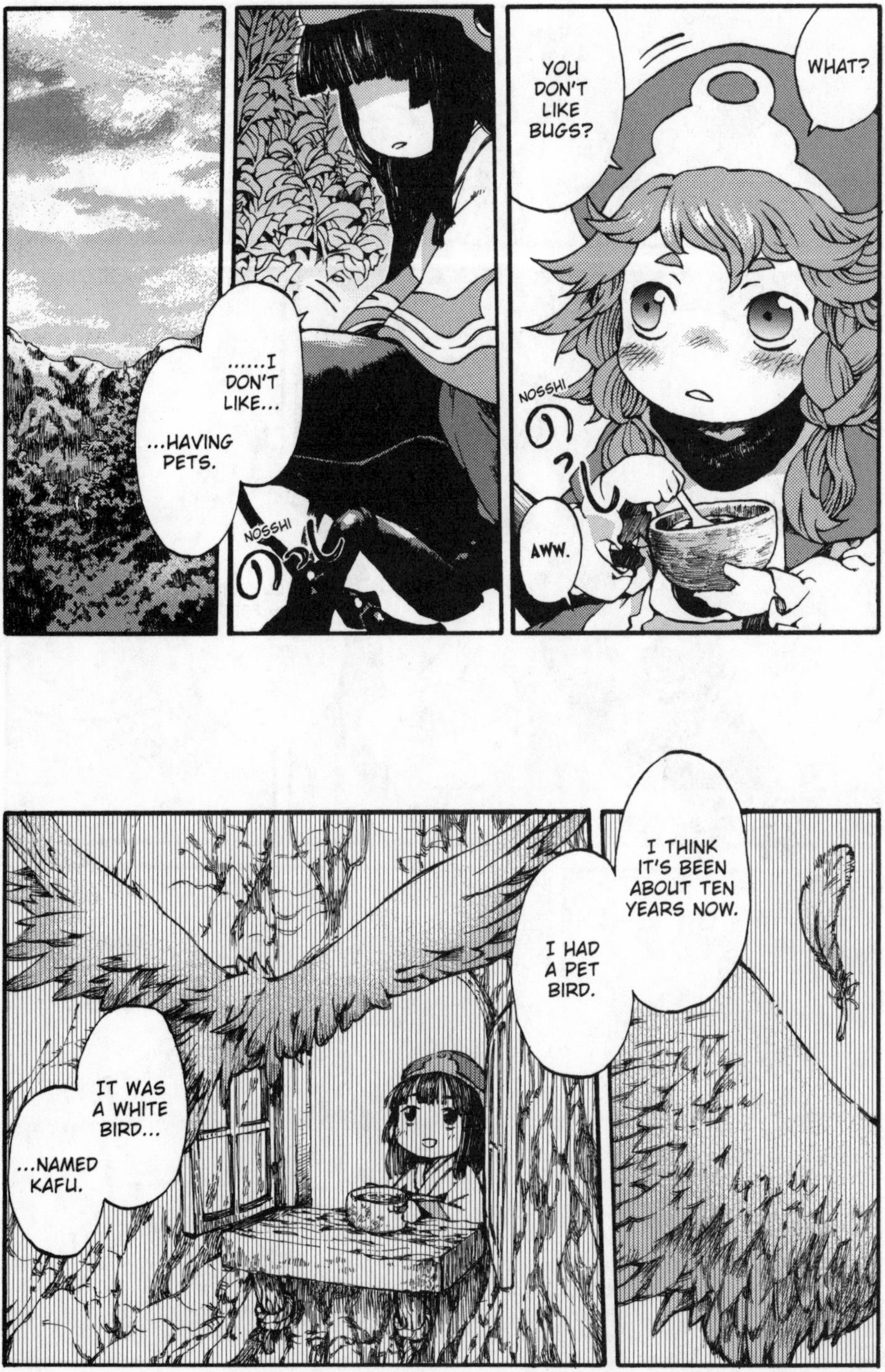
WHAT?
YOU DON'T LIKE BUGS?
NOSSHI
AWW.
NOSSHI
......I DON'T LIKE...
...HAVING PETS.
I THINK IT'S BEEN ABOUT TEN YEARS NOW.
I HAD A PET BIRD.
IT WAS A WHITE BIRD...
...NAMED KAFU.

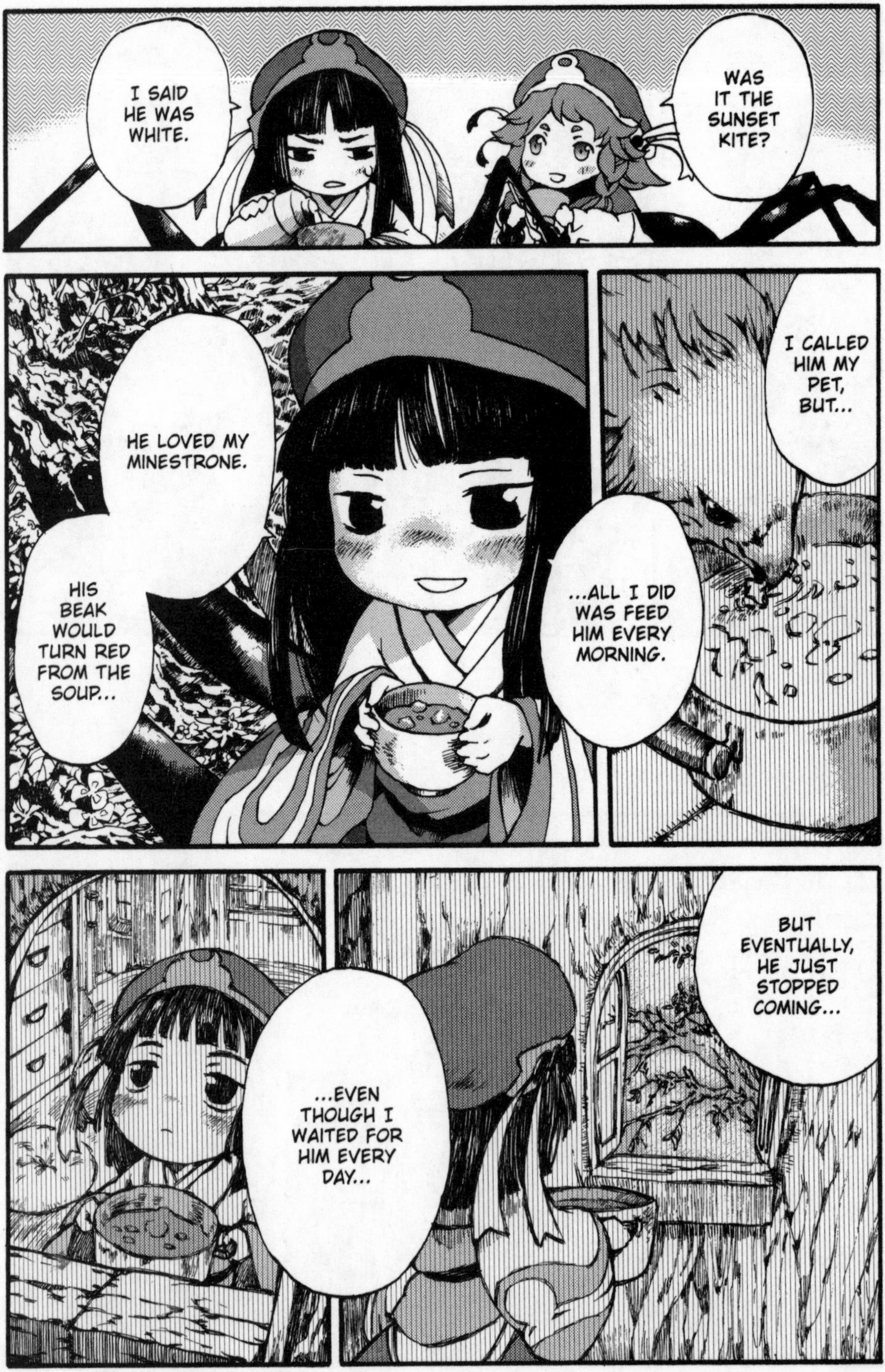
WAS IT THE SUNSET KITE?
I SAID HE WAS WHITE.
I CALLED HIM MY PET, BUT...
...ALL I DID WAS FEED HIM EVERY MORNING.
HE LOVED MY MINESTRONE.
HIS BEAK WOULD TURN RED FROM THE SOUP...
BUT EVENTUALLY, HE JUST STOPPED COMING...
...EVEN THOUGH I WAITED FOR HIM EVERY DAY...

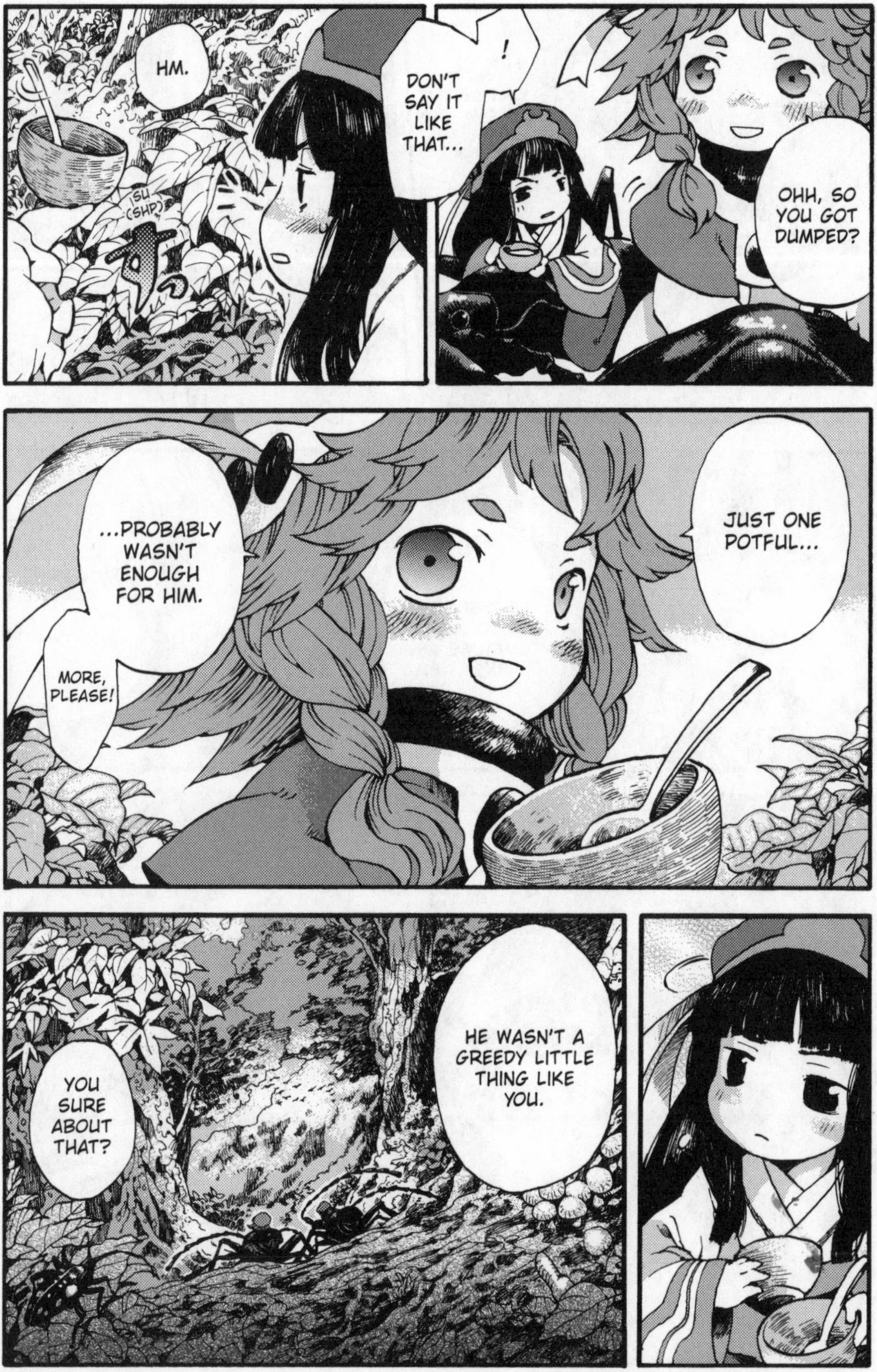
OHH, SO YOU GOT DUMPED?
!
DON'T SAY IT LIKE THAT...
HM.
SU (SHP)
JUST ONE POTFUL...
...PROBABLY WASN'T ENOUGH FOR HIM.
MORE, PLEASE!
HE WASN'T A GREEDY LITTLE THING LIKE YOU.
YOU SURE ABOUT THAT?

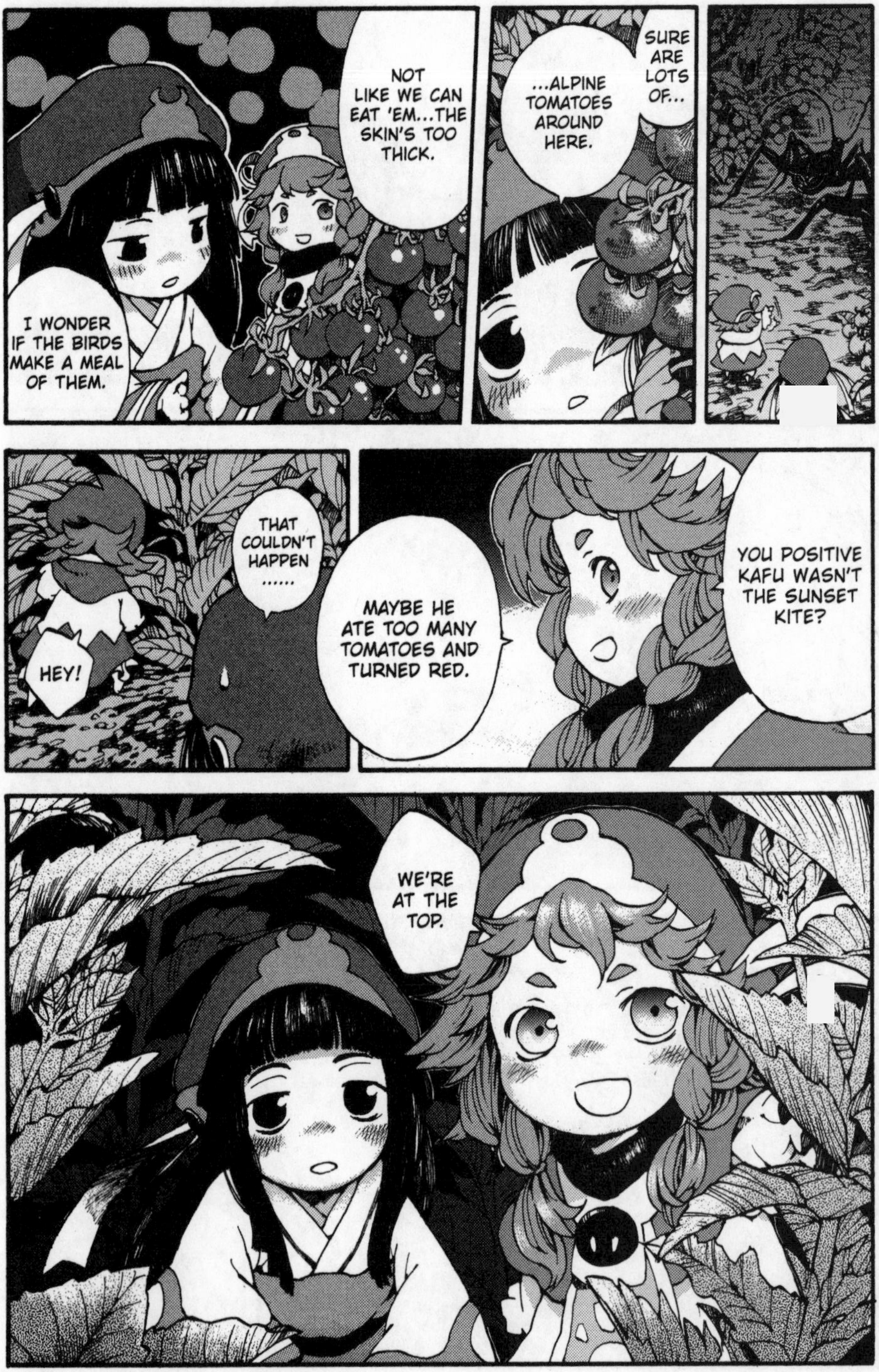
SURE ARE LOTS OF...
...ALPINE TOMATOES AROUND HERE.
NOT LIKE WE CAN EAT 'EM...THE SKIN'S TOO THICK.
I WONDER IF THE BIRDS MAKE A MEAL OF THEM.
YOU POSITIVE KAFU WASN'T THE SUNSET KITE?
MAYBE HE ATE TOO MANY TOMATOES AND TURNED RED.
THAT COULDN'T HAPPEN ......
HEY!
WE'RE AT THE TOP.

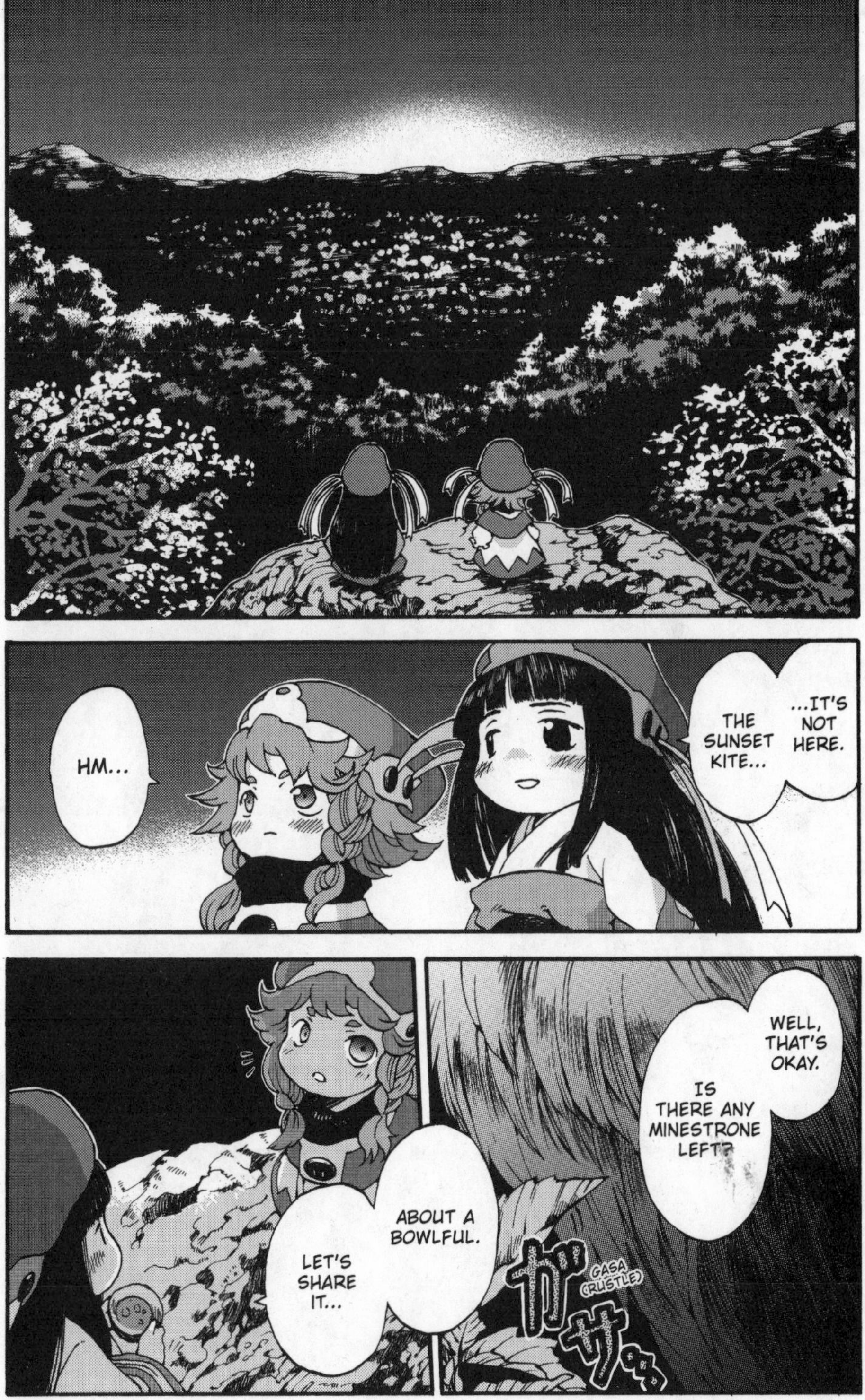
THE SUNSET KITE... ...IT'S NOT HERE.
HM...
WELL, THAT'S OKAY.
IS THERE ANY MINESTRONE LEFT?
GASA (RUSTLE)
ABOUT A BOWLFUL.
LET'S SHARE IT...

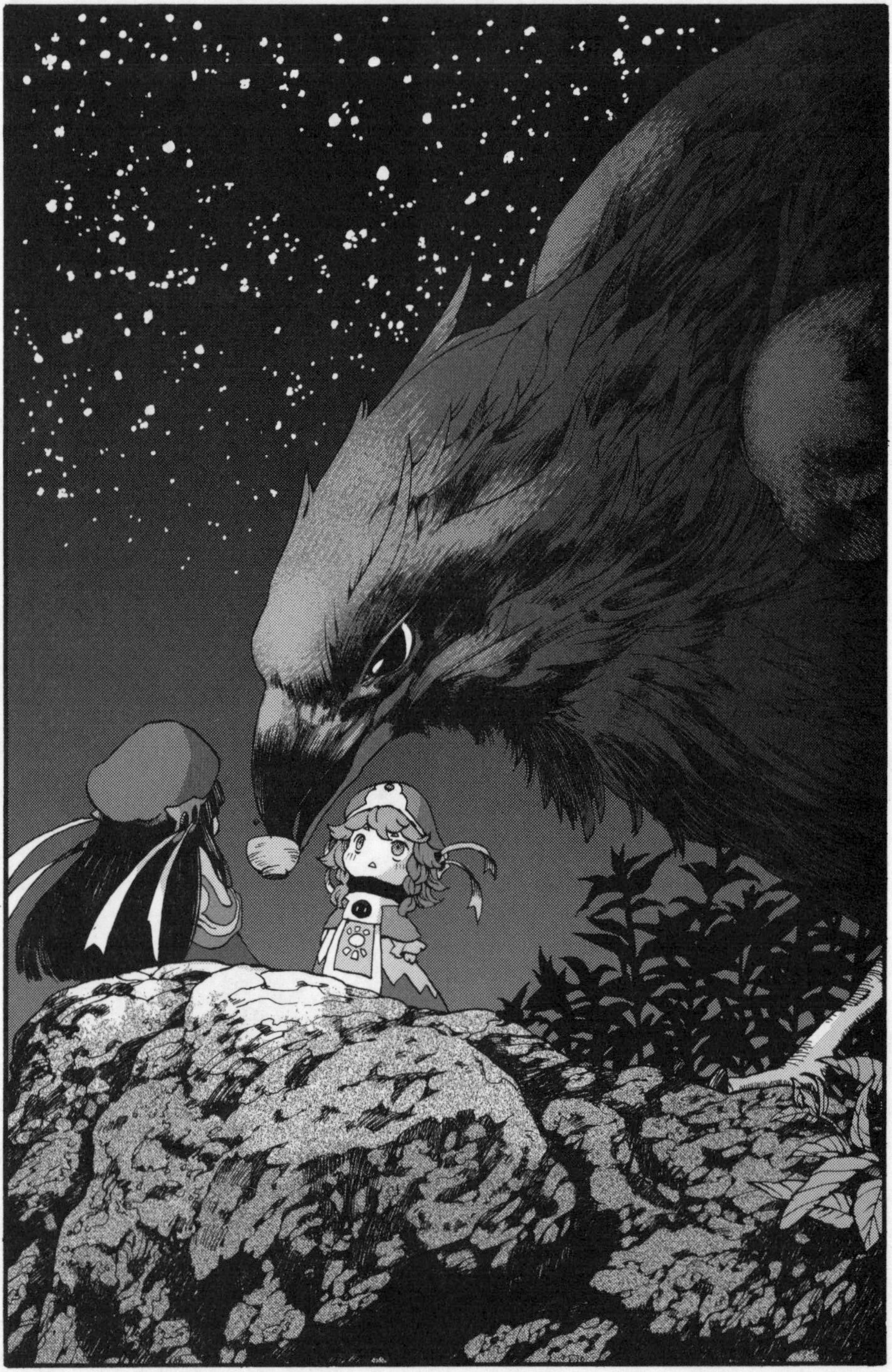

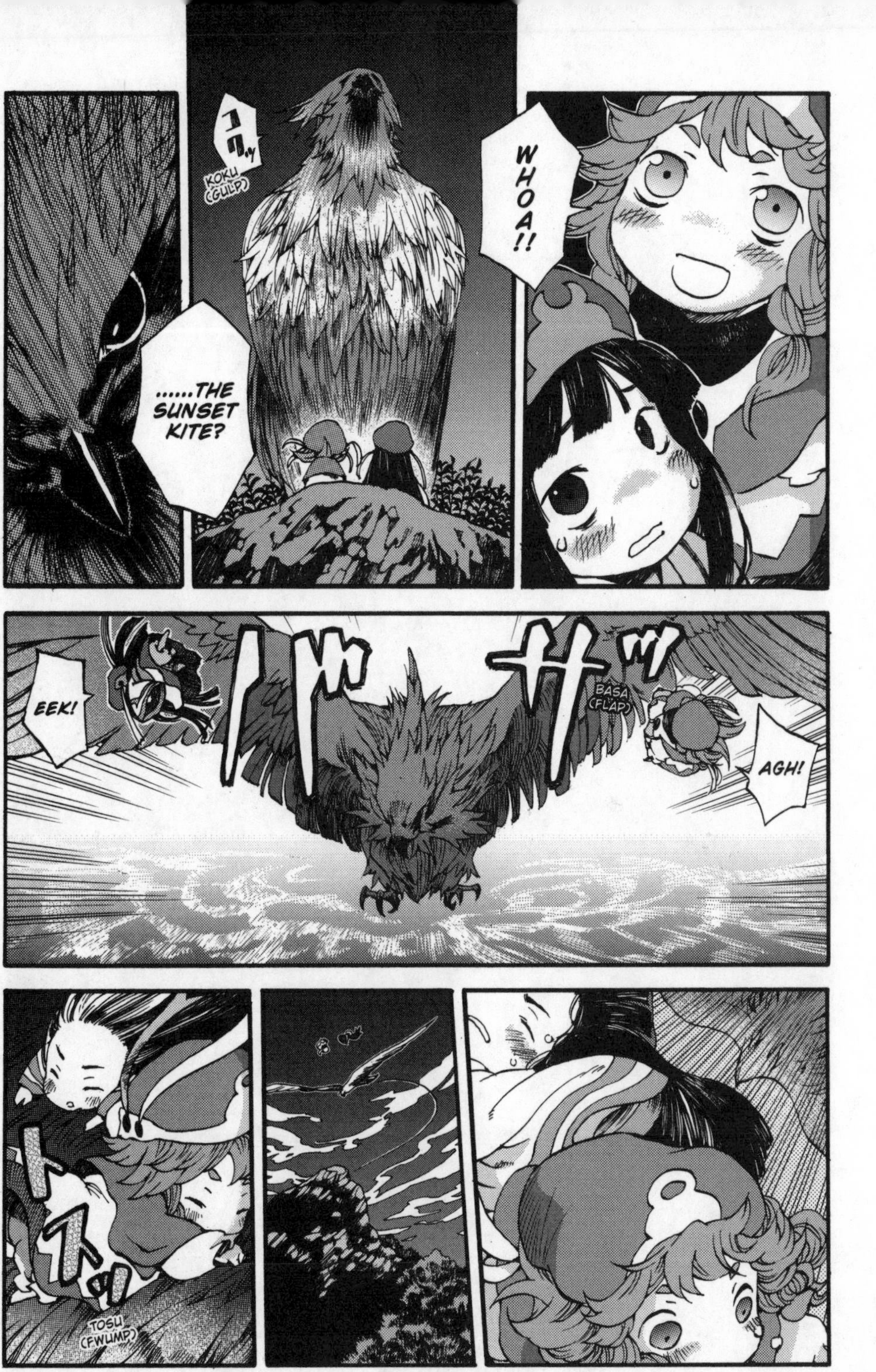
WHOA!!
KOKU (GULP)
......THE SUNSET KITE?
BASA (FLAP)
AGH!
EEK!
TOSU (FWUMP)

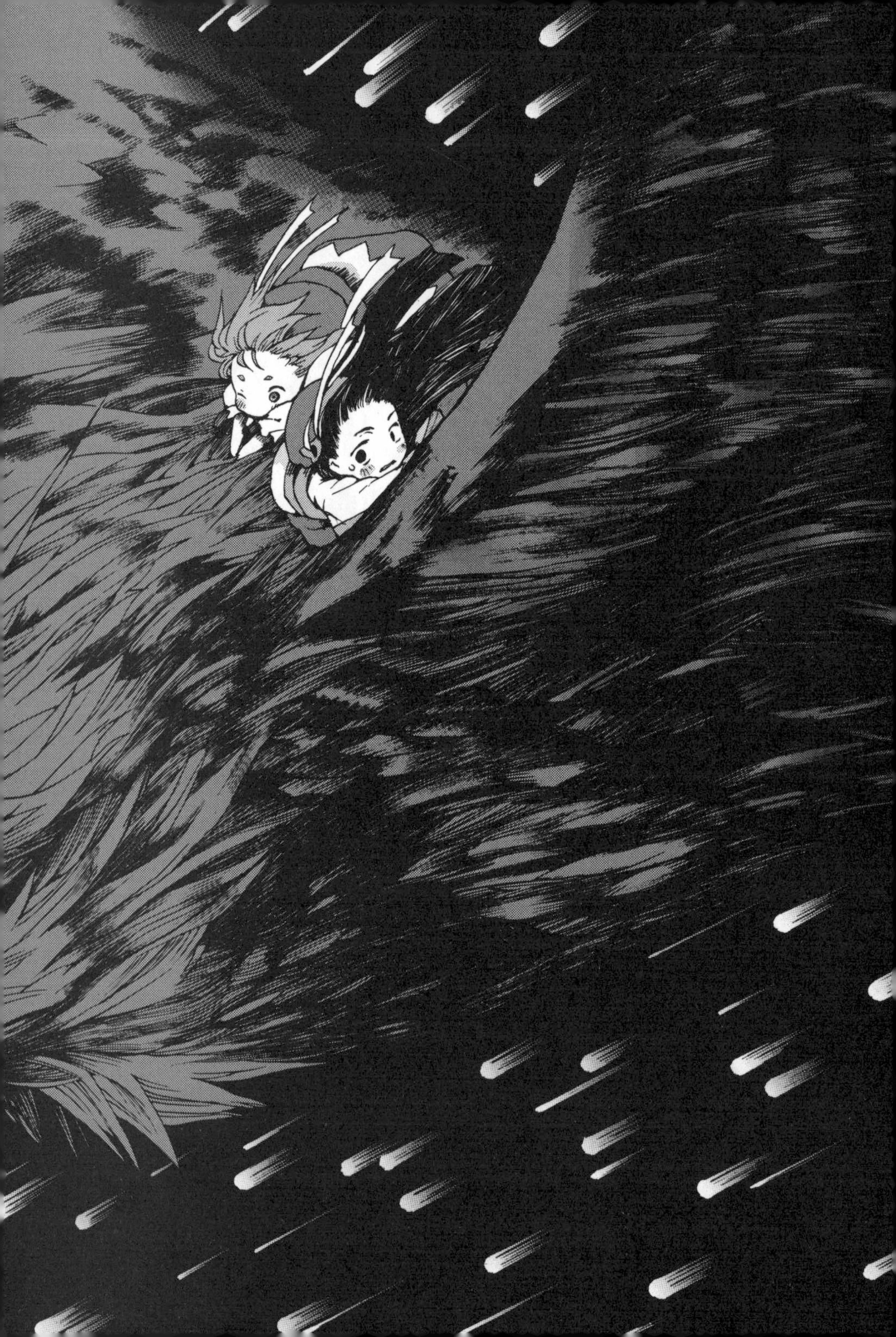

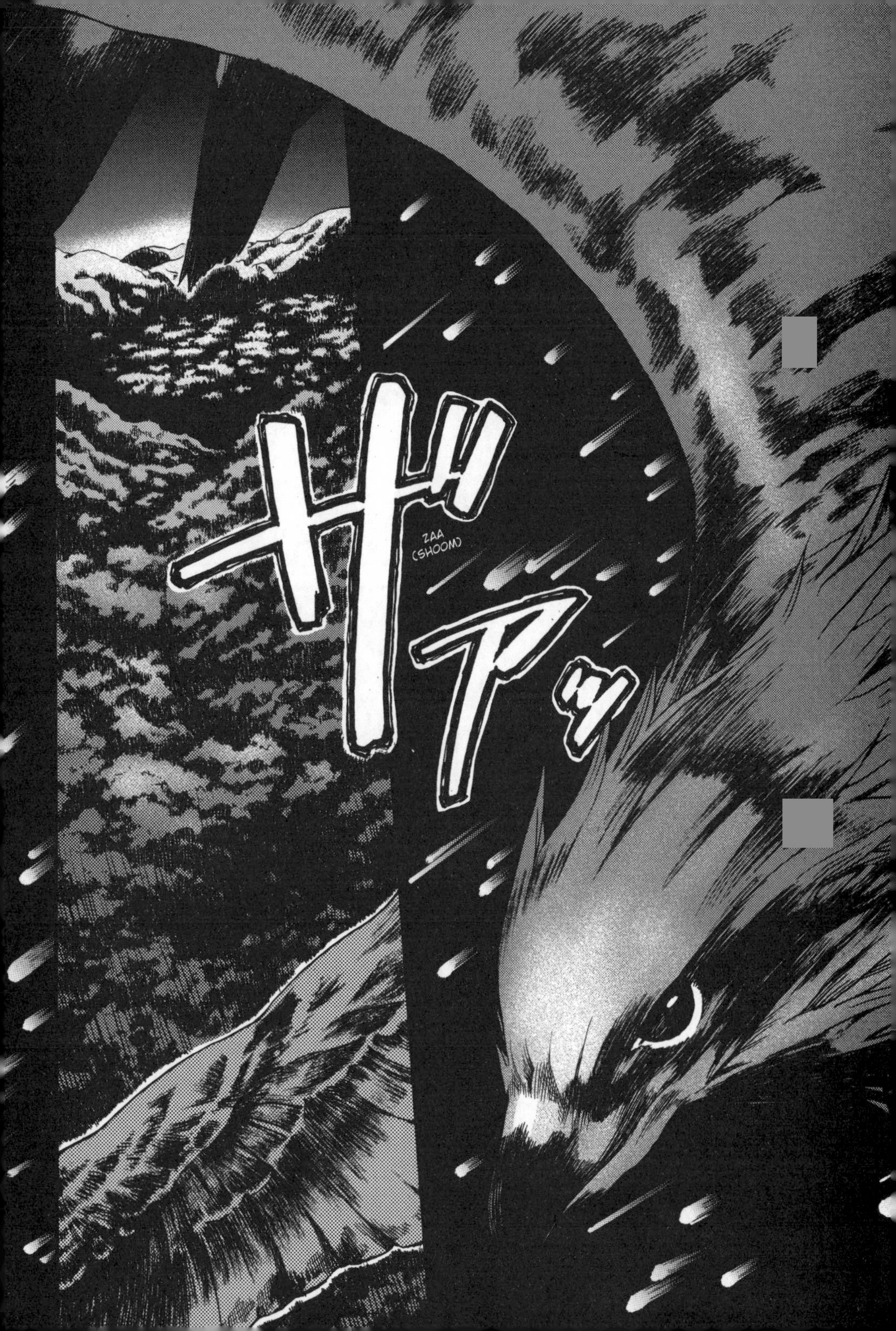
ザアッ
ZAA
(SHOOM)

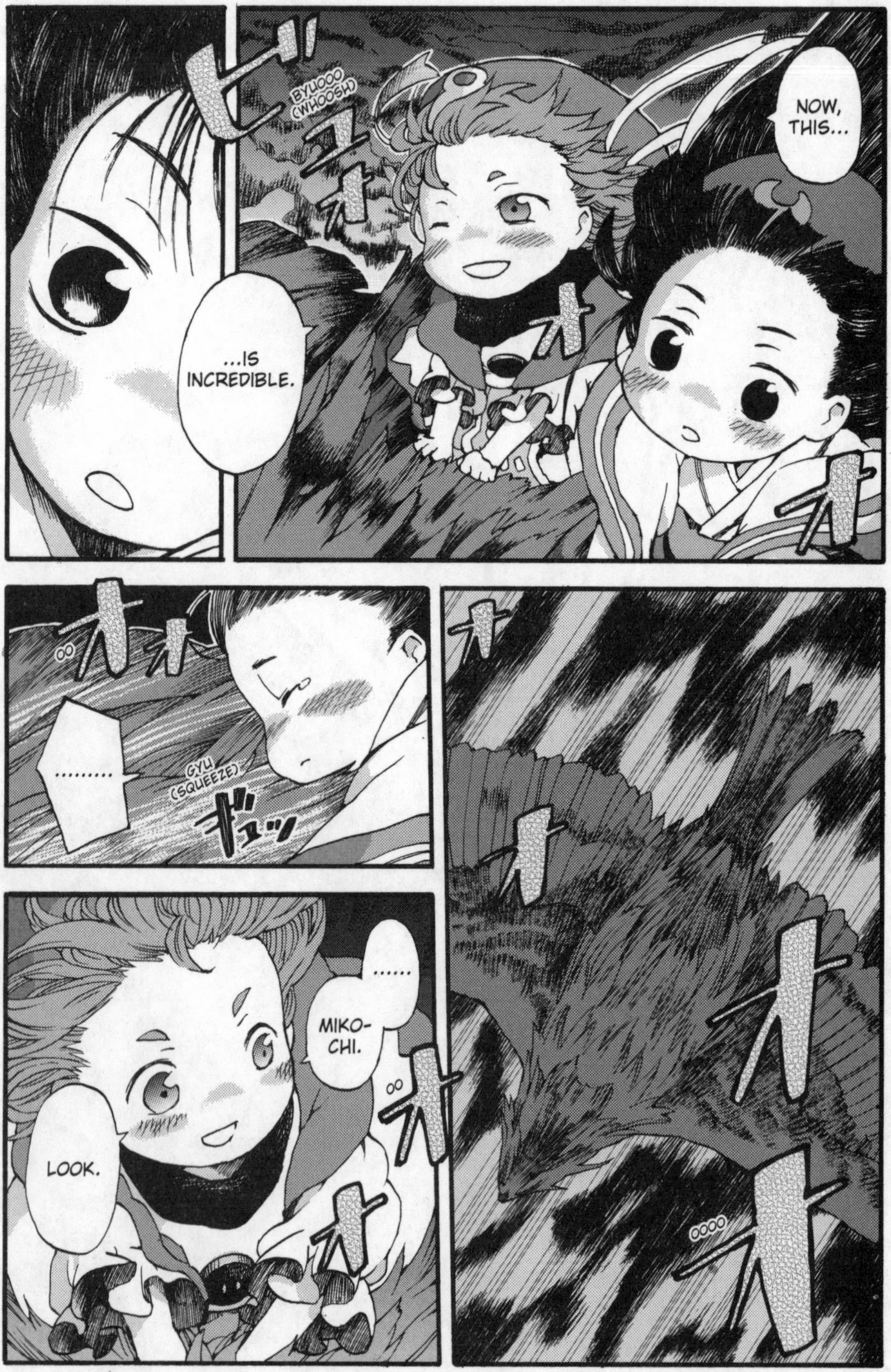
BYUOOO (WHOOSH)
NOW, THIS...
...IS INCREDIBLE.
OOOO
OO
....
GYU (SQUEEZE)
......
MIKO-CHI.
OO
LOOK.

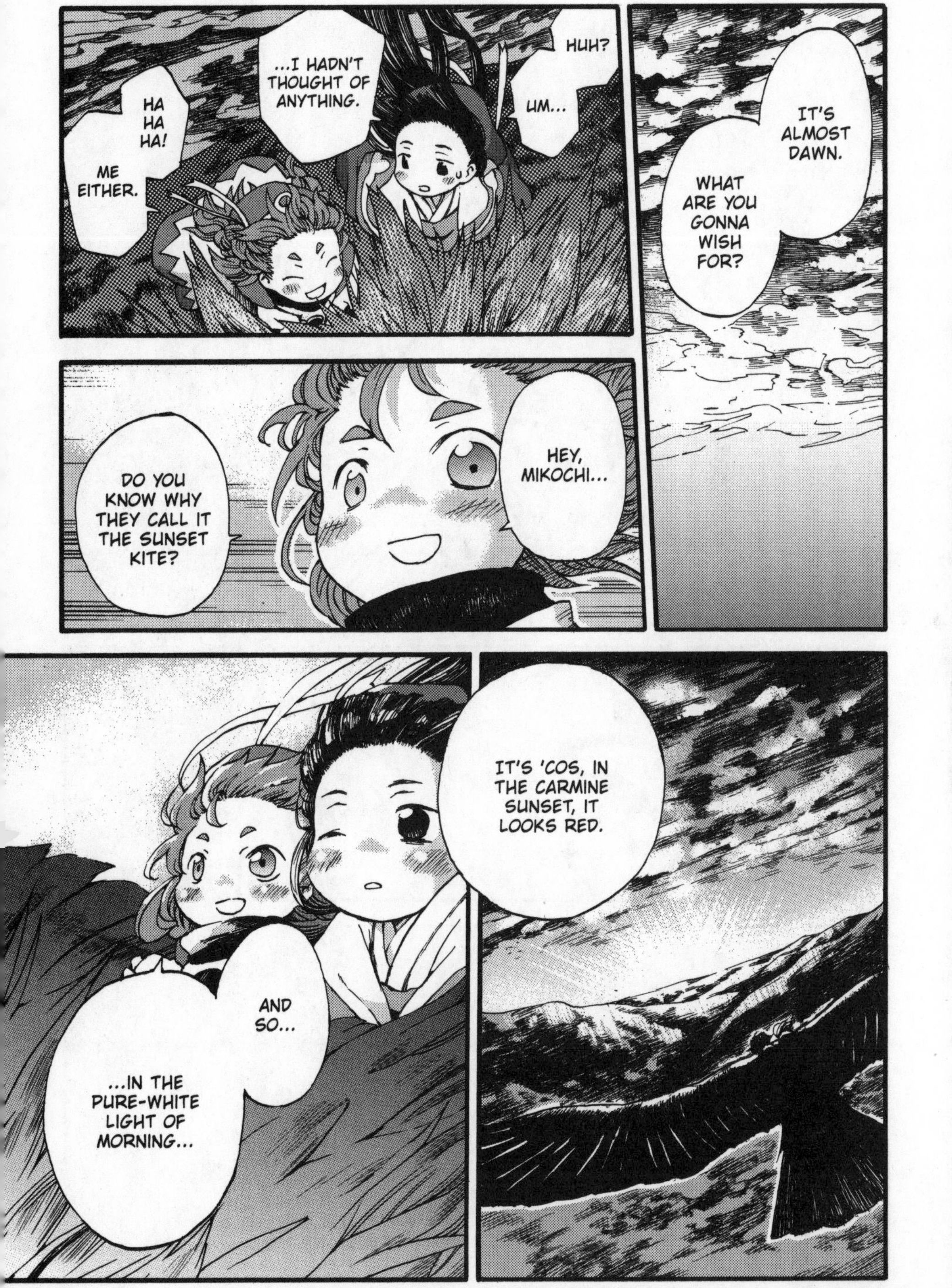
IT'S ALMOST DAWN.
WHAT ARE YOU GONNA WISH FOR?
HUH?
UM...
...I HADN'T THOUGHT OF ANYTHING.
HA HA HA!
ME EITHER.
HEY, MIKOCHI...
DO YOU KNOW WHY THEY CALL IT THE SUNSET KITE?
IT'S 'COS, IN THE CARMINE SUNSET, IT LOOKS RED.
AND SO...
...IN THE PURE-WHITE LIGHT OF MORNING...

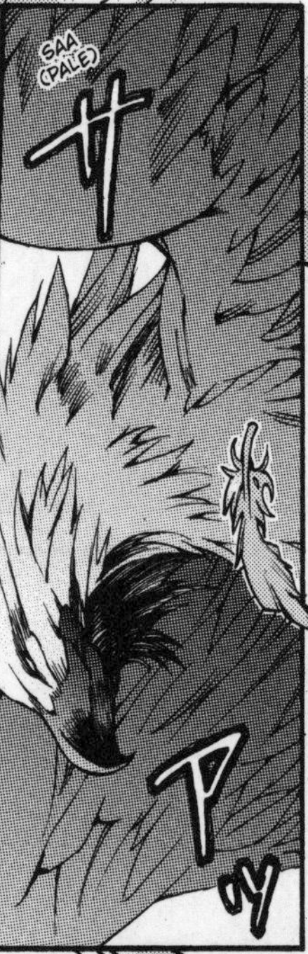
SAA (PALE)
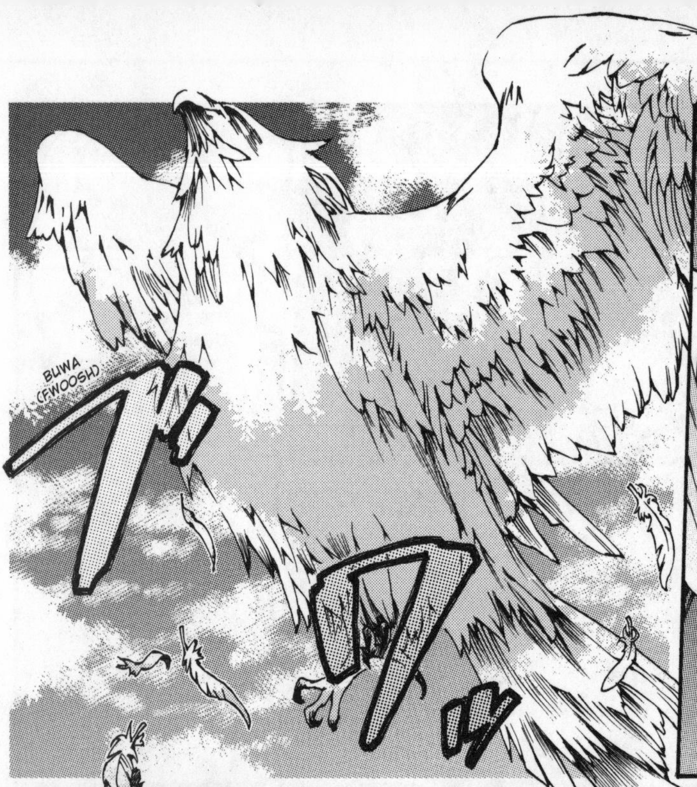
BUWA (FWOOSH)
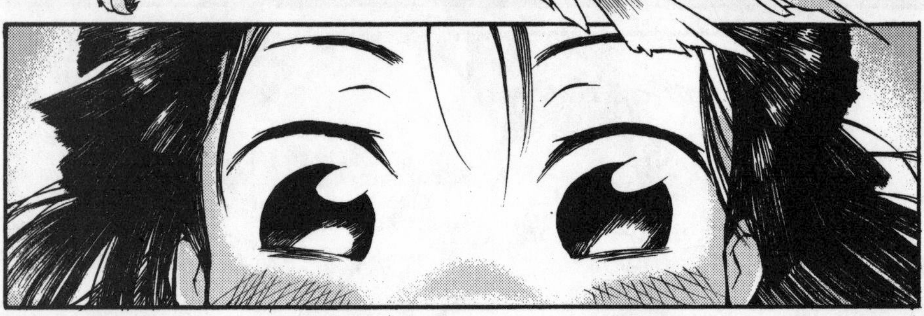
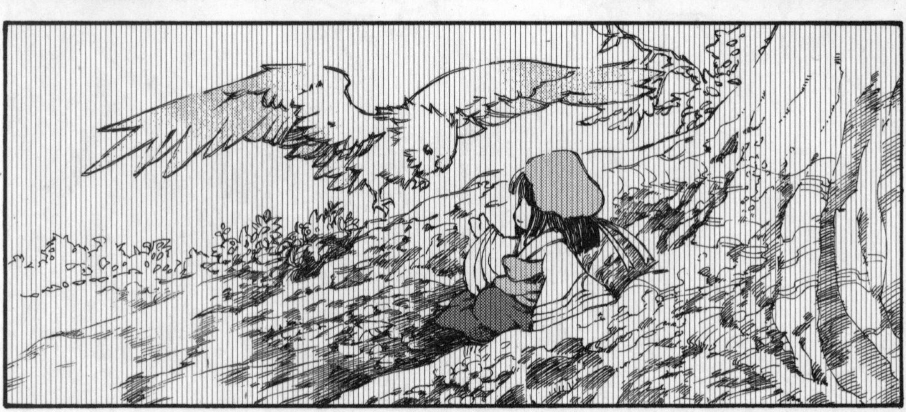

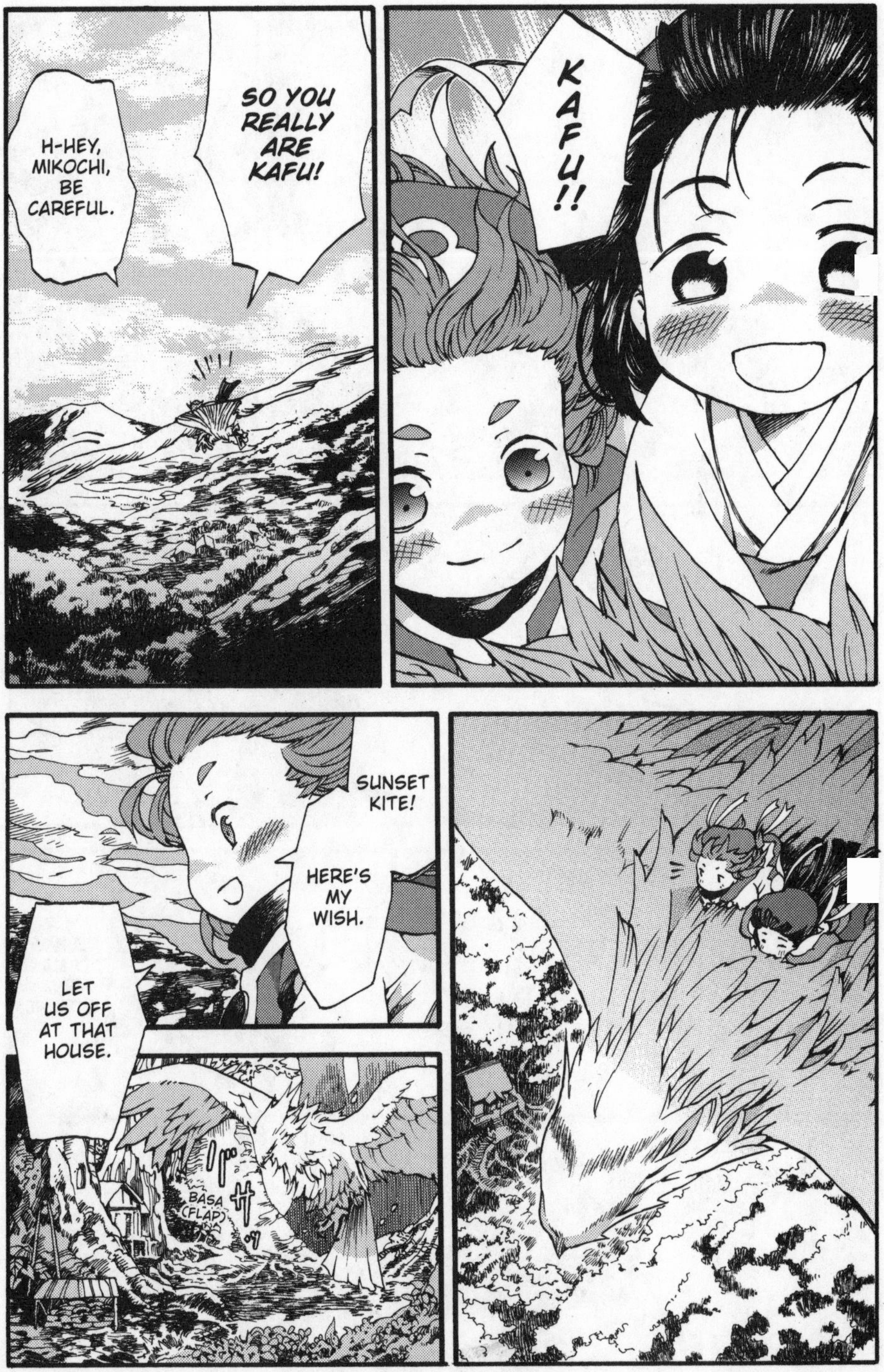
KAFU!!
SO YOU REALLY ARE KAFU!
H-HEY, MIKOCHI, BE CAREFUL.
SUNSET KITE!
HERE'S MY WISH.
LET US OFF AT THAT HOUSE.
BASA (FLAP)

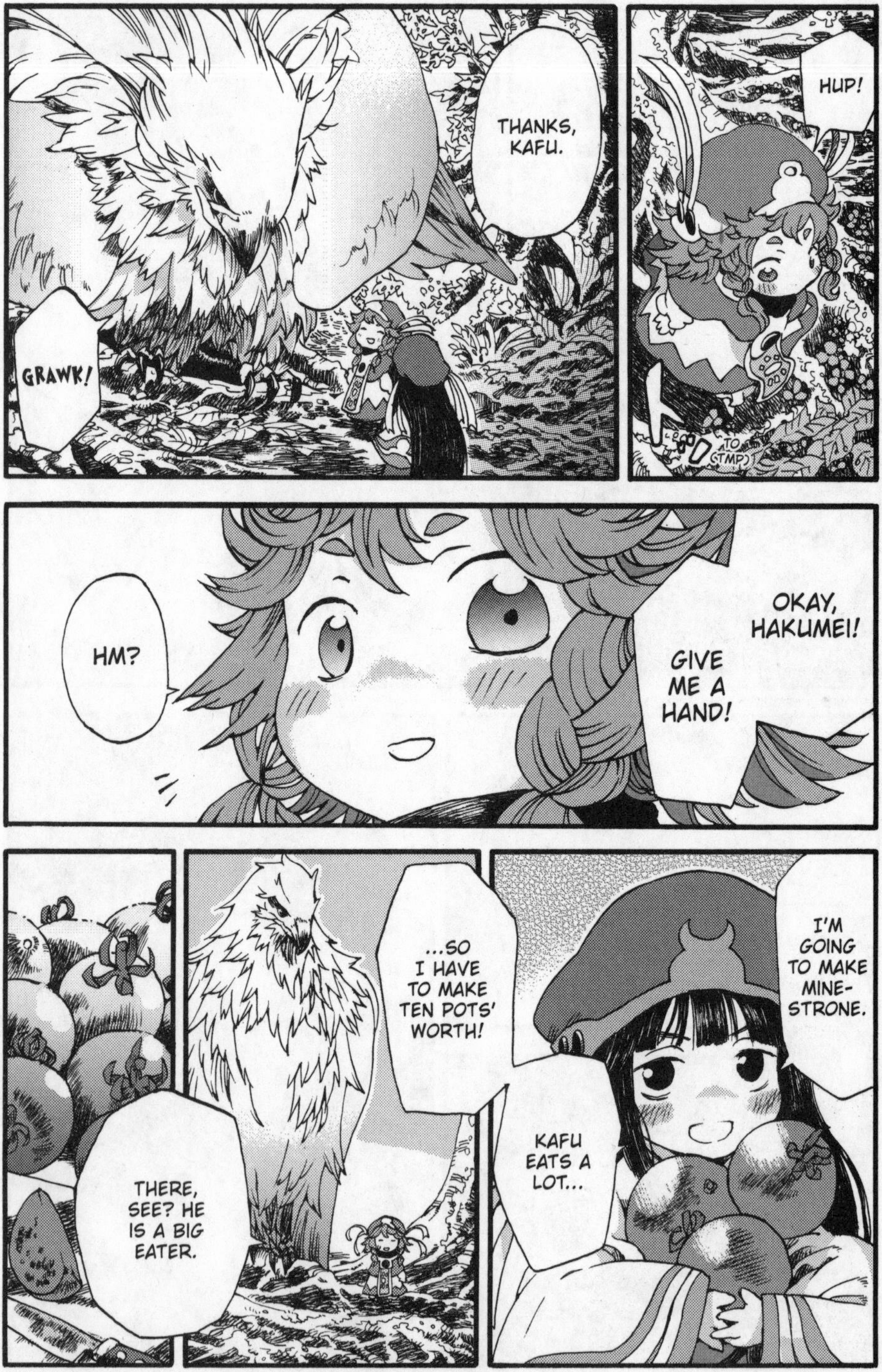
HUP!
TO (TMP)
THANKS, KAFU.
GRAWK!
OKAY, HAKUMEI!
GIVE ME A HAND!
HM?
I'M GOING TO MAKE MINE-STRONE.
KAFU EATS A LOT...
...SO I HAVE TO MAKE TEN POTS' WORTH!
THERE, SEE? HE IS A BIG EATER.

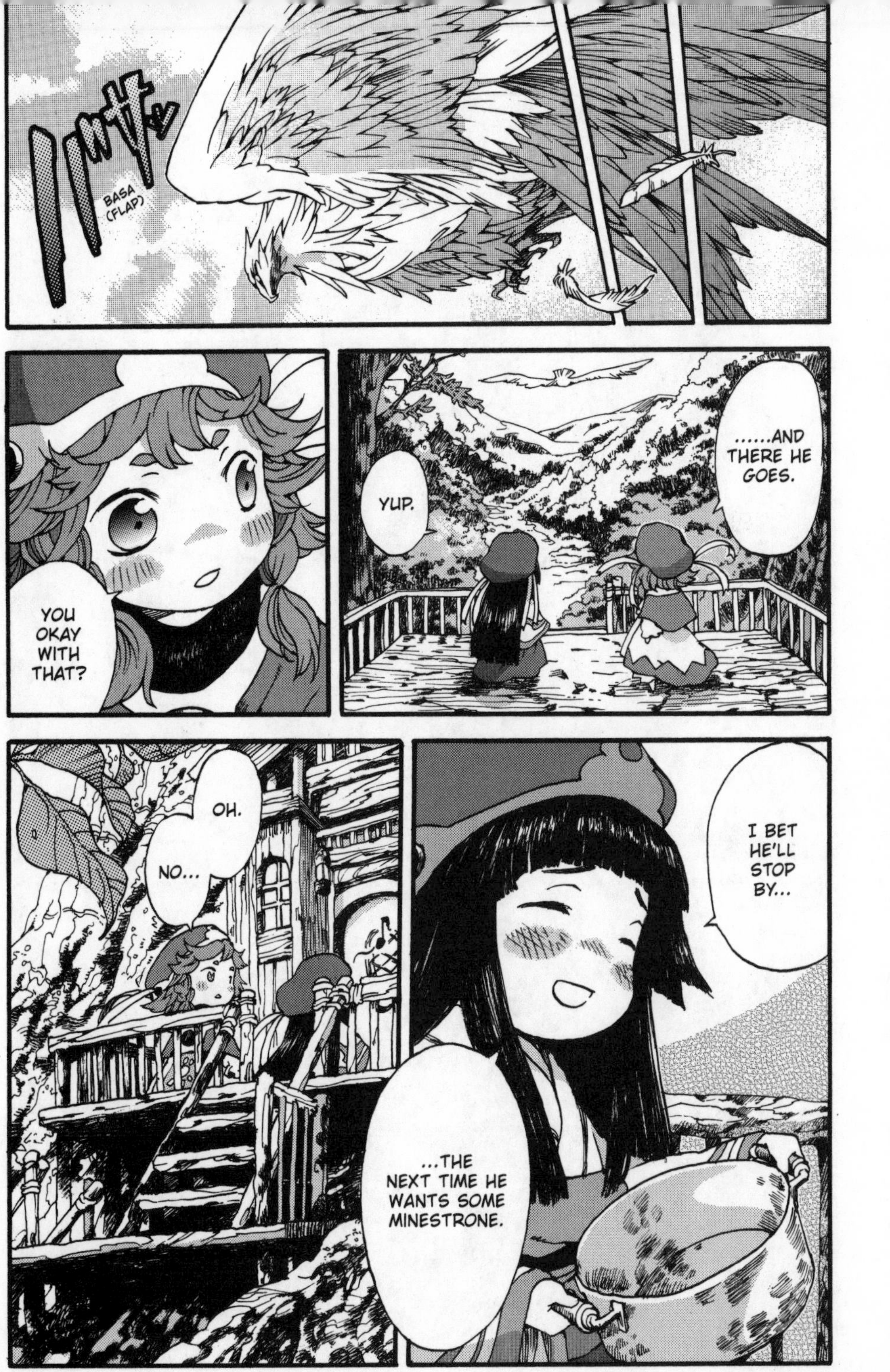
BASA (FLAP)
......AND THERE HE GOES.
YUP.
YOU OKAY WITH THAT?
I BET HE'LL STOP BY...
...THE NEXT TIME HE WANTS SOME MINESTRONE.
OH.
NO...

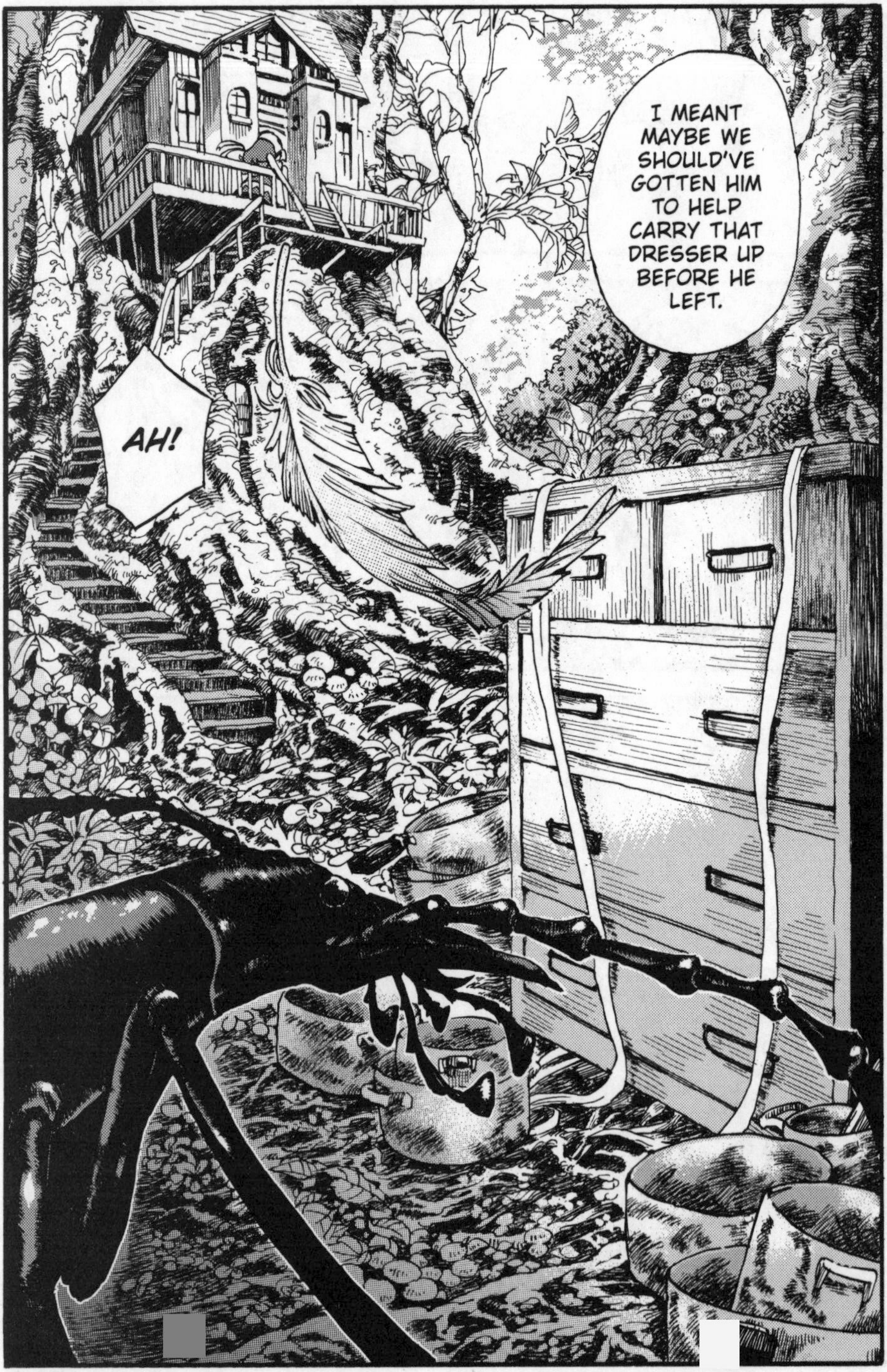
I MEANT MAYBE WE SHOULD'VE GOTTEN HIM TO HELP CARRY THAT DRESSER UP BEFORE HE LEFT.
AH!

Chapter 1 • End

The individual who spotted the Sunset Kite was one Mr. Yuga, a resident of Makinata's central district. After clocking out of his job at the papermaking workshop, he regularly climbs up the western hill with a spyglass and a telescope, having made it his daily task to confirm the veracity of the Stargazing Frog's Weather Forecast. Late on the night of April 29, following a stretch of overtime, he happened to see the Sunset Kite.

*

Although we attempted to interview Mr. Yuga, the individual in question was remarkably intoxicated and insistent that we write an article criticizing his place of employment, so we abandoned the effort. We plan to request an interview at a later date.

—Excerpt from the extra edition of the *Makinata Daily*

Chapter 2
The Two Songstresses

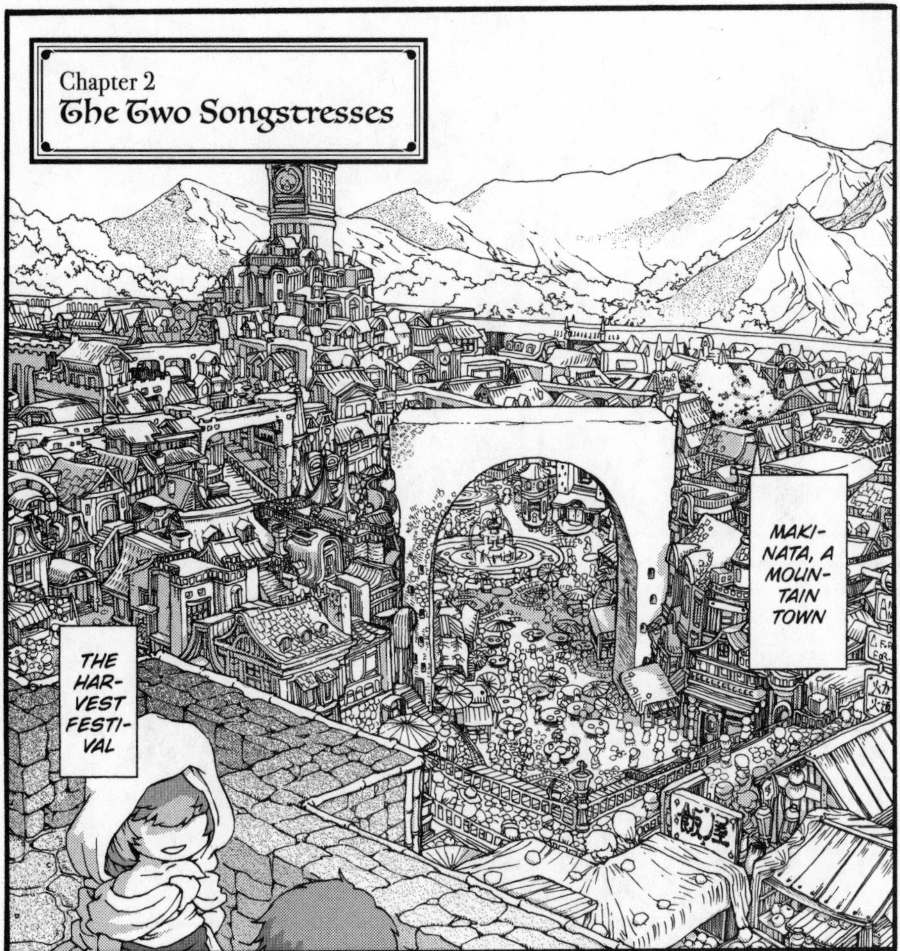
MAKINATA, A MOUNTAIN TOWN
THE HARVEST FESTIVAL

SIGN: PUB

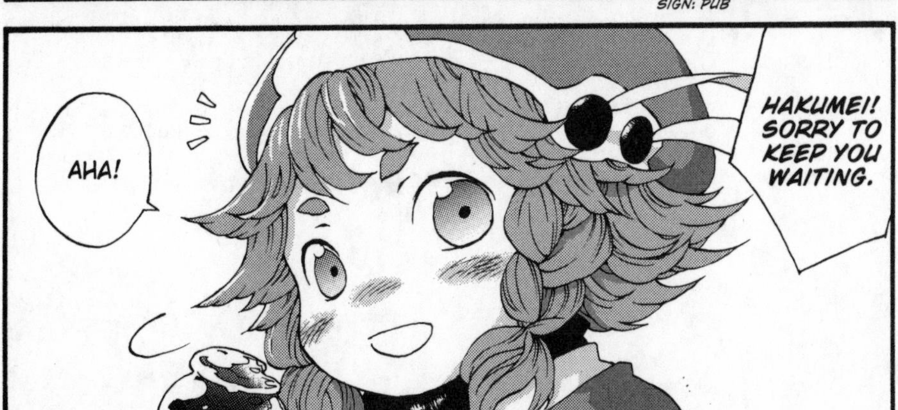
HAKUMEI! SORRY TO KEEP YOU WAITING.
AHA!

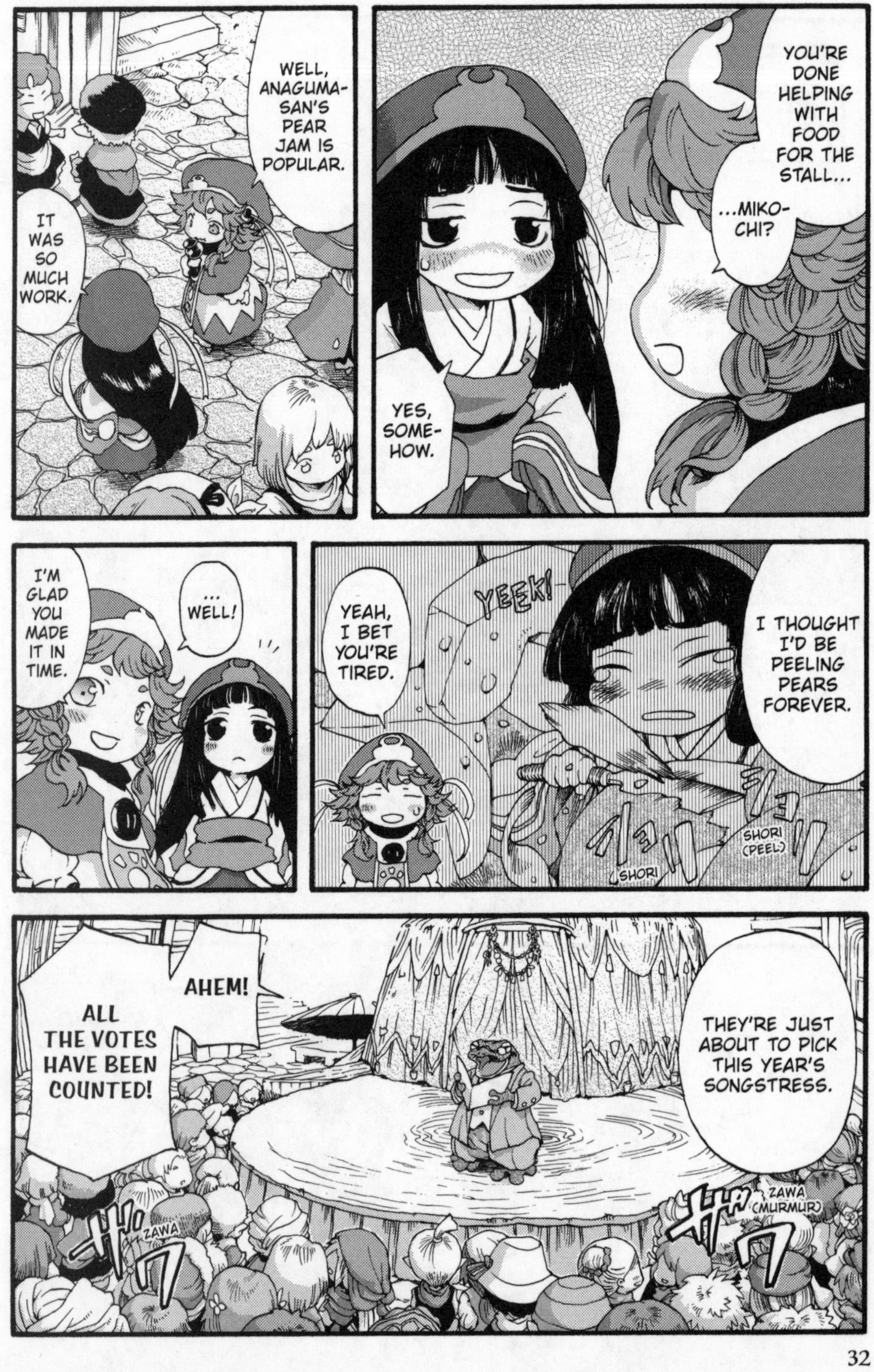
YOU'RE DONE HELPING WITH FOOD FOR THE STALL...
...MIKO-CHI?
YES, SOMEHOW.
WELL, ANAGUMA-SAN'S PEAR JAM IS POPULAR.
IT WAS SO MUCH WORK.
I THOUGHT I'D BE PEELING PEARS FOREVER.
YEEK!
SHORI (PEEL)
SHORI
YEAH, I BET YOU'RE TIRED.
... WELL!
I'M GLAD YOU MADE IT IN TIME.
THEY'RE JUST ABOUT TO PICK THIS YEAR'S SONGSTRESS.
ZAWA (MURMUR)
AHEM!
ALL THE VOTES HAVE BEEN COUNTED!
ZAWA

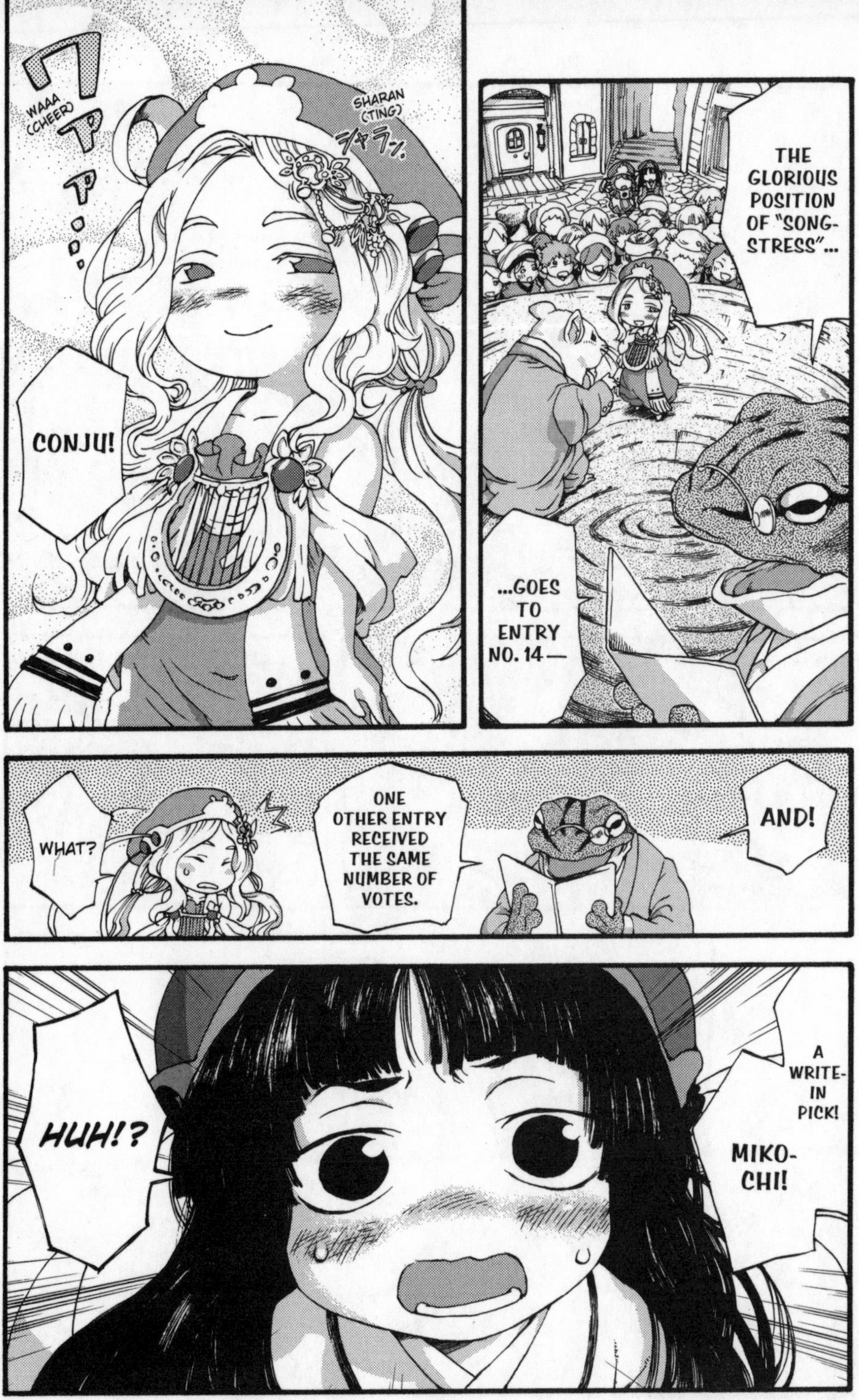
THE GLORIOUS POSITION OF "SONG-STRESS"...
...GOES TO ENTRY NO. 14—
SHARAN (TING)
シャラン
WAAA (CHEER)
ワァァ…
CONJU!
AND!
ONE OTHER ENTRY RECEIVED THE SAME NUMBER OF VOTES.
WHAT?
A WRITE-IN PICK!
MIKO-CHI!
HUH!?

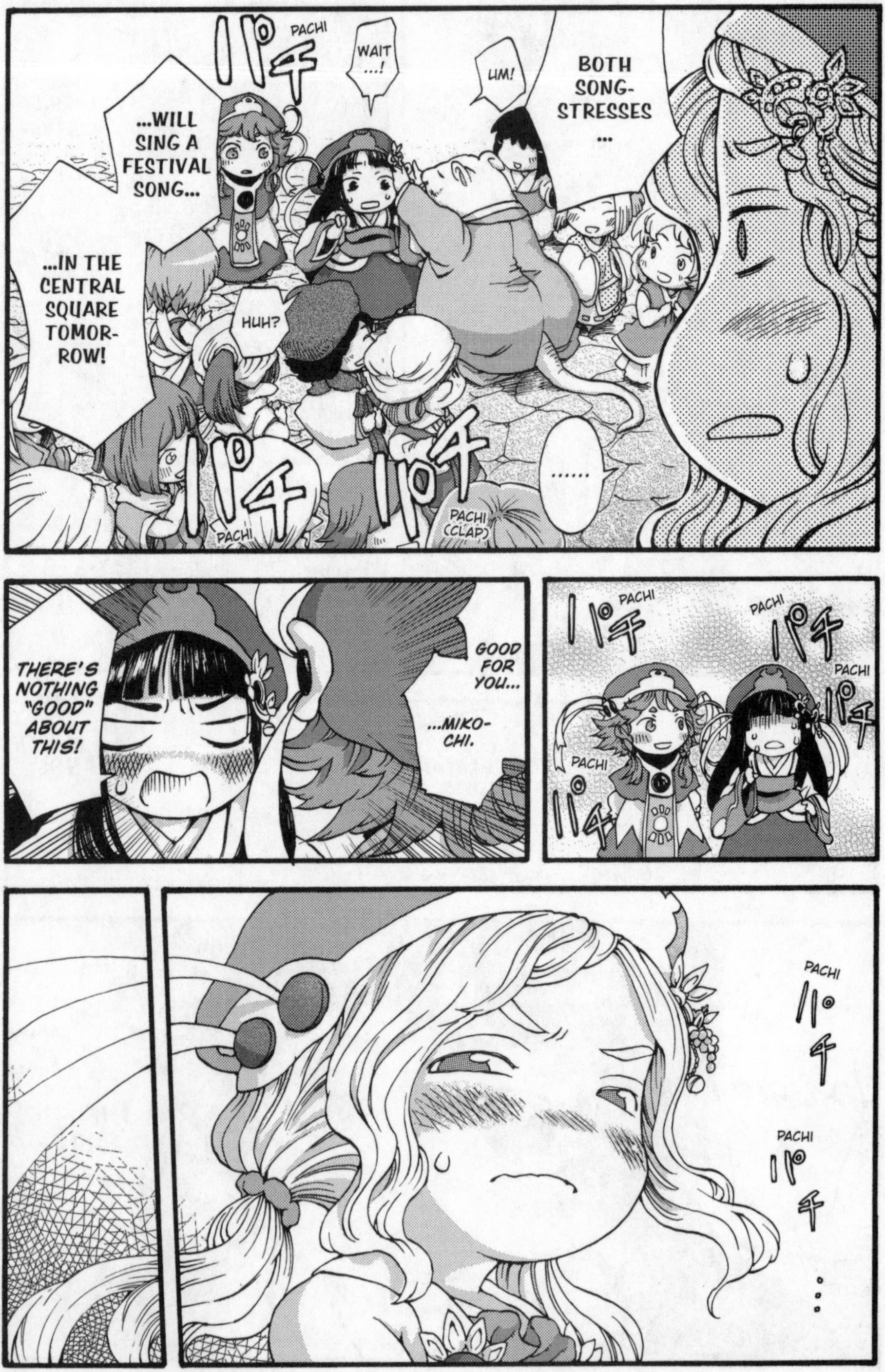
BOTH SONG-STRESSES ...
UM!
WAIT ...!
PACHI
...WILL SING A FESTIVAL SONG...
...IN THE CENTRAL SQUARE TOMOR-ROW!
HUH?
......
PACHI (CLAP)
PACHI
PACHI
PACHI
PACHI
PACHI
GOOD FOR YOU...
...MIKO-CHI.
THERE'S NOTHING "GOOD" ABOUT THIS!
PACHI
PACHI
...

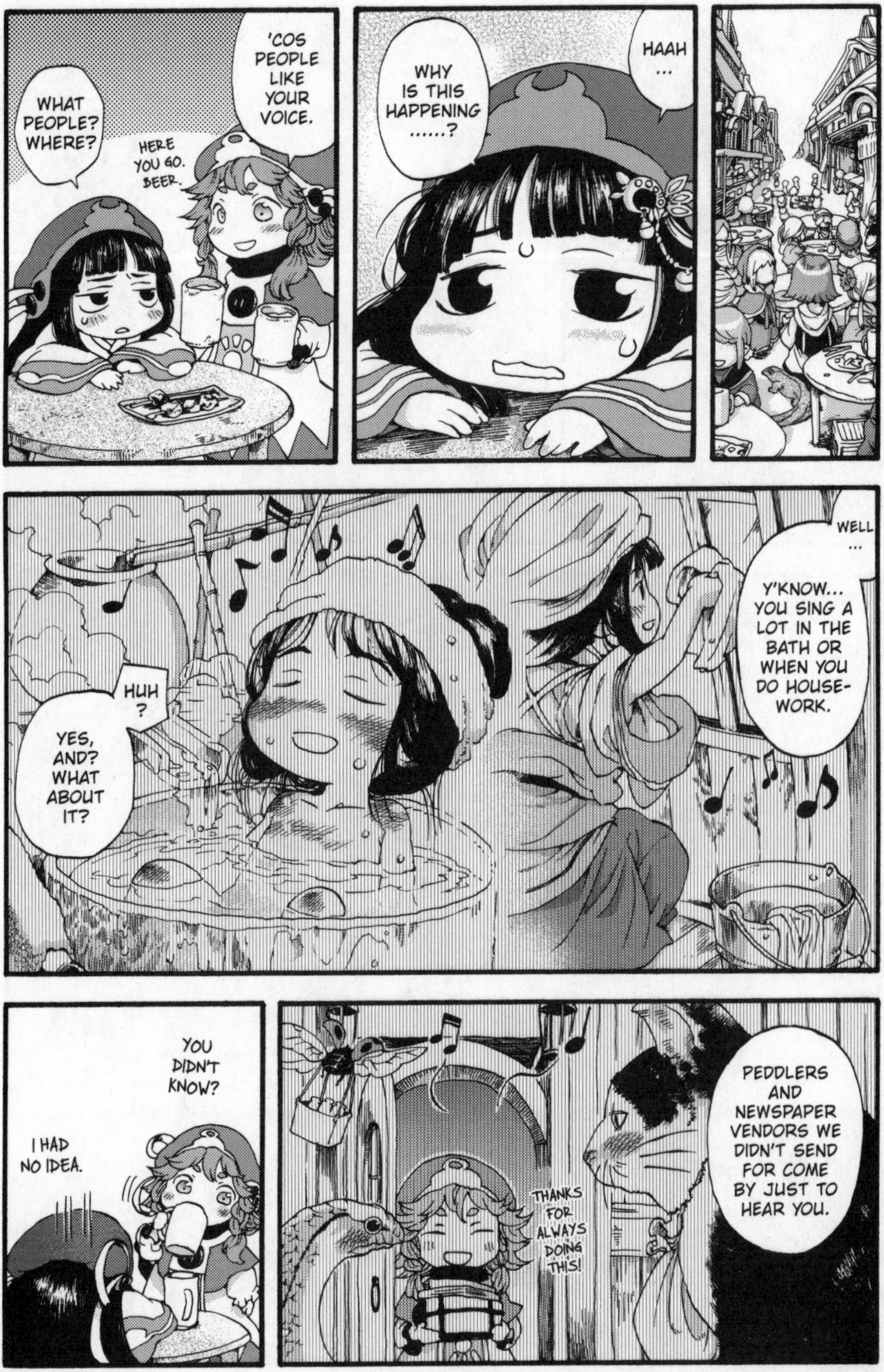
HAAH ...
WHY IS THIS HAPPENING ......?
'COS PEOPLE LIKE YOUR VOICE.
HERE YOU GO. BEER.
WHAT PEOPLE? WHERE?
WELL ...
Y'KNOW... YOU SING A LOT IN THE BATH OR WHEN YOU DO HOUSE-WORK.
HUH ?
YES, AND? WHAT ABOUT IT?
PEDDLERS AND NEWSPAPER VENDORS WE DIDN'T SEND FOR COME BY JUST TO HEAR YOU.
THANKS FOR ALWAYS DOING THIS!
YOU DIDN'T KNOW?
I HAD NO IDEA.

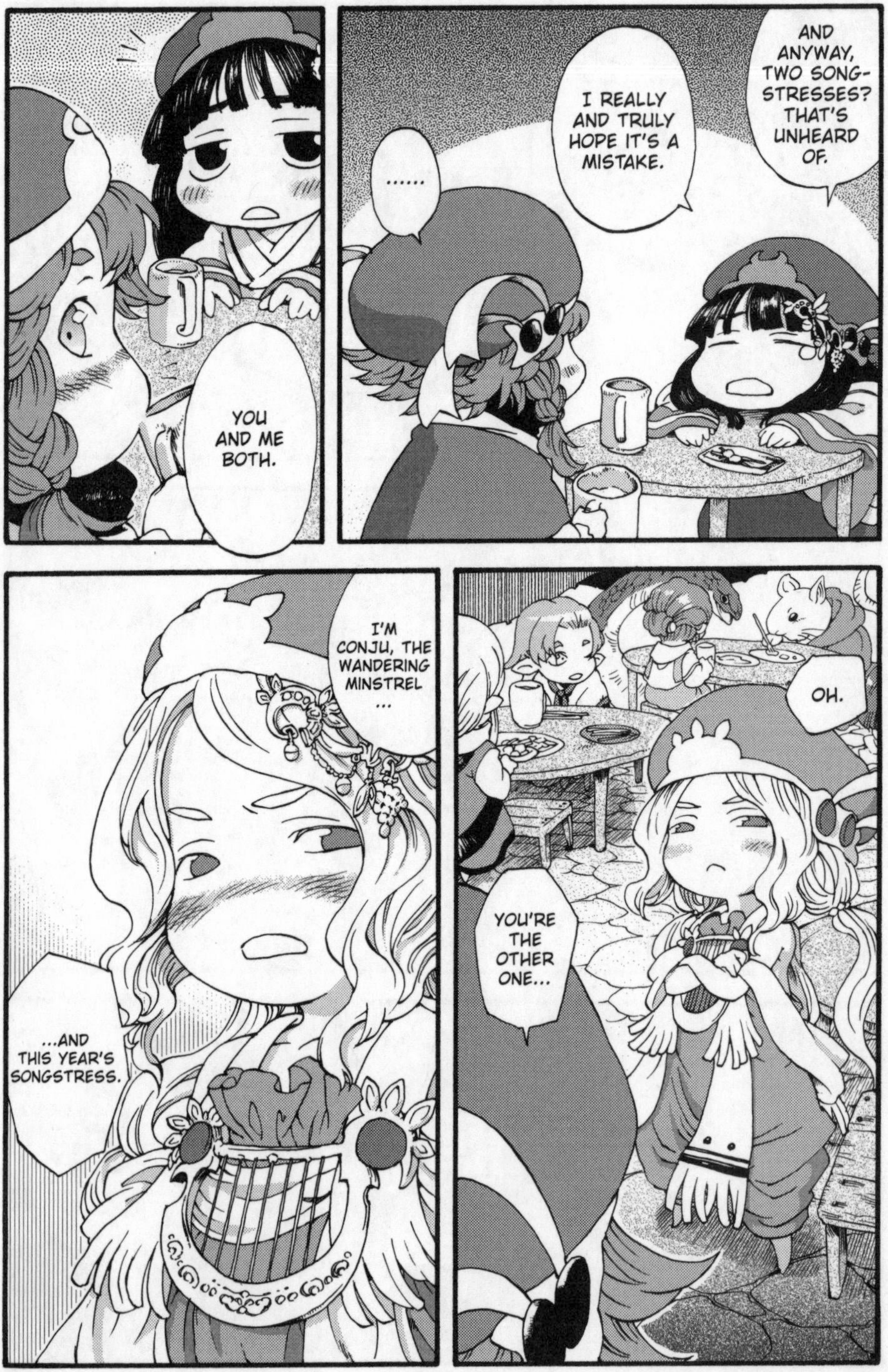
AND ANYWAY, TWO SONG-STRESSES? THAT'S UNHEARD OF.
I REALLY AND TRULY HOPE IT'S A MISTAKE.
......
YOU AND ME BOTH.
OH.
YOU'RE THE OTHER ONE...
I'M CONJU, THE WANDERING MINSTREL ...
...AND THIS YEAR'S SONGSTRESS.

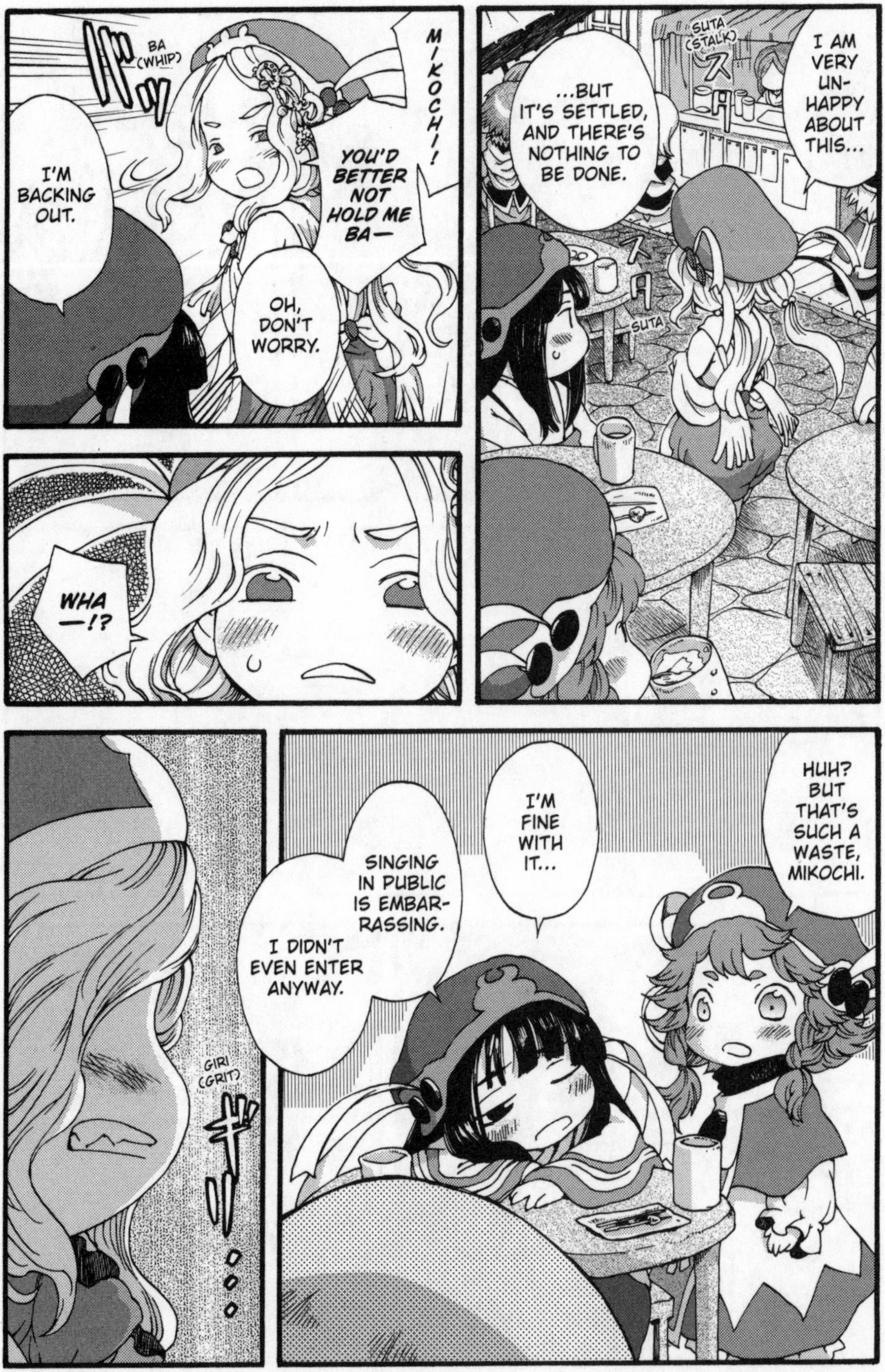
I AM VERY UN-HAPPY ABOUT THIS...
SUTA (STALK)
...BUT IT'S SETTLED, AND THERE'S NOTHING TO BE DONE.
SUTA
MIKOCHI!
YOU'D BETTER NOT HOLD ME BA—
BA (WHIP)
OH, DON'T WORRY.
I'M BACKING OUT.
WHA—!?
HUH? BUT THAT'S SUCH A WASTE, MIKOCHI.
I'M FINE WITH IT...
SINGING IN PUBLIC IS EMBARRASSING.
I DIDN'T EVEN ENTER ANYWAY.
GIRI (GRIT)

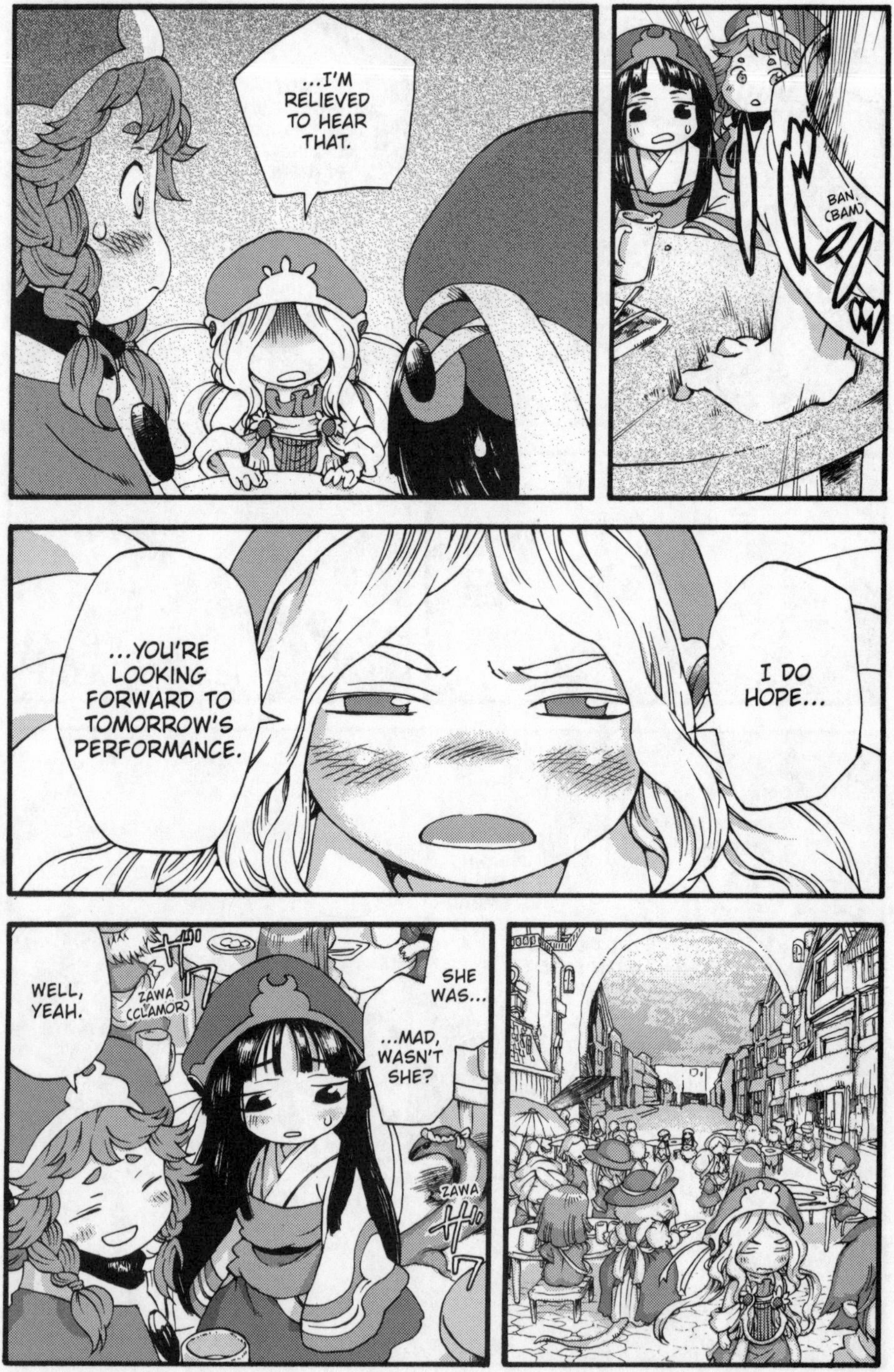
BAN (BAM)
...I'M RELIEVED TO HEAR THAT.
I DO HOPE...
...YOU'RE LOOKING FORWARD TO TOMORROW'S PERFORMANCE.
SHE WAS...
...MAD, WASN'T SHE?
ZAWA (CLAMOR)
WELL, YEAH.
ZAWA

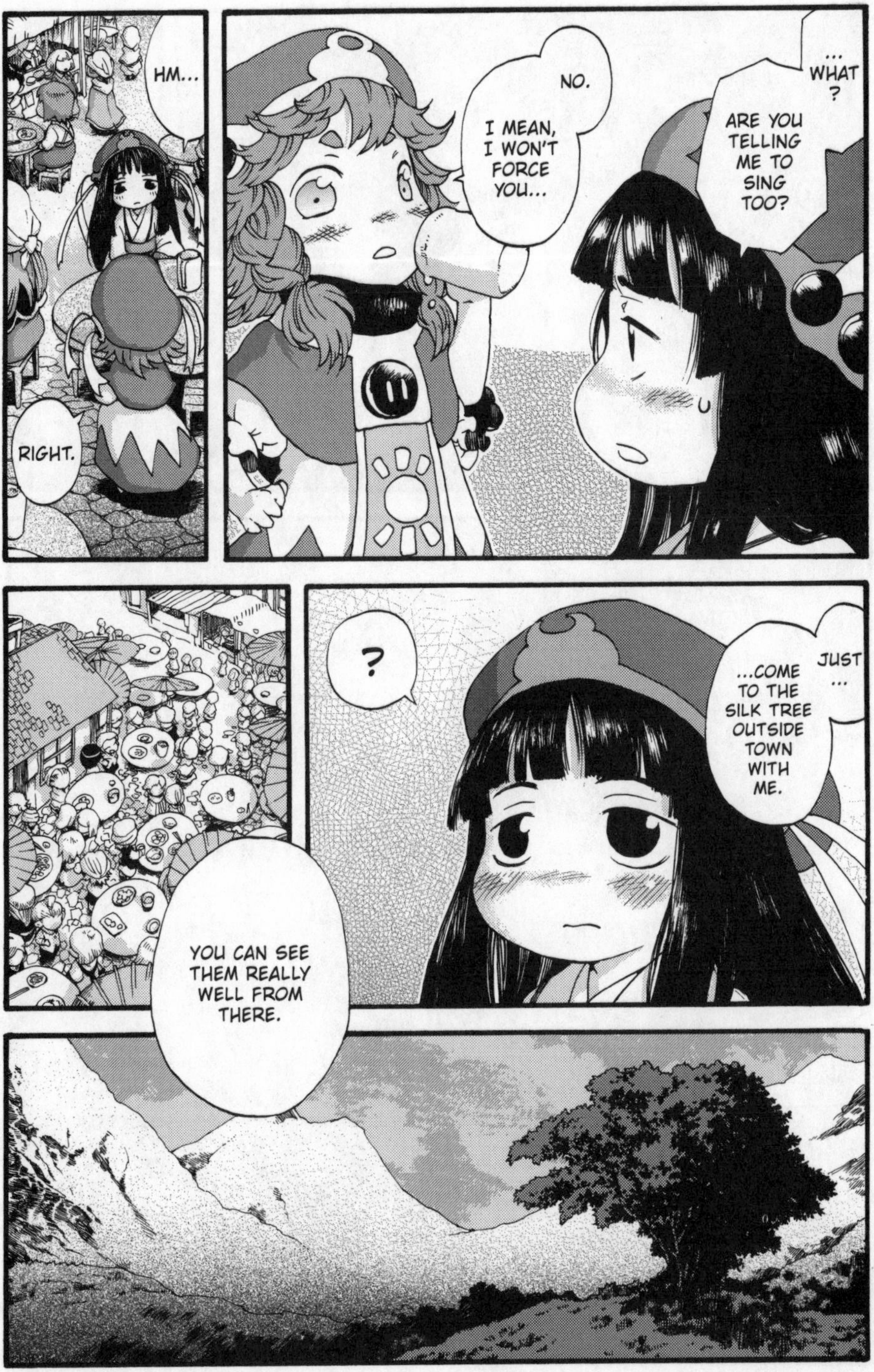
...WHAT?
ARE YOU TELLING ME TO SING TOO?
NO.
I MEAN, I WON'T FORCE YOU...
HM...
RIGHT.
JUST...
...COME TO THE SILK TREE OUTSIDE TOWN WITH ME.
?
YOU CAN SEE THEM REALLY WELL FROM THERE.

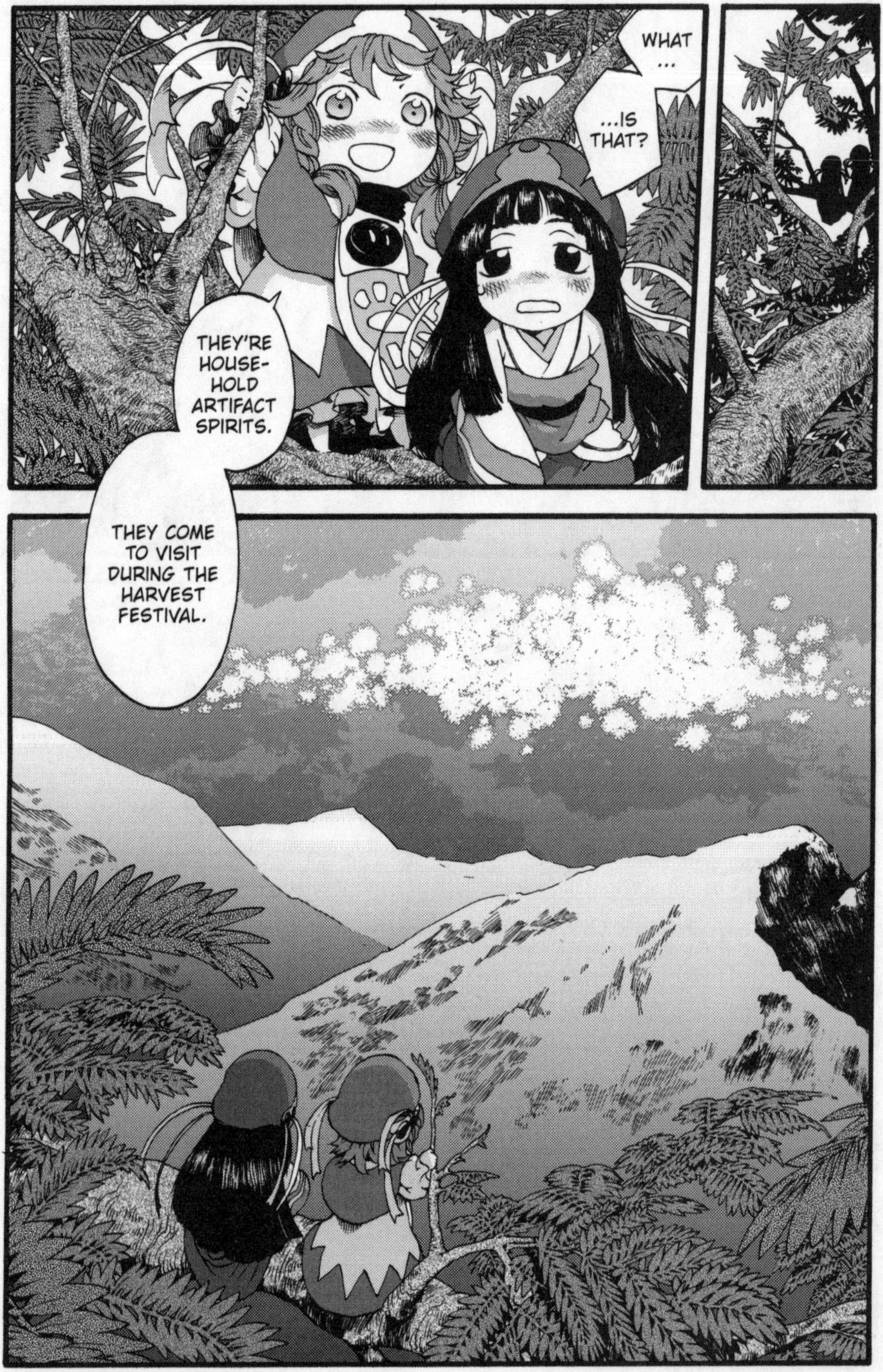
WHAT ...
...IS THAT?
THEY'RE HOUSEHOLD ARTIFACT SPIRITS.
THEY COME TO VISIT DURING THE HARVEST FESTIVAL.

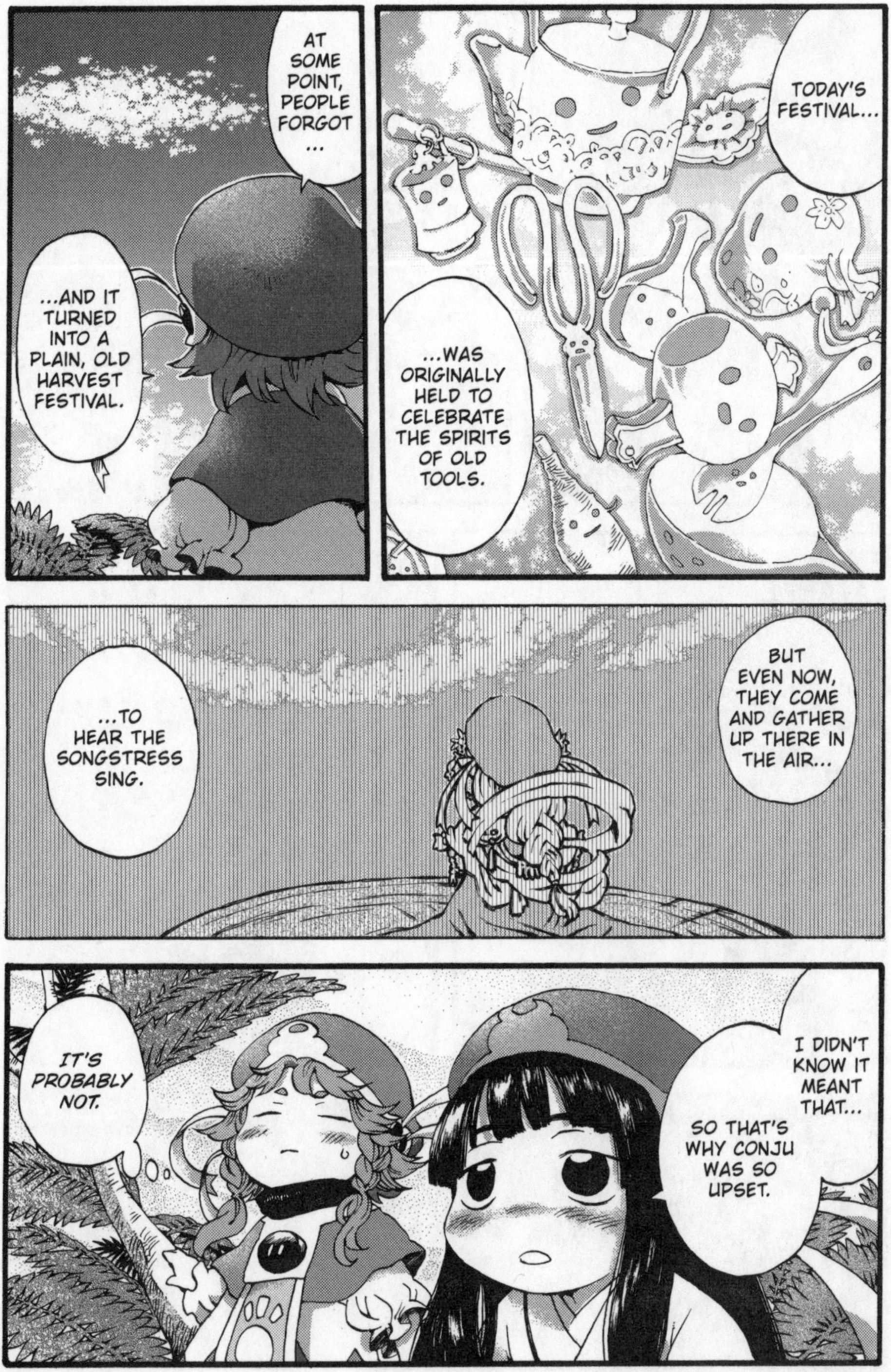
TODAY'S FESTIVAL...
...WAS ORIGINALLY HELD TO CELEBRATE THE SPIRITS OF OLD TOOLS.
AT SOME POINT, PEOPLE FORGOT...
...AND IT TURNED INTO A PLAIN, OLD HARVEST FESTIVAL.
BUT EVEN NOW, THEY COME AND GATHER UP THERE IN THE AIR...
...TO HEAR THE SONGSTRESS SING.
I DIDN'T KNOW IT MEANT THAT...
SO THAT'S WHY CONJU WAS SO UPSET.
IT'S PROBABLY NOT.

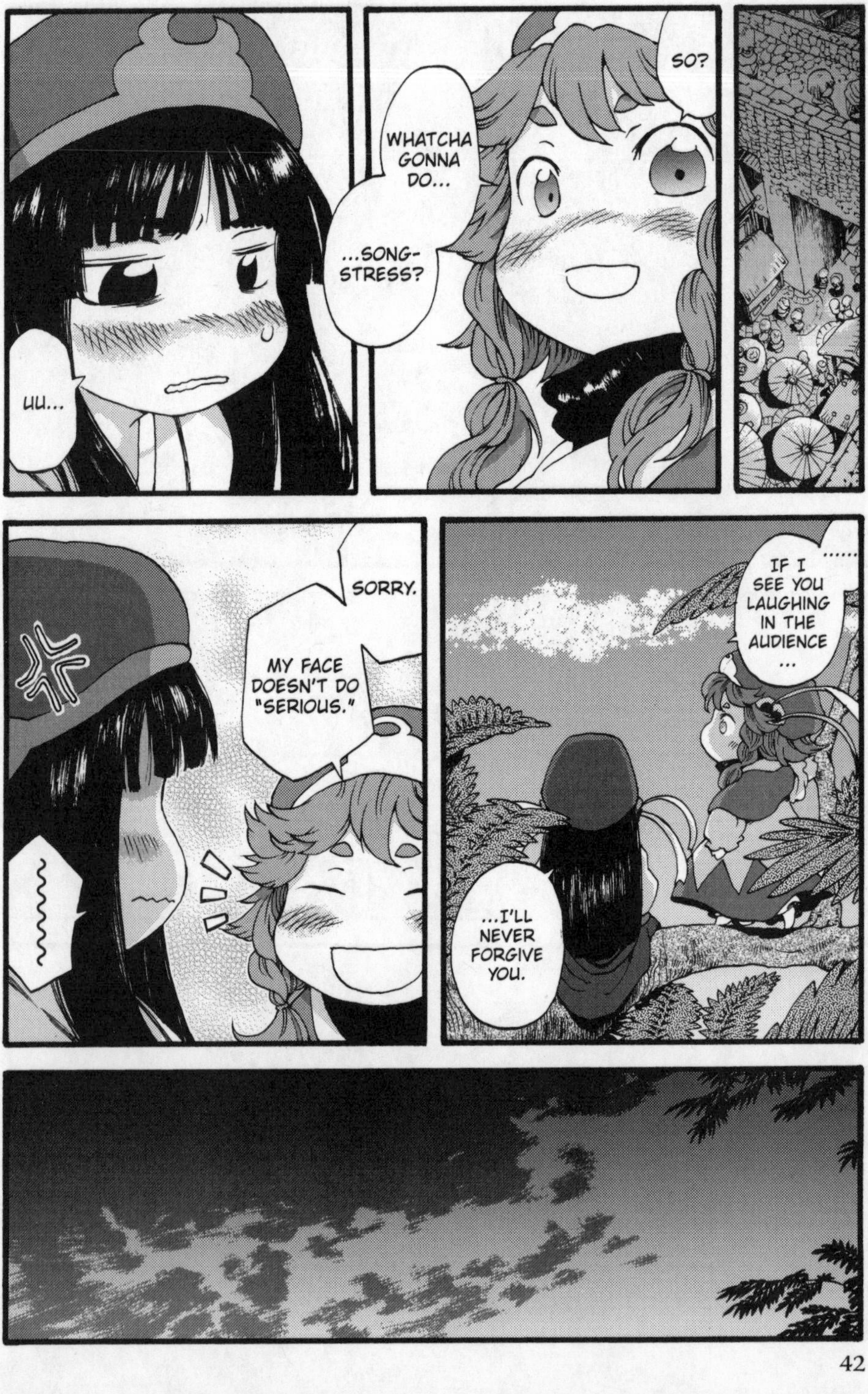
SO?
WHATCHA GONNA DO...
...SONG-STRESS?
UU...
......
IF I SEE YOU LAUGHING IN THE AUDIENCE ...
...I'LL NEVER FORGIVE YOU.
SORRY.
MY FACE DOESN'T DO "SERIOUS."

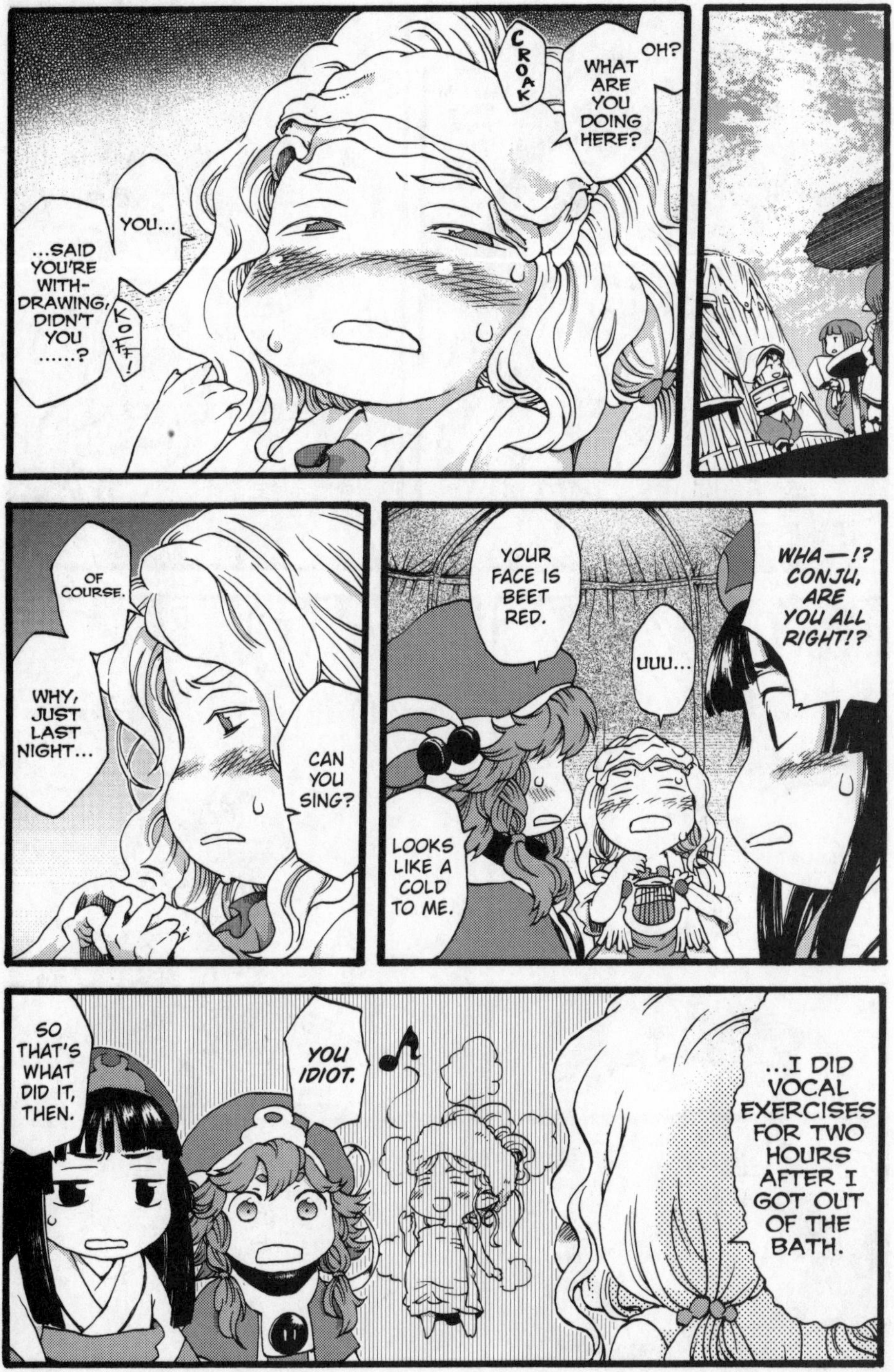
OH? WHAT ARE YOU DOING HERE?
CROAK
YOU...
...SAID YOU'RE WITH-DRAWING, DIDN'T YOU ......?
KOFF!
WHA—!? CONJU, ARE YOU ALL RIGHT!?
YOUR FACE IS BEET RED.
UUU...
LOOKS LIKE A COLD TO ME.
CAN YOU SING?
OF COURSE.
WHY, JUST LAST NIGHT...
...I DID VOCAL EXERCISES FOR TWO HOURS AFTER I GOT OUT OF THE BATH.
YOU IDIOT.
SO THAT'S WHAT DID IT, THEN.

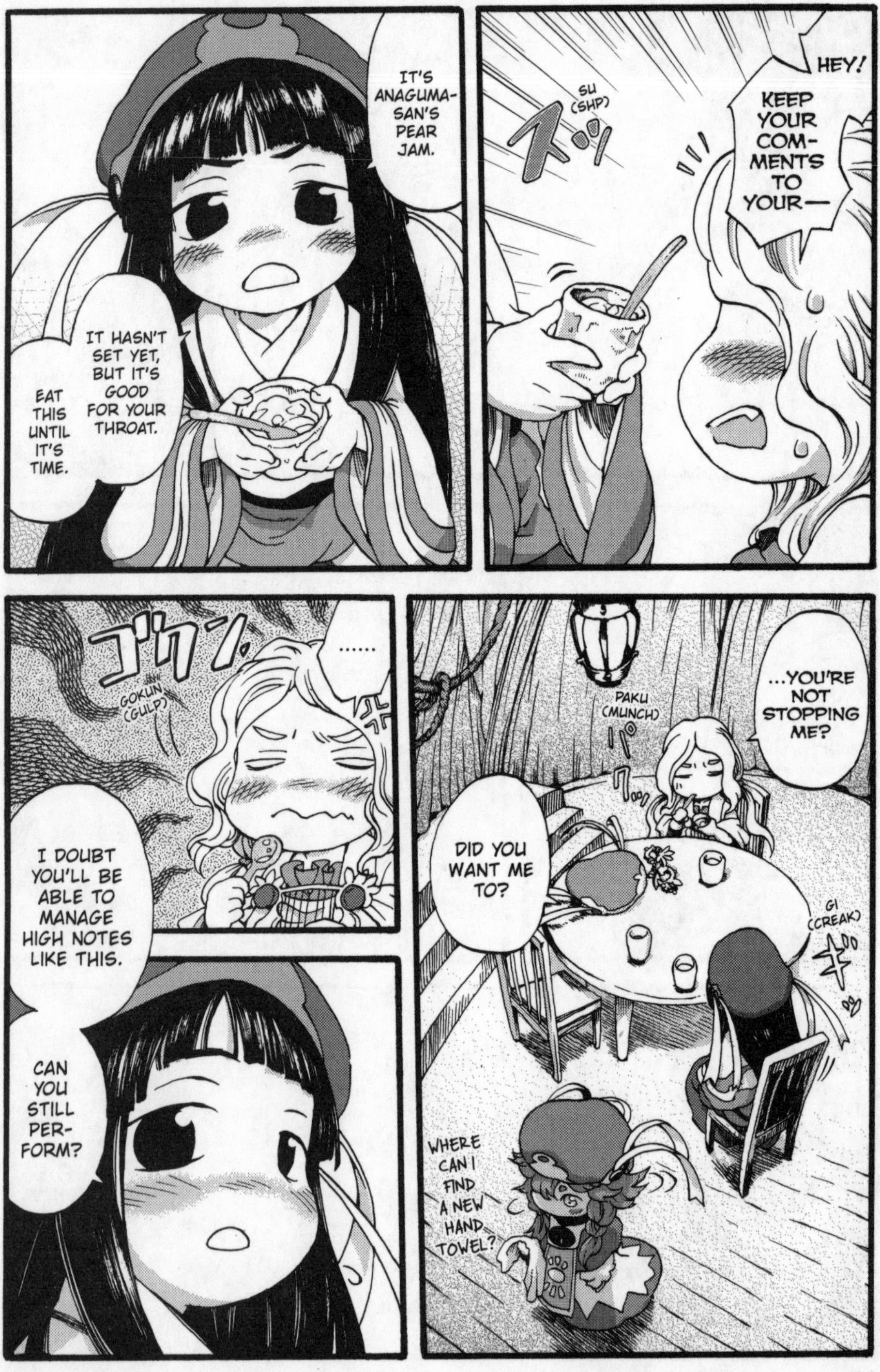
HEY!
KEEP YOUR COM-MENTS TO YOUR—
SU (SHP)
IT'S ANAGUMA-SAN'S PEAR JAM.
IT HASN'T SET YET, BUT IT'S GOOD FOR YOUR THROAT.
EAT THIS UNTIL IT'S TIME.
...YOU'RE NOT STOPPING ME?
PAKU (MUNCH)
DID YOU WANT ME TO?
GI (CREAK)
WHERE CAN I FIND A NEW HAND TOWEL?
......
GOKUN (GULP)
I DOUBT YOU'LL BE ABLE TO MANAGE HIGH NOTES LIKE THIS.
CAN YOU STILL PER-FORM?

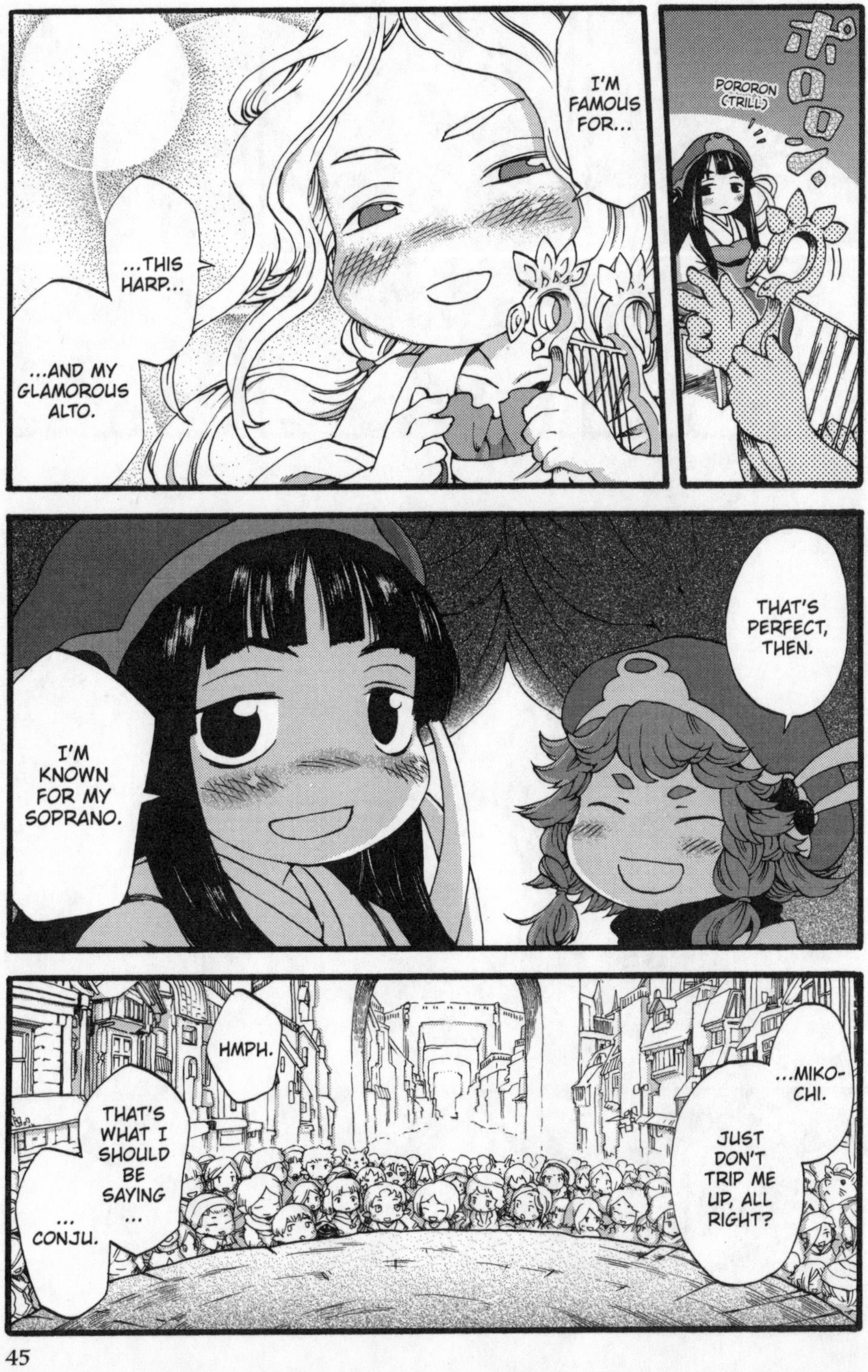
POROROR (TRILL)
I'M FAMOUS FOR...
...THIS HARP...
...AND MY GLAMOROUS ALTO.
THAT'S PERFECT, THEN.
I'M KNOWN FOR MY SOPRANO.
...MIKO-CHI.
JUST DON'T TRIP ME UP, ALL RIGHT?
HMPH.
THAT'S WHAT I SHOULD BE SAYING ...
... CONJU.

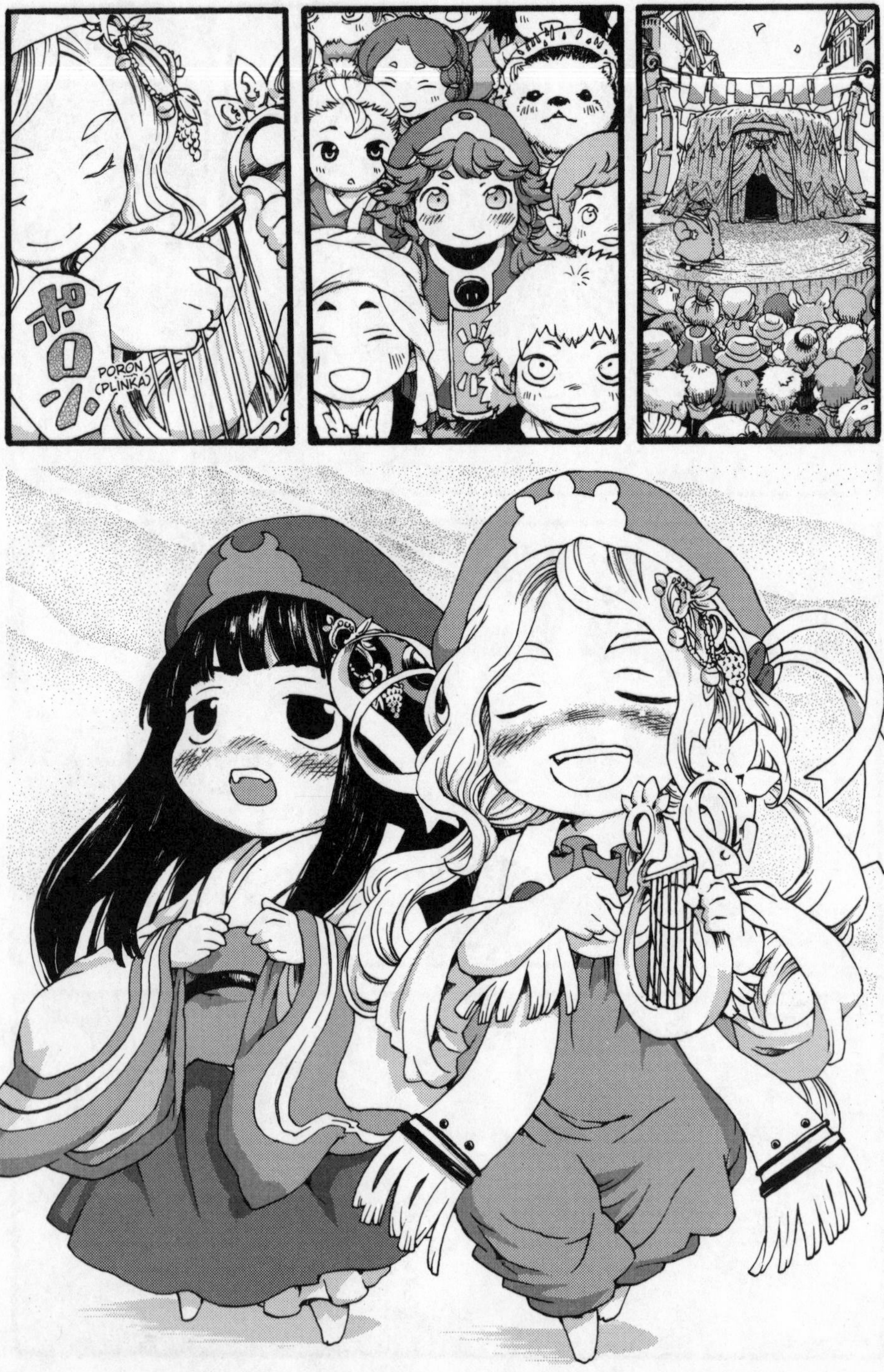
ポロン
PORON (PLINKA)

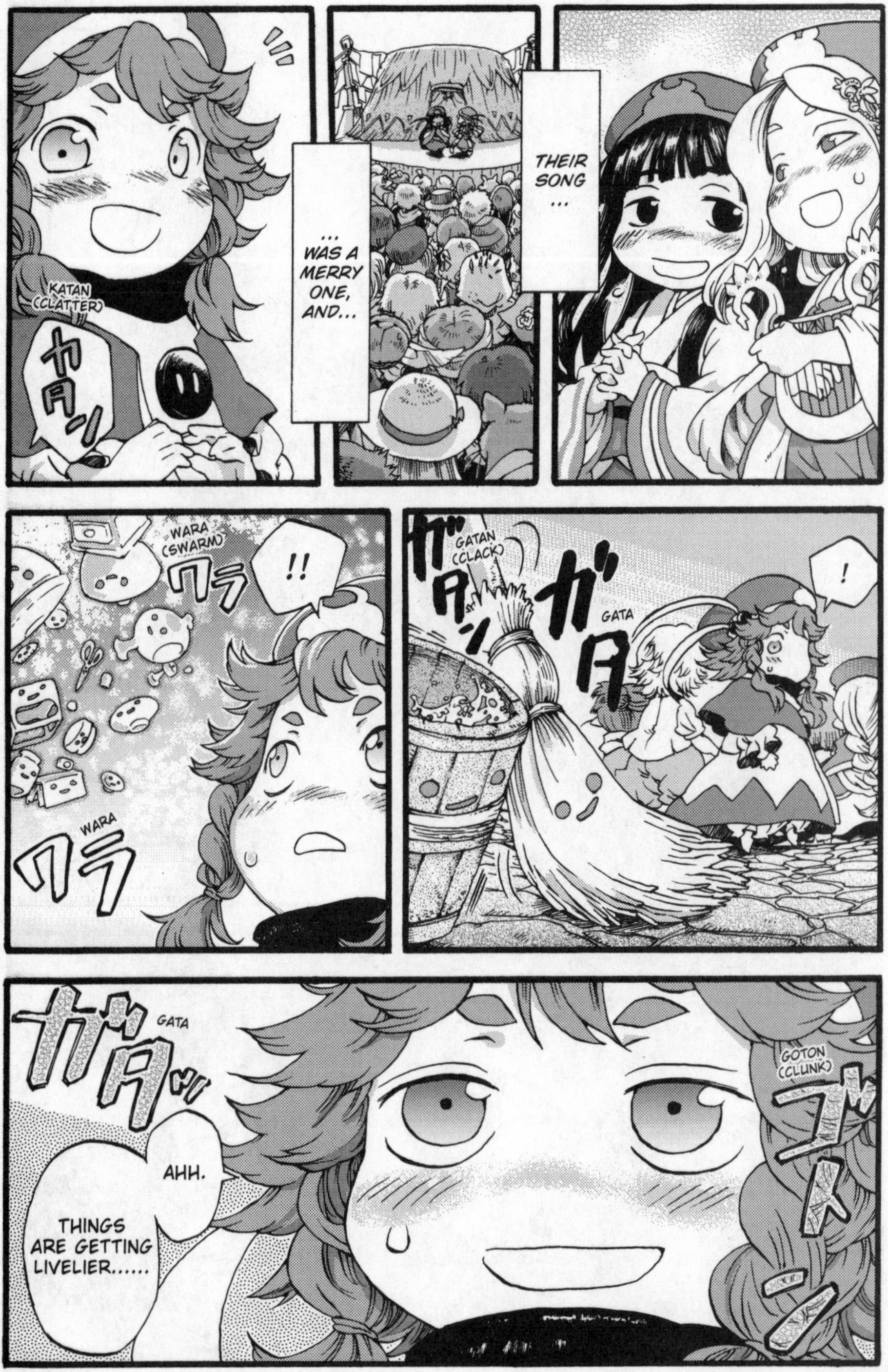
THEIR SONG ...
... WAS A MERRY ONE, AND...
KATAN (CLATTER)
!
GATAN (CLACK)
GATA
!!
WARA (SWARM)
WARA
GOTON (CLUNK)
GATA
AHH.
THINGS ARE GETTING LIVELIER......

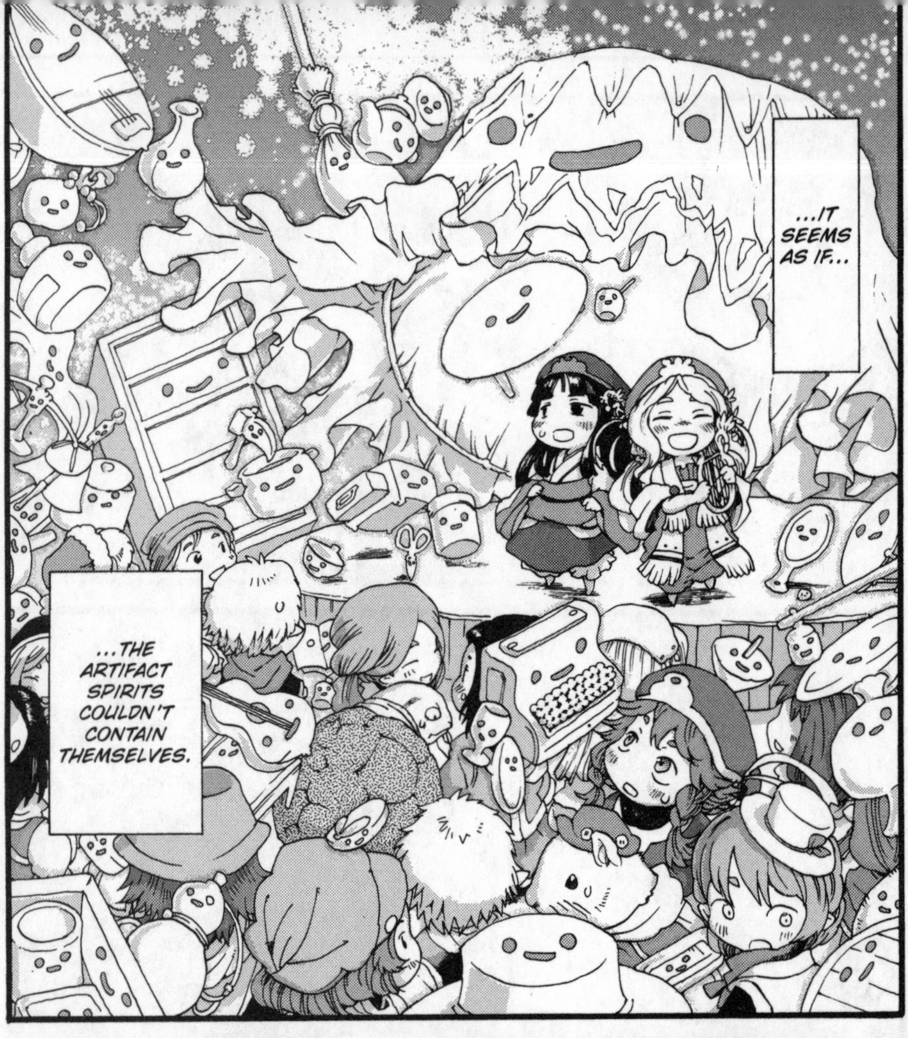
...IT SEEMS AS IF...
...THE ARTIFACT SPIRITS COULDN'T CONTAIN THEMSELVES.

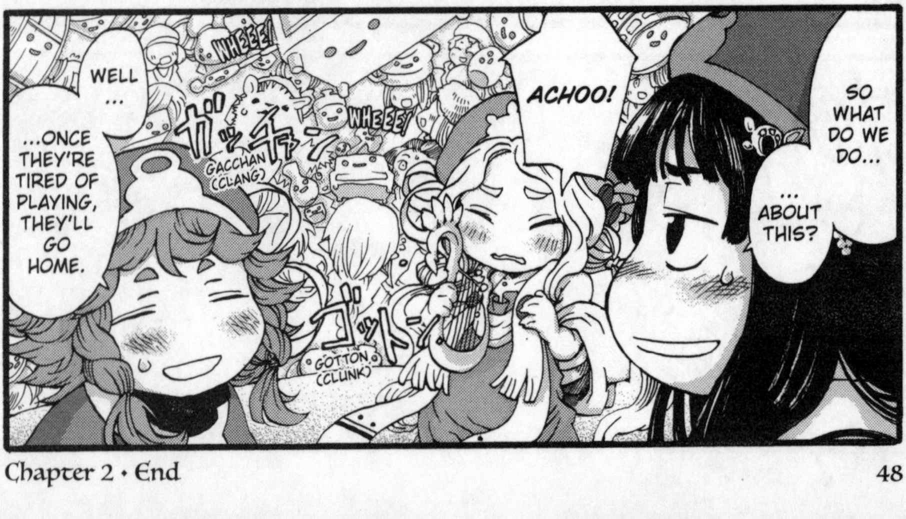
SO WHAT DO WE DO...
...ABOUT THIS?
ACHOO!
WHEEE!
WHEEE!
GACCHAN (CLANG)
GOTTON (CLUNK)
WELL ...
...ONCE THEY'RE TIRED OF PLAYING, THEY'LL GO HOME.

Chapter 2 • End

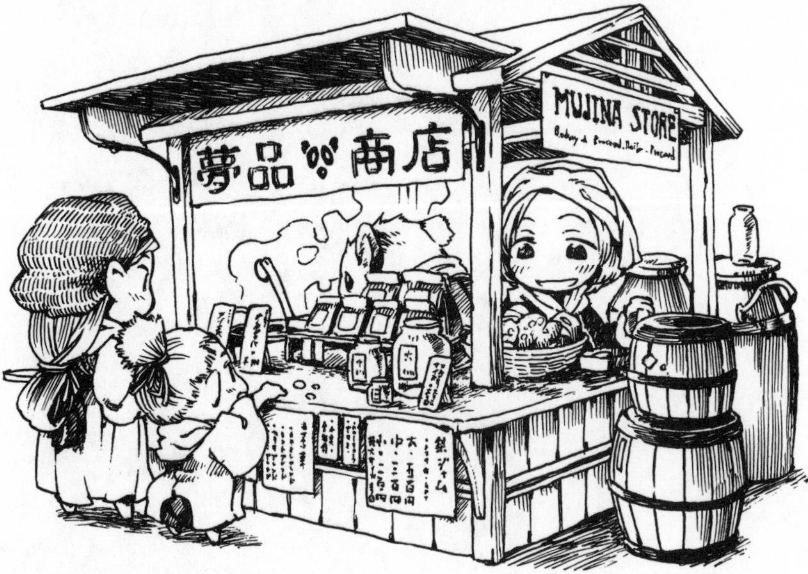
商店
MUJINA STORE
大・五百円
中・三百円
小・二百円

The Makinata harvest festival features approximately six thousand street stalls and booths. Of these, the Mujina Store stall attracts particular attention. The Mujina flagship store is located in Jaga Valley, where they sell household goods, preserved foods, bread, and sweets. However, exclusively during the harvest festival, their offerings include a secret customer favorite: pear jam.

The jam is made from large pears from the south of Arabi. You can enjoy its robust sweetness, fresh fragrance, and texture as is. However, the recommended way to eat it is between two slices of multigrain bread (also sold at the stall) while having a stroll. A large pear jam will set you back ¥500, a medium ¥300, and a small ¥200.

Since the stall also sells things like bagels and yogurt, you can try the jam in lots of different ways.

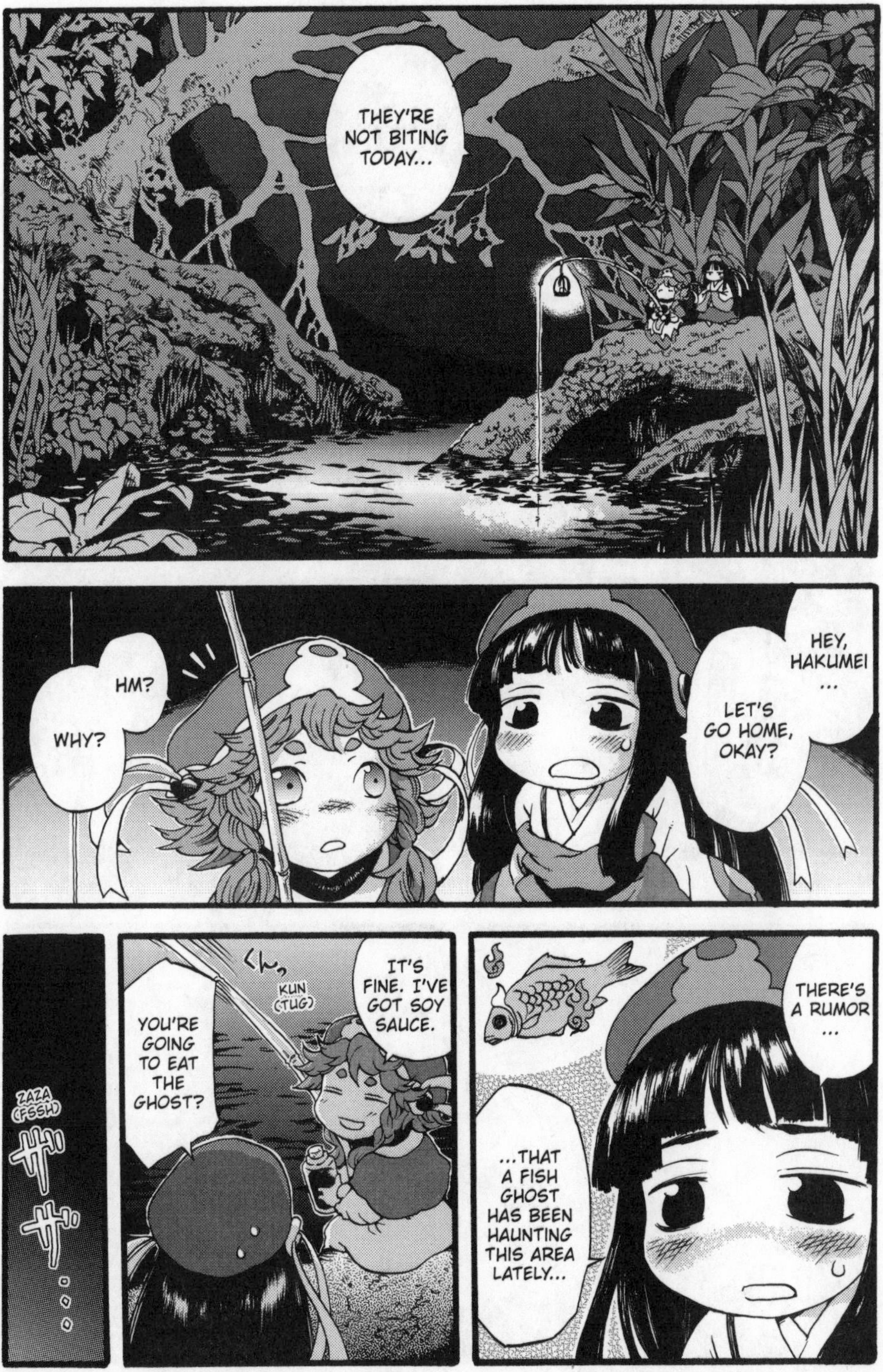
THEY'RE NOT BITING TODAY...
HEY, HAKUMEI ...
LET'S GO HOME, OKAY?
HM?
WHY?
THERE'S A RUMOR ...
...THAT A FISH GHOST HAS BEEN HAUNTING THIS AREA LATELY...
IT'S FINE. I'VE GOT SOY SAUCE.
KUN (TUG)
YOU'RE GOING TO EAT THE GHOST?
ZAZA (FSSH)

Chapter 3
The Glass Lamp

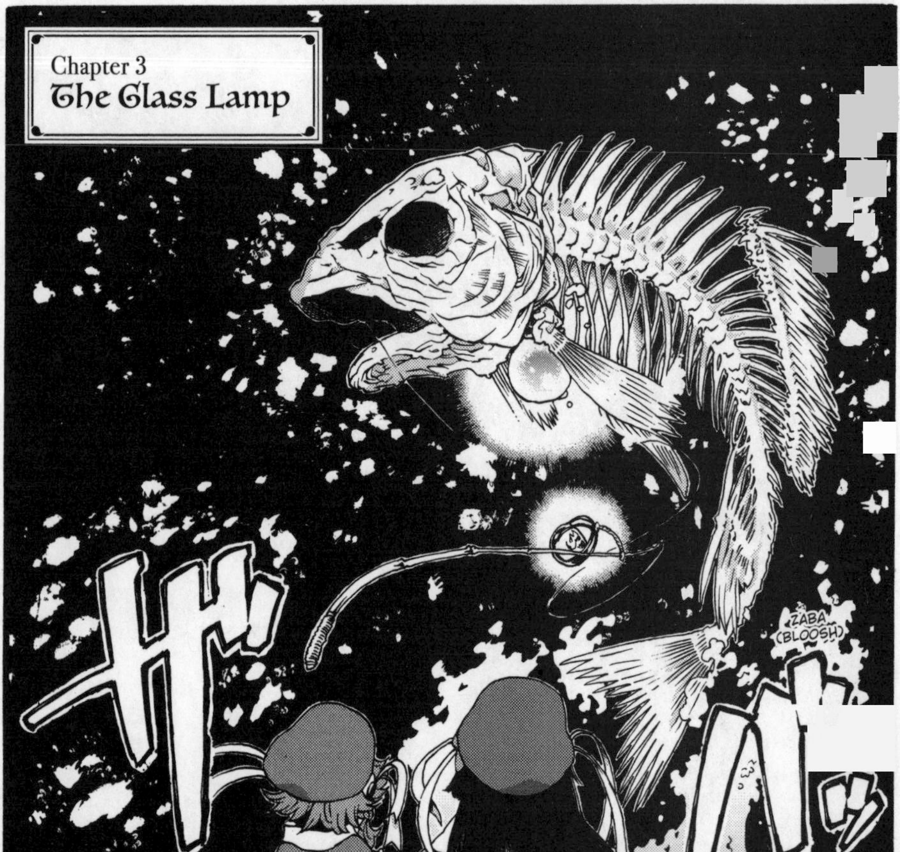
ZABA
(BLOOSH)

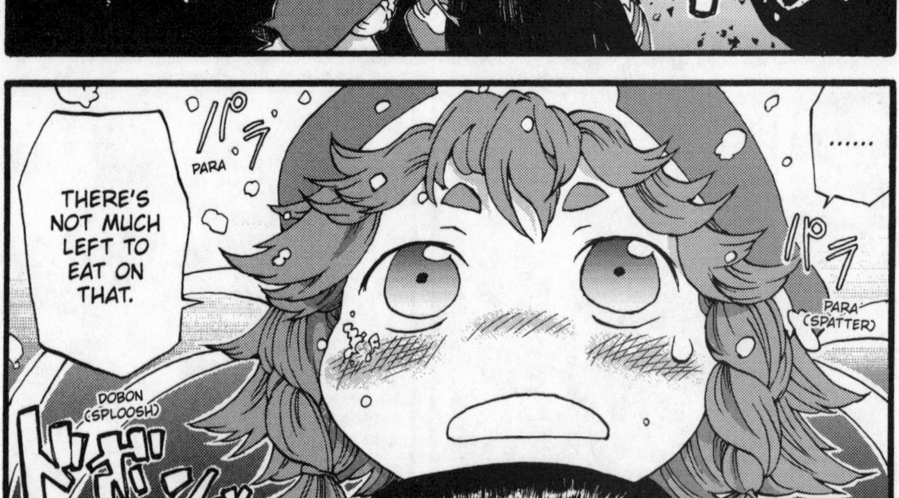
......
PARA
(SPATTER)
PARA
THERE'S NOT MUCH LEFT TO EAT ON THAT.
DOBON
(SPLOOSH)

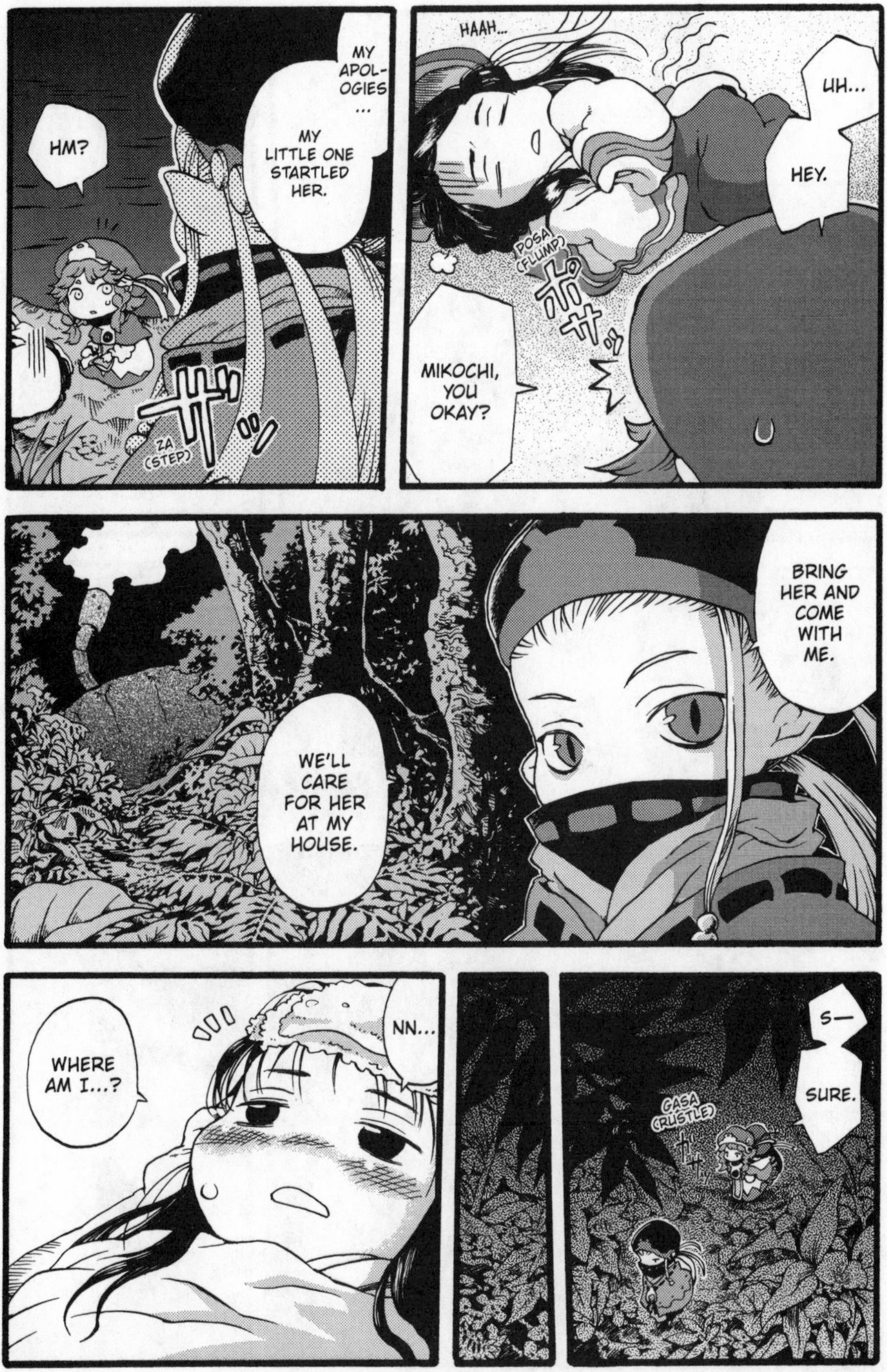
UH...
HEY.
HAAH...
POSA (FLUMP)
MIKOCHI, YOU OKAY?
MY APOLOGIES...
MY LITTLE ONE STARTLED HER.
HM?
ZA (STEP)
BRING HER AND COME WITH ME.
WE'LL CARE FOR HER AT MY HOUSE.
S—
SURE.
GASA (RUSTLE)
NN...
WHERE AM I...?

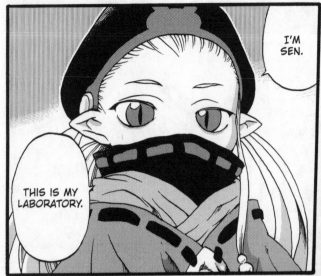

YOU'RE AWAKE, HMM?
I'M SEN.
THIS IS MY LABORATORY.
UM...
I THINK MY FRIEND WAS WITH ME...
OUT-SIDE?
GI (CREAK)
ギッ
HEY!
MIKO-CHI!
ぬっ
NU (LOOM)

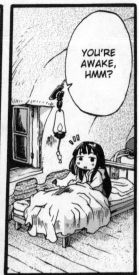

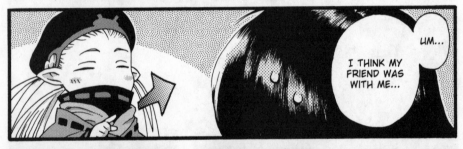

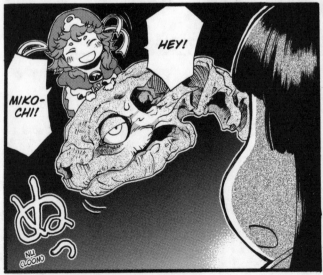

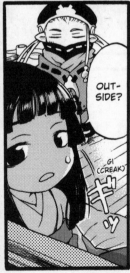

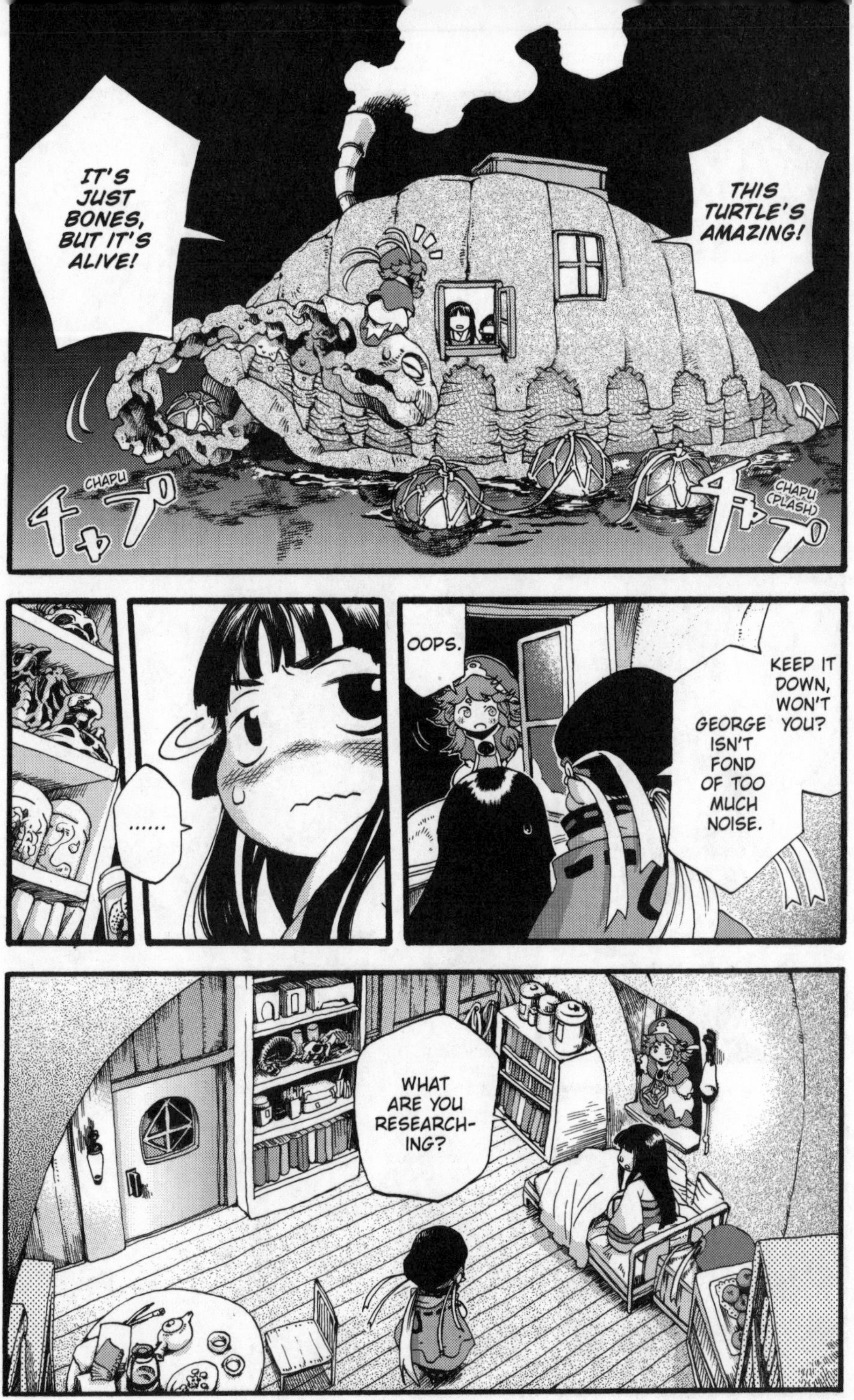
THIS TURTLE'S AMAZING!
IT'S JUST BONES, BUT IT'S ALIVE!
チャプ
CHAPU (PLASH)
チャプ
CHAPU
KEEP IT DOWN, WON'T YOU? GEORGE ISN'T FOND OF TOO MUCH NOISE.
OOPS.
......
WHAT ARE YOU RESEARCHING?

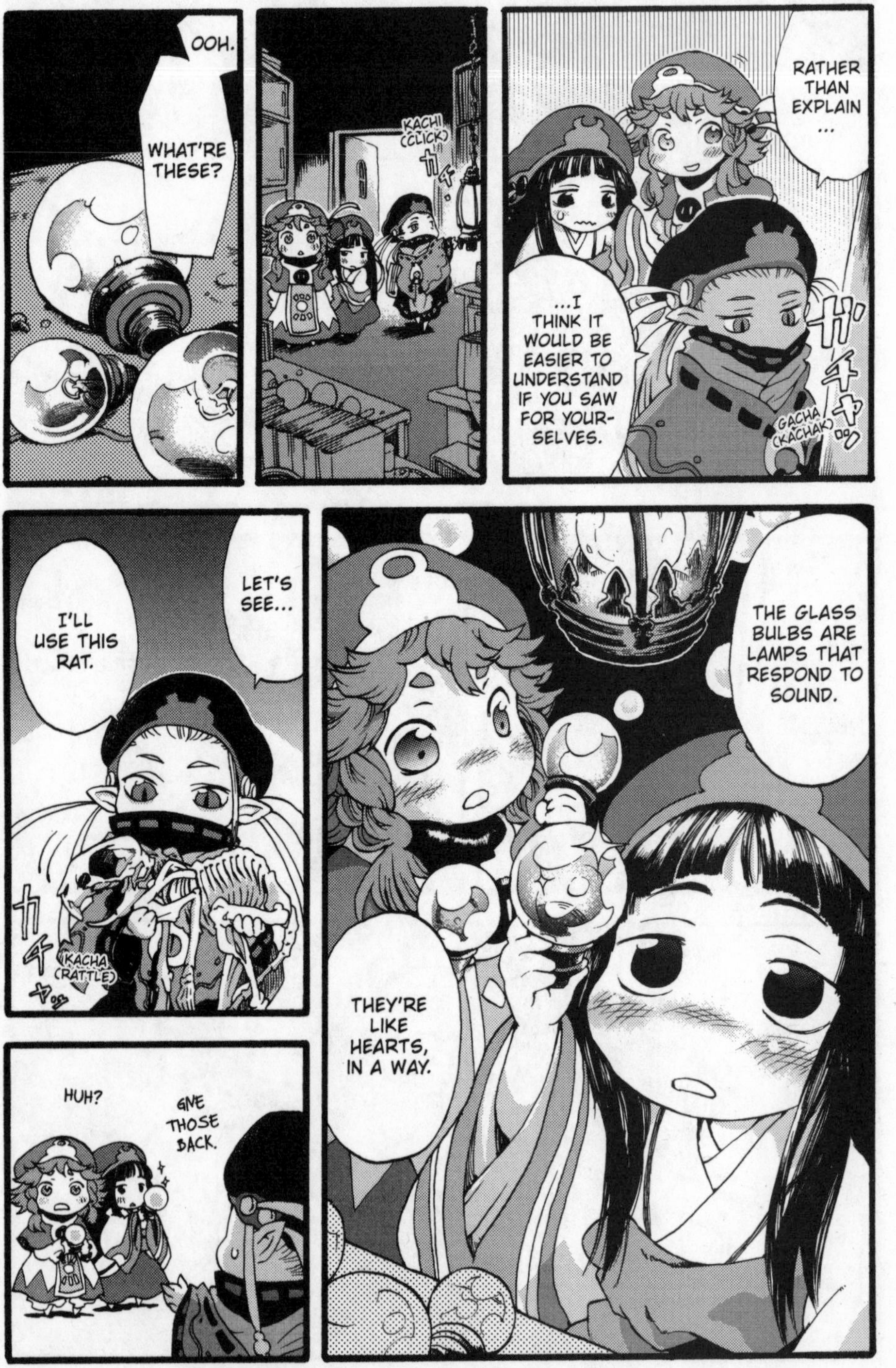
RATHER THAN EXPLAIN ...
...I THINK IT WOULD BE EASIER TO UNDERSTAND IF YOU SAW FOR YOUR-SELVES.
GACHA (KACHAK)
KACHI (CLICK)
OOH.
WHAT'RE THESE?
THE GLASS BULBS ARE LAMPS THAT RESPOND TO SOUND.
THEY'RE LIKE HEARTS, IN A WAY.
LET'S SEE...
I'LL USE THIS RAT.
KACHA (RATTLE)
GIVE THOSE BACK.
HUH?

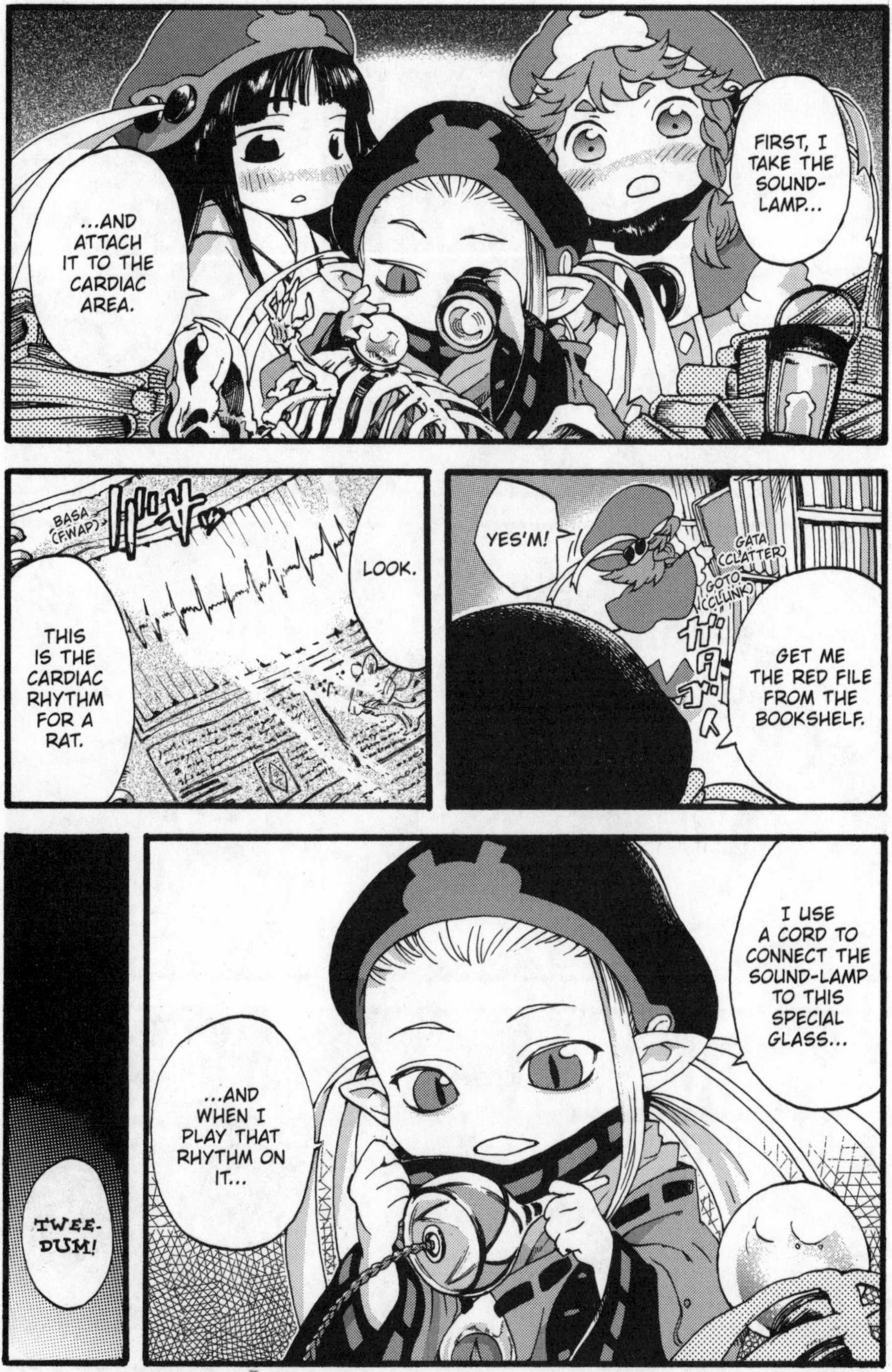
FIRST, I TAKE THE SOUND-LAMP...
...AND ATTACH IT TO THE CARDIAC AREA.
GET ME THE RED FILE FROM THE BOOKSHELF.
YES'M!
GATA (CLATTER)
GOTO (CLUNK)
BASA (F.WAP)
LOOK.
THIS IS THE CARDIAC RHYTHM FOR A RAT.
I USE A CORD TO CONNECT THE SOUND-LAMP TO THIS SPECIAL GLASS...
...AND WHEN I PLAY THAT RHYTHM ON IT...
TWEE-DUM!

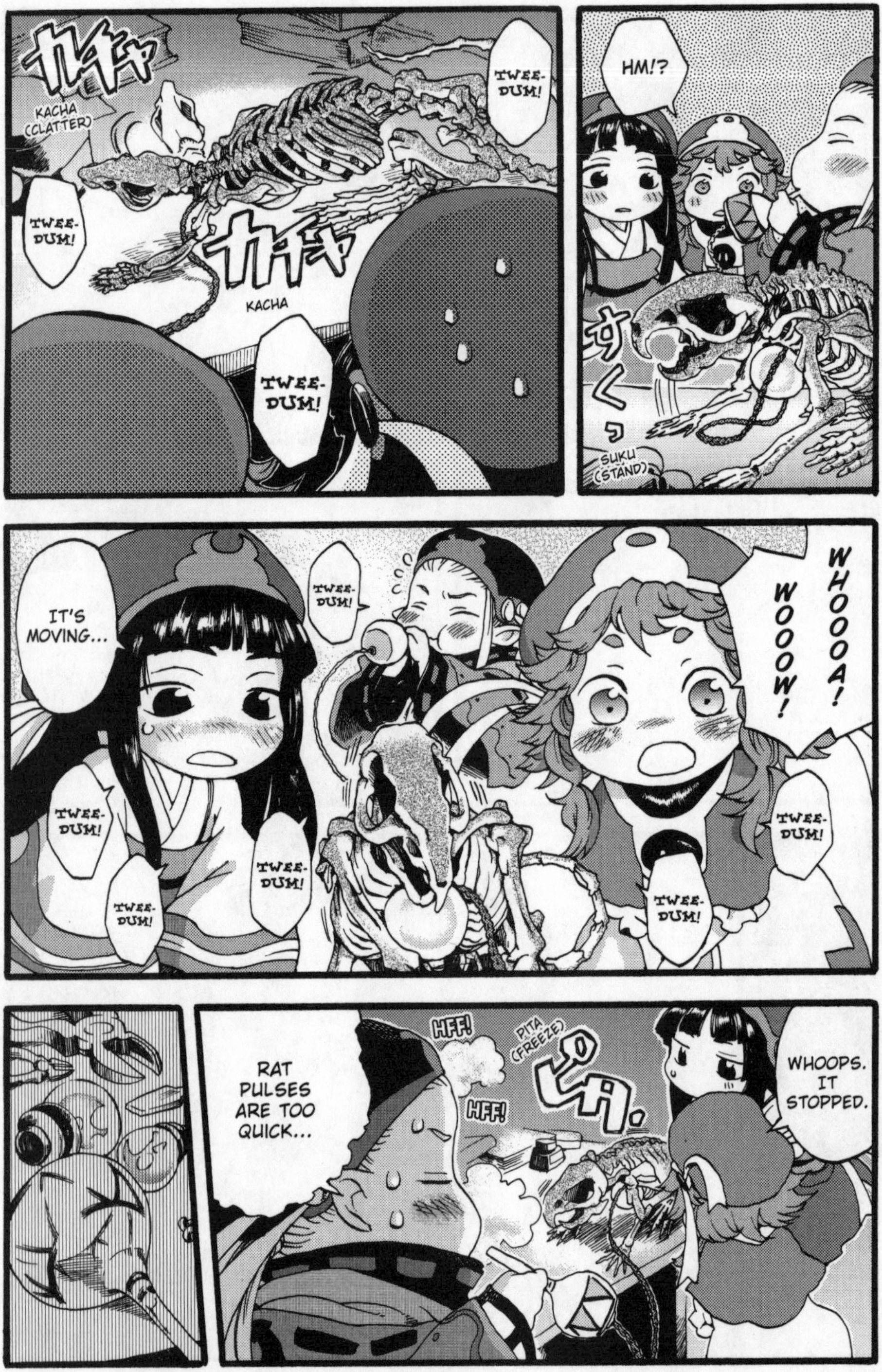
HM!?
すくっ
SUKU (STAND)
カチャ
KACHA (CLATTER)
TWEE-DUM!
TWEE-DUM!
カチャ
KACHA
TWEE-DUM!
WHOOOOA! WOOOOW!
TWEE-DUM!
TWEE-DUM!
TWEE-DUM!
IT'S MOVING...
TWEE-DUM!
TWEE-DUM!
TWEE-DUM!
WHOOPS. IT STOPPED.
PITA (FREEZE)
ピタ。
HFF!
HFF!
RAT PULSES ARE TOO QUICK...

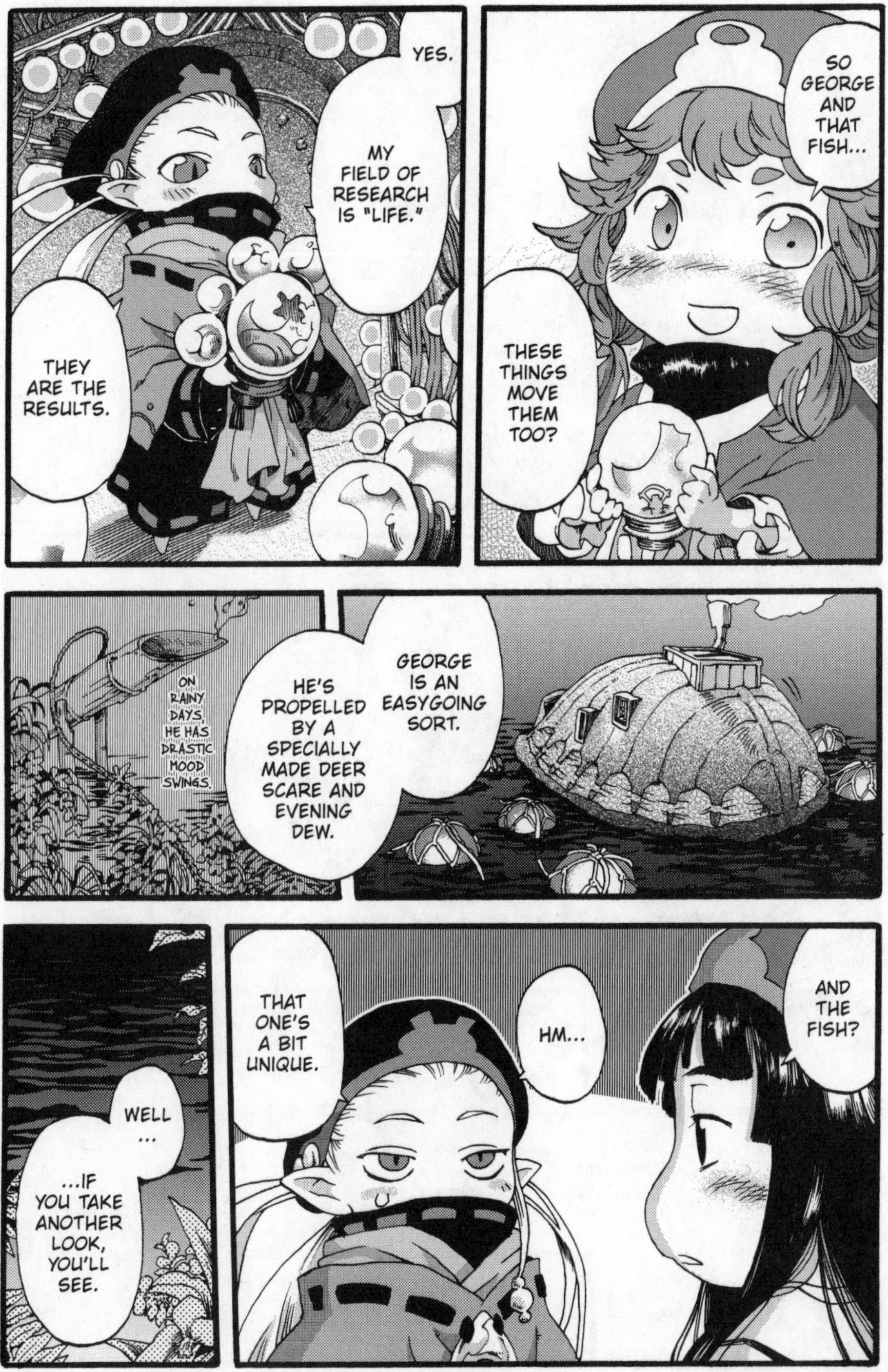
SO GEORGE AND THAT FISH...
THESE THINGS MOVE THEM TOO?
YES.
MY FIELD OF RESEARCH IS "LIFE."
THEY ARE THE RESULTS.
GEORGE IS AN EASYGOING SORT.
HE'S PROPELLED BY A SPECIALLY MADE DEER SCARE AND EVENING DEW.
ON RAINY DAYS, HE HAS DRASTIC MOOD SWINGS.
AND THE FISH?
HM...
THAT ONE'S A BIT UNIQUE.
WELL...
...IF YOU TAKE ANOTHER LOOK, YOU'LL SEE.

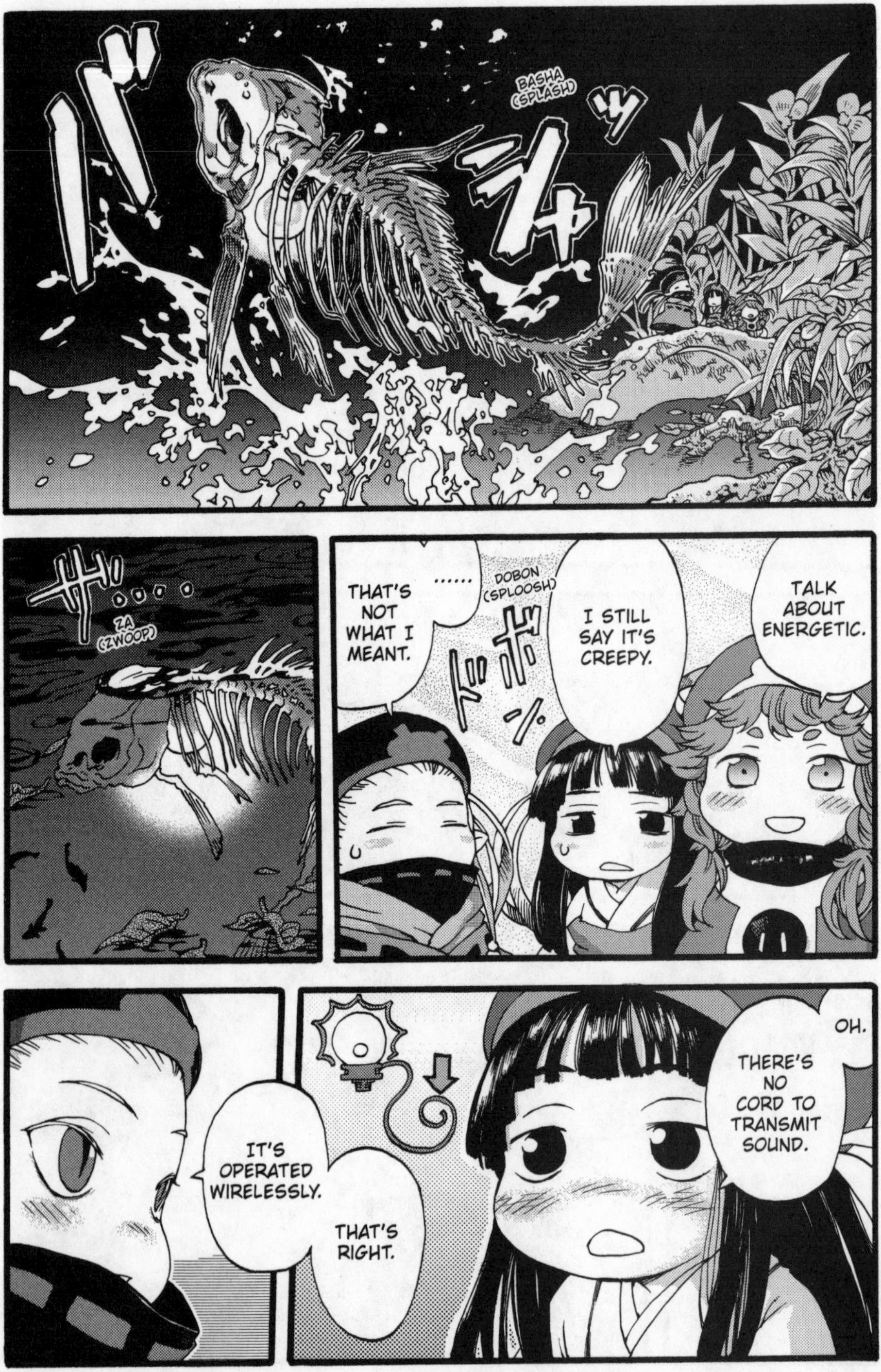
BASHA (SPLASH)
TALK ABOUT ENERGETIC.
I STILL SAY IT'S CREEPY.
DOBON (SPLOOSH)
......
THAT'S NOT WHAT I MEANT.
ZA (ZWOOP)
OH.
THERE'S NO CORD TO TRANSMIT SOUND.
IT'S OPERATED WIRELESSLY.
THAT'S RIGHT.

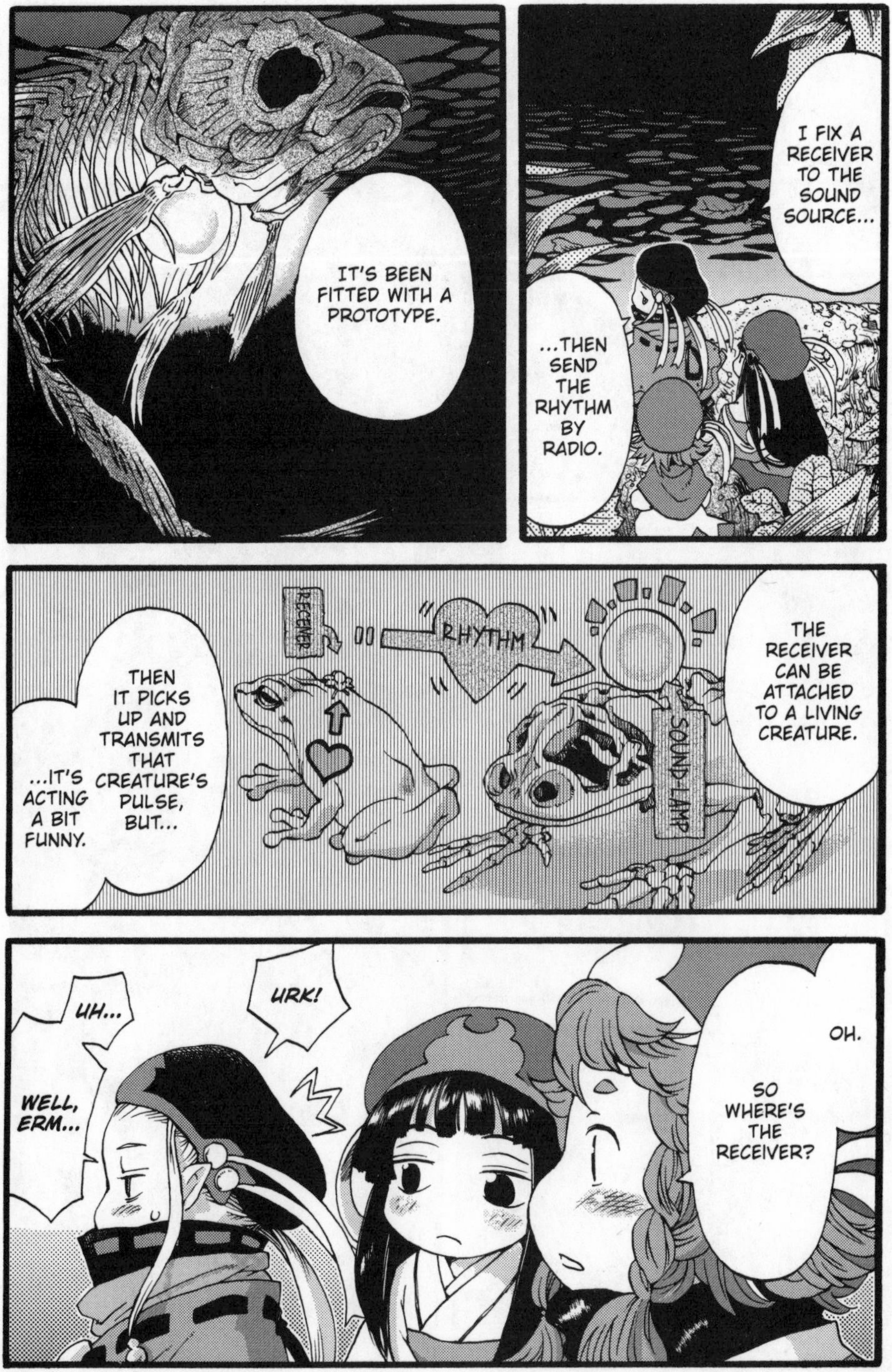
I FIX A RECEIVER TO THE SOUND SOURCE...
...THEN SEND THE RHYTHM BY RADIO.
IT'S BEEN FITTED WITH A PROTOTYPE.
THE RECEIVER CAN BE ATTACHED TO A LIVING CREATURE.
SOUND LAMP
RHYTHM
RECEIVER
THEN IT PICKS UP AND TRANSMITS THAT CREATURE'S PULSE, BUT...
...IT'S ACTING A BIT FUNNY.
OH.
SO WHERE'S THE RECEIVER?
URK!
UH...
WELL, ERM...

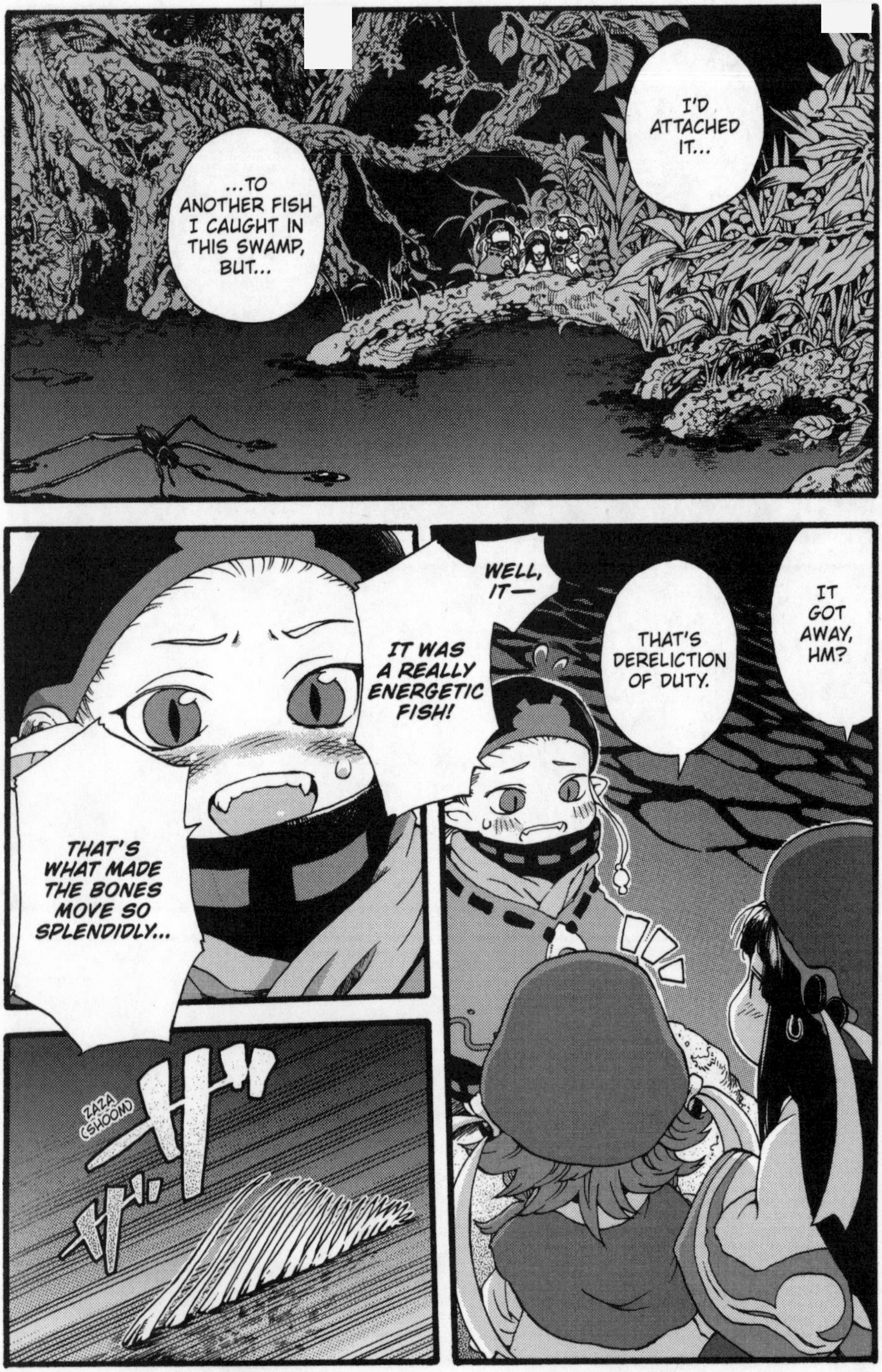
I'D ATTACHED IT...
...TO ANOTHER FISH I CAUGHT IN THIS SWAMP, BUT...
IT GOT AWAY, HM?
THAT'S DERELICTION OF DUTY.
WELL, IT—
IT WAS A REALLY ENERGETIC FISH!
THAT'S WHAT MADE THE BONES MOVE SO SPLENDIDLY...
ZAZA (SHOOM)

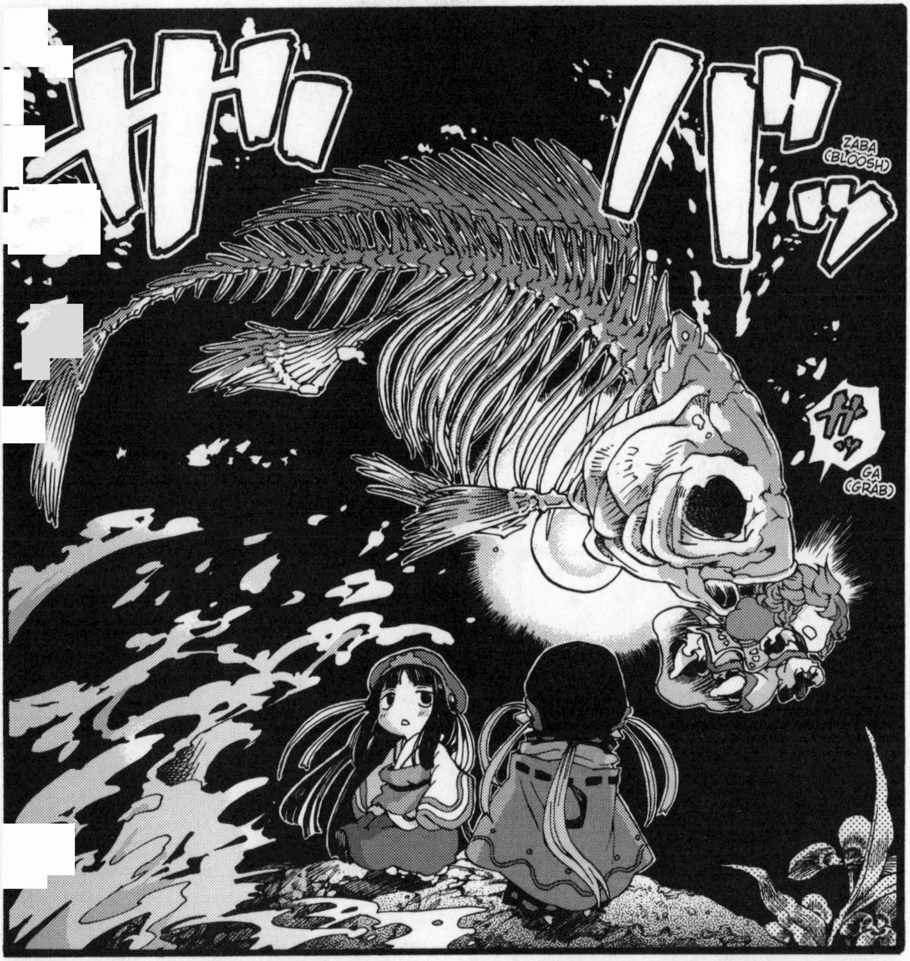
ZABA (BLOOSH)
GA (GRAB)

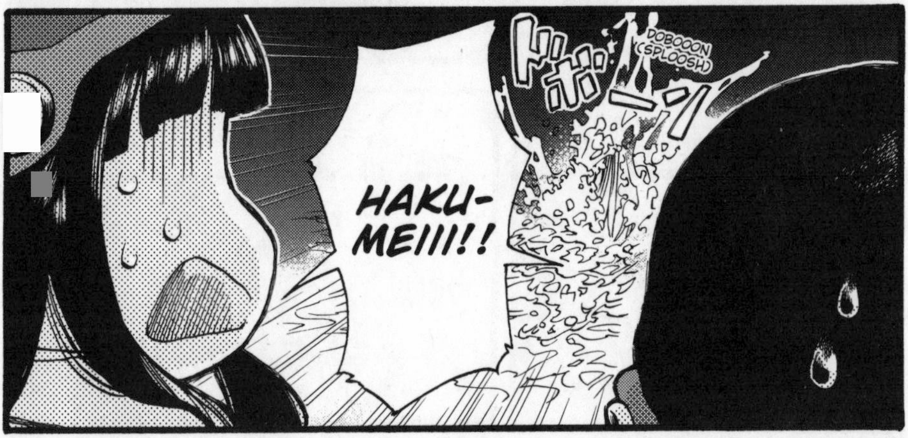
DOBOOON (SPLOOSH)
HAKU-MEIII!!

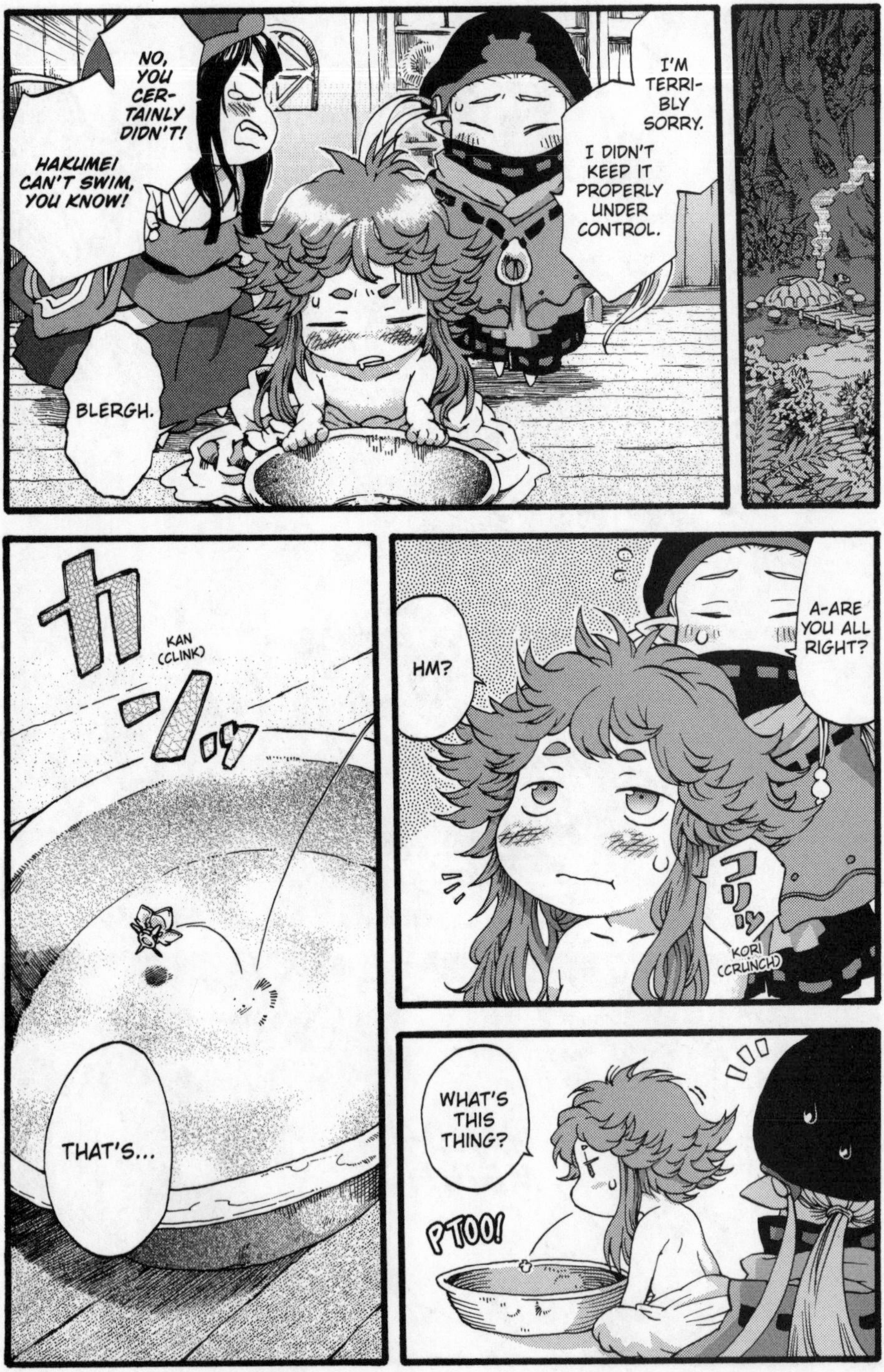
I'M TERRIBLY SORRY.
I DIDN'T KEEP IT PROPERLY UNDER CONTROL.
NO, YOU CERTAINLY DIDN'T!
HAKUMEI CAN'T SWIM, YOU KNOW!
BLERGH.
A-ARE YOU ALL RIGHT?
HM?
KORI (CRUNCH)
WHAT'S THIS THING?
PTOO!
KAN (CLINK)
THAT'S...

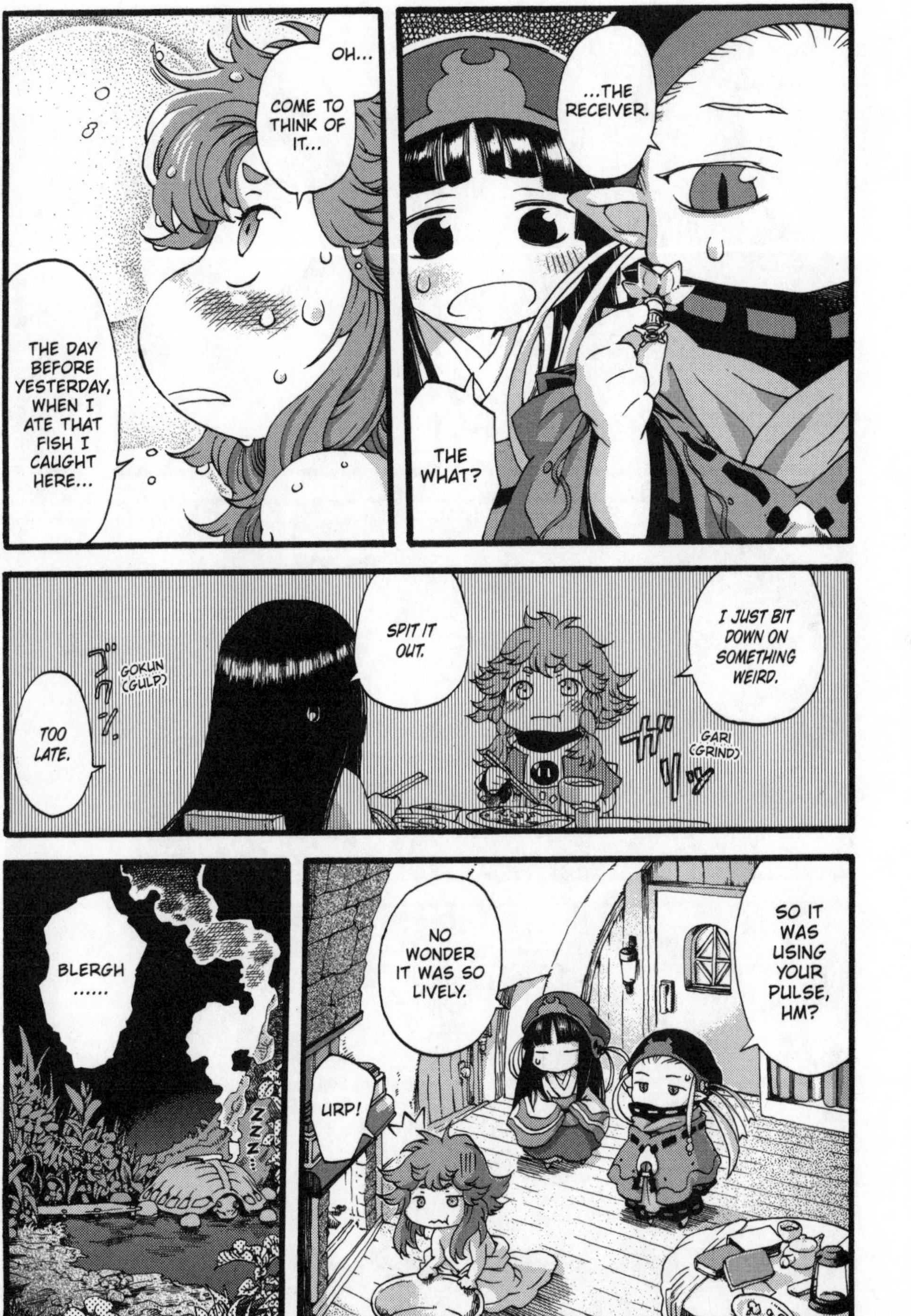
...THE RECEIVER.
THE WHAT?
OH... COME TO THINK OF IT...
THE DAY BEFORE YESTERDAY, WHEN I ATE THAT FISH I CAUGHT HERE...
I JUST BIT DOWN ON SOMETHING WEIRD.
GARI (GRIND)
SPIT IT OUT.
GOKUN (GULP)
TOO LATE.
SO IT WAS USING YOUR PULSE, HM?
NO WONDER IT WAS SO LIVELY.
URP!
BLERGH ......
ZZZ...

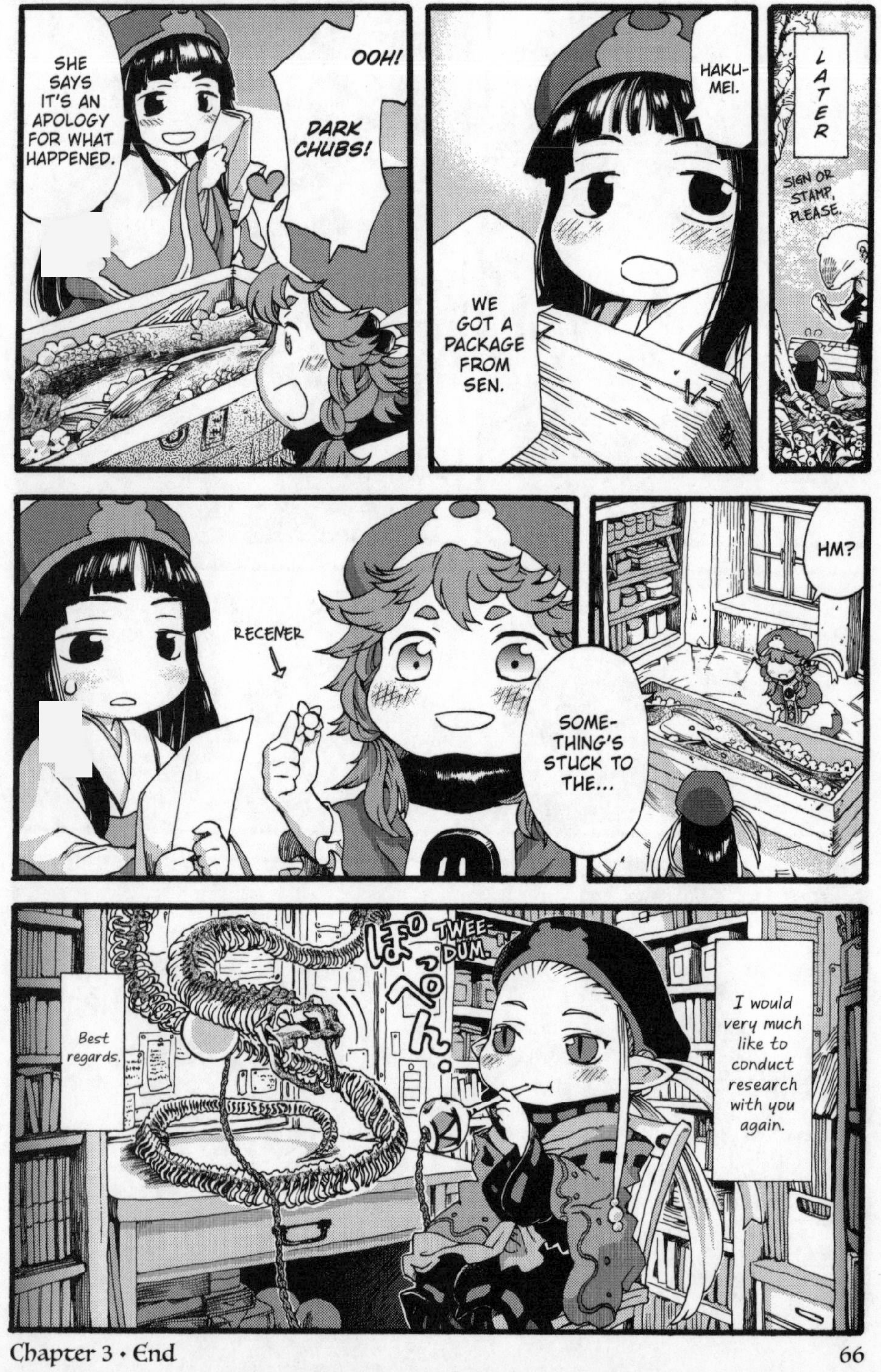
LATER
SIGN OR STAMP, PLEASE.
HAKU-MEI.
WE GOT A PACKAGE FROM SEN.
SHE SAYS IT'S AN APOLOGY FOR WHAT HAPPENED.
OOH!
DARK CHUBS!
HM?
SOME-THING'S STUCK TO THE...
RECEIVER
I would very much like to conduct research with you again.
TWEE-DUM.
ぽっぺん。
Best regards.

"'Did you hear the rumor about the fish ghost?'"

"'Ohh, the one that supposedly haunts the eastern swamp, right? My friend says he saw it.'"

"'I saw it a little while ago. A pale woman with red eyes, dressed in pitch-black clothes, was controlling the fish ghost and using it to drag someone into the swamp...'"

"—That's what the kids were saying anyway. But I've never seen her once, and I live in that swamp."

"O-oh, is that right......?"

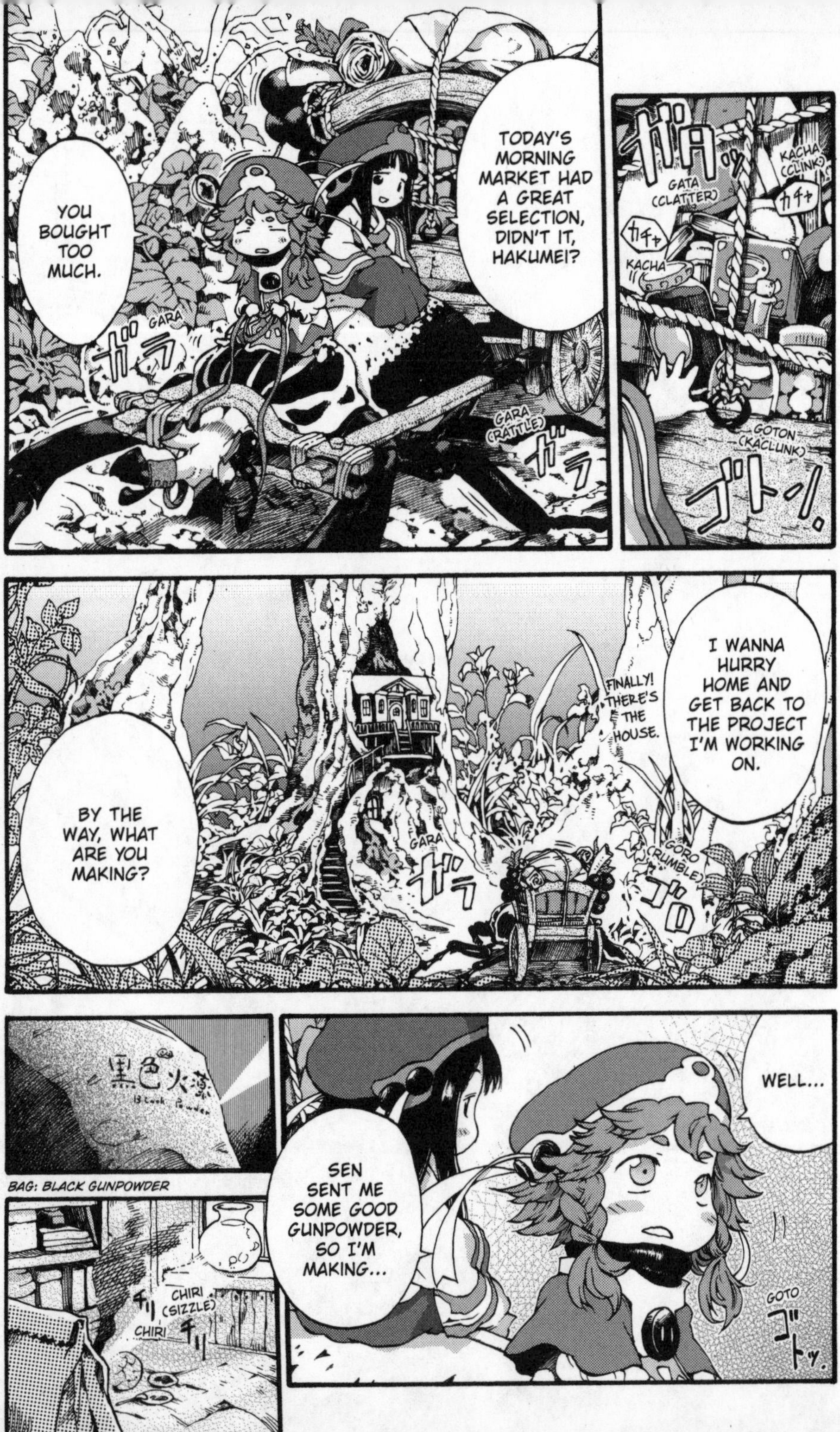
ガタッ
GATA (CLATTER)
KACHA (CLINK)
カチャ
カチャ
KACHA
GOTON (KACLUNK)
ゴトン。
TODAY'S MORNING MARKET HAD A GREAT SELECTION, DIDN'T IT, HAKUMEI?
YOU BOUGHT TOO MUCH.
GARA
ガラ
GARA (RATTLE)
ガラ
I WANNA HURRY HOME AND GET BACK TO THE PROJECT I'M WORKING ON.
FINALLY! THERE'S THE HOUSE.
GORO (RUMBLE)
ゴロ
GARA
ガラ
BY THE WAY, WHAT ARE YOU MAKING?
WELL...
SEN SENT ME SOME GOOD GUNPOWDER, SO I'M MAKING...
GOTO
ゴトッ。
黒色火薬
Black Powder
BAG: BLACK GUNPOWDER
チリ
CHIRI (SIZZLE)
CHIRI
チリ

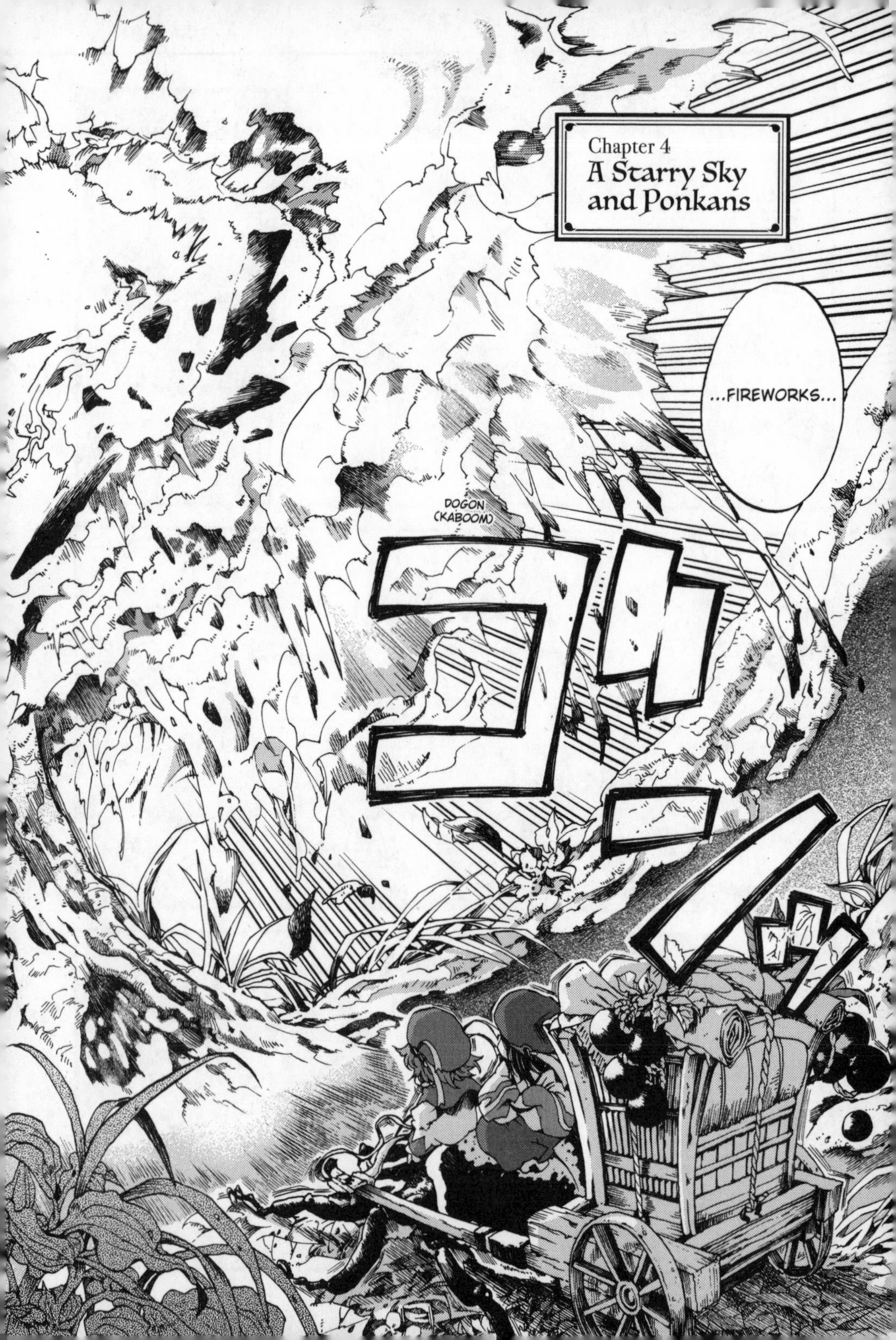
Chapter 4
A Starry Sky and Ponkans
...FIREWORKS...
DOGON (KABOOM)

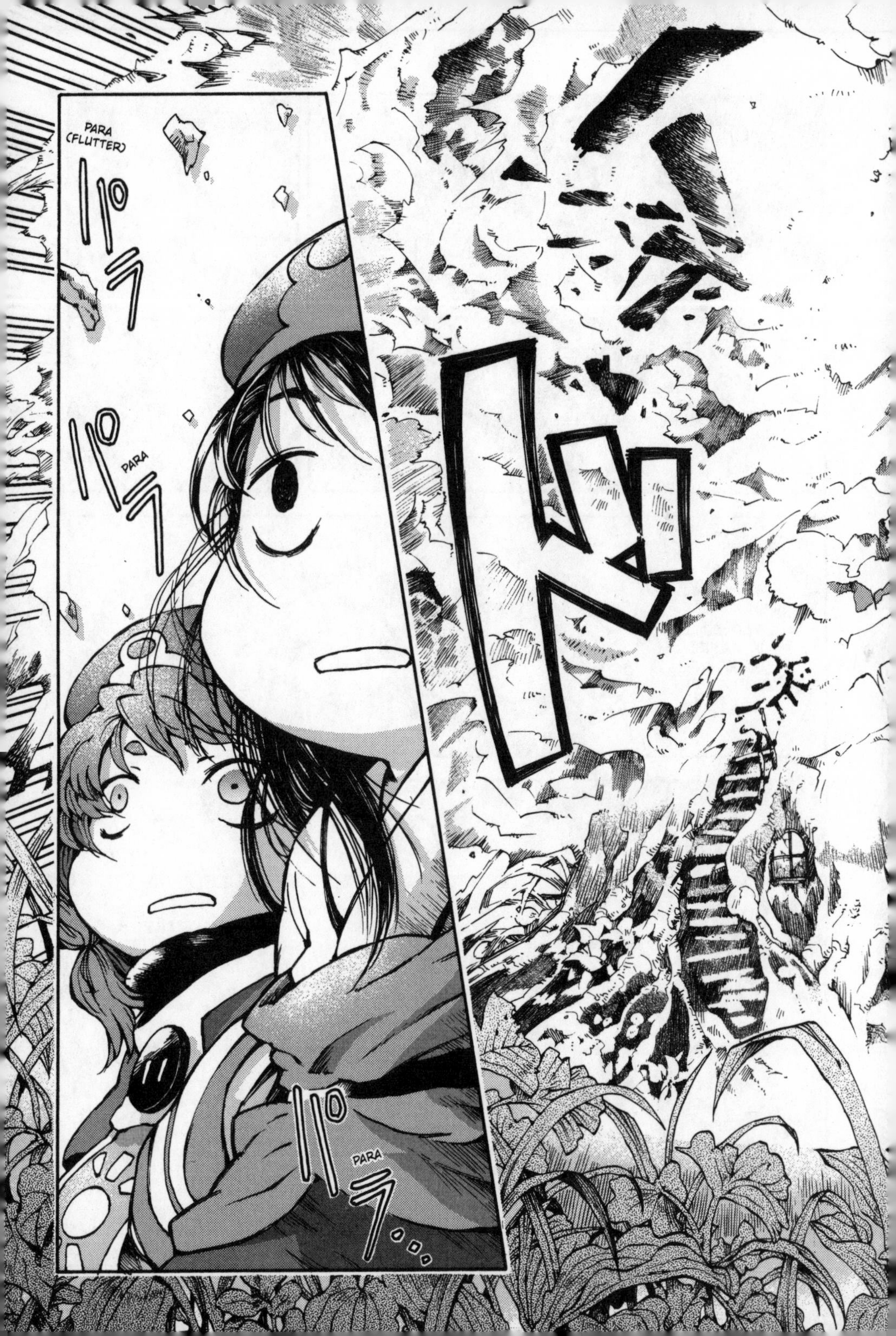
PARA (FLUTTER)
PARA
PARA

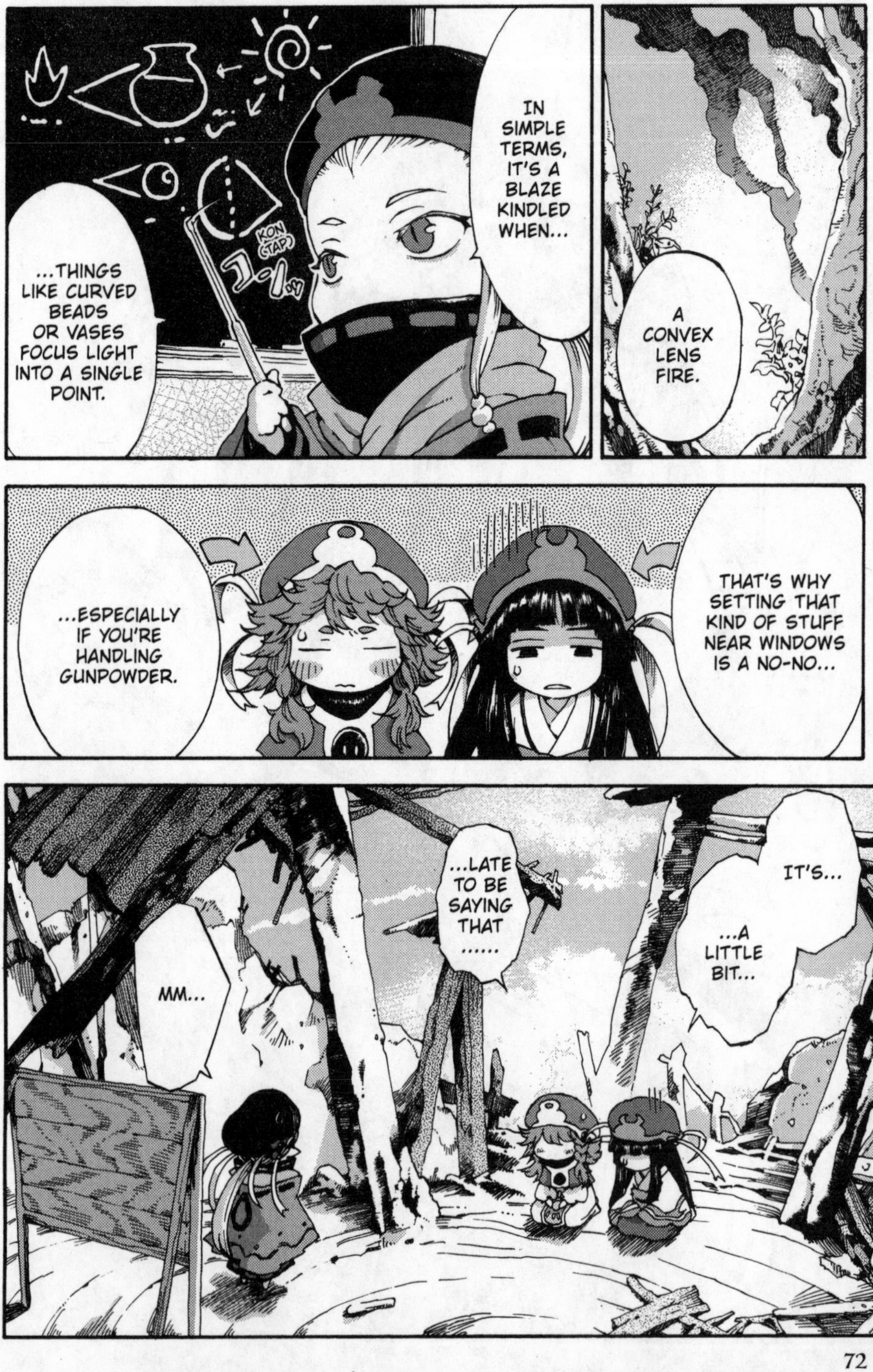
A CONVEX LENS FIRE.
IN SIMPLE TERMS, IT'S A BLAZE KINDLED WHEN...
KON (TAP)
...THINGS LIKE CURVED BEADS OR VASES FOCUS LIGHT INTO A SINGLE POINT.
THAT'S WHY SETTING THAT KIND OF STUFF NEAR WINDOWS IS A NO-NO...
...ESPECIALLY IF YOU'RE HANDLING GUNPOWDER.
IT'S...
...A LITTLE BIT...
...LATE TO BE SAYING THAT ......
MM...

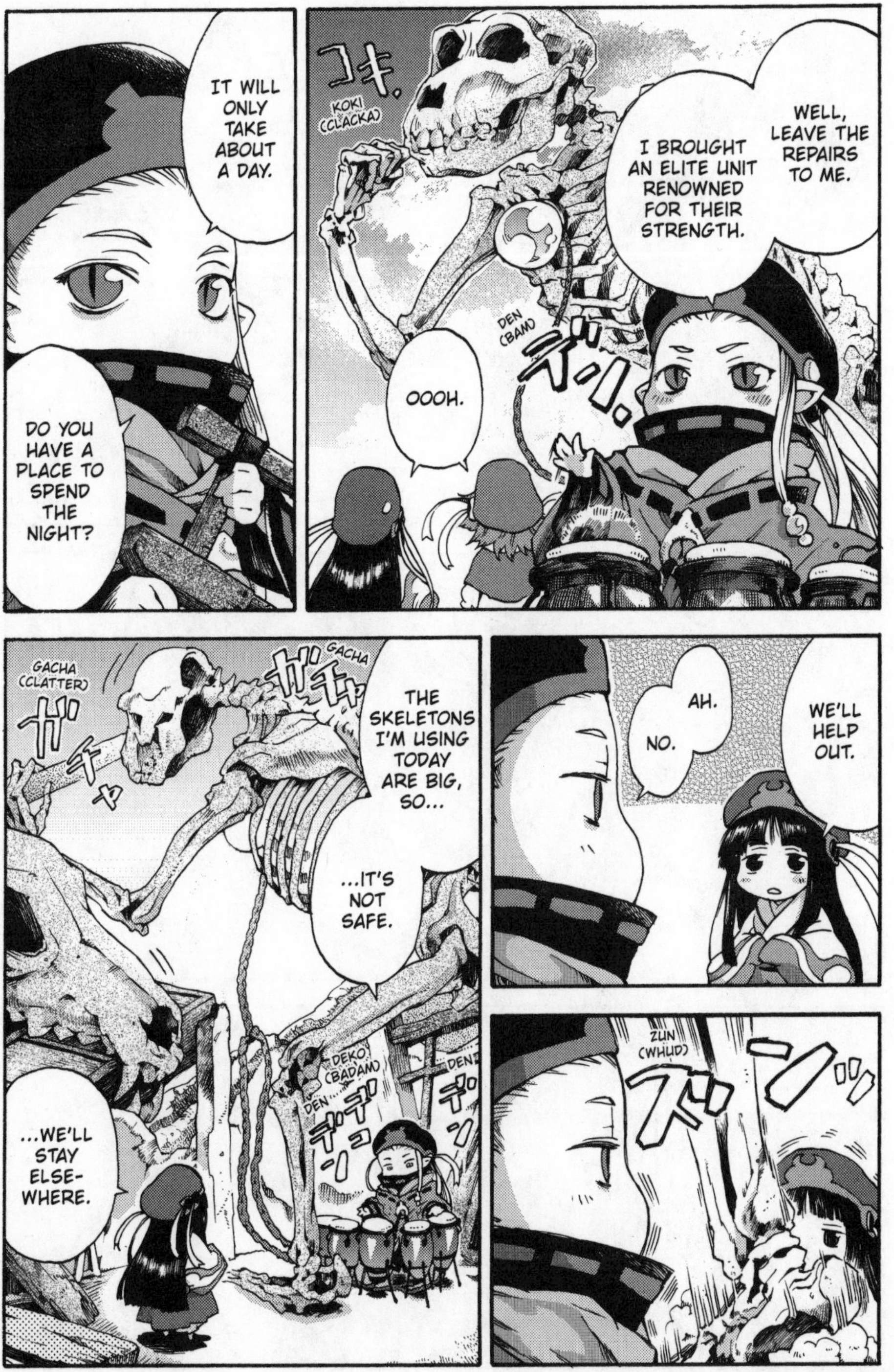
WELL, LEAVE THE REPAIRS TO ME.
I BROUGHT AN ELITE UNIT RENOWNED FOR THEIR STRENGTH.
KOKI (CLACKA)
DEN (BAM)
OOOH.
IT WILL ONLY TAKE ABOUT A DAY.
DO YOU HAVE A PLACE TO SPEND THE NIGHT?
WE'LL HELP OUT.
AH.
NO.
ZUN (WHUD)
GACHA
THE SKELETONS I'M USING TODAY ARE BIG, SO...
...IT'S NOT SAFE.
GACHA (CLATTER)
DEN
DEKO (BADAM)
DEN
...WE'LL STAY ELSE-WHERE.

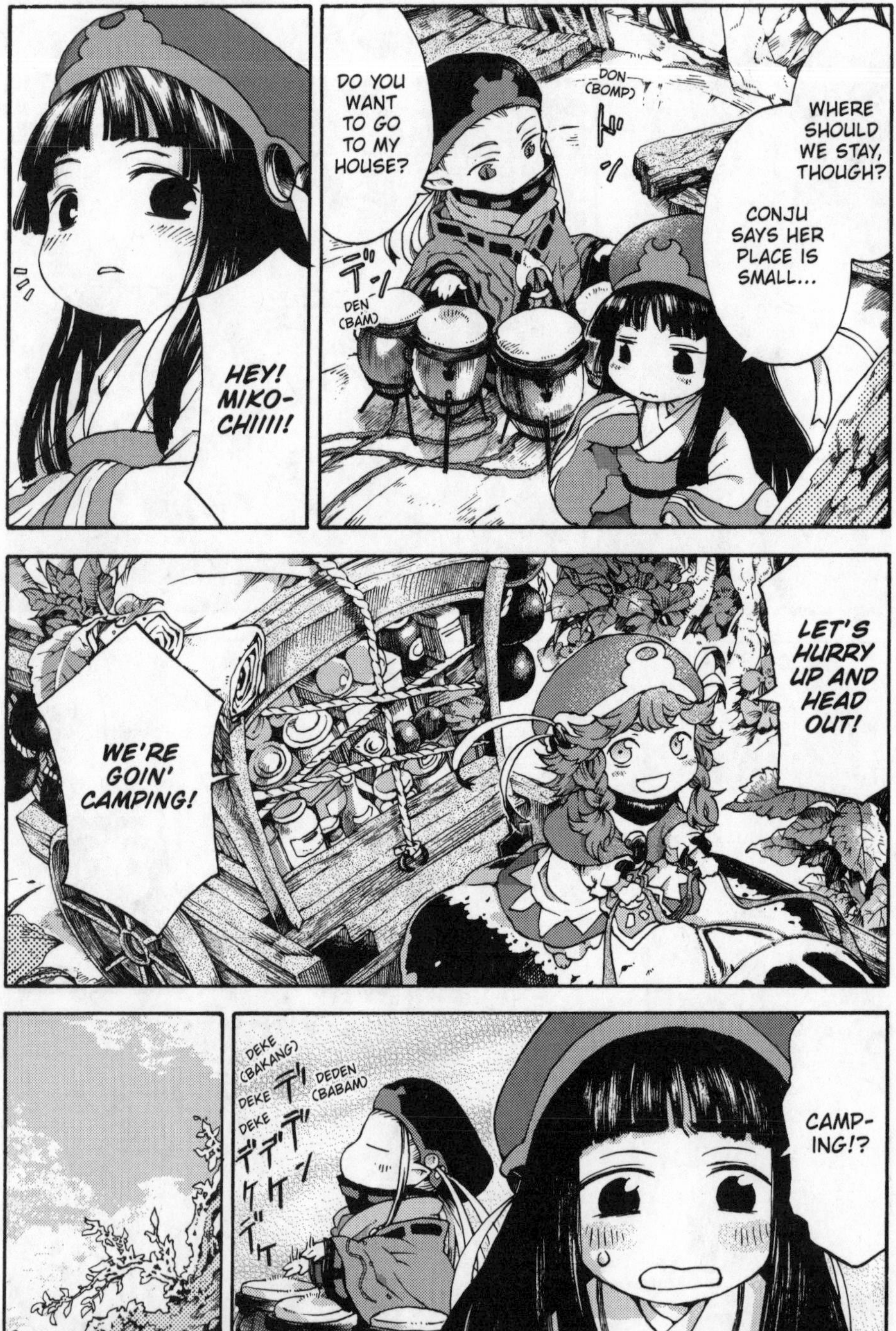
WHERE SHOULD WE STAY, THOUGH?
CONJU SAYS HER PLACE IS SMALL...
DON (BOMP)
DO YOU WANT TO GO TO MY HOUSE?
DEN (BAM)
HEY! MIKO-CHI!!!!!
LET'S HURRY UP AND HEAD OUT!
WE'RE GOIN' CAMPING!
CAMP-ING!?
DEDEN (BABAM)
DEKE (BAKANG)
DEKE
DEKE

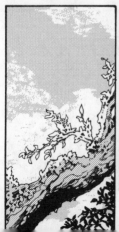

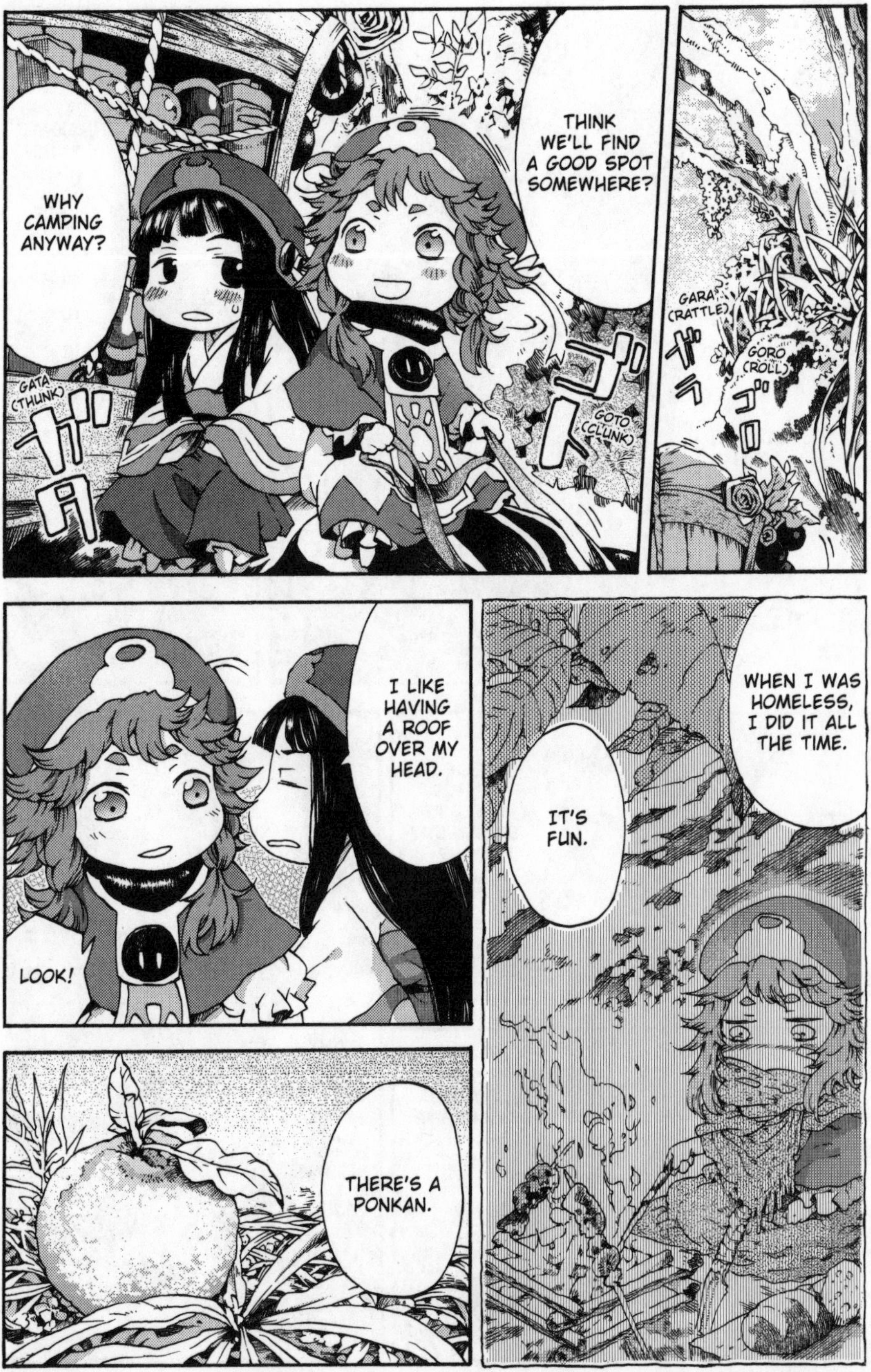
GARA (RATTLE)
GORO (ROLL)
THINK WE'LL FIND A GOOD SPOT SOMEWHERE?
GOTO (CLUNK)
WHY CAMPING ANYWAY?
GATA (THUNK)
WHEN I WAS HOMELESS, I DID IT ALL THE TIME.
IT'S FUN.
I LIKE HAVING A ROOF OVER MY HEAD.
LOOK!
THERE'S A PONKAN.

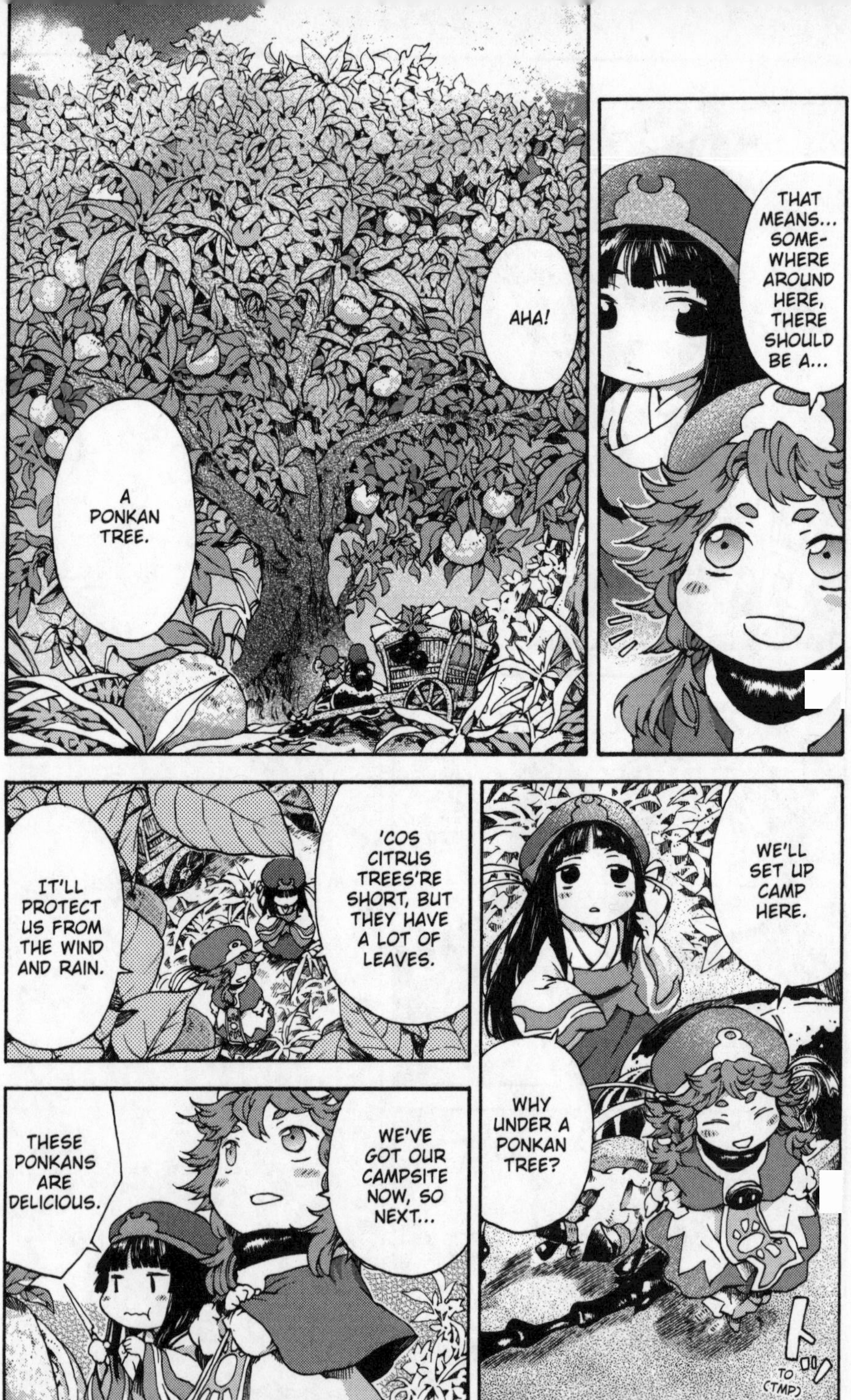
THAT MEANS... SOME-WHERE AROUND HERE, THERE SHOULD BE A...
AHA!
A PONKAN TREE.
WE'LL SET UP CAMP HERE.
WHY UNDER A PONKAN TREE?
TO (TMP)
'COS CITRUS TREES'RE SHORT, BUT THEY HAVE A LOT OF LEAVES.
IT'LL PROTECT US FROM THE WIND AND RAIN.
WE'VE GOT OUR CAMPSITE NOW, SO NEXT...
THESE PONKANS ARE DELICIOUS.

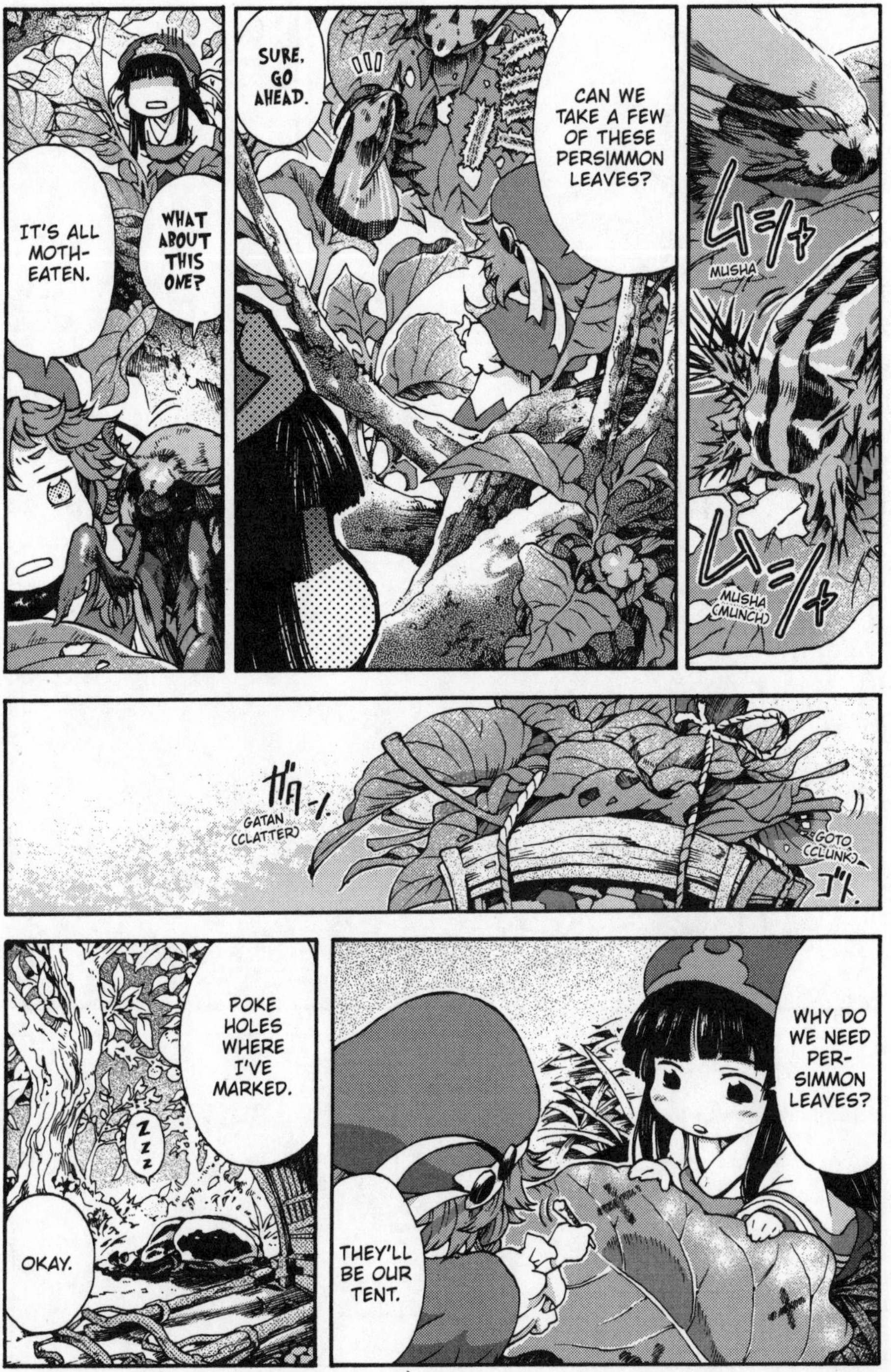
ムシャ
MUSHA
ムシャ
MUSHA (MUNCH)
CAN WE TAKE A FEW OF THESE PERSIMMON LEAVES?
SURE, GO AHEAD.
WHAT ABOUT THIS ONE?
IT'S ALL MOTH-EATEN.
ゴト
GOTO (CLUNK)
GATAN (CLATTER)
WHY DO WE NEED PER-SIMMON LEAVES?
THEY'LL BE OUR TENT.
POKE HOLES WHERE I'VE MARKED.
ZZZ
OKAY.

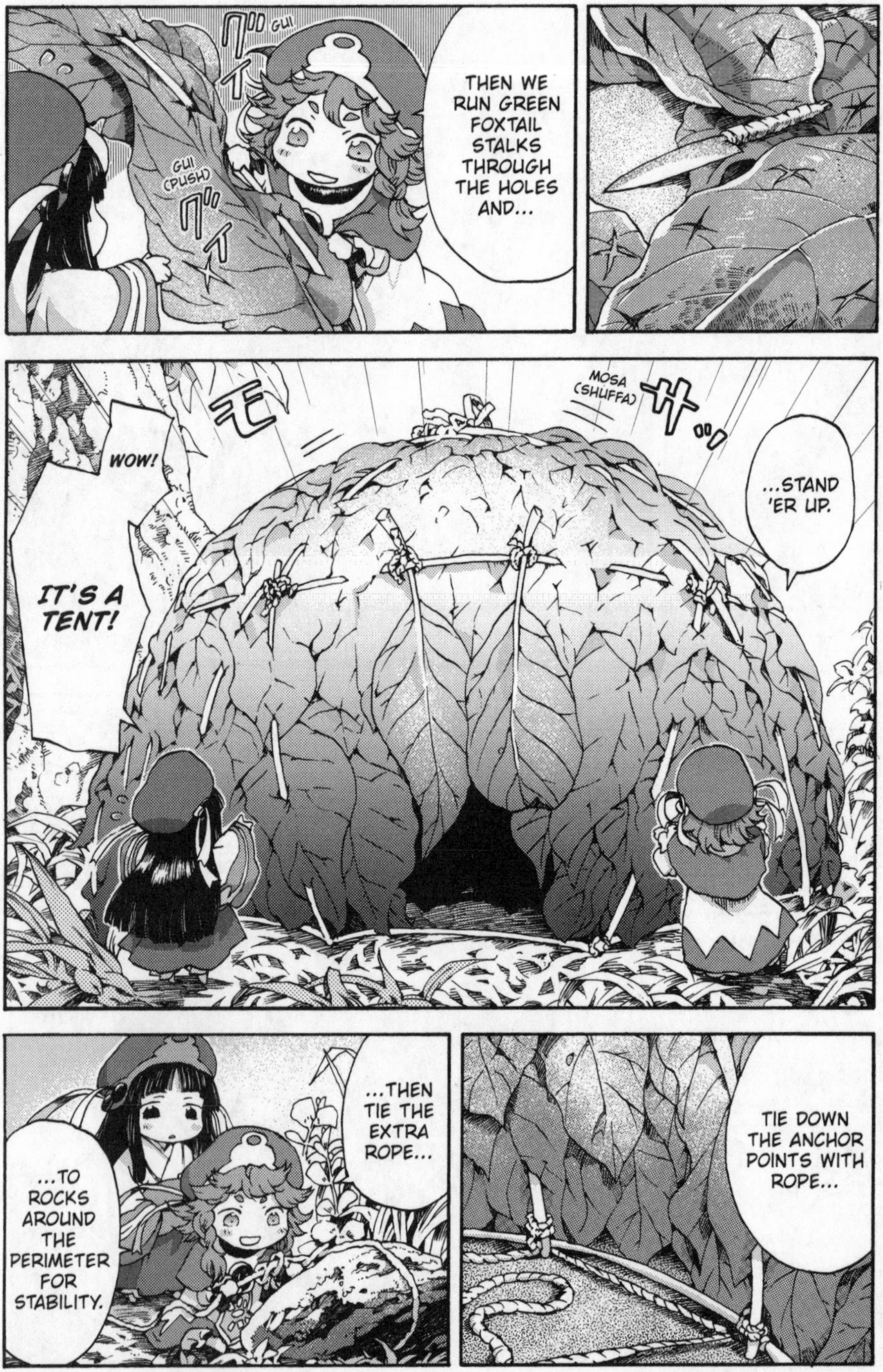
GUI
GUI (PUSH)
THEN WE RUN GREEN FOXTAIL STALKS THROUGH THE HOLES AND...
MOSA (SHUFFA)
...STAND 'ER UP.
WOW!
IT'S A TENT!
TIE DOWN THE ANCHOR POINTS WITH ROPE...
...THEN TIE THE EXTRA ROPE...
...TO ROCKS AROUND THE PERIMETER FOR STABILITY.

DOSA (WHUMP)

YOU TACKLE THESE, MIKOCHI.

CATCH.

IT'S HARD. I'LL DO IT.

NO, NO.

WANT ME TO DO THE OTHER SIDE, HAKUMEI?

GYU (TUG)

GICHI (TIGHT)

ROAST THEM WHOLE, OR WRAP THEM AND ROAST THEM...

THAT'S PRACTICALLY THE SAME THING.

I FOUND THEM EARLIER.

USE THEM FOR DINNER.

WILD ONION BULBS?

GUUU (YANK)

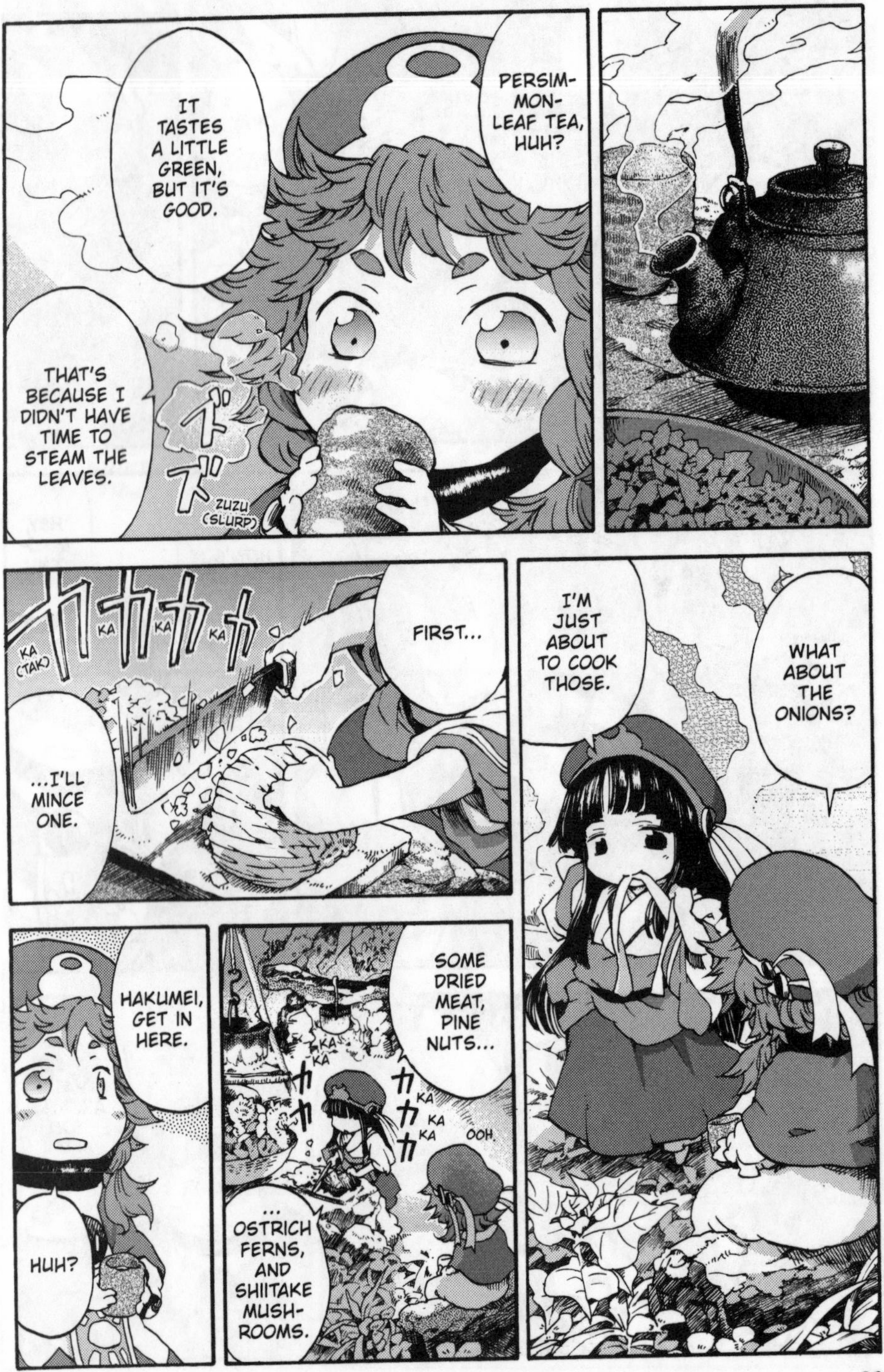
PERSIMMON-LEAF TEA, HUH?
IT TASTES A LITTLE GREEN, BUT IT'S GOOD.
THAT'S BECAUSE I DIDN'T HAVE TIME TO STEAM THE LEAVES.
ZUZU (SLURP)
WHAT ABOUT THE ONIONS?
I'M JUST ABOUT TO COOK THOSE.
FIRST...
KA KA KA KA KA (TAK)
...I'LL MINCE ONE.
SOME DRIED MEAT, PINE NUTS...
KA KA KA
KA KA
OOH.
... OSTRICH FERNS, AND SHIITAKE MUSHROOMS.
HAKUMEI, GET IN HERE.
HUH?

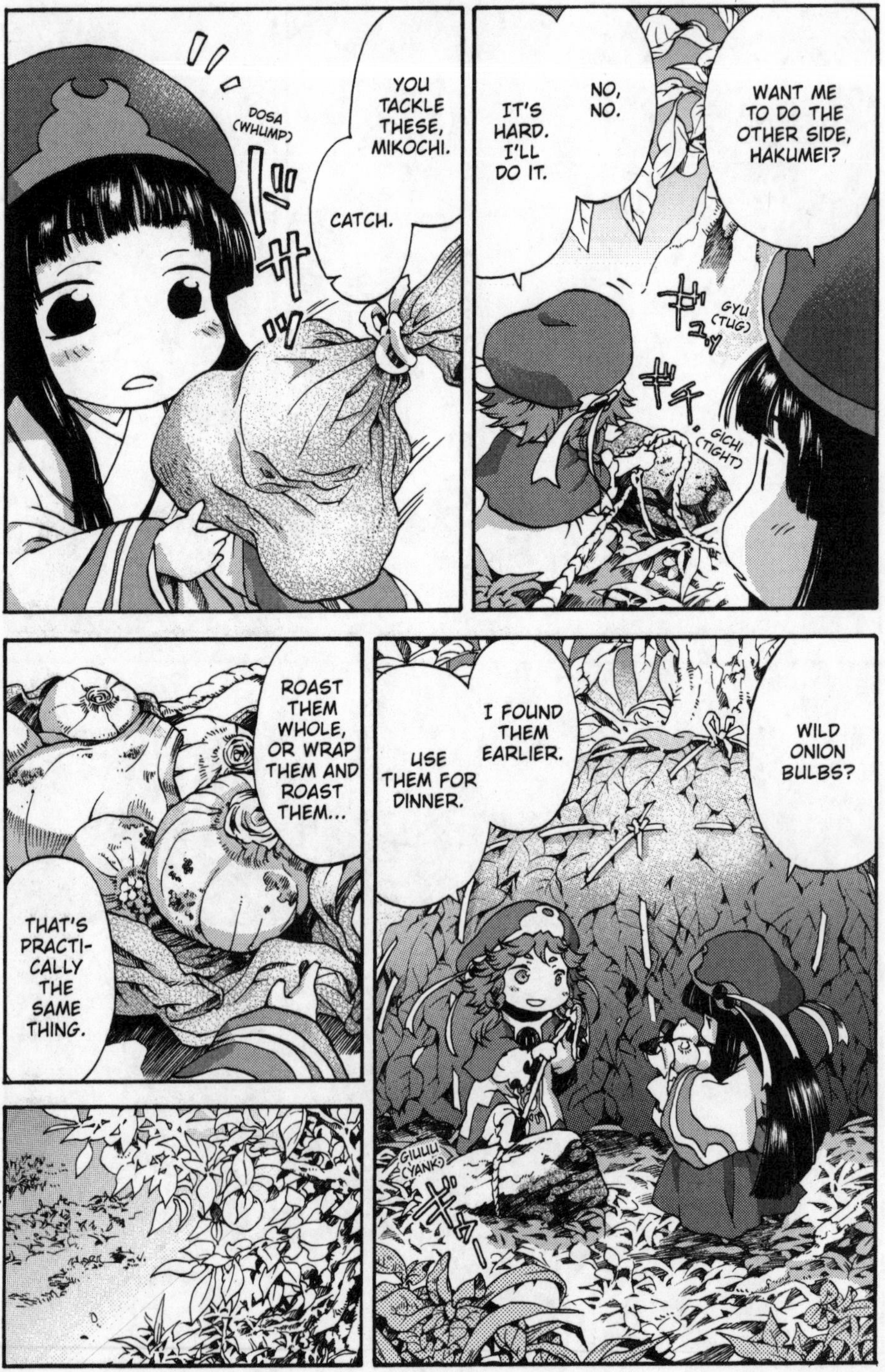
WANT ME TO DO THE OTHER SIDE, HAKUMEI?
NO, NO.
IT'S HARD. I'LL DO IT.
GYU (TUG)
GICHI (TIGHT)
YOU TACKLE THESE, MIKOCHI.
CATCH.
DOSA (WHUMP)
WILD ONION BULBS?
I FOUND THEM EARLIER.
USE THEM FOR DINNER.
GIUUU (YANK)
ROAST THEM WHOLE, OR WRAP THEM AND ROAST THEM...
THAT'S PRACTI-CALLY THE SAME THING.

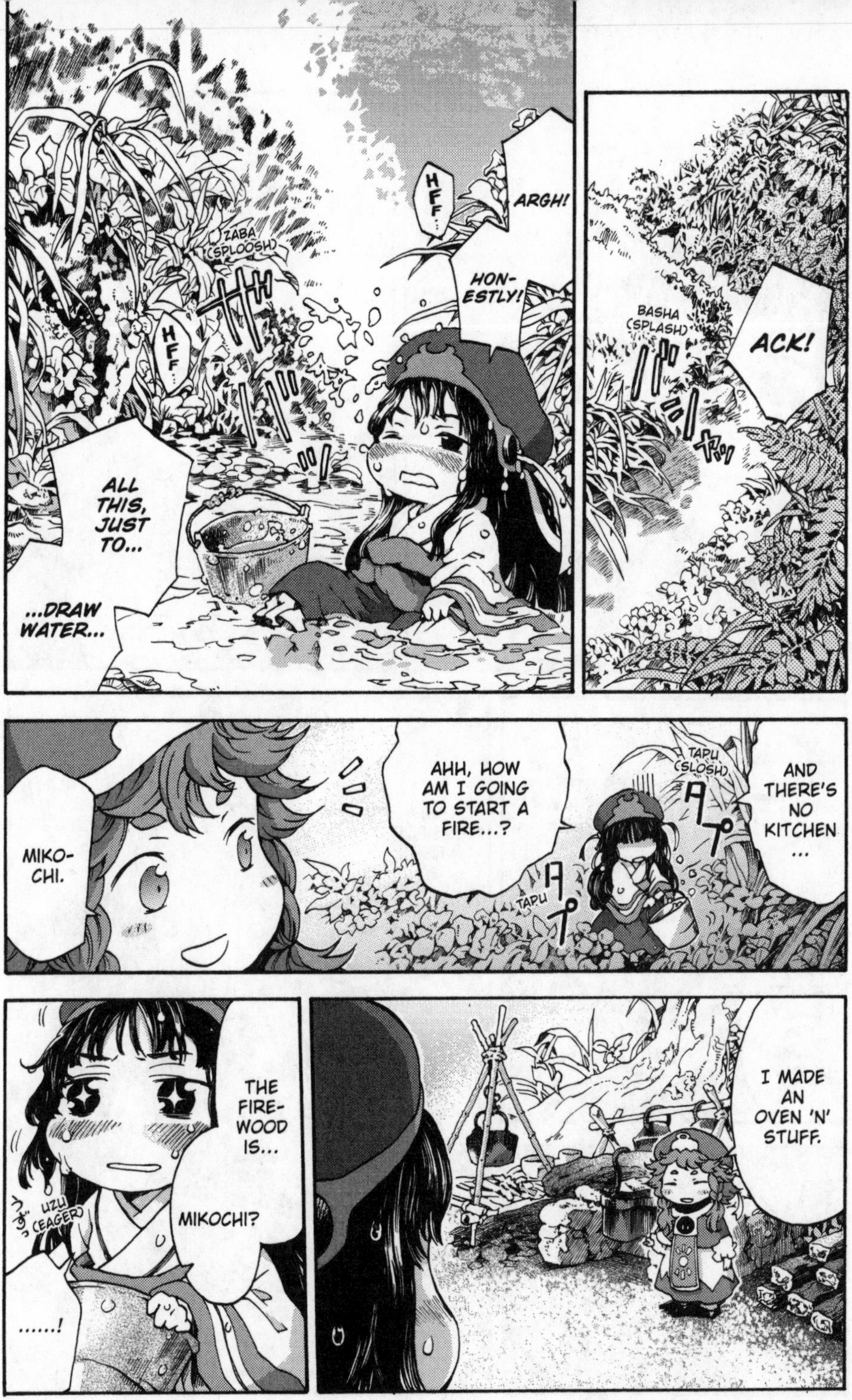
BASHA (SPLASH)
ACK!
ARGH!
HON-ESTLY!
HFF...
ZABA (SPLOOSH)
HFF...
ALL THIS, JUST TO...
...DRAW WATER...
AND THERE'S NO KITCHEN ...
TAPU (SLOSH)
AHH, HOW AM I GOING TO START A FIRE...?
TAPU
MIKO-CHI.
I MADE AN OVEN 'N' STUFF.
THE FIRE-WOOD IS...
MIKOCHI?
UZU (EAGER)
......!

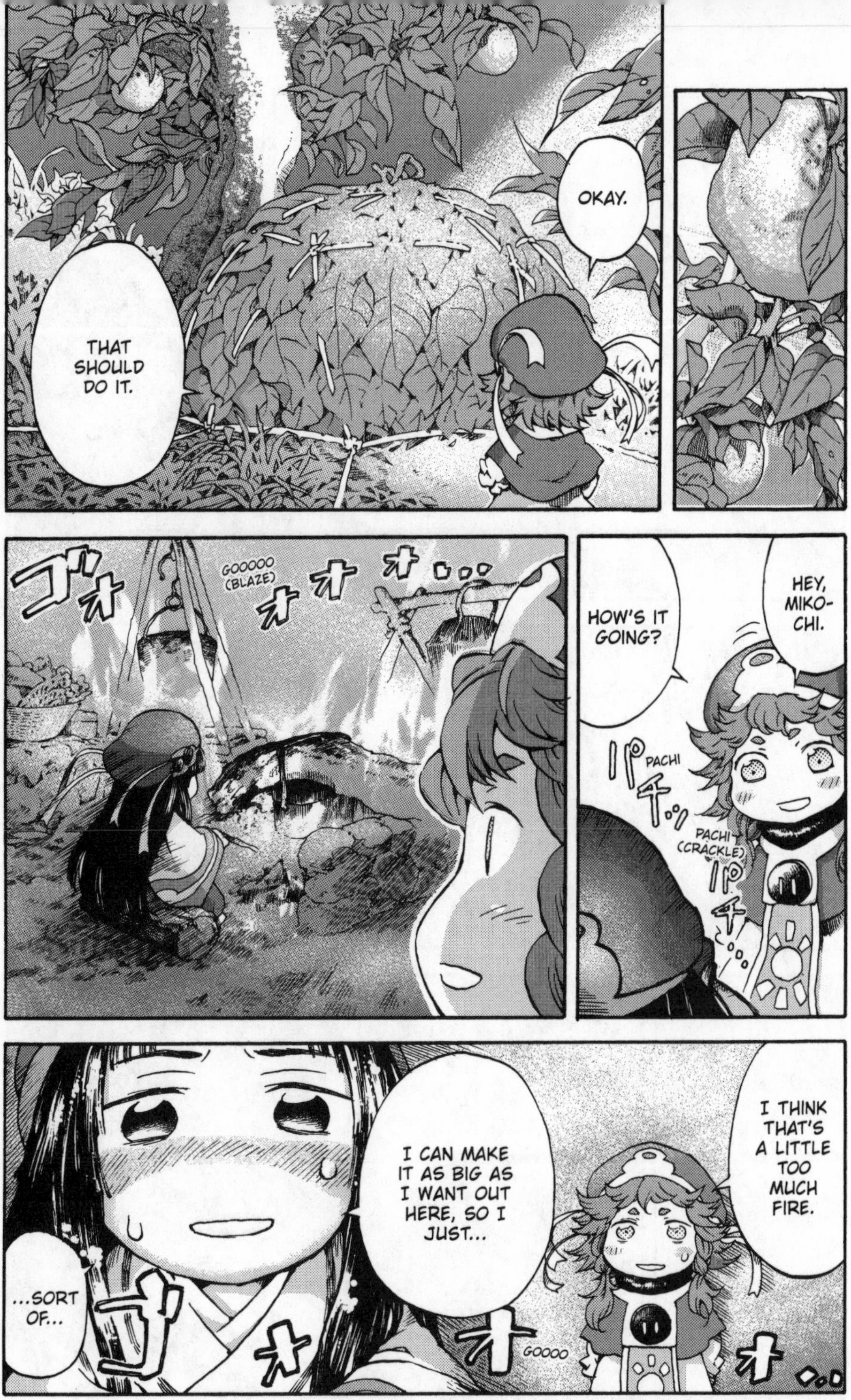
OKAY.
THAT SHOULD DO IT.
HEY, MIKO-CHI.
HOW'S IT GOING?
PACHI
PACHI (CRACKLE)
GOOOOO (BLAZE)
I THINK THAT'S A LITTLE TOO MUCH FIRE.
I CAN MAKE IT AS BIG AS I WANT OUT HERE, SO I JUST...
GOOOO
...SORT OF...

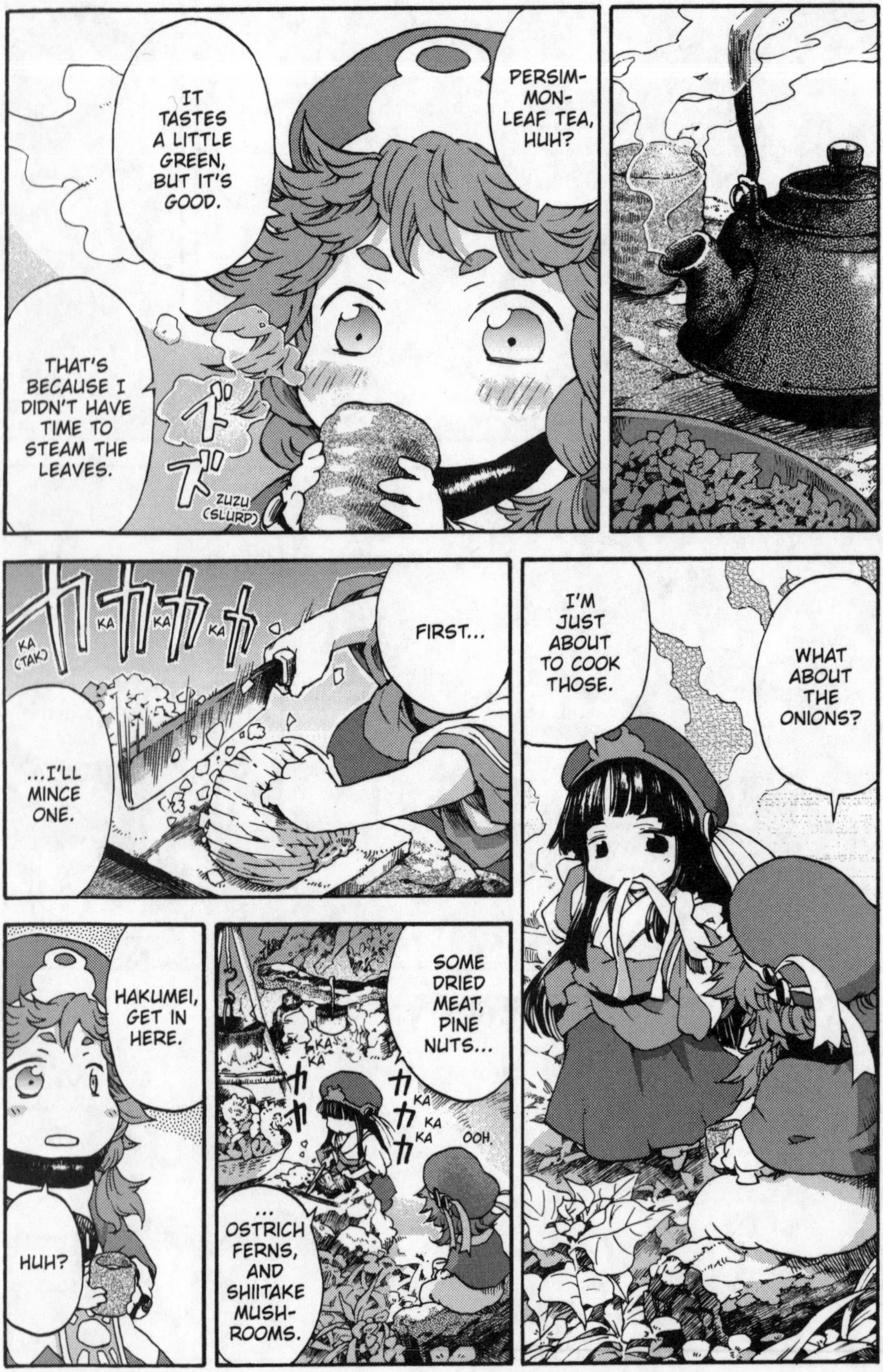
PERSIM-MON-LEAF TEA, HUH?
IT TASTES A LITTLE GREEN, BUT IT'S GOOD.
THAT'S BECAUSE I DIDN'T HAVE TIME TO STEAM THE LEAVES.
ZUZU (SLURP)
WHAT ABOUT THE ONIONS?
I'M JUST ABOUT TO COOK THOSE.
FIRST...
KA (TAK) KA KA KA
...I'LL MINCE ONE.
SOME DRIED MEAT, PINE NUTS...
KA KA
KA KA KA
OOH.
...OSTRICH FERNS, AND SHIITAKE MUSH-ROOMS.
HAKUMEI, GET IN HERE.
HUH?

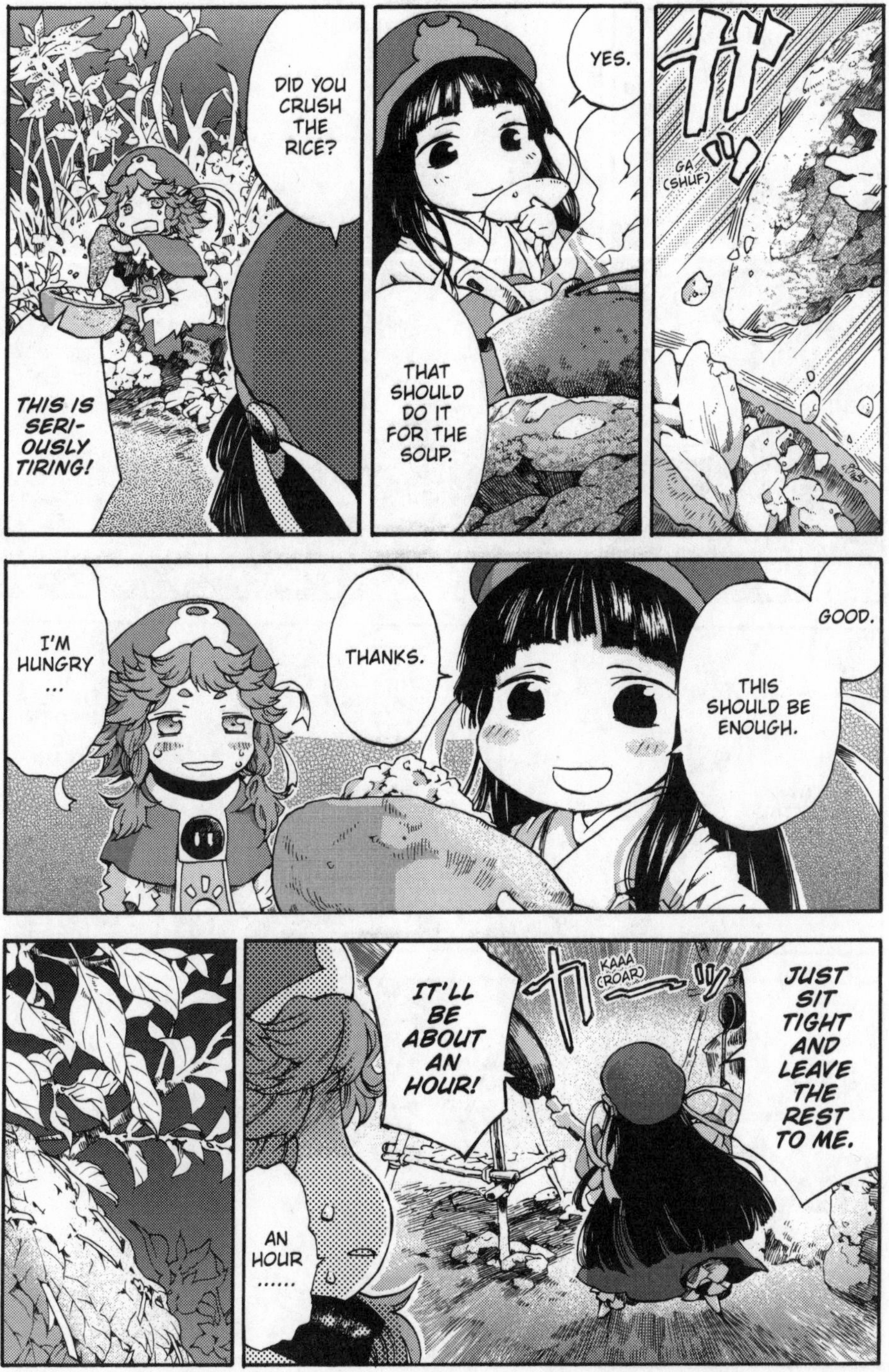
GA (SHUF)
YES.
THAT SHOULD DO IT FOR THE SOUP.
DID YOU CRUSH THE RICE?
THIS IS SERIOUSLY TIRING!
GOOD.
THIS SHOULD BE ENOUGH.
THANKS.
I'M HUNGRY ...
KAAA (ROAR)
JUST SIT TIGHT AND LEAVE THE REST TO ME.
IT'LL BE ABOUT AN HOUR!
AN HOUR ......

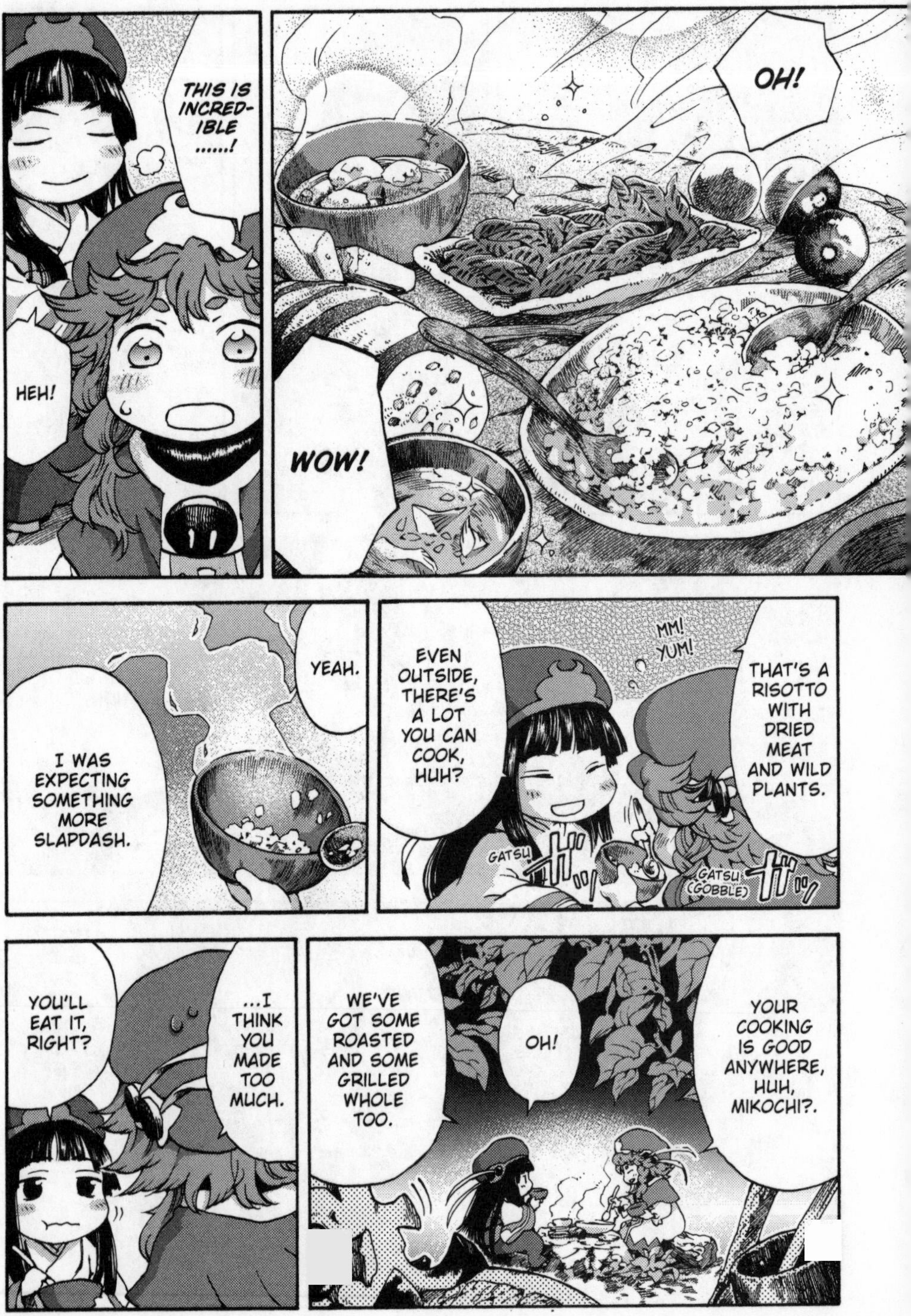
OH!
WOW!
THIS IS INCREDIBLE ......!
HEH!
THAT'S A RISOTTO WITH DRIED MEAT AND WILD PLANTS.
MM! YUM!
EVEN OUTSIDE, THERE'S A LOT YOU CAN COOK, HUH?
GATSU (GOBBLE)
GATSU
YEAH.
I WAS EXPECTING SOMETHING MORE SLAPDASH.
YOUR COOKING IS GOOD ANYWHERE, HUH, MIKOCHI?.
OH!
WE'VE GOT SOME ROASTED AND SOME GRILLED WHOLE TOO.
...I THINK YOU MADE TOO MUCH.
YOU'LL EAT IT, RIGHT?

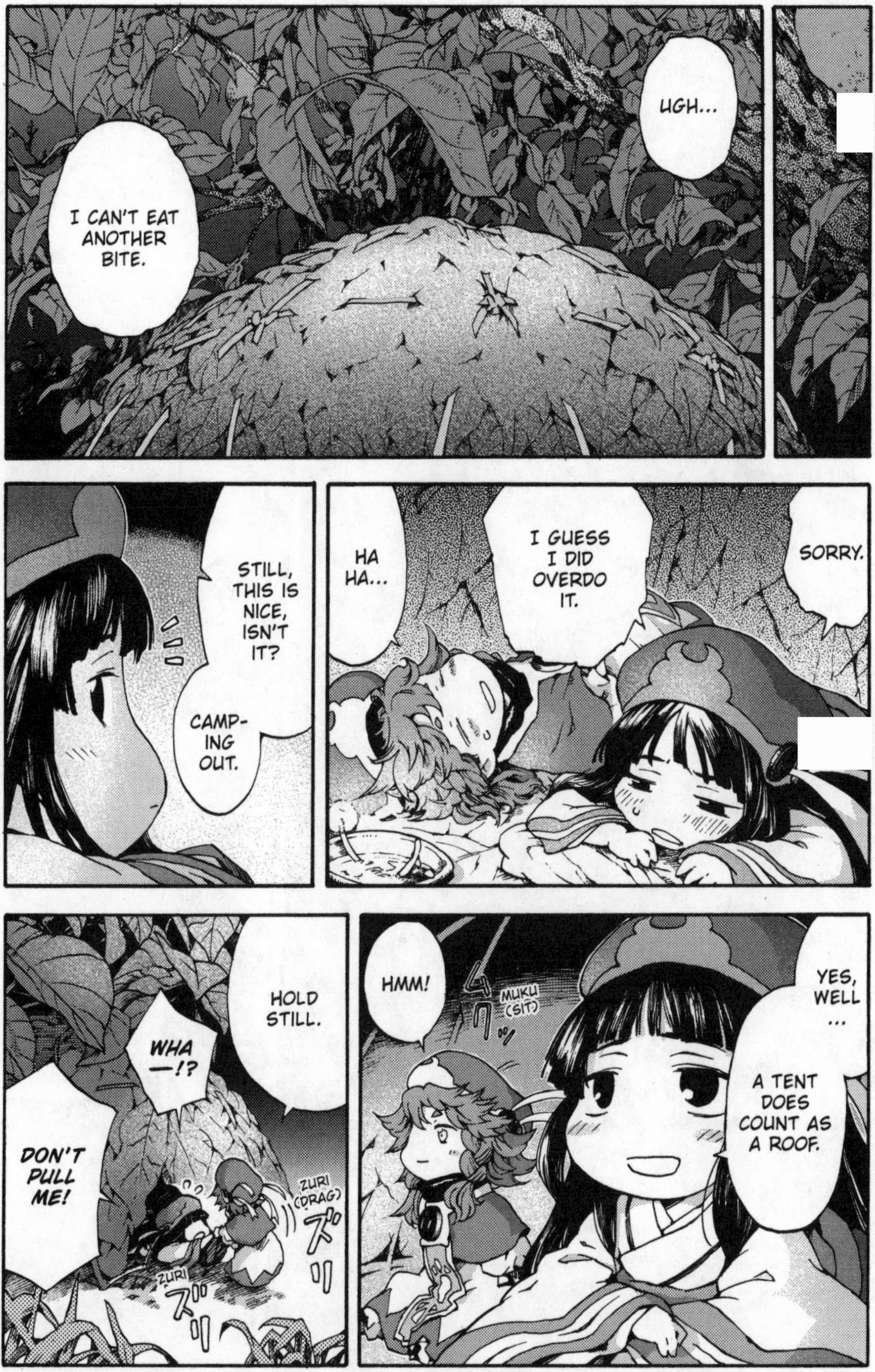
UGH...
I CAN'T EAT ANOTHER BITE.
SORRY.
I GUESS I DID OVERDO IT.
HA HA...
STILL, THIS IS NICE, ISN'T IT?
CAMP-ING OUT.
YES, WELL ...
A TENT DOES COUNT AS A ROOF.
MUKU (SIT)
HMM!
HOLD STILL.
WHA—!?
ZURI (DRAG)
ZURI
DON'T PULL ME!

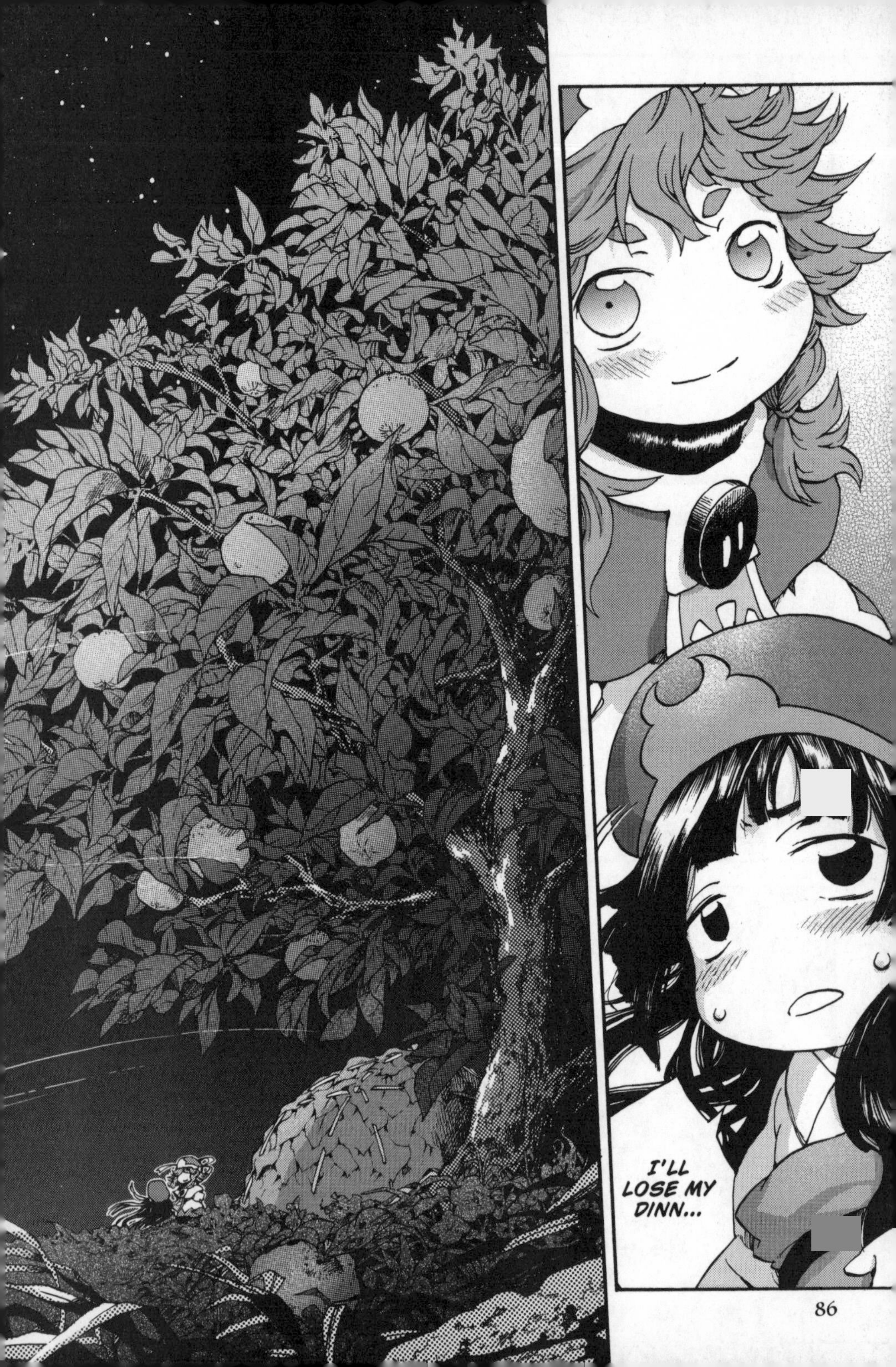
I'LL LOSE MY DINN...

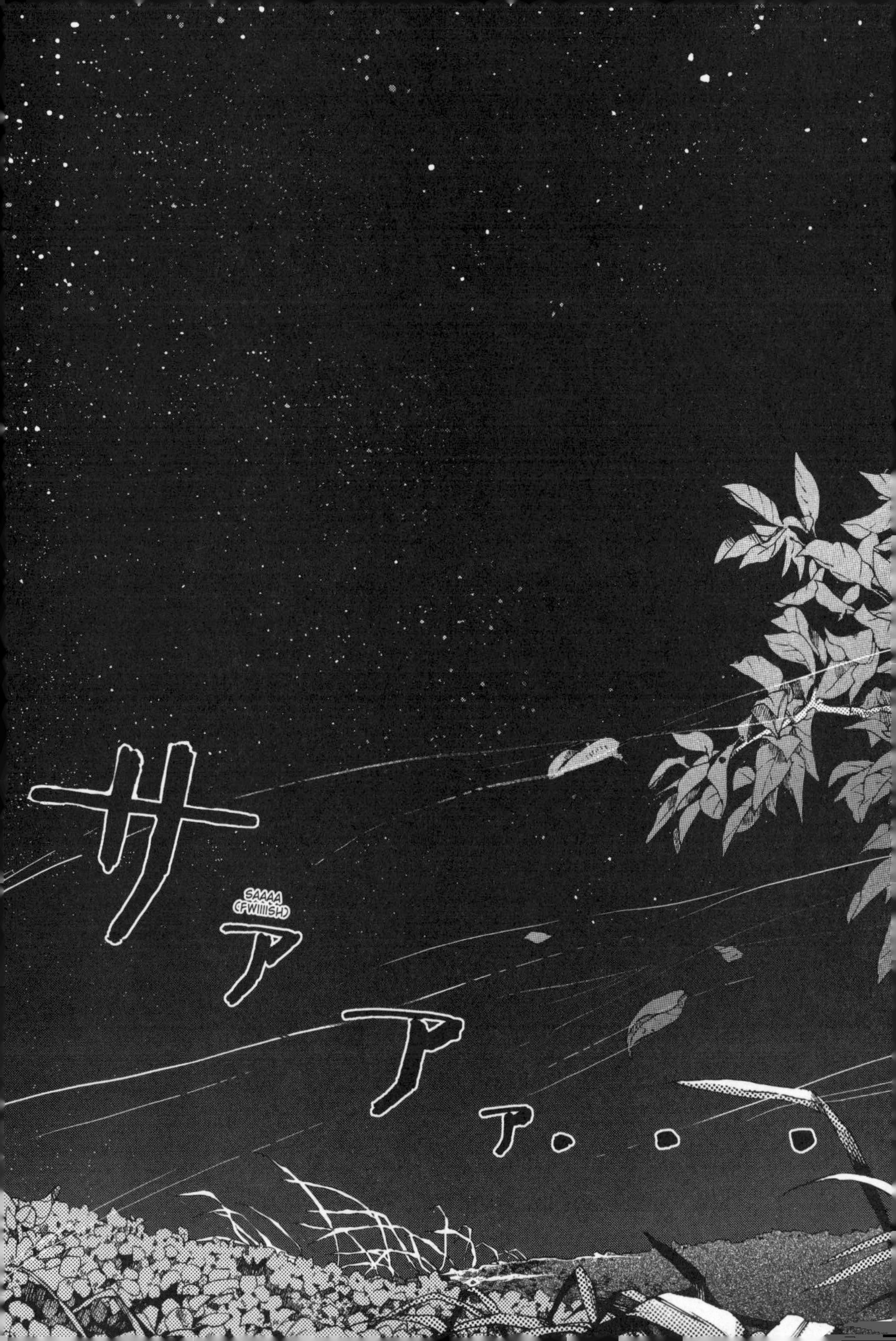
サァァァ。。。
SAAAA
(FWIIIISH)

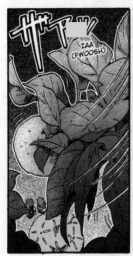

ZAA
(FWOOSH)

WE HAVE ALL THIS...

...FOR OUR ROOF.

PUCHI (SNAP)

ISN'T IT?

OHHH, HOW...

...ENCHANTING.

BICHA (DRENCH)

DOBU (SPLAT)

88

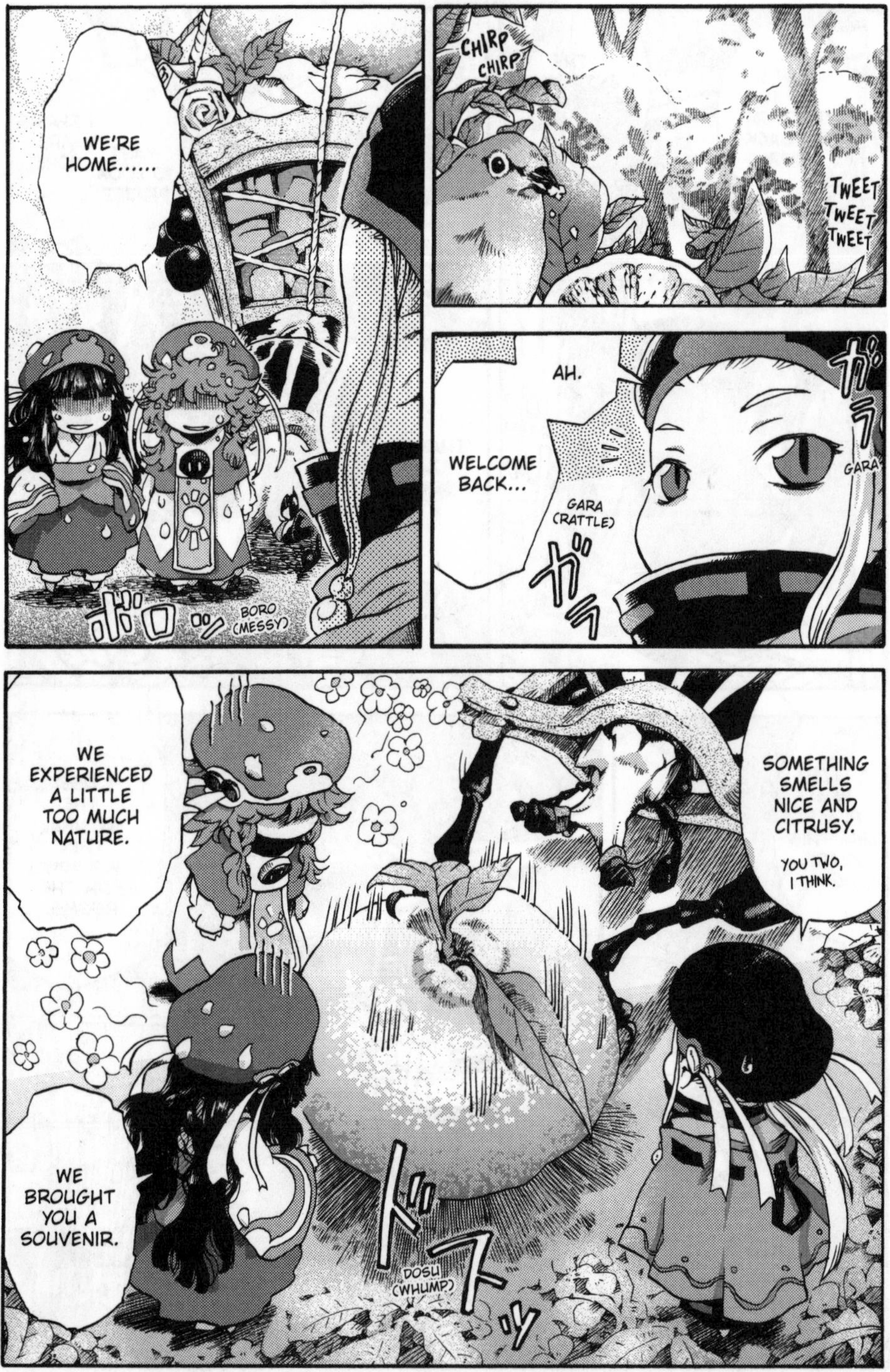
WE'RE HOME......
ボロ
BORO (MESSY)
CHIRP CHIRP
TWEET TWEET TWEET
AH.
WELCOME BACK...
ガラ
GARA (RATTLE)
ガラ
GARA
WE EXPERIENCED A LITTLE TOO MUCH NATURE.
SOMETHING SMELLS NICE AND CITRUSY.
YOU TWO, I THINK.
WE BROUGHT YOU A SOUVENIR.
ドスッ
DOSU (WHUMP)

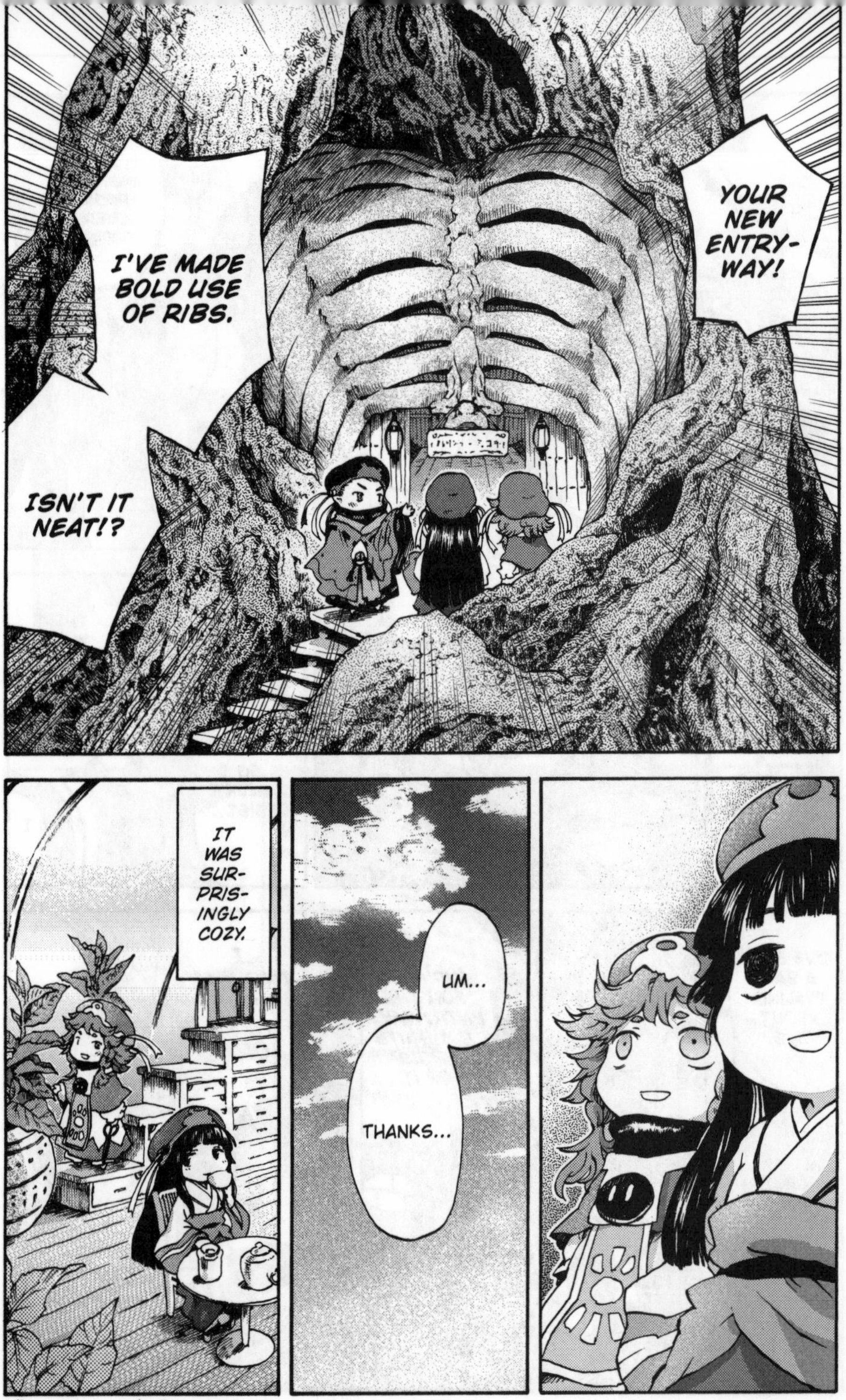
YOUR NEW ENTRY-WAY!
I'VE MADE BOLD USE OF RIBS.
ISN'T IT NEAT!?
UM...
THANKS...
IT WAS SURPRISINGLY COZY.

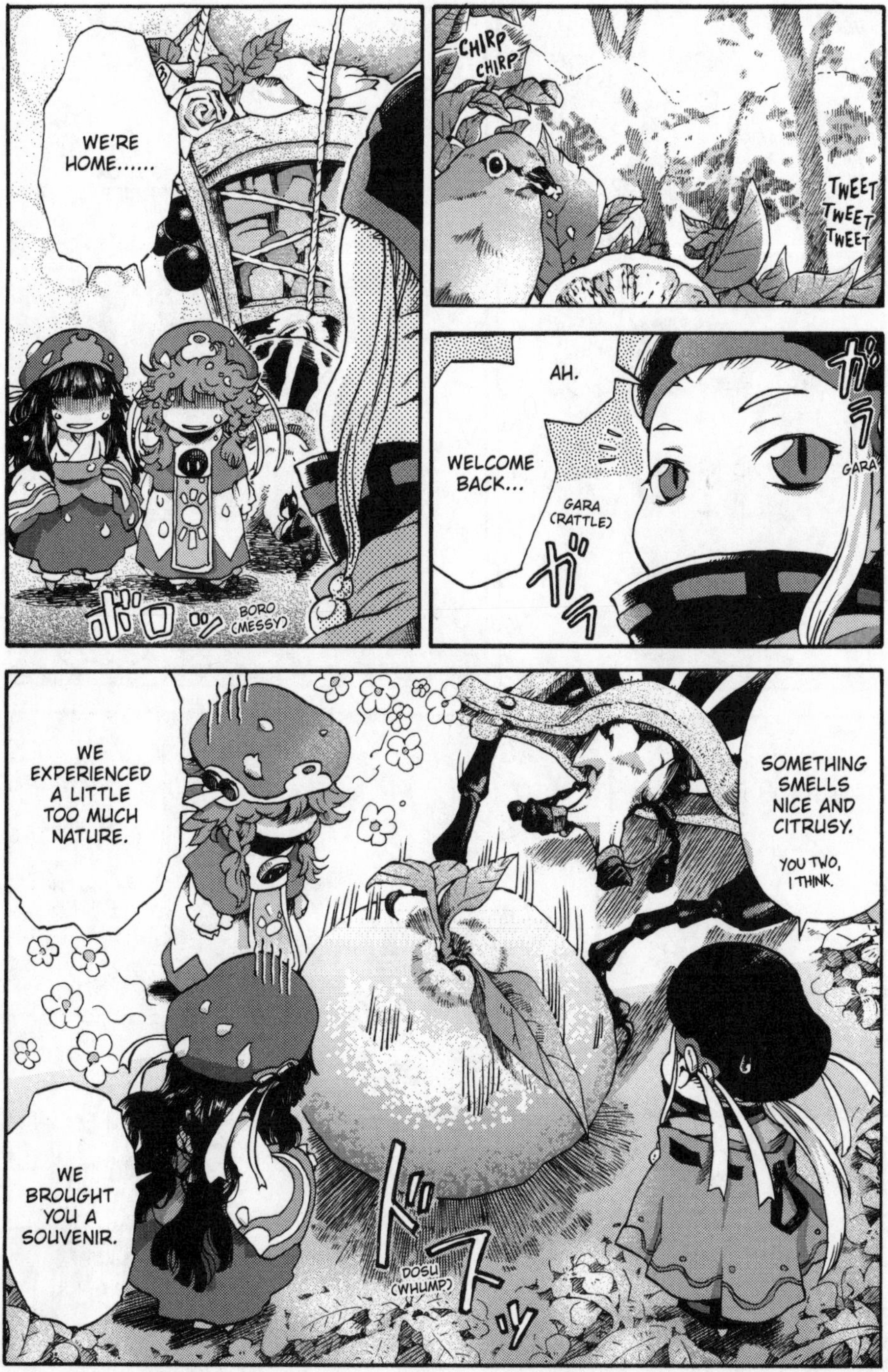
CHIRP CHIRP
TWEET TWEET TWEET
GARA
AH.
WELCOME BACK...
GARA (RATTLE)
WE'RE HOME......
BORO (MESSY)
SOMETHING SMELLS NICE AND CITRUSY.
YOU TWO, I THINK.
WE EXPERIENCED A LITTLE TOO MUCH NATURE.
WE BROUGHT YOU A SOUVENIR.
DOSU (WHUMP)

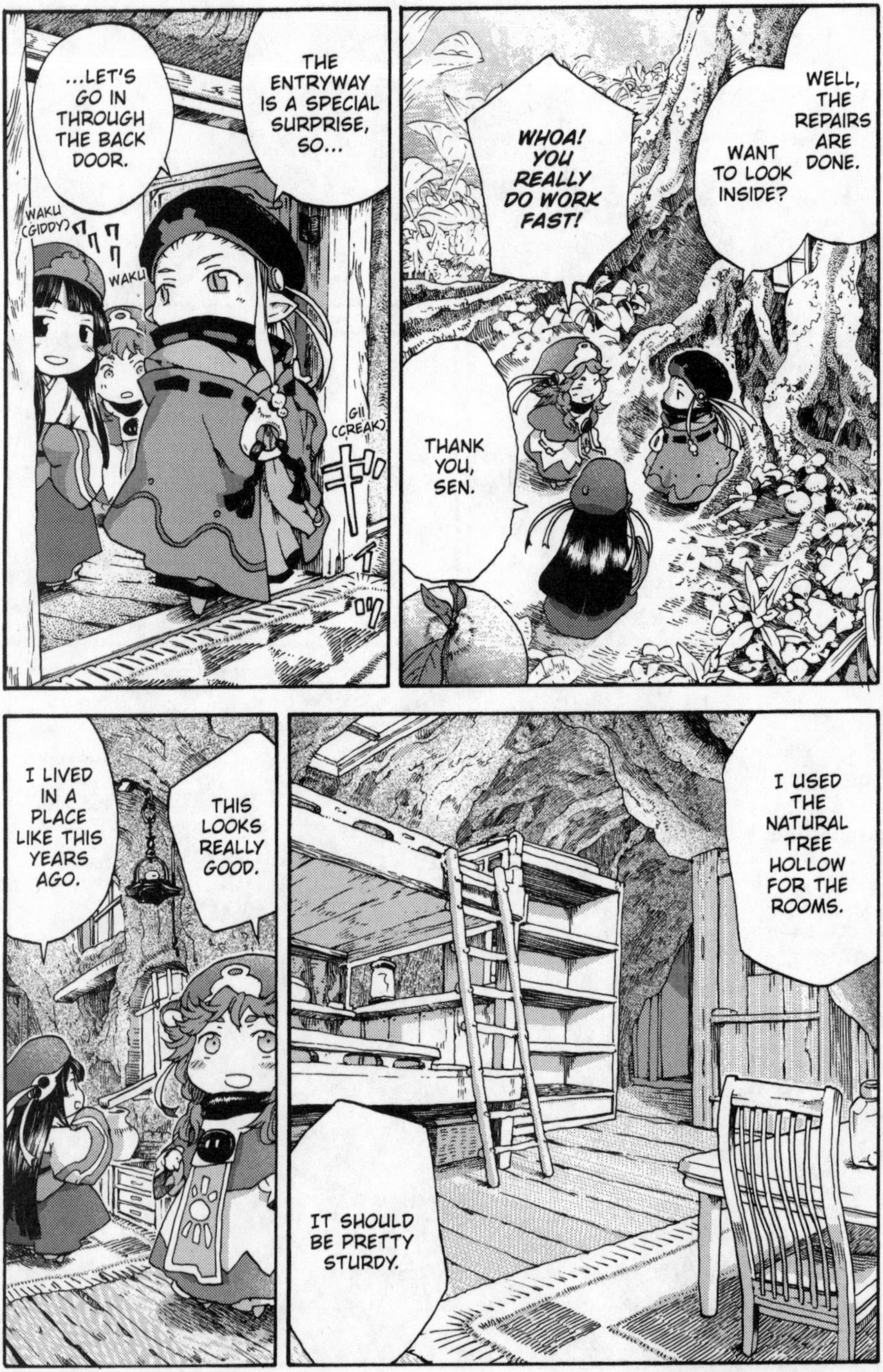
WELL, THE REPAIRS ARE DONE.
WANT TO LOOK INSIDE?
WHOA! YOU REALLY DO WORK FAST!
THANK YOU, SEN.
THE ENTRYWAY IS A SPECIAL SURPRISE, SO...
...LET'S GO IN THROUGH THE BACK DOOR.
WAKU (GIDDY)
WAKU
GII (CREAK)
I USED THE NATURAL TREE HOLLOW FOR THE ROOMS.
IT SHOULD BE PRETTY STURDY.
THIS LOOKS REALLY GOOD.
I LIVED IN A PLACE LIKE THIS YEARS AGO.

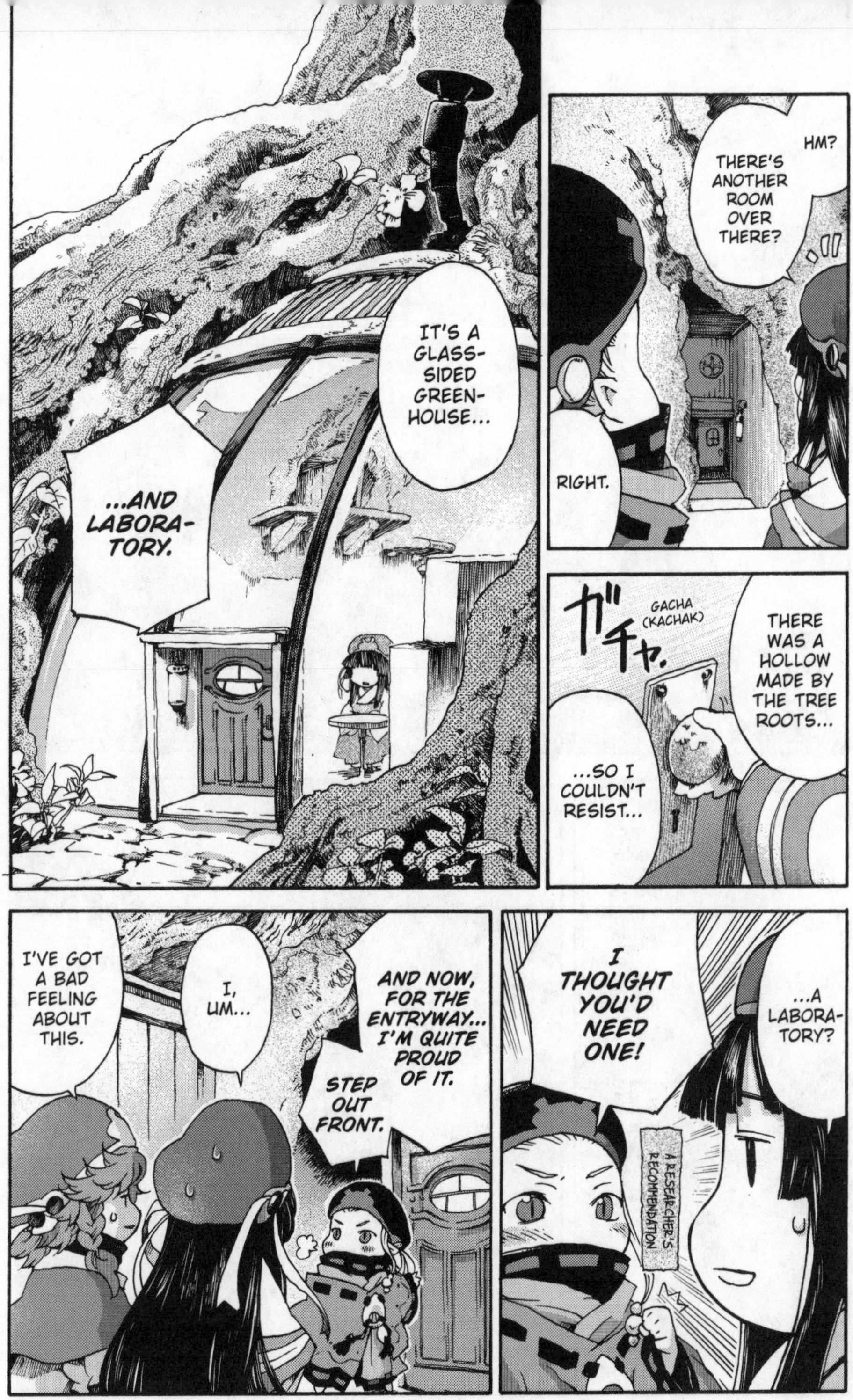
HM? THERE'S ANOTHER ROOM OVER THERE?
RIGHT.
ガチャ.
GACHA (KACHAK)
THERE WAS A HOLLOW MADE BY THE TREE ROOTS...
...SO I COULDN'T RESIST...
IT'S A GLASS-SIDED GREEN-HOUSE...
...AND LABORA-TORY.
...A LABORA-TORY?
I THOUGHT YOU'D NEED ONE!
A RESEARCHER'S RECOMMENDATION
AND NOW, FOR THE ENTRYWAY... I'M QUITE PROUD OF IT.
STEP OUT FRONT.
I, UM...
I'VE GOT A BAD FEELING ABOUT THIS.

YOUR NEW ENTRY-WAY!

I'VE MADE BOLD USE OF RIBS.

ISN'T IT NEAT!?

IT WAS SUR-PRIS-INGLY COZY.

UM...

THANKS...

Chapter 4 • End

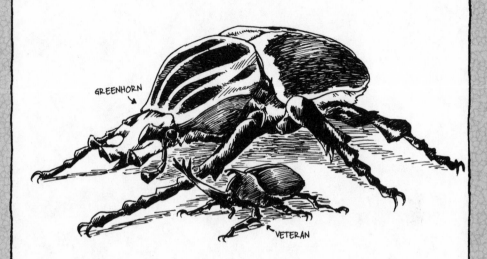

GREENHORN

VETERAN

With a length of more than one hundred millimeters, goliath beetles are the world's heaviest insect. Big-bodied and strong, they often end up working exclusively in the transportation industry.

As a rule, they tend to work independently, without joining unions. Their shipping costs are a mixed bag, but it's possible to pay them with material goods. If you treat them to a tasty meal, they'll undertake jobs with no objection.

Rhinoceros beetles are involved in the same business, handling things like small transport and solo travel.

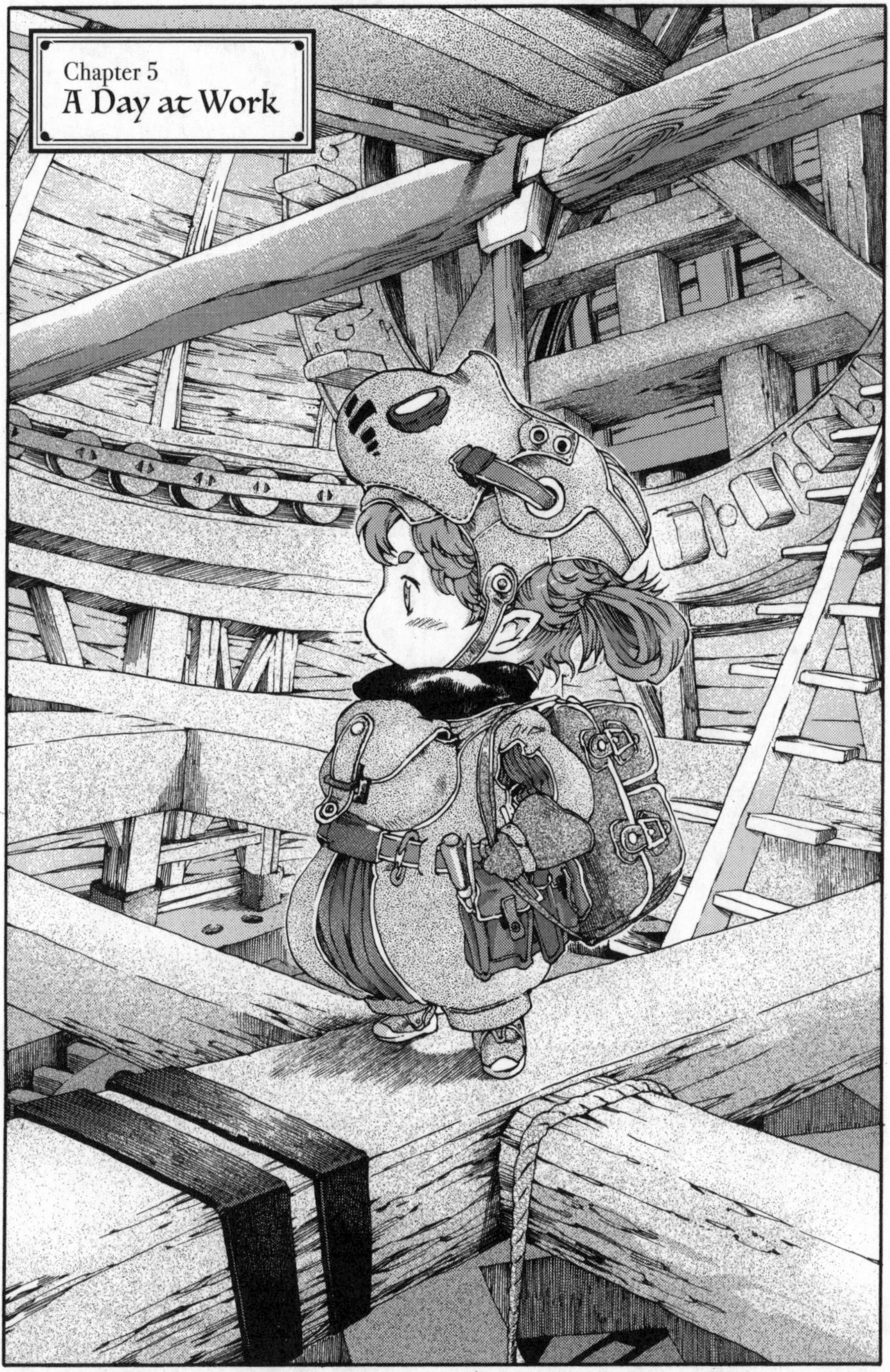
Chapter 5
A Day at Work

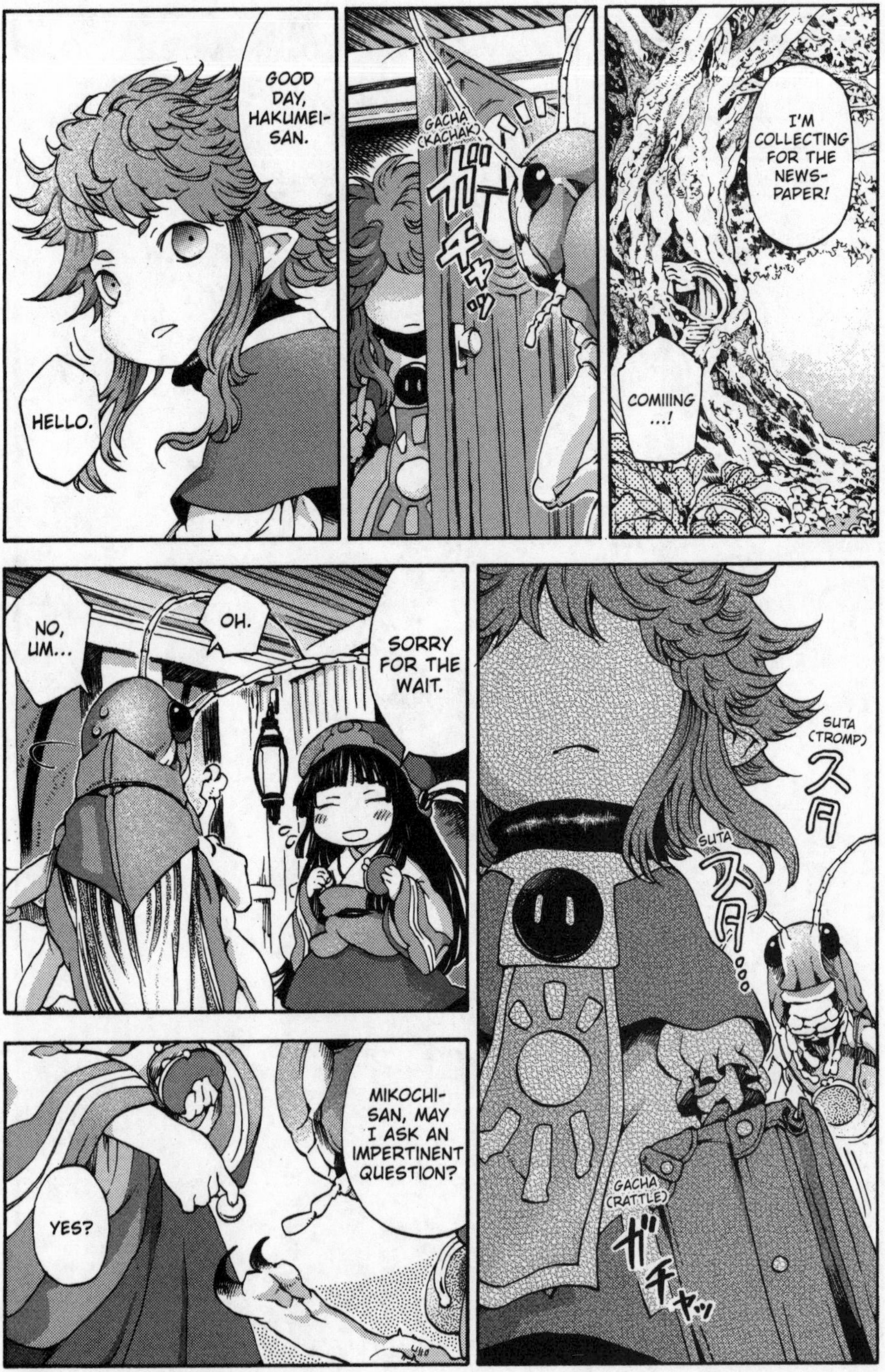
I'M COLLECTING FOR THE NEWS-PAPER!
COMIIING ...!
GACHA (KACHAK)
ガチャッ
GOOD DAY, HAKUMEI-SAN.
HELLO.
SUTA (TROMP)
スタ
SUTA
スタ
GACHA (RATTLE)
ガチャッ
SORRY FOR THE WAIT.
OH.
NO, UM...
MIKOCHI-SAN, MAY I ASK AN IMPERTINENT QUESTION?
YES?

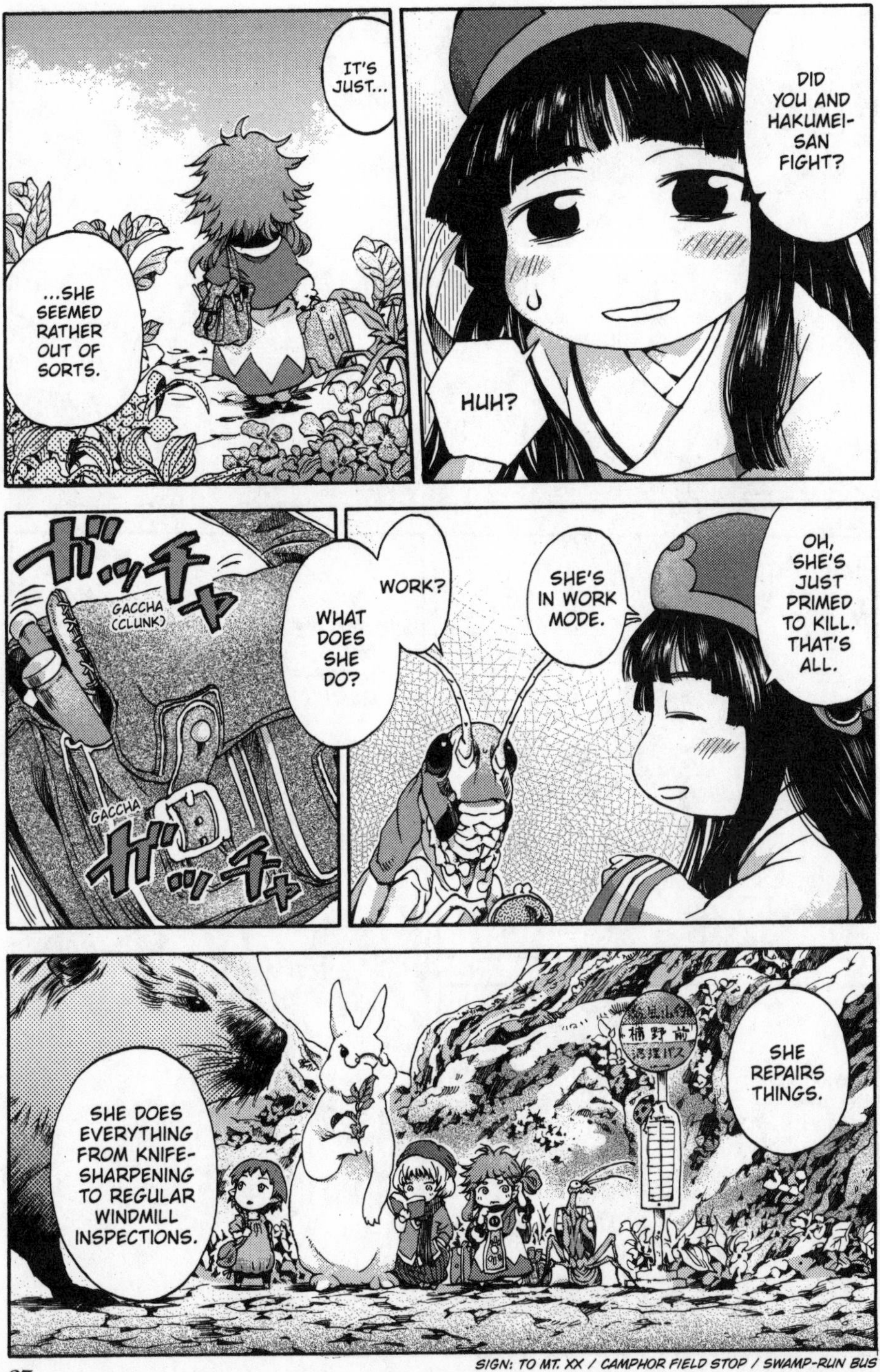
DID YOU AND HAKUMEI-SAN FIGHT?
HUH?
IT'S JUST...
...SHE SEEMED RATHER OUT OF SORTS.
OH, SHE'S JUST PRIMED TO KILL. THAT'S ALL.
SHE'S IN WORK MODE.
WORK?
WHAT DOES SHE DO?
ガッチャ
GACCHA (CLUNK)
GACCHA
ガッチャ
SHE REPAIRS THINGS.
SHE DOES EVERYTHING FROM KNIFE-SHARPENING TO REGULAR WINDMILL INSPECTIONS.

SIGN: TO MT. XX / CAMPHOR FIELD STOP / SWAMP-RUN BUS

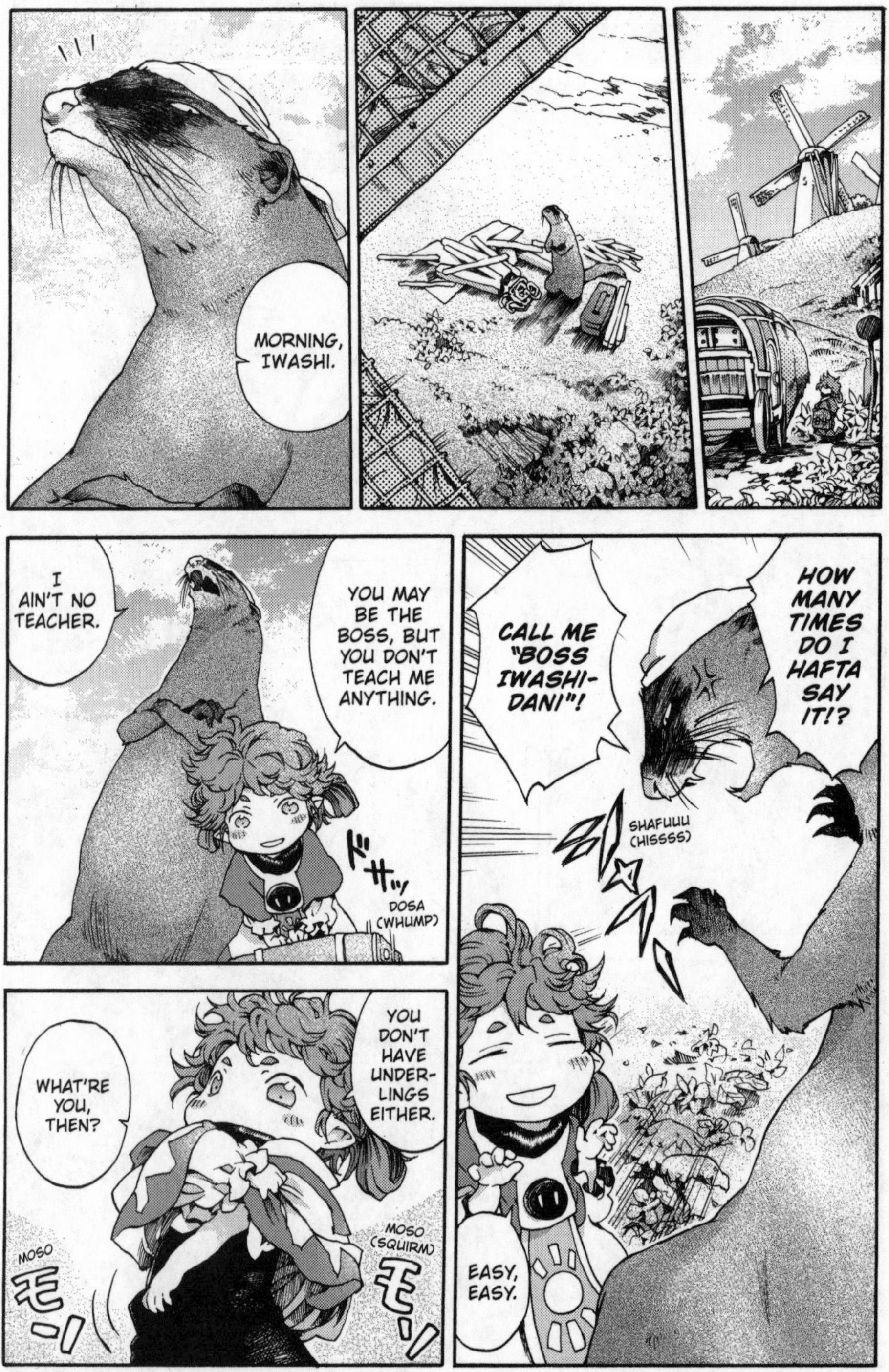
MORNING, IWASHI.
YOU MAY BE THE BOSS, BUT YOU DON'T TEACH ME ANYTHING.
I AIN'T NO TEACHER.
ドサッ
DOSA (WHUMP)
YOU DON'T HAVE UNDER-LINGS EITHER.
WHAT'RE YOU, THEN?
モソ
MOSO (SQUIRM)
モソ
MOSO
CALL ME "BOSS IWASHI-DANI"!
HOW MANY TIMES DO I HAFTA SAY IT!?
SHAFUUU (HISSSS)
EASY, EASY.

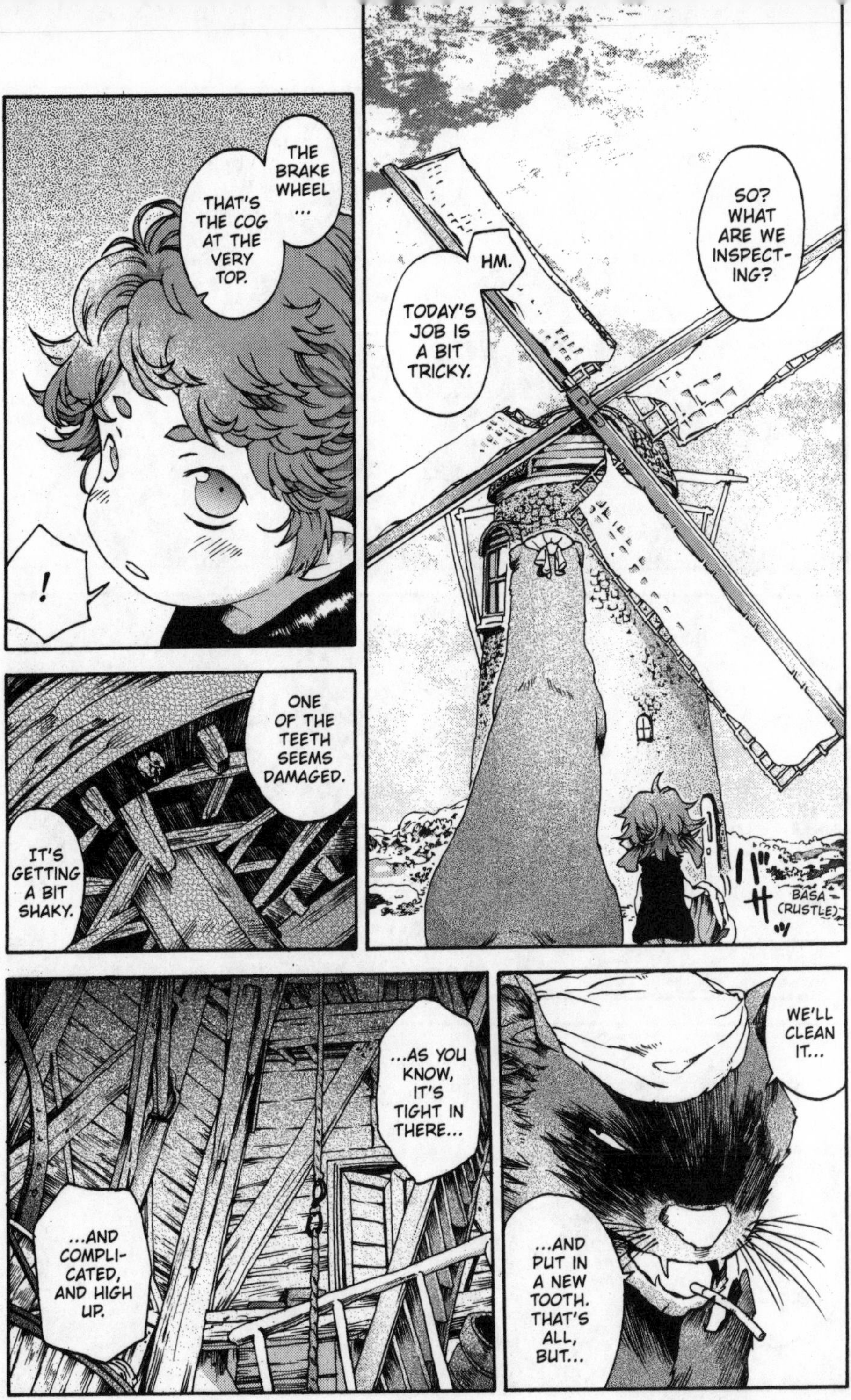
SO? WHAT ARE WE INSPECTING?
HM.
TODAY'S JOB IS A BIT TRICKY.
BASA (RUSTLE)
THE BRAKE WHEEL...
THAT'S THE COG AT THE VERY TOP.
!
ONE OF THE TEETH SEEMS DAMAGED.
IT'S GETTING A BIT SHAKY.
WE'LL CLEAN IT...
...AND PUT IN A NEW TOOTH. THAT'S ALL, BUT...
...AS YOU KNOW, IT'S TIGHT IN THERE...
...AND COMPLICATED, AND HIGH UP.

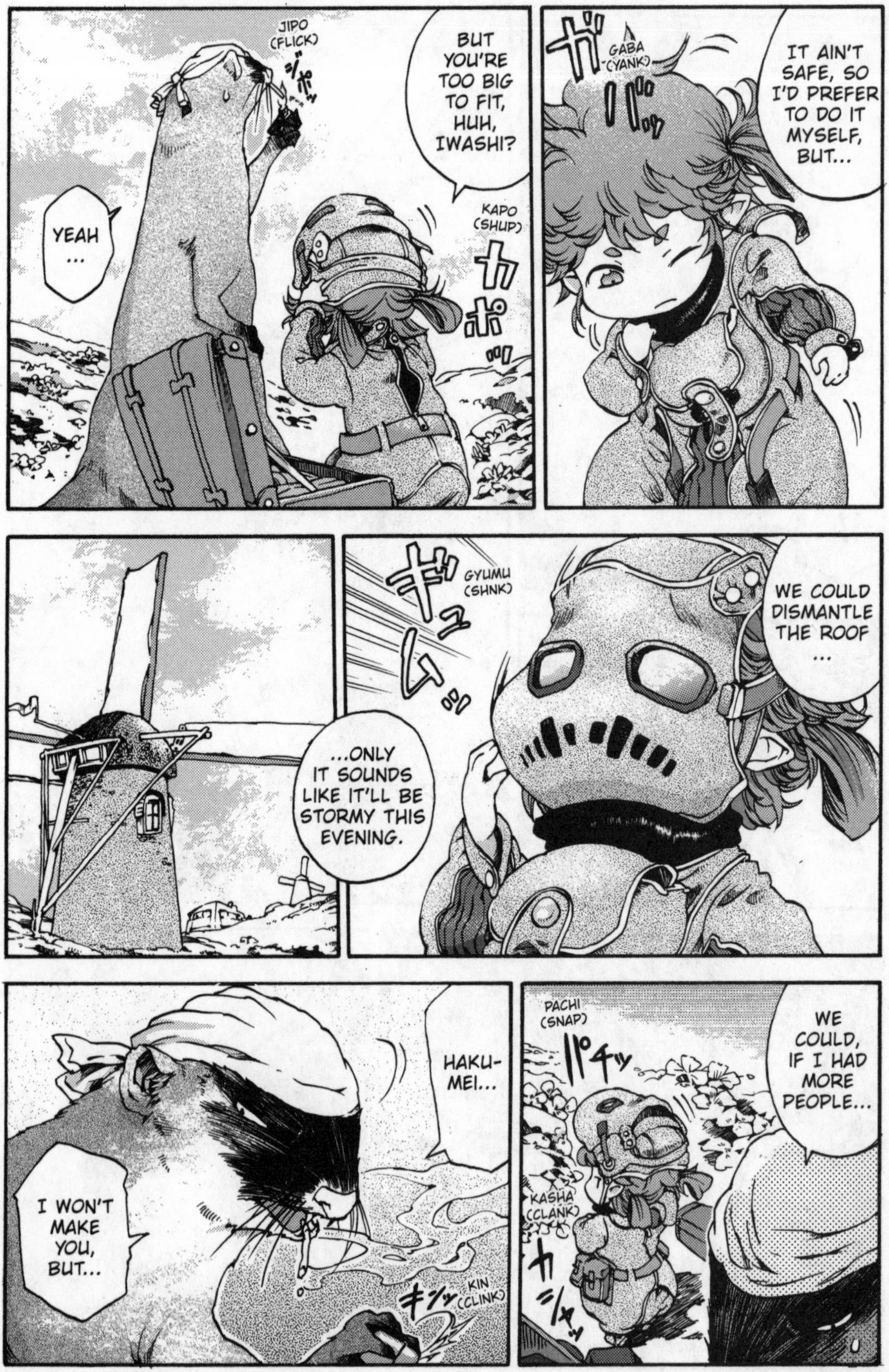
GABA (YANK)
IT AIN'T SAFE, SO I'D PREFER TO DO IT MYSELF, BUT...
BUT YOU'RE TOO BIG TO FIT, HUH, IWASHI?
JIPO (FLICK)
KAPO (SHUP)
YEAH ...
GYUMU (SHNK)
WE COULD DISMANTLE THE ROOF ...
...ONLY IT SOUNDS LIKE IT'LL BE STORMY THIS EVENING.
PACHI (SNAP)
WE COULD, IF I HAD MORE PEOPLE...
KASHA (CLANK)
HAKU-MEI...
I WON'T MAKE YOU, BUT...
KIN (CLINK)

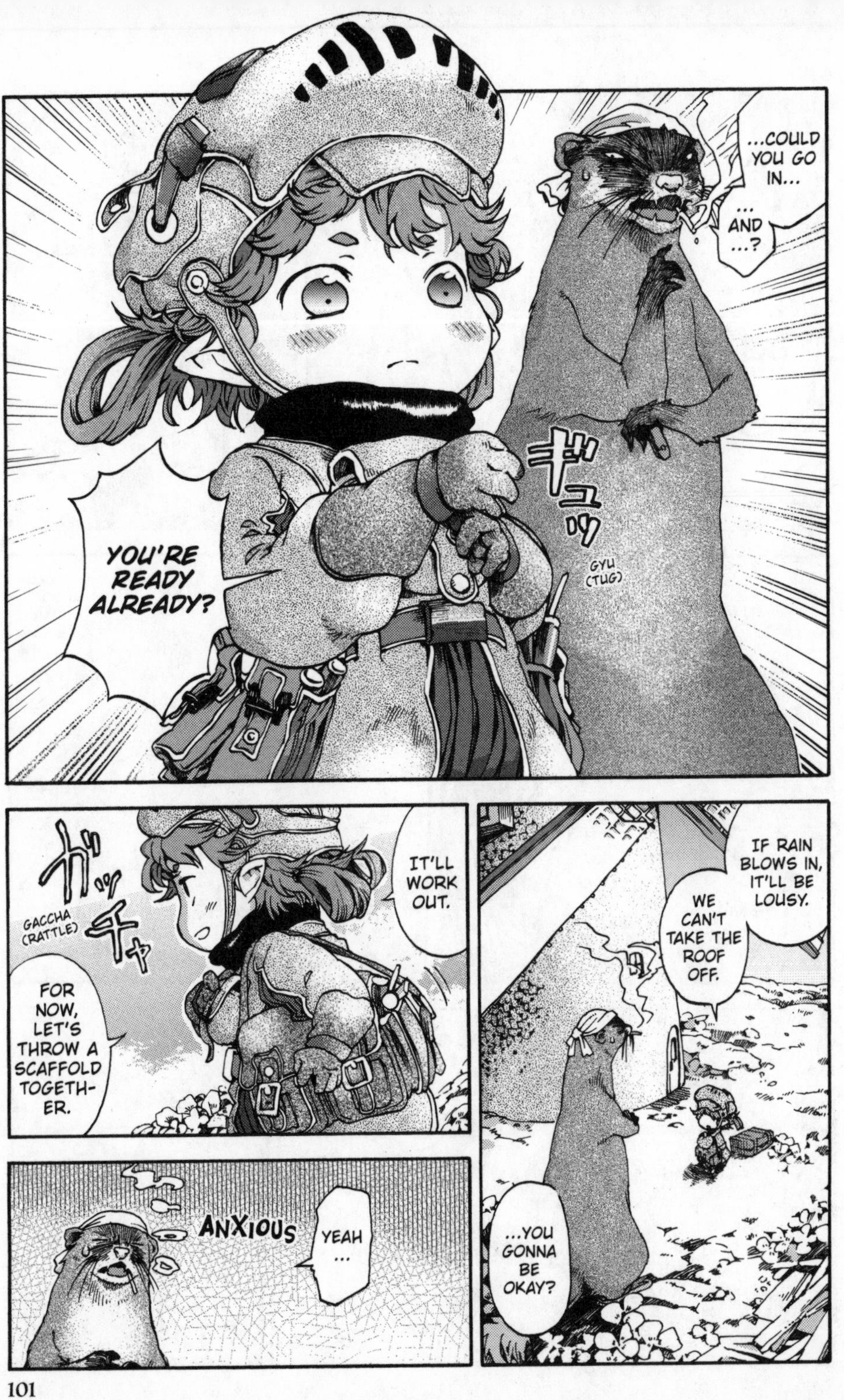

...COULD YOU GO IN...
...AND ...?
YOU'RE READY ALREADY?
ギュッ
GYU (TUG)
IF RAIN BLOWS IN, IT'LL BE LOUSY.
WE CAN'T TAKE THE ROOF OFF.
IT'LL WORK OUT.
ガッチャ
GACCHA (RATTLE)
FOR NOW, LET'S THROW A SCAFFOLD TOGETHER.
...YOU GONNA BE OKAY?
ANXIOUS
YEAH ...

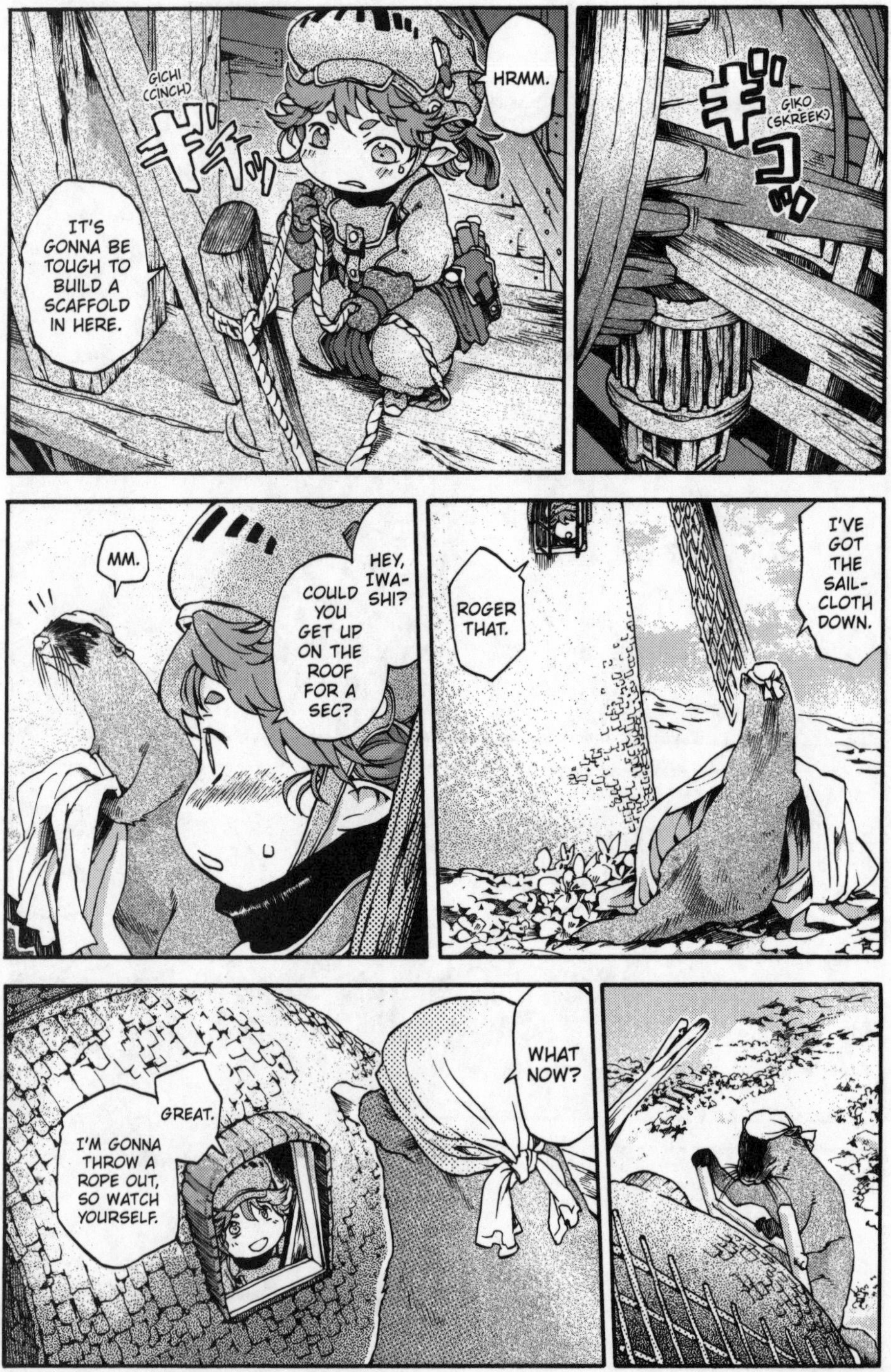
GIKO (SKREEK)
HRMM.
GICHI (CINCH)
IT'S GONNA BE TOUGH TO BUILD A SCAFFOLD IN HERE.
I'VE GOT THE SAIL-CLOTH DOWN.
ROGER THAT.
HEY, IWASHI? COULD YOU GET UP ON THE ROOF FOR A SEC?
MM.
WHAT NOW?
GREAT. I'M GONNA THROW A ROPE OUT, SO WATCH YOURSELF.

SURE.

I WANT TO HAUL UP A BEAM, GIVE IT A TUG FOR ME. BUT IT'S HEAVY.

I'M ON IT.

IT'S OUT.

HUP!

HYUN (SWISH)

ピューッ

WHOA!

FAST!

GAKON (CLONK)

GUOO (FOOM)

GARI (SCRAPE)

ガコン

グォォ

ガリ

ガリ

AND HEAVE...

GU (YANK)

グッ

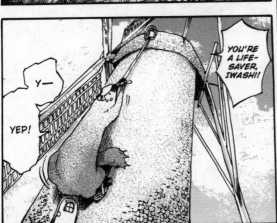

Y—

YEP!

YOU'RE A LIFE-SAVER, IWASHI!

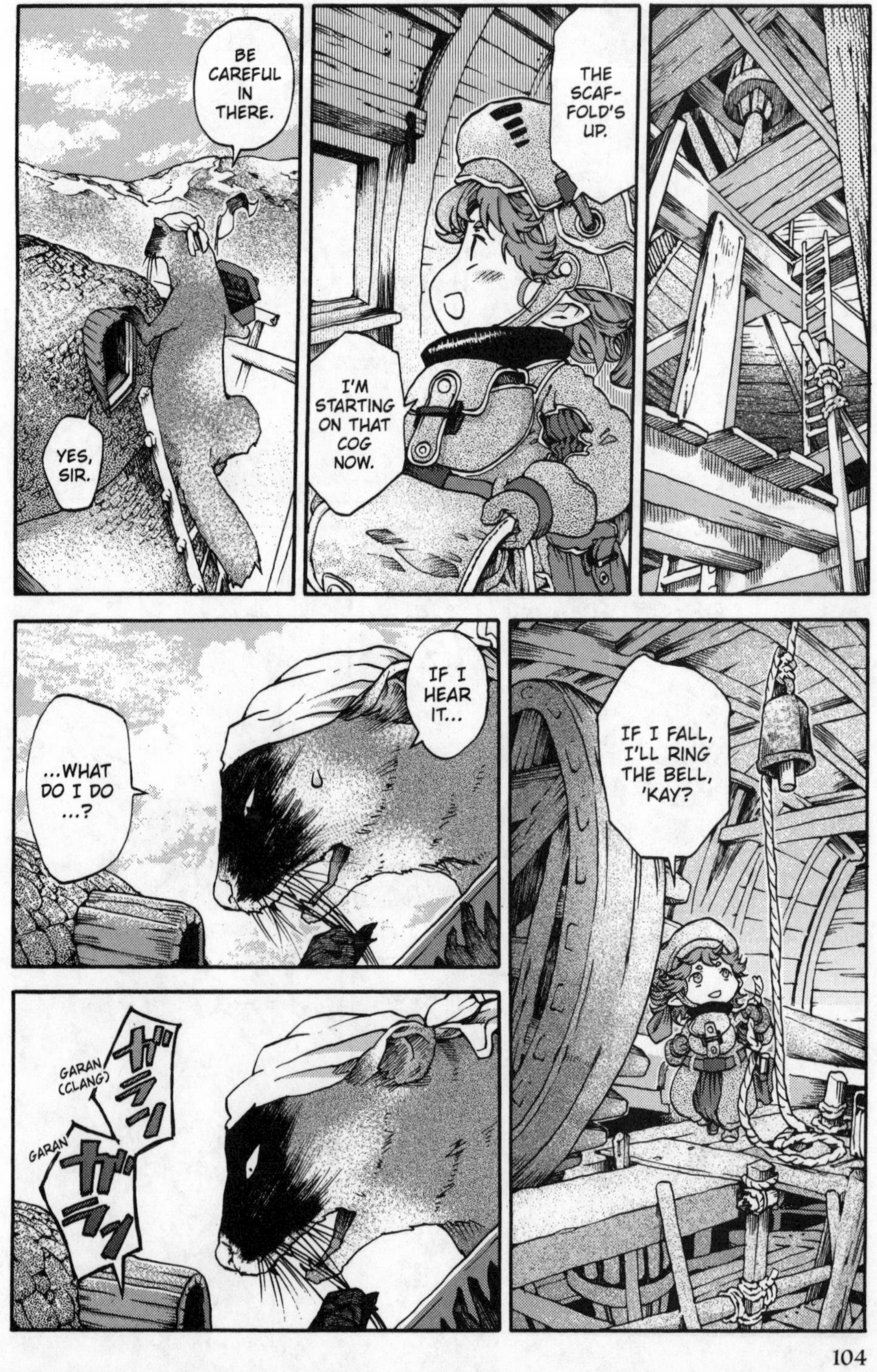
THE SCAF-FOLD'S UP.
I'M STARTING ON THAT COG NOW.
BE CAREFUL IN THERE.
YES, SIR.
IF I FALL, I'LL RING THE BELL, 'KAY?
IF I HEAR IT...
...WHAT DO I DO ...?
GARAN (CLANG)
GARAN

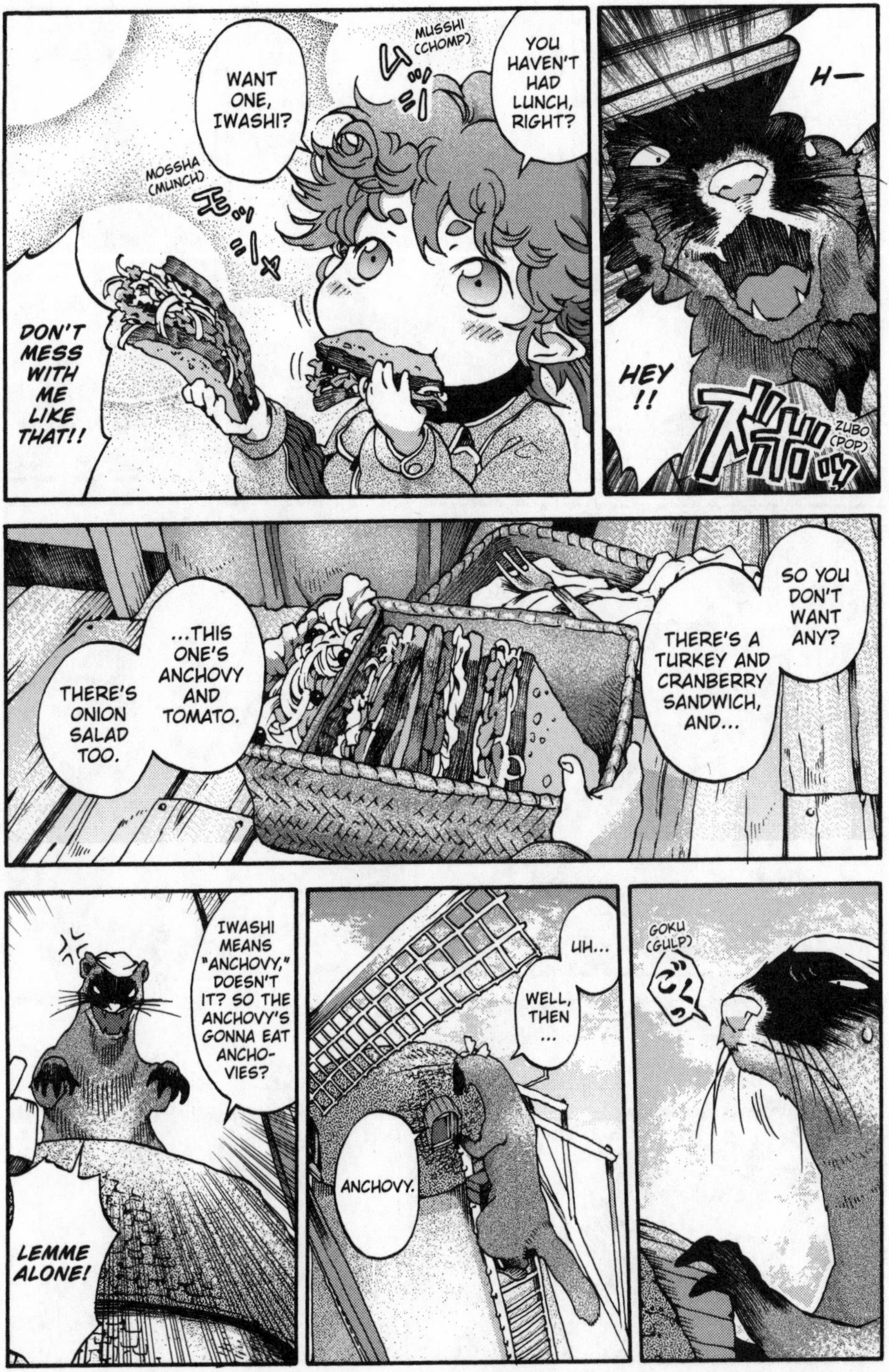
H—
HEY!!
ZUBO (POP)
YOU HAVEN'T HAD LUNCH, RIGHT?
MUSSHI (CHOMP)
WANT ONE, IWASHI?
MOSSHA (MUNCH)
DON'T MESS WITH ME LIKE THAT!!
SO YOU DON'T WANT ANY?
THERE'S A TURKEY AND CRANBERRY SANDWICH, AND...
...THIS ONE'S ANCHOVY AND TOMATO.
THERE'S ONION SALAD TOO.
GOKU (GULP)
UH...
WELL, THEN ...
ANCHOVY.
IWASHI MEANS "ANCHOVY," DOESN'T IT? SO THE ANCHOVY'S GONNA EAT ANCHO-VIES?
LEMME ALONE!

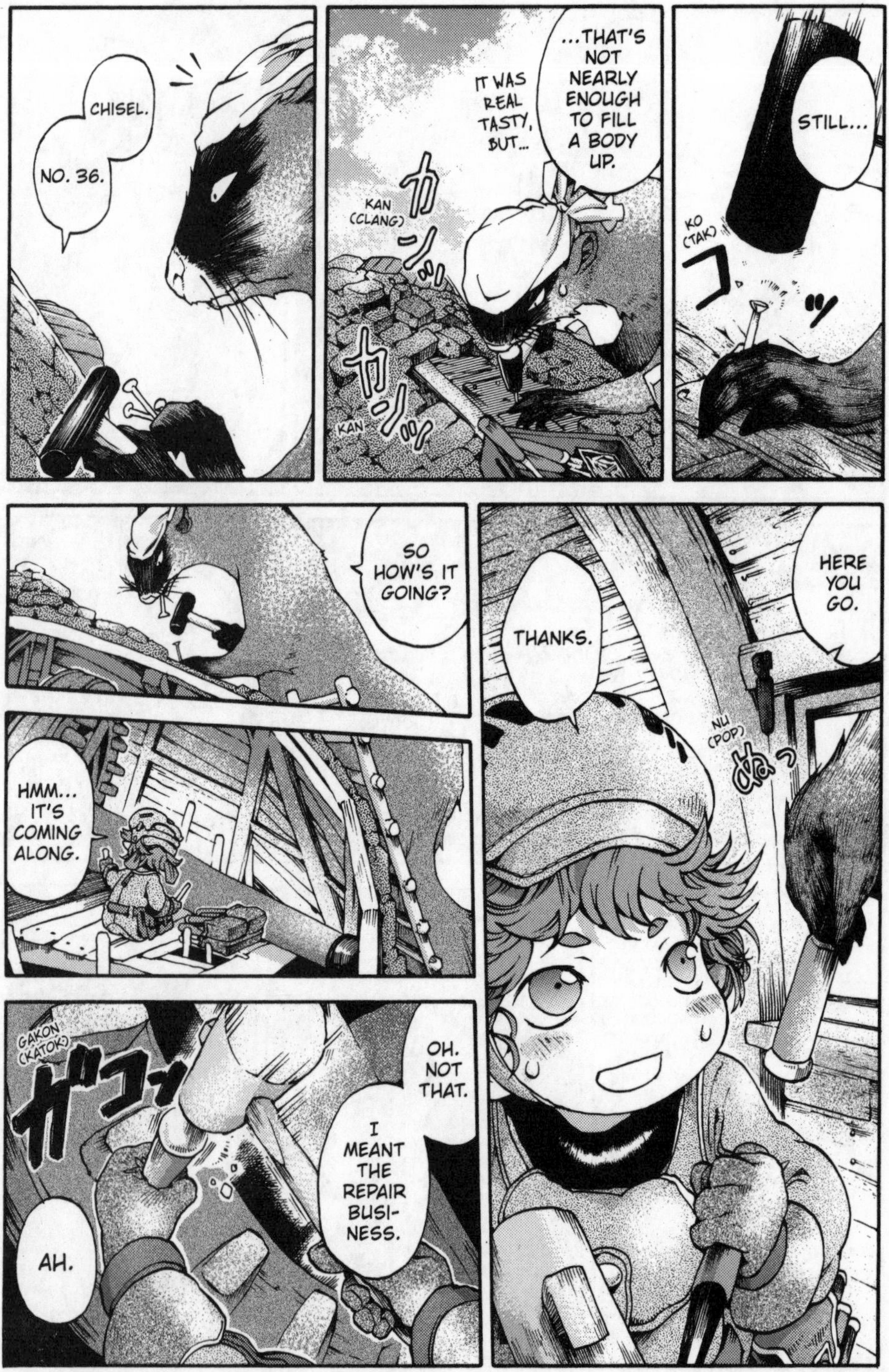
STILL...
KO (TAK)
IT WAS REAL TASTY, BUT...
...THAT'S NOT NEARLY ENOUGH TO FILL A BODY UP.
KAN (CLANG)
KAN
CHISEL.
NO. 36.
HERE YOU GO.
THANKS.
NU (POP)
SO HOW'S IT GOING?
HMM... IT'S COMING ALONG.
OH. NOT THAT.
I MEANT THE REPAIR BUSINESS.
GAKON (KATOK)
AH.

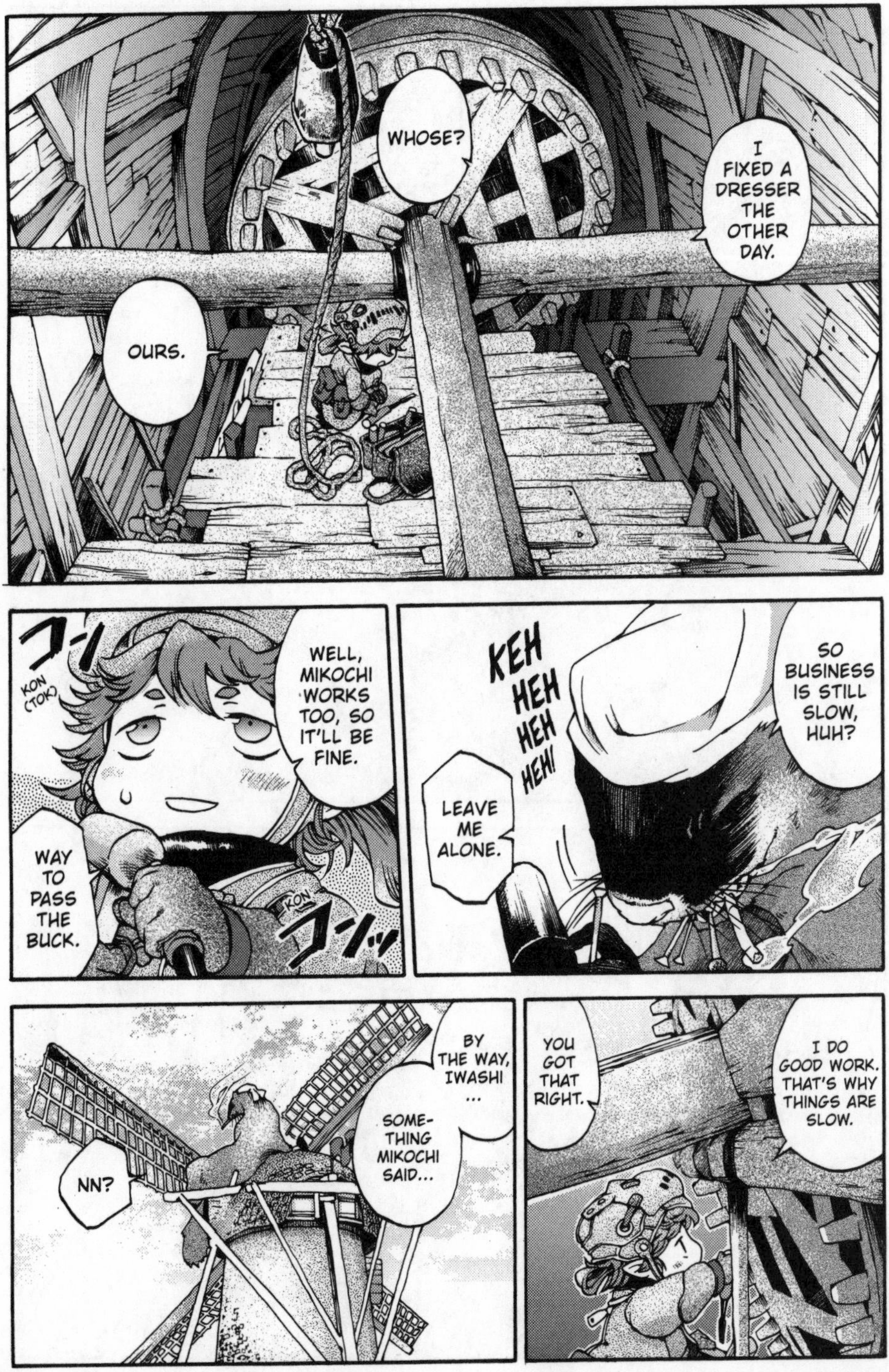
I FIXED A DRESSER THE OTHER DAY.
WHOSE?
OURS.
SO BUSINESS IS STILL SLOW, HUH?
KEH HEH HEH HEH!
LEAVE ME ALONE.
WELL, MIKOCHI WORKS TOO, SO IT'LL BE FINE.
コーン
KON (TOK)
WAY TO PASS THE BUCK.
KON
コンッ
I DO GOOD WORK. THAT'S WHY THINGS ARE SLOW.
YOU GOT THAT RIGHT.
BY THE WAY, IWASHI...
SOME-THING MIKOCHI SAID...
NN?

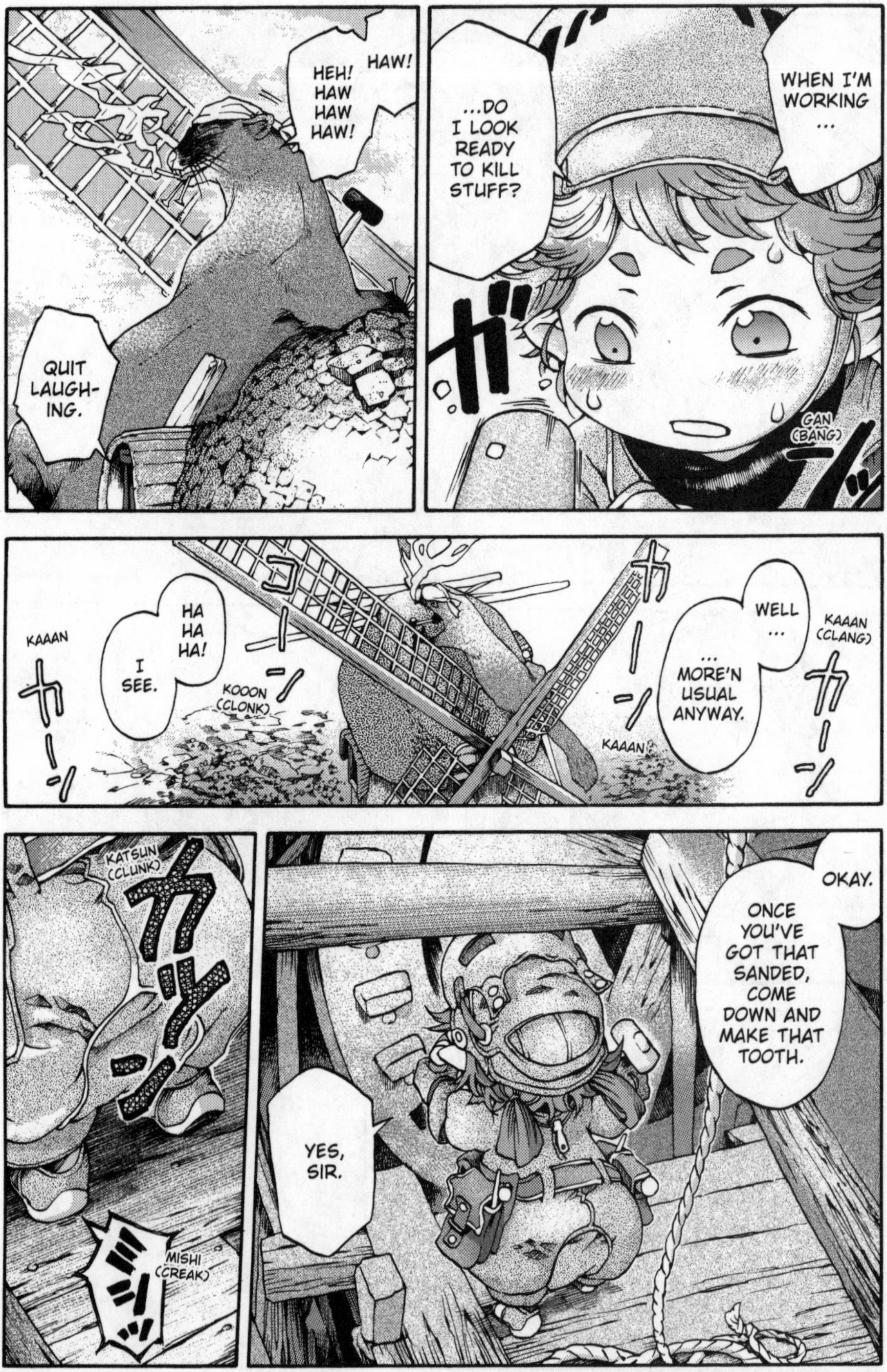
WHEN I'M WORKING ...
...DO I LOOK READY TO KILL STUFF?
GAN (BANG)
HAW!
HEH! HAW HAW HAW!
QUIT LAUGHING.
KAAAN (CLANG)
WELL ...
... MORE'N USUAL ANYWAY.
KAAAN
KOOON (CLONK)
HA HA HA! I SEE.
KAAAN
OKAY.
ONCE YOU'VE GOT THAT SANDED, COME DOWN AND MAKE THAT TOOTH.
YES, SIR.
KATSUN (CLUNK)
MISHI (CREAK)

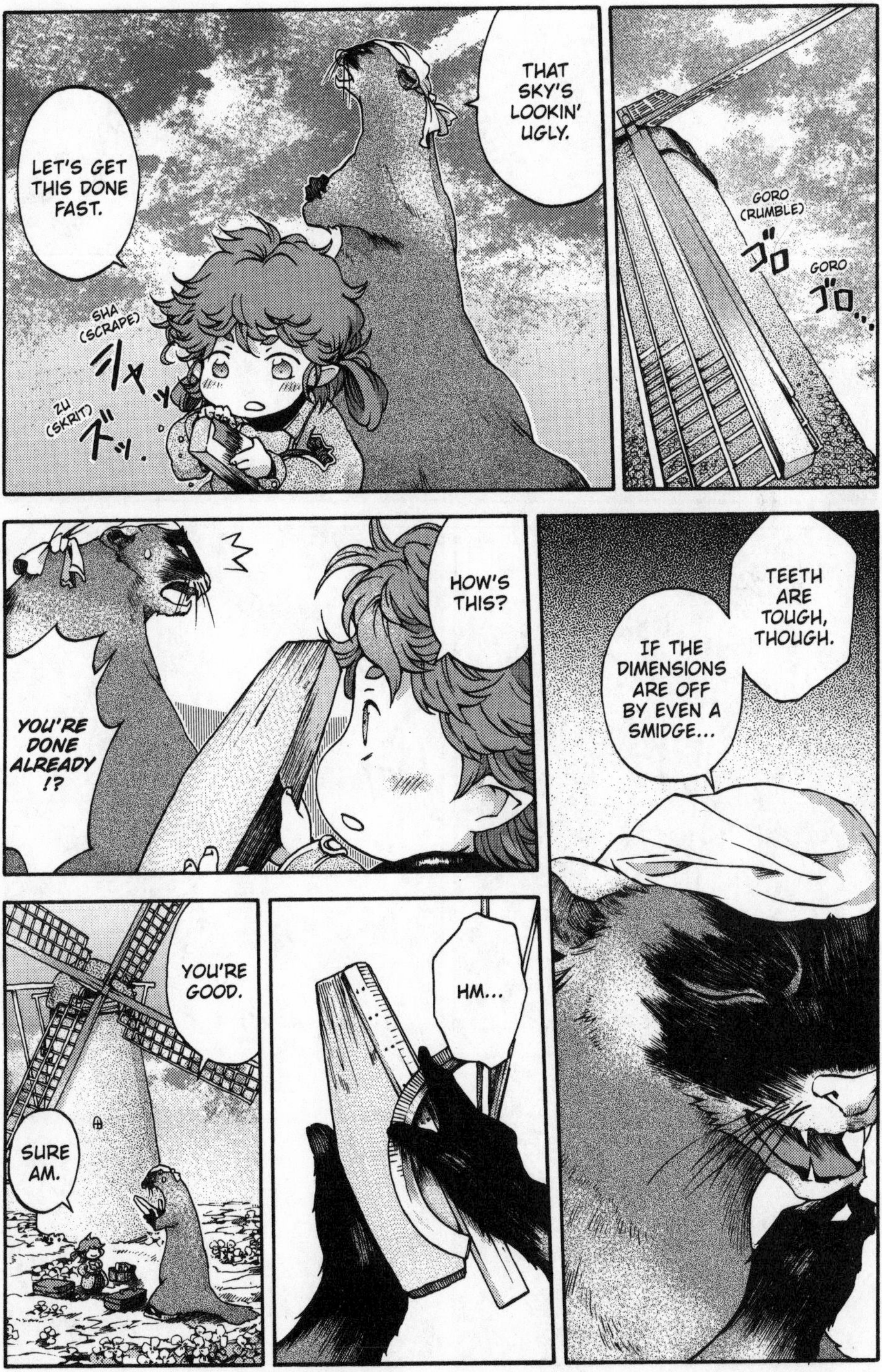
GORO (RUMBLE)
ゴロ
GORO
ゴロ…
THAT SKY'S LOOKIN' UGLY.
LET'S GET THIS DONE FAST.
SHA (SCRAPE)
シャッ
ZU (SKRIT)
ズッ.
HOW'S THIS?
YOU'RE DONE ALREADY!?
HM…
TEETH ARE TOUGH, THOUGH.
IF THE DIMENSIONS ARE OFF BY EVEN A SMIDGE…
YOU'RE GOOD.
SURE AM.

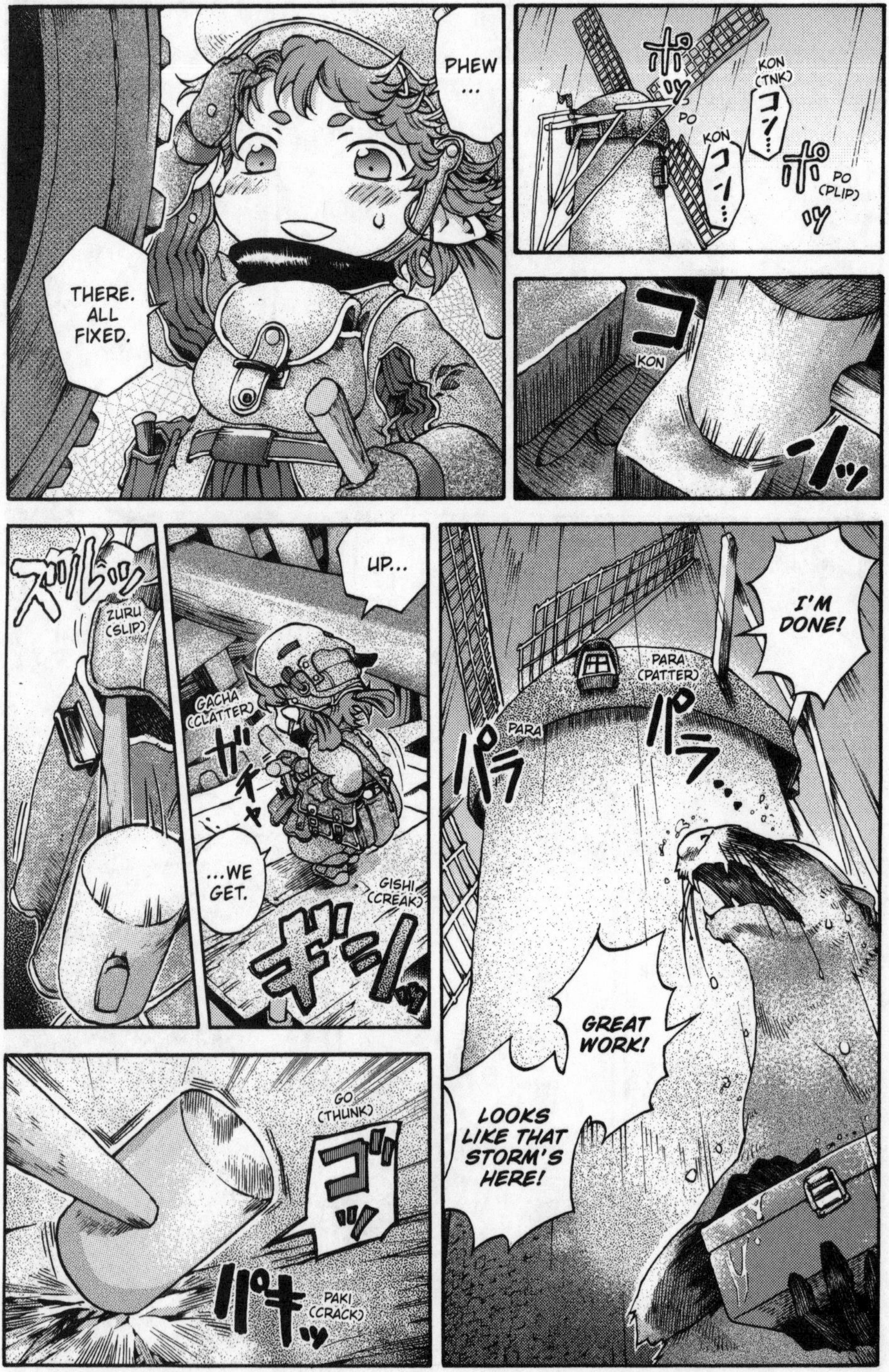
KON (TNK)
PO
KON
PO (PLIP)
KON
PHEW...
THERE. ALL FIXED.
I'M DONE!
PARA (PATTER)
PARA
GREAT WORK!
LOOKS LIKE THAT STORM'S HERE!
UP...
GACHA (CLATTER)
...WE GET.
GISHI (CREAK)
ZURU (SLIP)
GO (THUNK)
PAKI (CRACK)

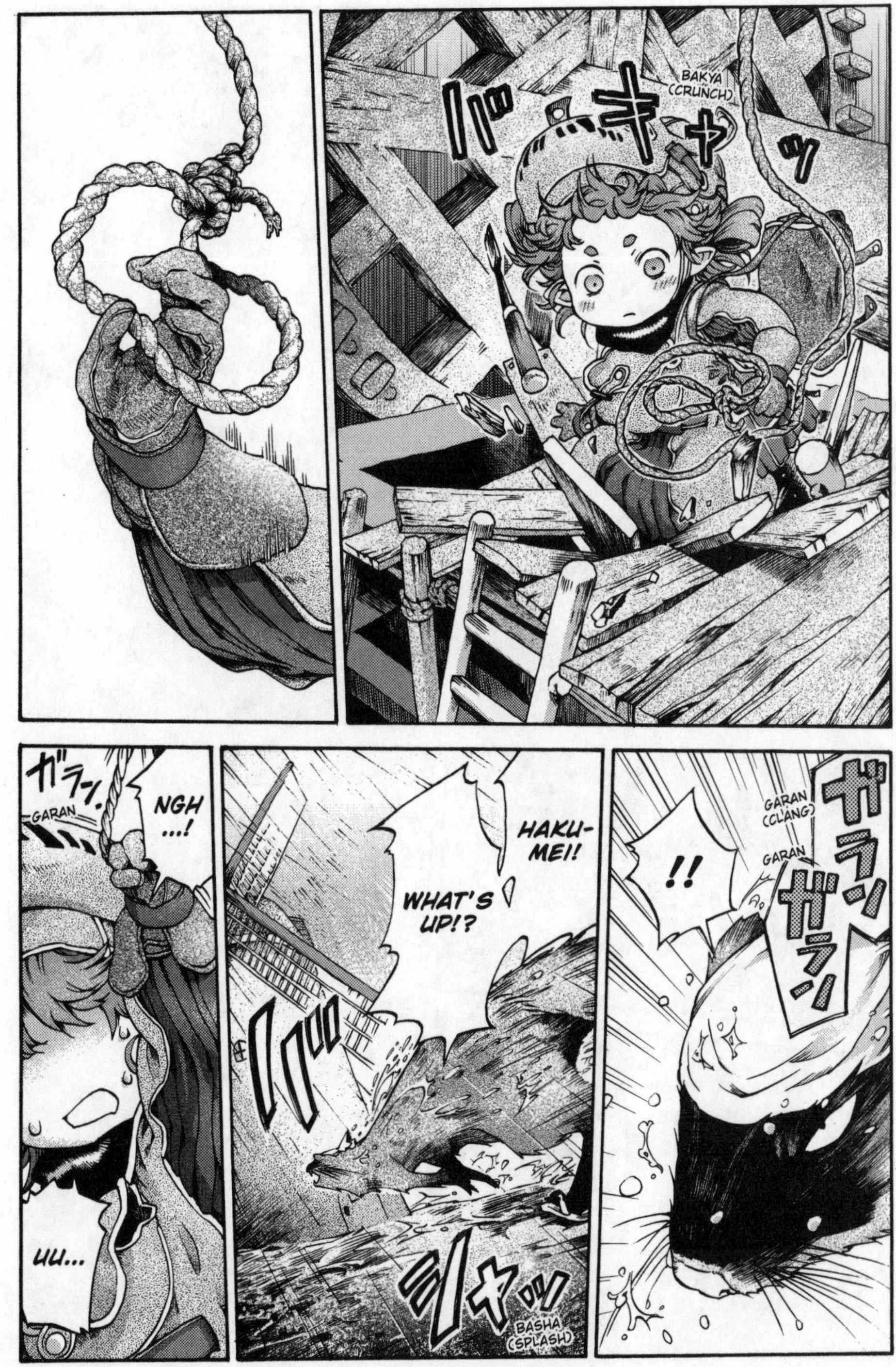
BAKYA (CRUNCH)
GARAN (CLANG)
GARAN
!!
HAKU-MEI!!
WHAT'S UP!?
BASHA (SPLASH)
GARAN
NGH ...!
UU...

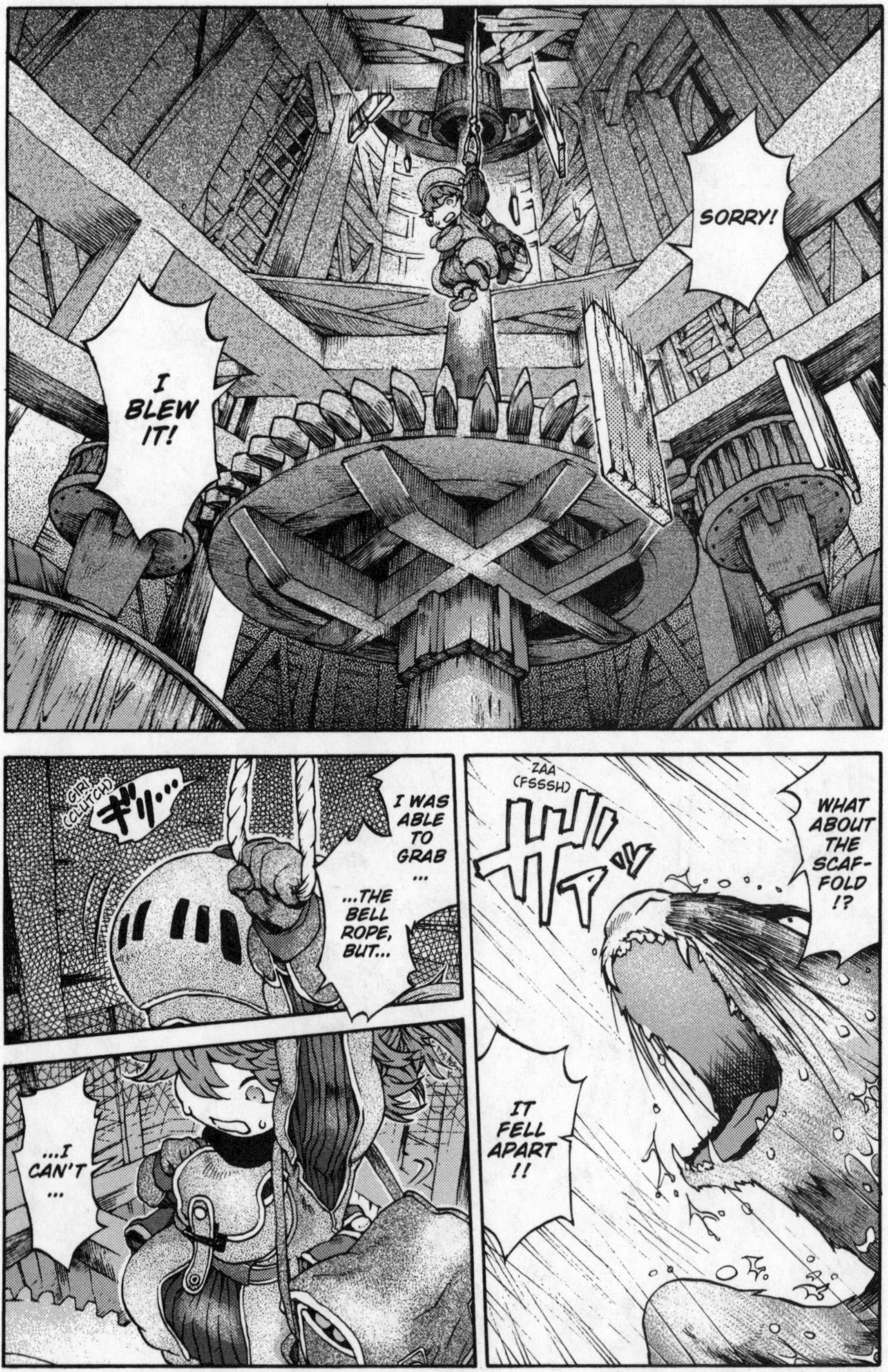
SORRY!
I BLEW IT!
ZAA (FSSSH)
ザァッ
WHAT ABOUT THE SCAF-FOLD !?
IT FELL APART !!
GIRI (CLUTCH)
ギリ…
I WAS ABLE TO GRAB ...
...THE BELL ROPE, BUT...
...I CAN'T ...

GI (CREAK)

GI (CREAK)

GI

GA (CLEAP)

ZAAA

BASHA (SPLASH)

AAAGH, DAMMIT!

BASHA

BOSS
...!

B—

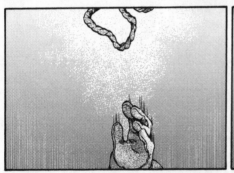

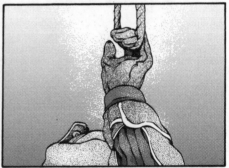

DOGA (CRUNCH)

GARAN

GARAN (CLANG)

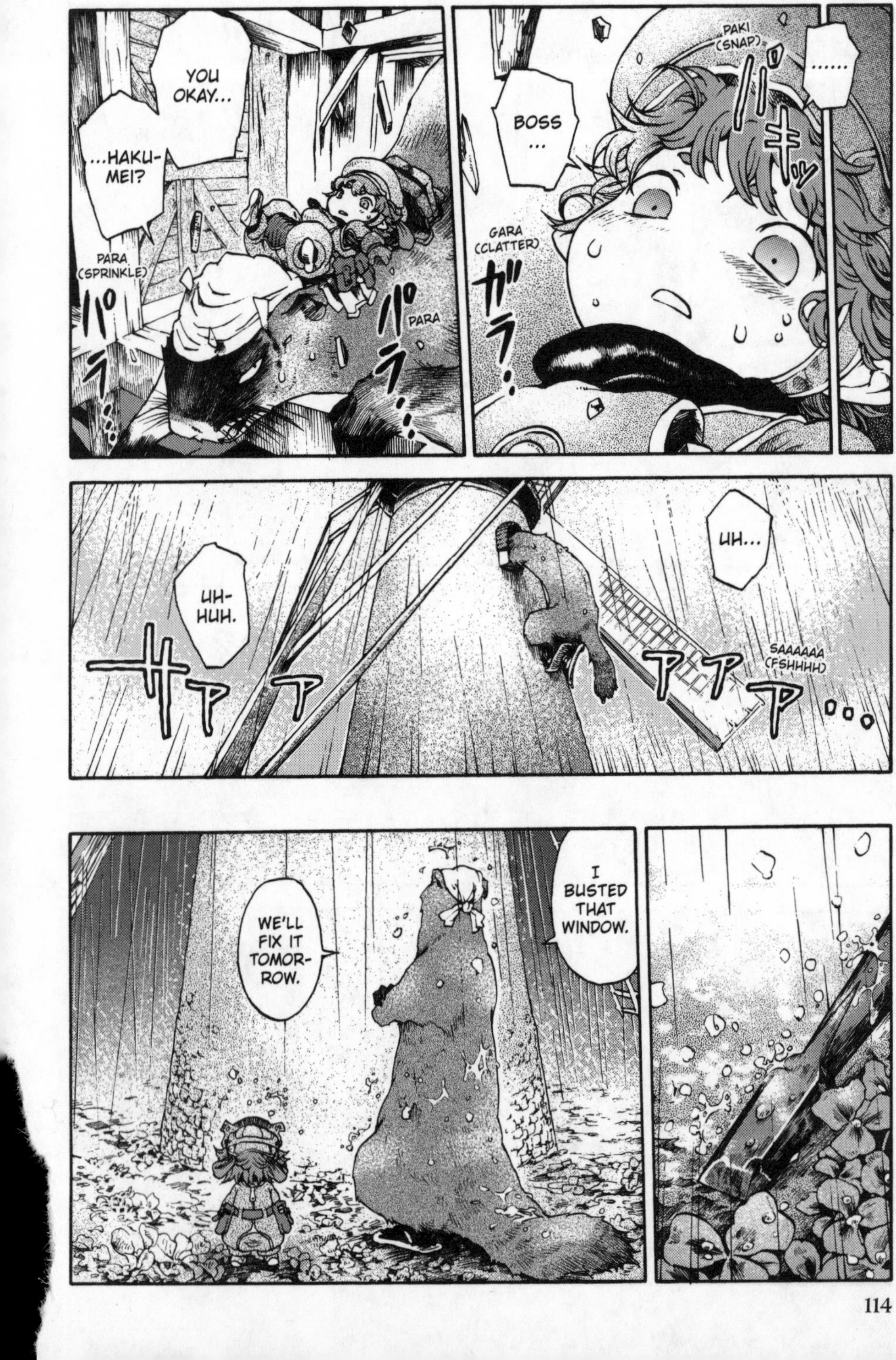
......
PAKI (SNAP)
BOSS ...
GARA (CLATTER)
YOU OKAY...
...HAKUMEI?
PARA (SPRINKLE)
PARA
UH...
SAAAAAA (FSHHHH)
UH-HUH.
I BUSTED THAT WINDOW.
WE'LL FIX IT TOMORROW.

YEAH.

THE THONG SNAPPED, HUH?

パタタ (PATTER)

ヮヮ....

WELL, THAT'S OKAY.

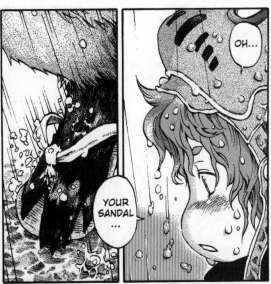

YOUR SANDAL...

OH...

BOSS...

I'M SORRY.

ポト (PLOP)

ト

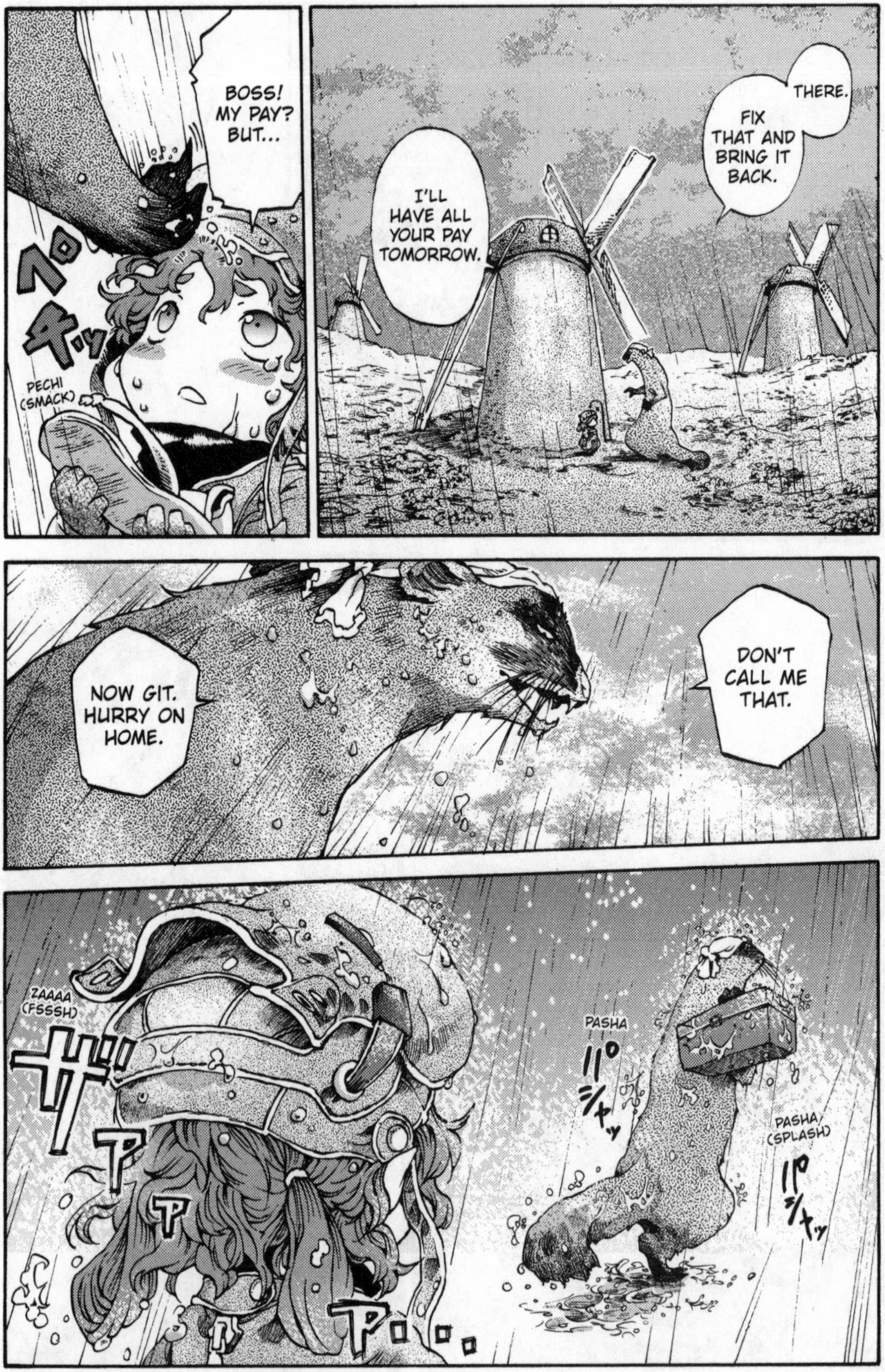
THERE.
FIX THAT AND BRING IT BACK.
I'LL HAVE ALL YOUR PAY TOMORROW.
BOSS! MY PAY? BUT...
PECHI (SMACK)
DON'T CALL ME THAT.
NOW GIT. HURRY ON HOME.
PASHA (SPLASH)
PASHA
ZAAAA (FSSSH)

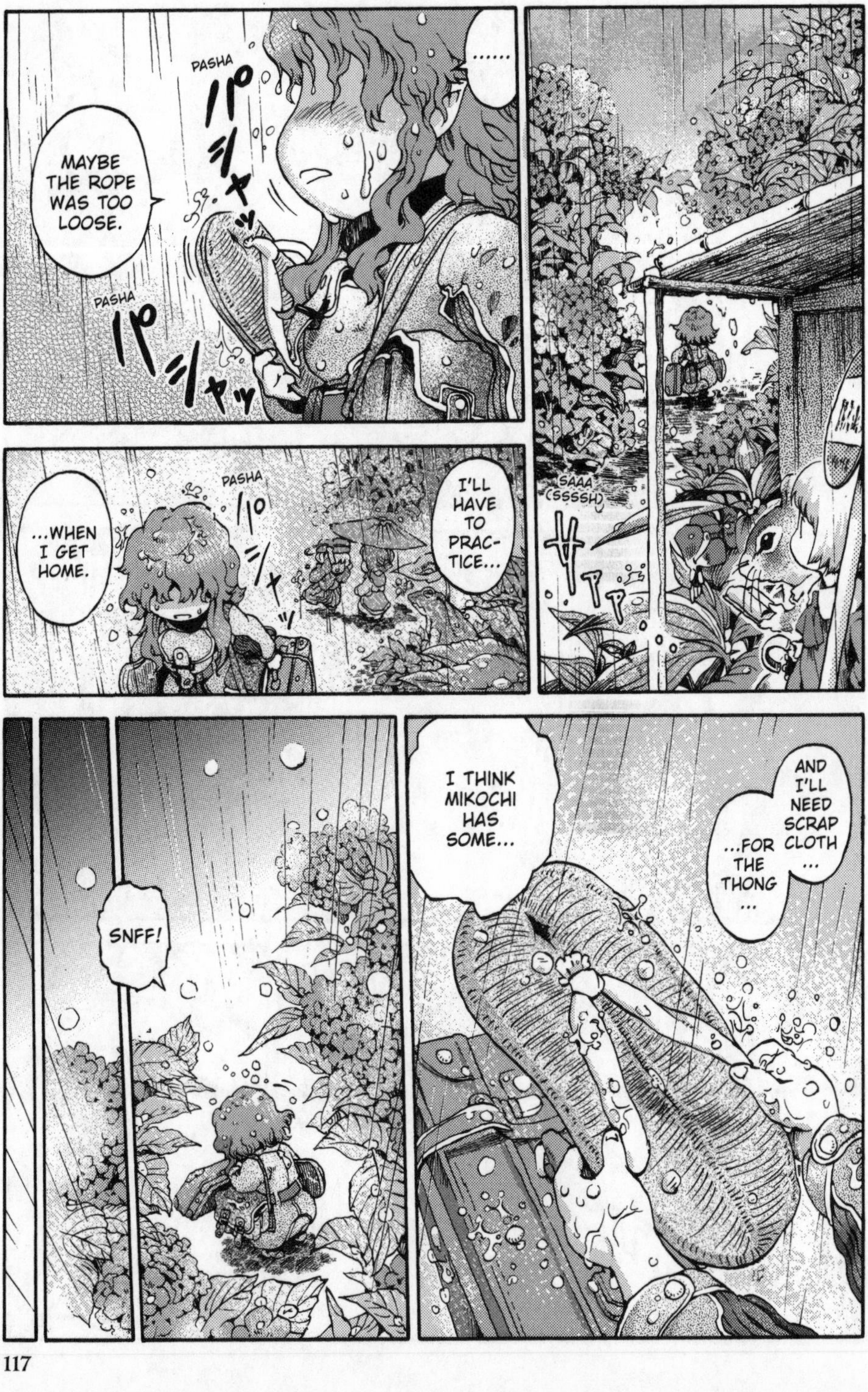
SAAA (SSSSH)
......
PASHA
MAYBE THE ROPE WAS TOO LOOSE.
PASHA
I'LL HAVE TO PRACTICE...
PASHA
...WHEN I GET HOME.
AND I'LL NEED SCRAP CLOTH...
...FOR THE THONG...
I THINK MIKOCHI HAS SOME...
SNFF!

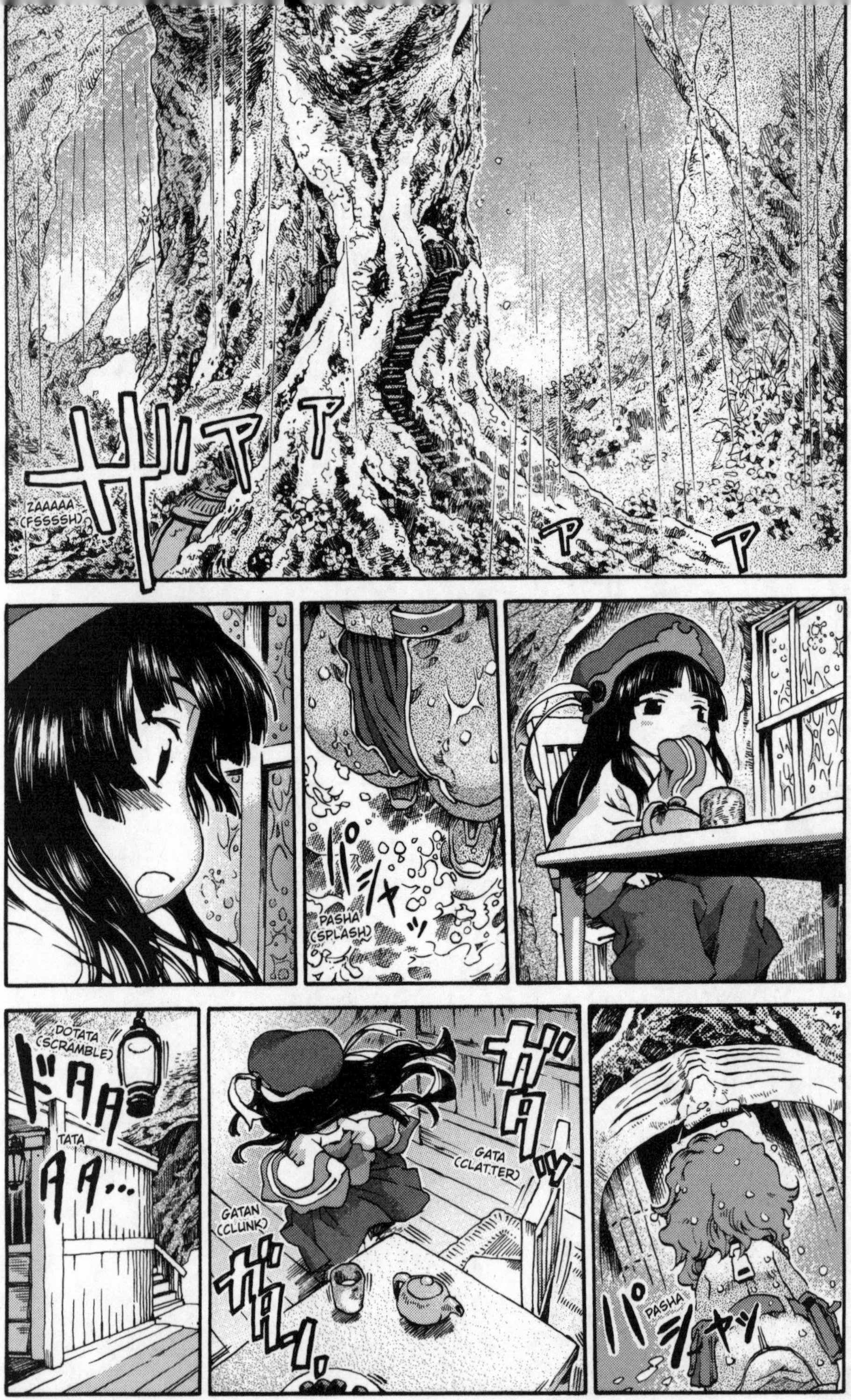
ZAAAAA (FSSSSH)
PASHA (SPLASH)
PASHA
GATA (CLATTER)
GATAN (CLUNK)
DOTATA (SCRAMBLE)
TATA...

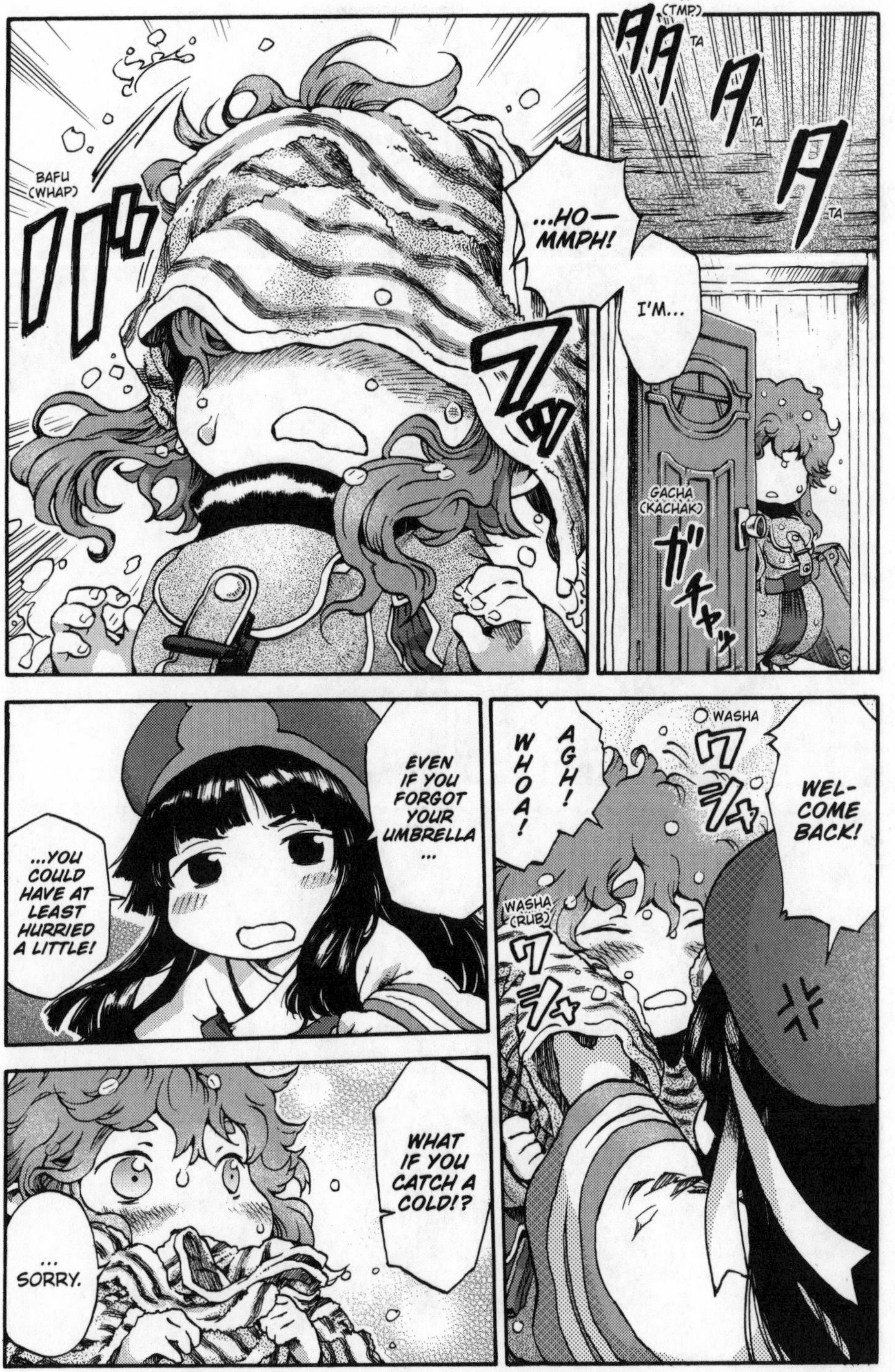
TA (TMP.)
TA
TA
TA
GACHA (KACHAK)
I'M...
...HO—MMPH!
BAFU (WHAP)
WASHA
AGH! WHOA!
WEL-COME BACK!
WASHA (RUB)
EVEN IF YOU FORGOT YOUR UMBRELLA...
...YOU COULD HAVE AT LEAST HURRIED A LITTLE!
WHAT IF YOU CATCH A COLD!?
...SORRY.

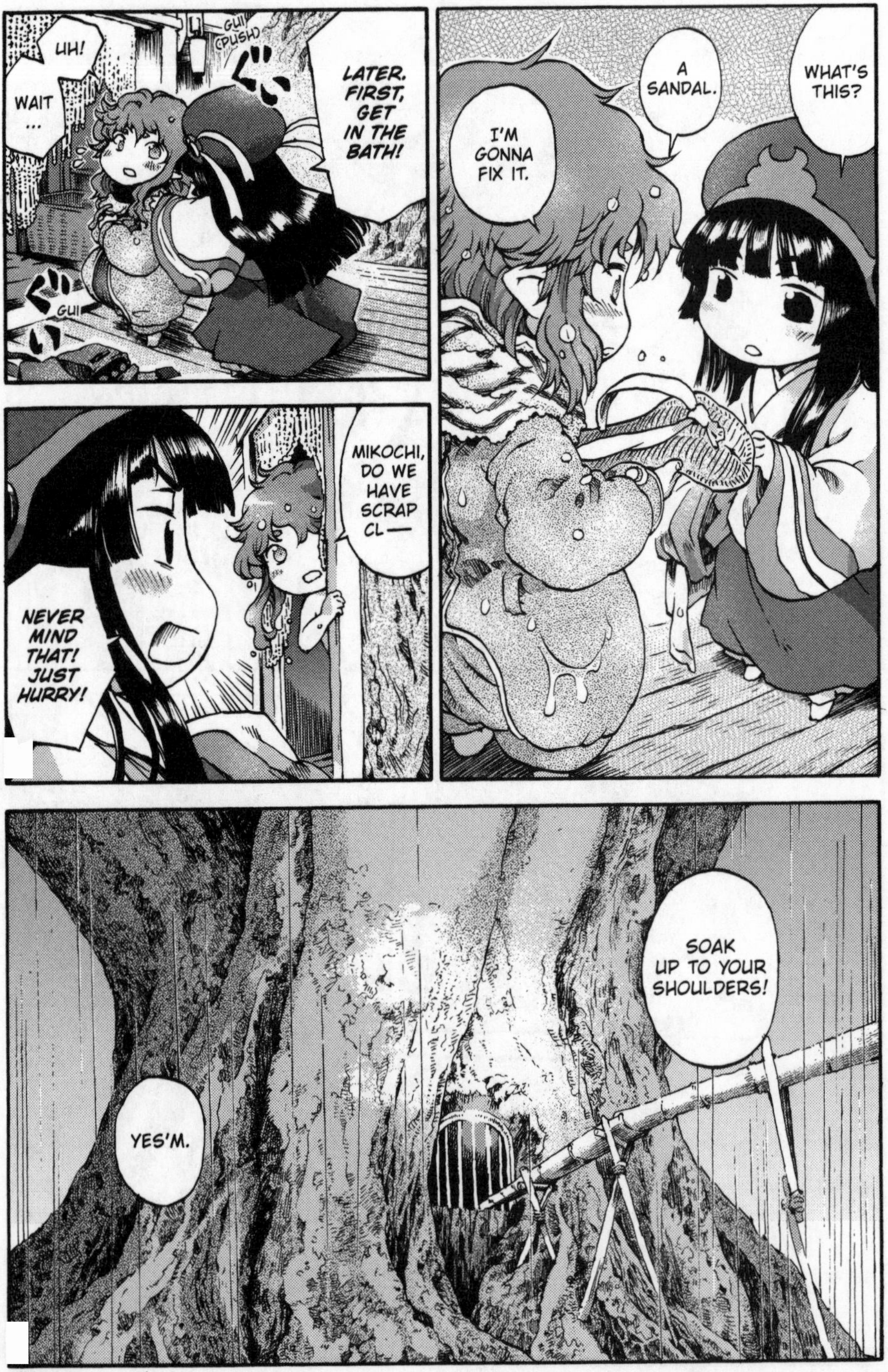
WHAT'S THIS?
A SANDAL.
I'M GONNA FIX IT.
GUI (PUSH)
UH!
WAIT ...
LATER. FIRST, GET IN THE BATH!
GUI
MIKOCHI, DO WE HAVE SCRAP CL—
NEVER MIND THAT! JUST HURRY!
SOAK UP TO YOUR SHOULDERS!
YES'M.

"Hm? What's with this little thing?"

"I'm Hakumei. This is my first day on-site. I'm looking forward to working with you, mister."

"Oh yeah. You're the helper they were talking about, huh? Can you even do carpentry? You're a pip-squeak."

"I fixed the shutter over on the other side and replaced the bricks without asking first. Was that okay?"

"…Yeah, I guess that'll do."

"I'll start helping over here, then. I'm gonna go get changed."

"Sure thing. I'm Boss Iwashidani."

"So you're an anchovy, even though you're a weasel?"

"Shaddup."

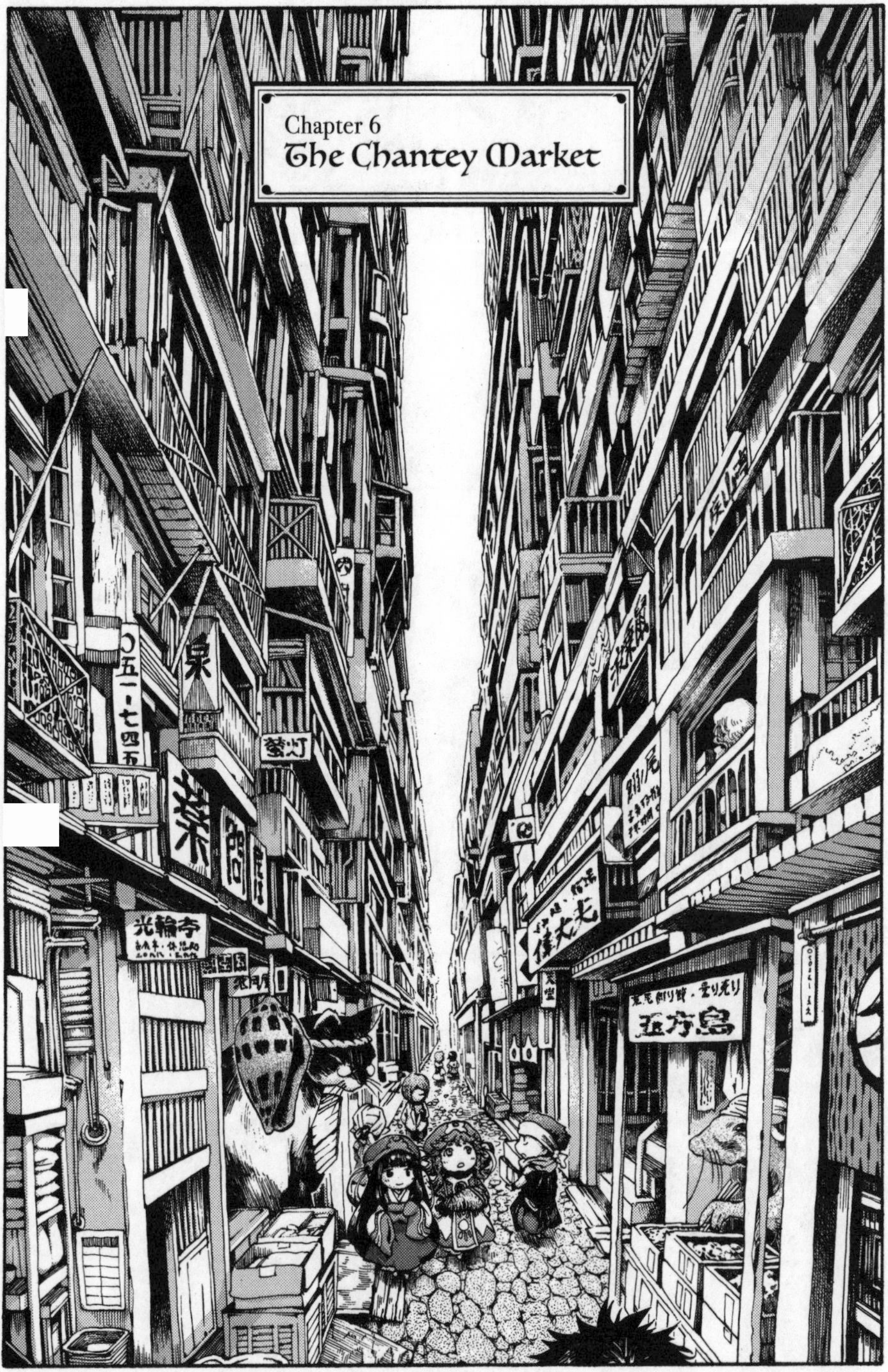
Chapter 6
The Chantey Market

SIGNS: FISHING / BLOWFISH MEAT

SIGNS: CRIMSON TUNA / EYE

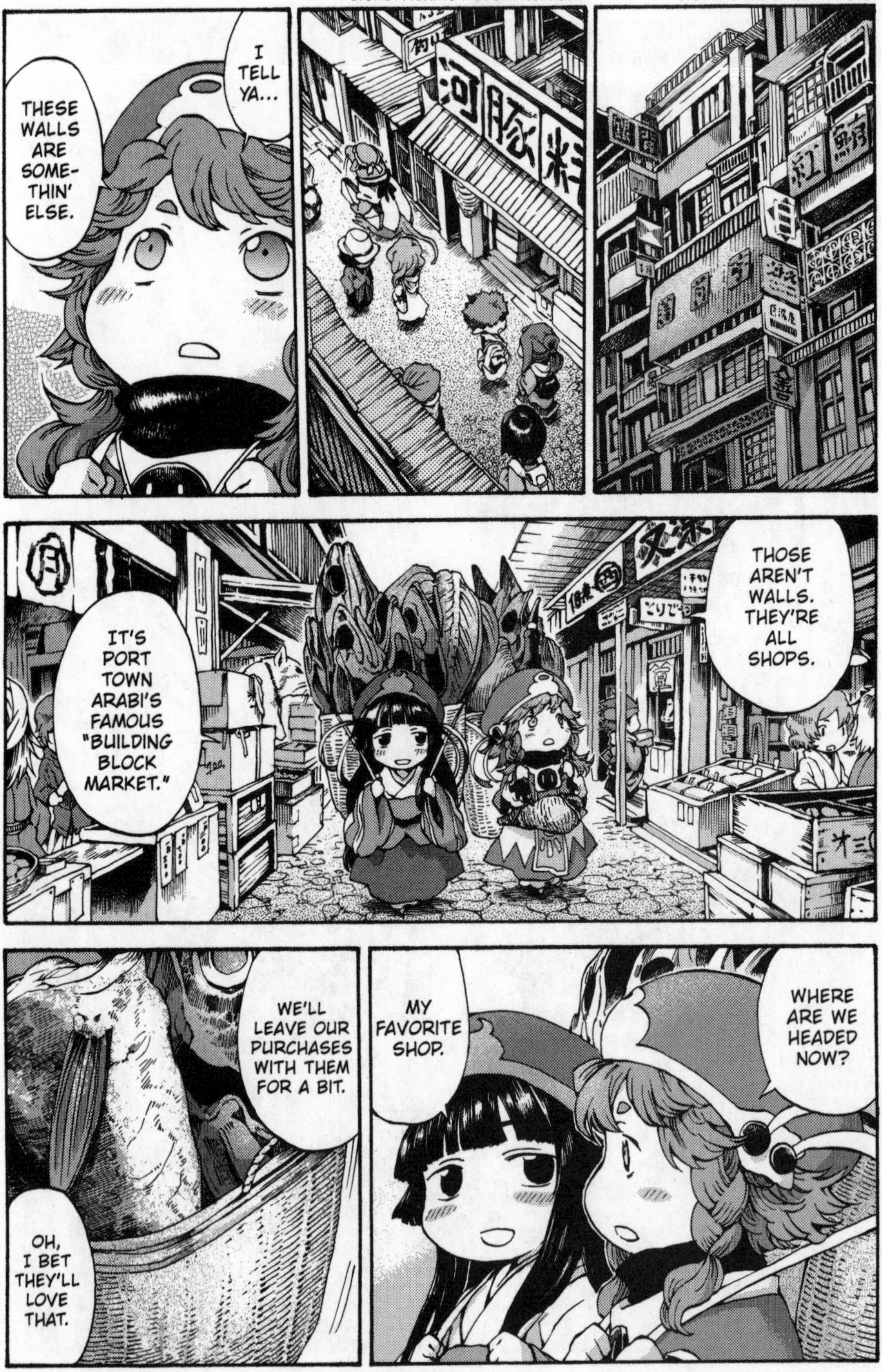
I TELL YA...
THESE WALLS ARE SOMETHIN' ELSE.
THOSE AREN'T WALLS. THEY'RE ALL SHOPS.
IT'S PORT TOWN ARABI'S FAMOUS "BUILDING BLOCK MARKET."
WHERE ARE WE HEADED NOW?
MY FAVORITE SHOP.
WE'LL LEAVE OUR PURCHASES WITH THEM FOR A BIT.
OH, I BET THEY'LL LOVE THAT.

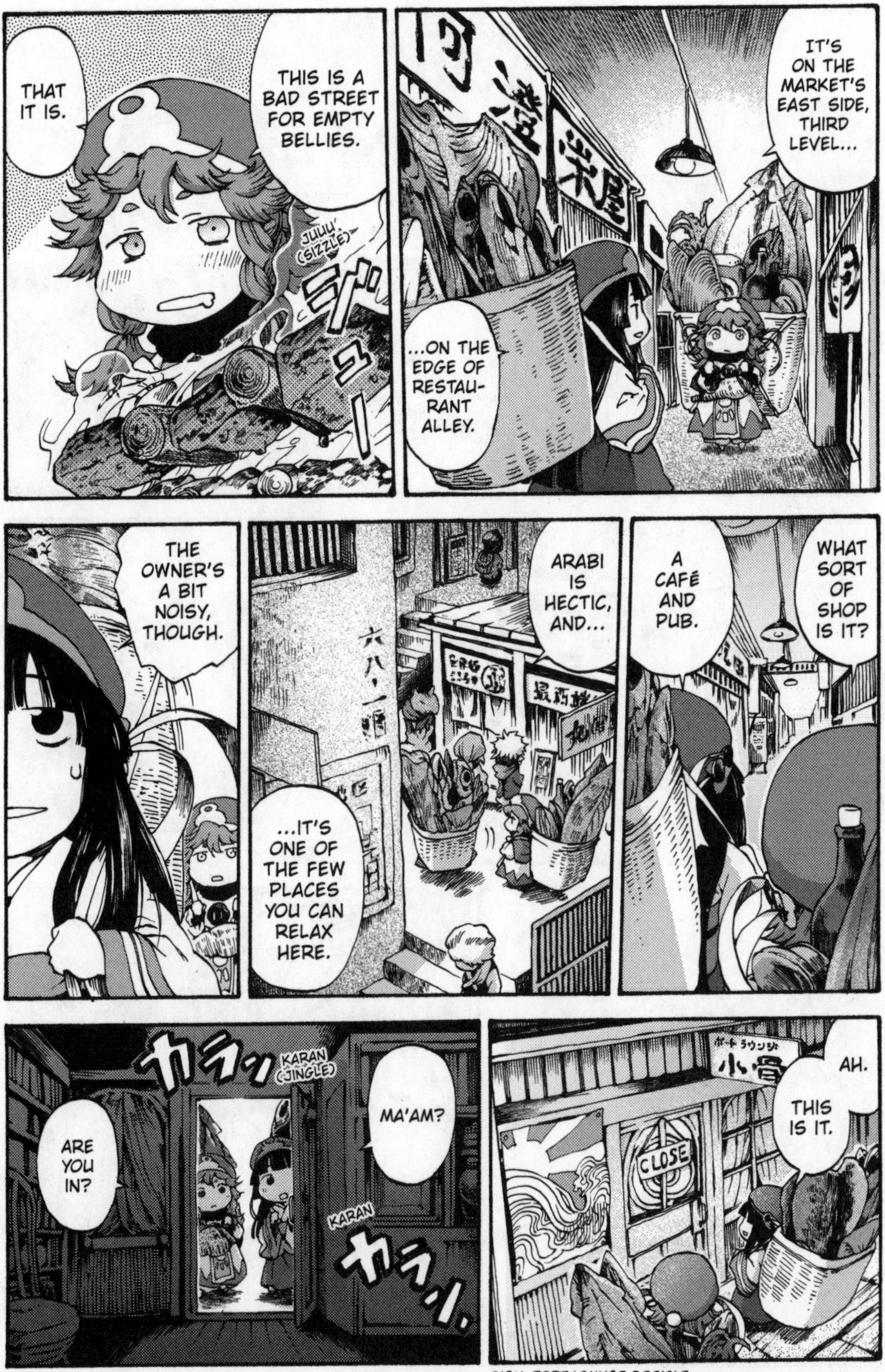
IT'S ON THE MARKET'S EAST SIDE, THIRD LEVEL...
...ON THE EDGE OF RESTAURANT ALLEY.
THIS IS A BAD STREET FOR EMPTY BELLIES.
THAT IT IS.
JUUU (SIZZLE)
WHAT SORT OF SHOP IS IT?
A CAFÉ AND PUB.
ARABI IS HECTIC, AND...
...IT'S ONE OF THE FEW PLACES YOU CAN RELAX HERE.
THE OWNER'S A BIT NOISY, THOUGH.
AH.
THIS IS IT.
CLOSE
KARAN (JINGLE)
MA'AM?
ARE YOU IN?
KARAN

SIGN: PORT LOUNGE OSSICLE

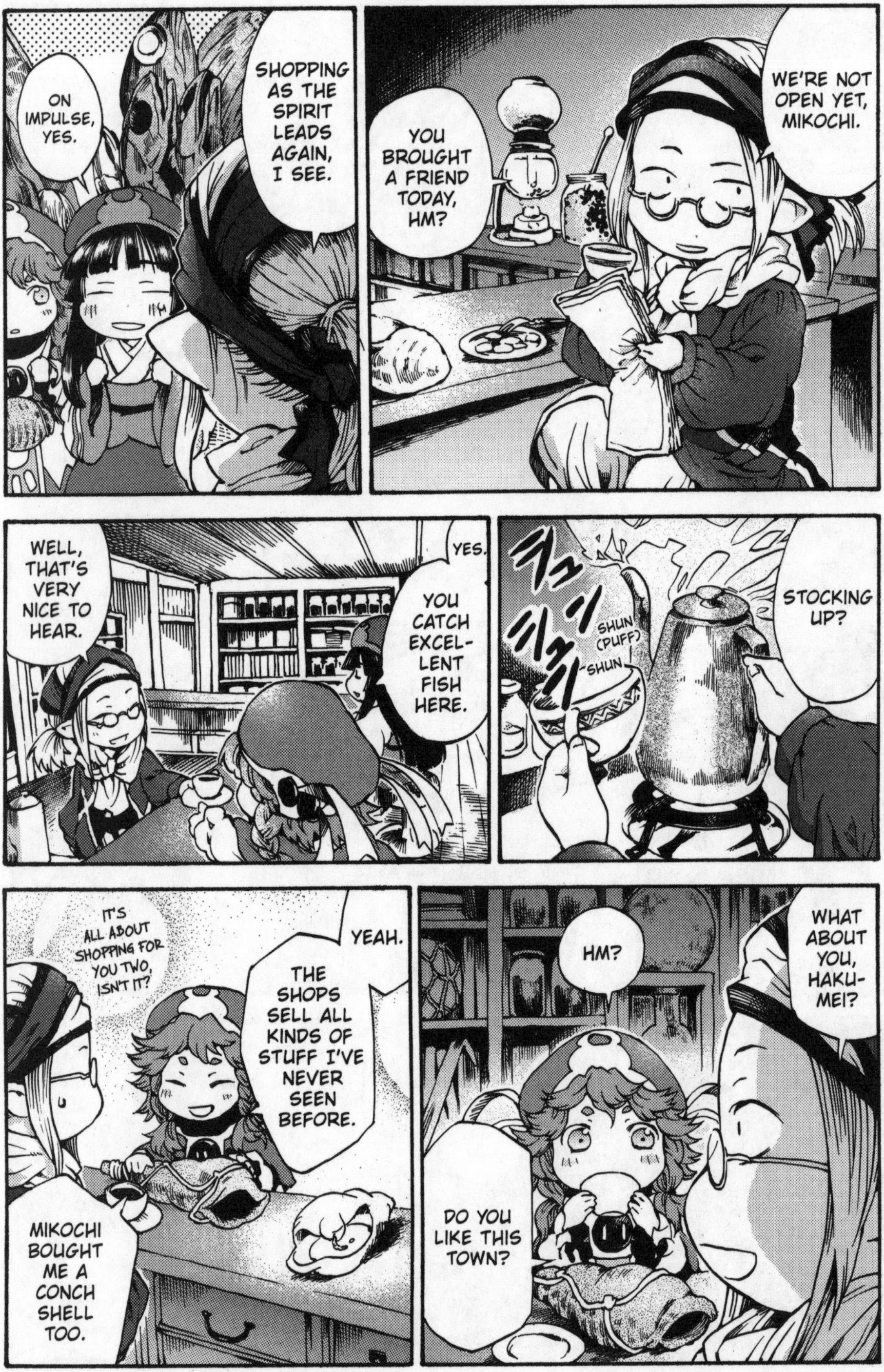
WE'RE NOT OPEN YET, MIKOCHI.
YOU BROUGHT A FRIEND TODAY, HM?
SHOPPING AS THE SPIRIT LEADS AGAIN, I SEE.
ON IMPULSE, YES.
STOCKING UP?
SHUN (PUFF)
SHUN
YES.
YOU CATCH EXCEL-LENT FISH HERE.
WELL, THAT'S VERY NICE TO HEAR.
WHAT ABOUT YOU, HAKU-MEI?
HM?
DO YOU LIKE THIS TOWN?
YEAH.
THE SHOPS SELL ALL KINDS OF STUFF I'VE NEVER SEEN BEFORE.
IT'S ALL ABOUT SHOPPING FOR YOU TWO, ISN'T IT?
MIKOCHI BOUGHT ME A CONCH SHELL TOO.

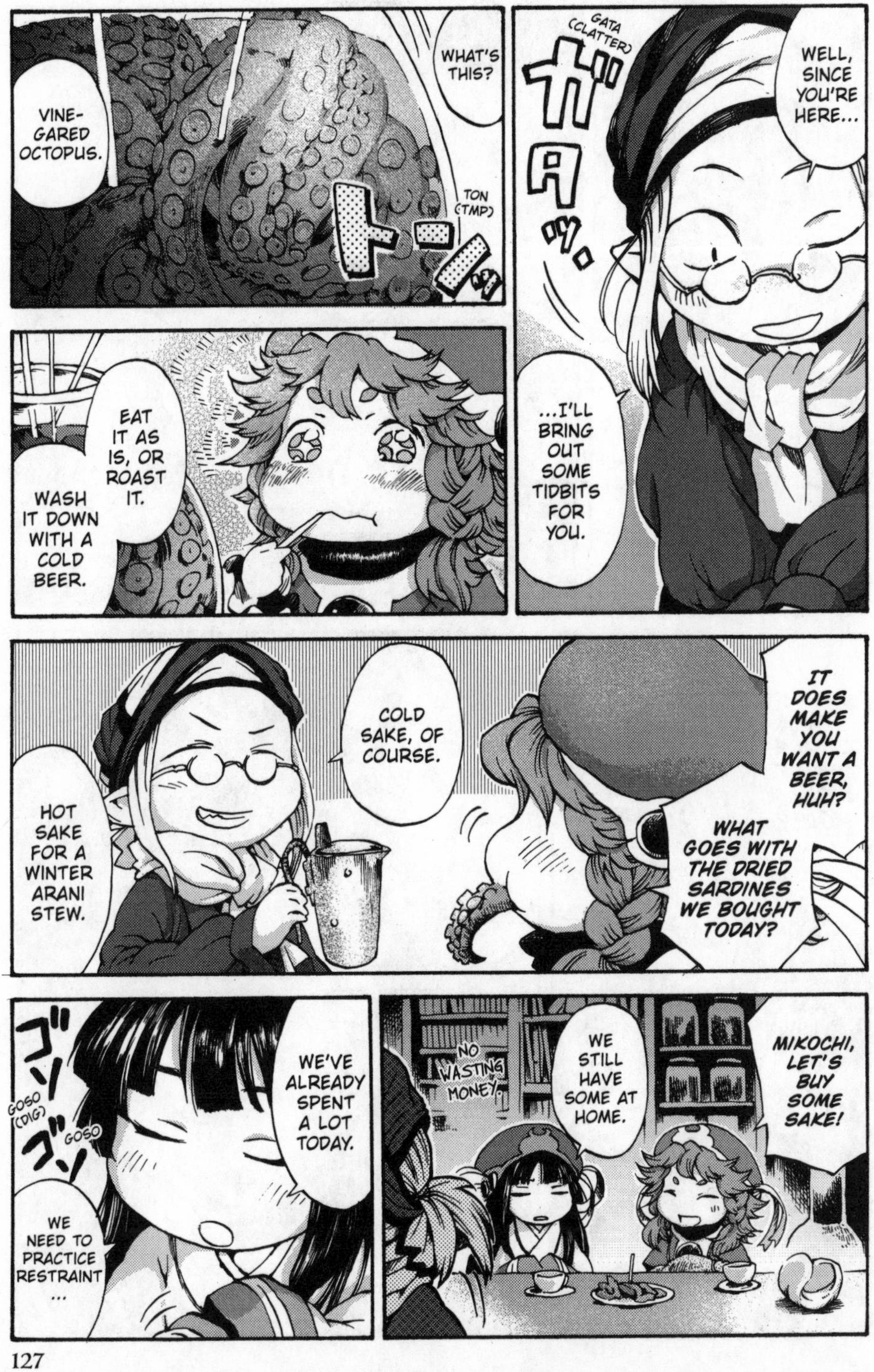
GATA (CLATTER)
WELL, SINCE YOU'RE HERE...
...I'LL BRING OUT SOME TIDBITS FOR YOU.
WHAT'S THIS?
TON (TMP)
VINE-GARED OCTOPUS.
EAT IT AS IS, OR ROAST IT.
WASH IT DOWN WITH A COLD BEER.
IT DOES MAKE YOU WANT A BEER, HUH?
WHAT GOES WITH THE DRIED SARDINES WE BOUGHT TODAY?
COLD SAKE, OF COURSE.
HOT SAKE FOR A WINTER ARANI STEW.
MIKOCHI, LET'S BUY SOME SAKE!
WE STILL HAVE SOME AT HOME.
NO WASTING MONEY
WE'VE ALREADY SPENT A LOT TODAY.
GOSO (DIG)
GOSO
WE NEED TO PRACTICE RESTRAINT ...

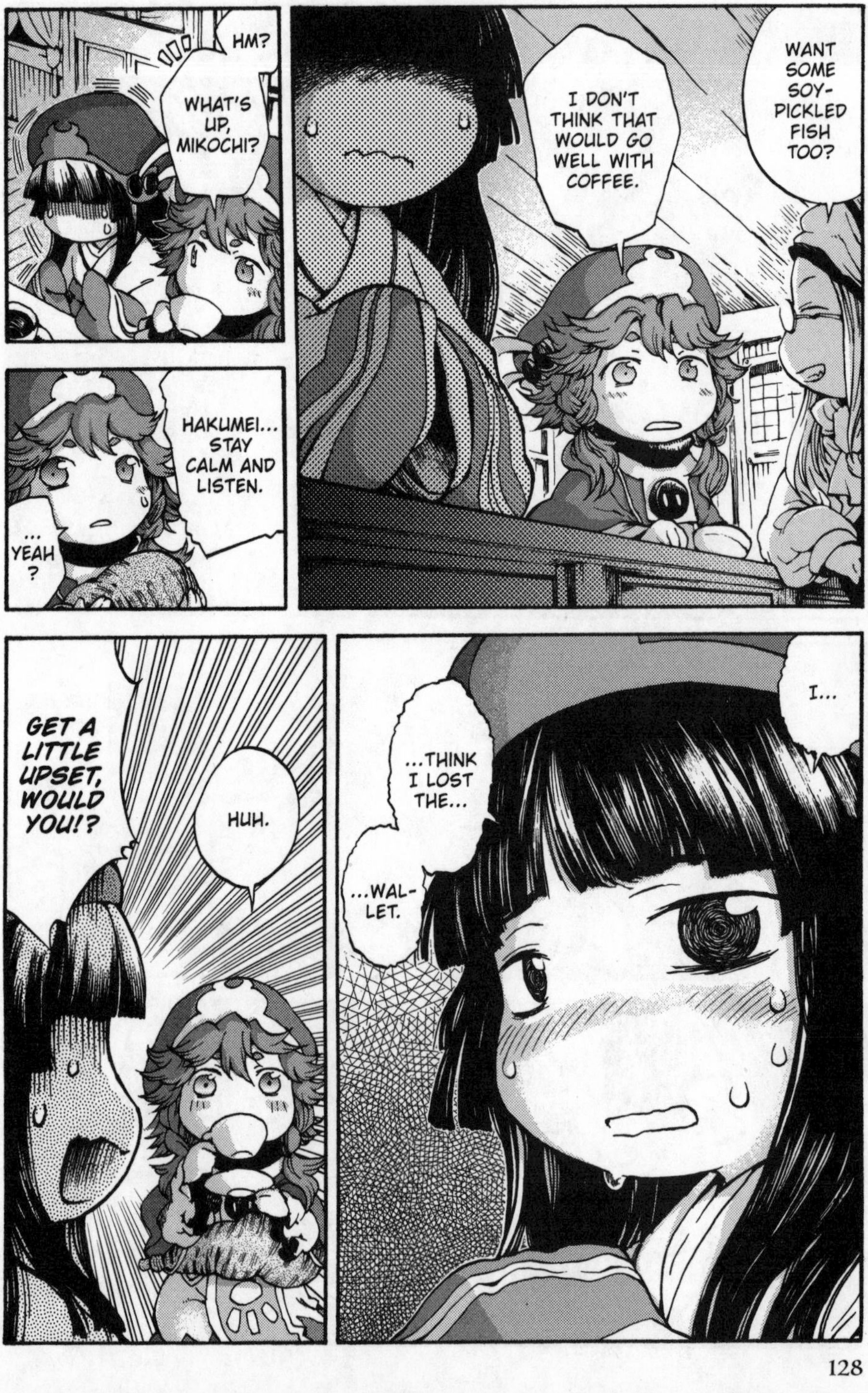
WANT SOME SOY-PICKLED FISH TOO?
I DON'T THINK THAT WOULD GO WELL WITH COFFEE.
HM?
WHAT'S UP, MIKOCHI?
HAKUMEI... STAY CALM AND LISTEN.
...YEAH?
I...
...THINK I LOST THE...
...WAL-LET.
HUH.
GET A LITTLE UPSET, WOULD YOU!?

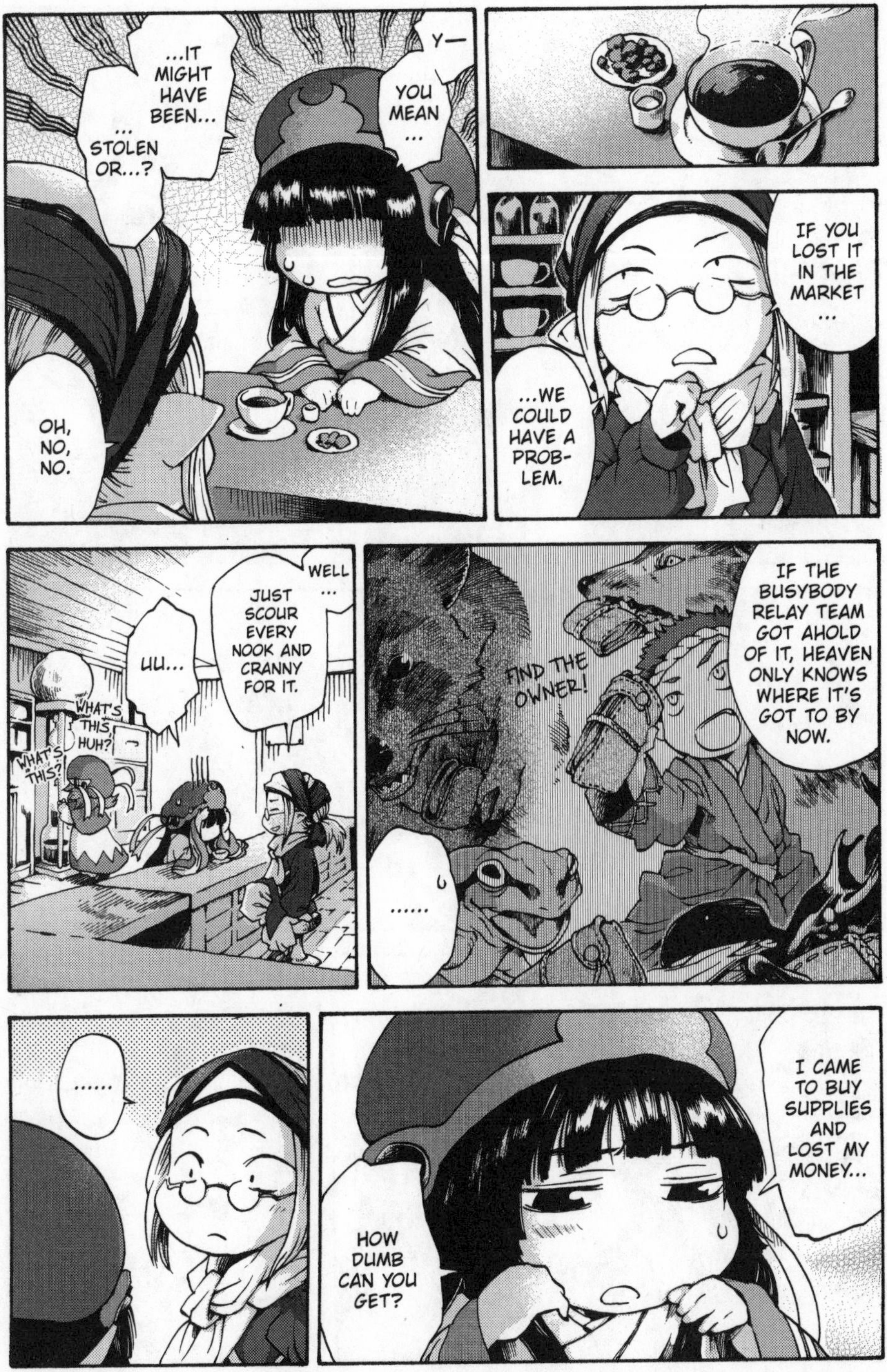
IF YOU LOST IT IN THE MARKET ...
...WE COULD HAVE A PROB-LEM.
Y—
YOU MEAN ...
...IT MIGHT HAVE BEEN... ...STOLEN OR...?
OH, NO, NO.
IF THE BUSYBODY RELAY TEAM GOT AHOLD OF IT, HEAVEN ONLY KNOWS WHERE IT'S GOT TO BY NOW.
FIND THE OWNER!
......
WELL ...
JUST SCOUR EVERY NOOK AND CRANNY FOR IT.
UU...
WHAT'S THIS, HUH?
WHAT'S THIS?
I CAME TO BUY SUPPLIES AND LOST MY MONEY...
HOW DUMB CAN YOU GET?
......

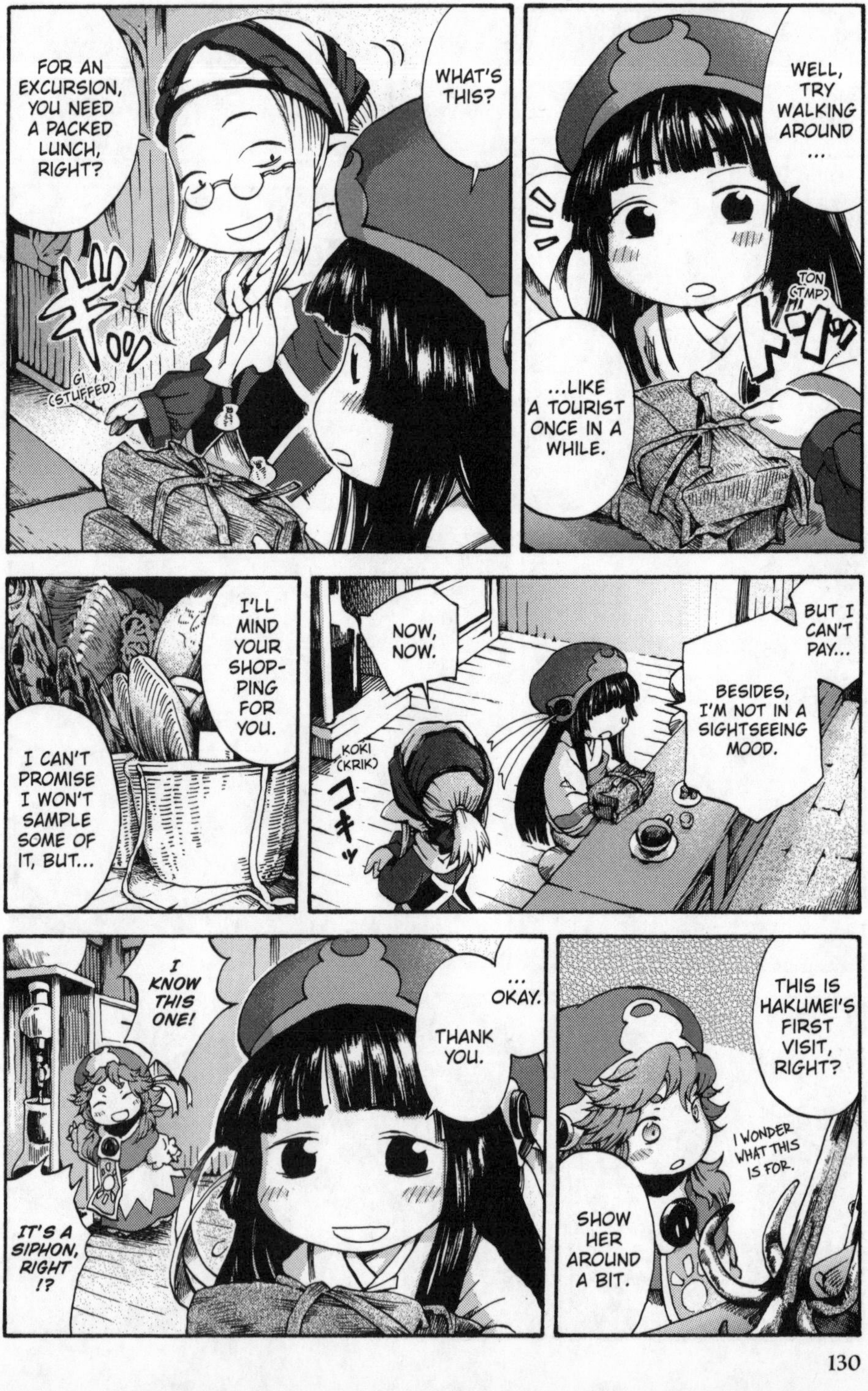
WELL, TRY WALKING AROUND ...
...LIKE A TOURIST ONCE IN A WHILE.
TON (TMP)
WHAT'S THIS?
FOR AN EXCURSION, YOU NEED A PACKED LUNCH, RIGHT?
GI (STUFFED)
BUT I CAN'T PAY...
BESIDES, I'M NOT IN A SIGHTSEEING MOOD.
NOW, NOW.
KOKI (KRIK)
I'LL MIND YOUR SHOP-PING FOR YOU.
I CAN'T PROMISE I WON'T SAMPLE SOME OF IT, BUT...
THIS IS HAKUMEI'S FIRST VISIT, RIGHT?
I WONDER WHAT THIS IS FOR.
SHOW HER AROUND A BIT.
...OKAY.
THANK YOU.
I KNOW THIS ONE!
IT'S A SIPHON, RIGHT!?

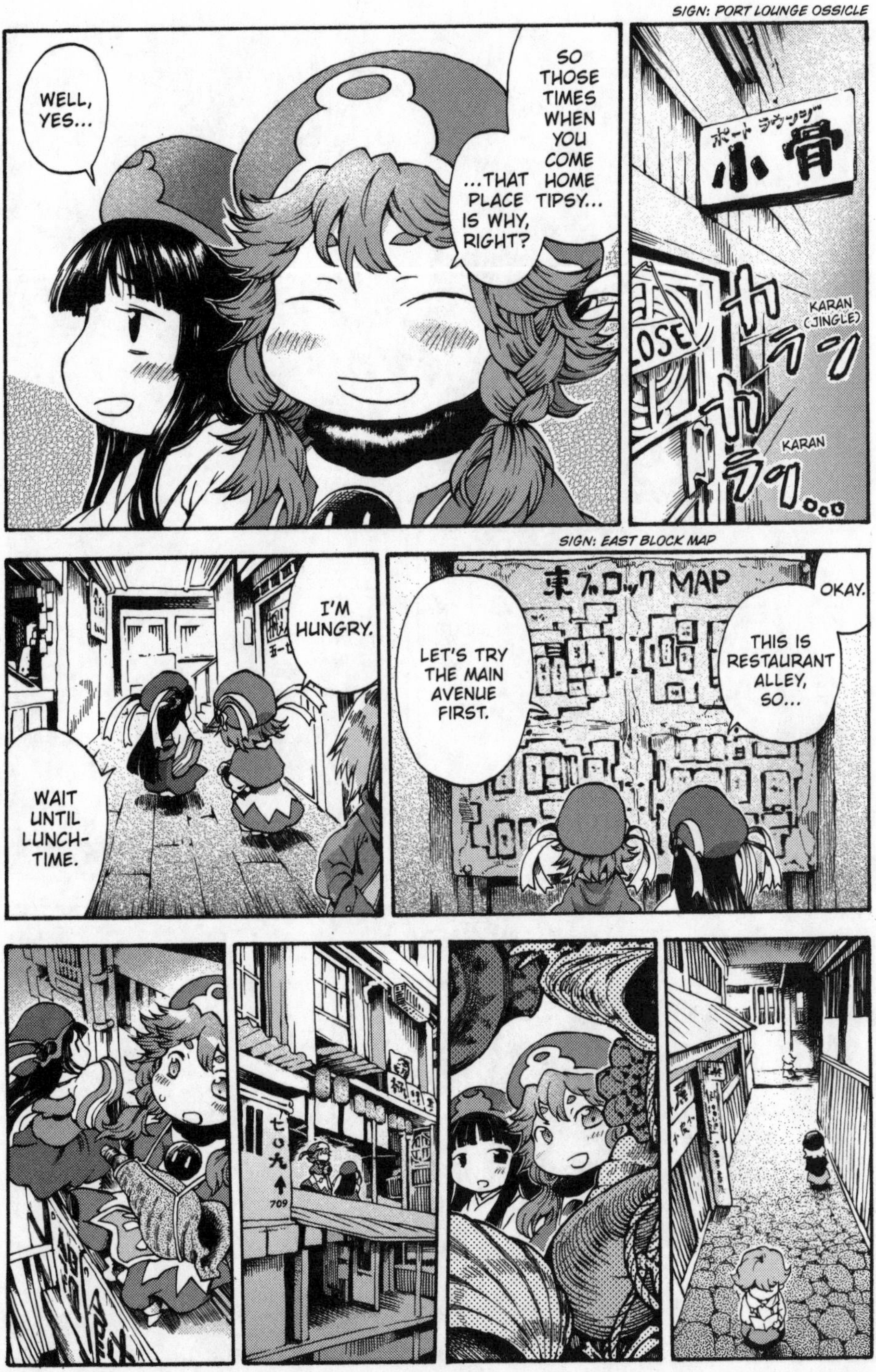
SIGN: PORT LOUNGE OSSICLE
KARAN (JINGLE)
KARAN
SO THOSE TIMES WHEN YOU COME HOME TIPSY...
...THAT PLACE IS WHY, RIGHT?
WELL, YES...
SIGN: EAST BLOCK MAP
OKAY.
THIS IS RESTAURANT ALLEY, SO...
LET'S TRY THE MAIN AVENUE FIRST.
I'M HUNGRY.
WAIT UNTIL LUNCH-TIME.

BANNER: LOYAL

SIGN: NAMIBE SUSHI

SIGN: FISH

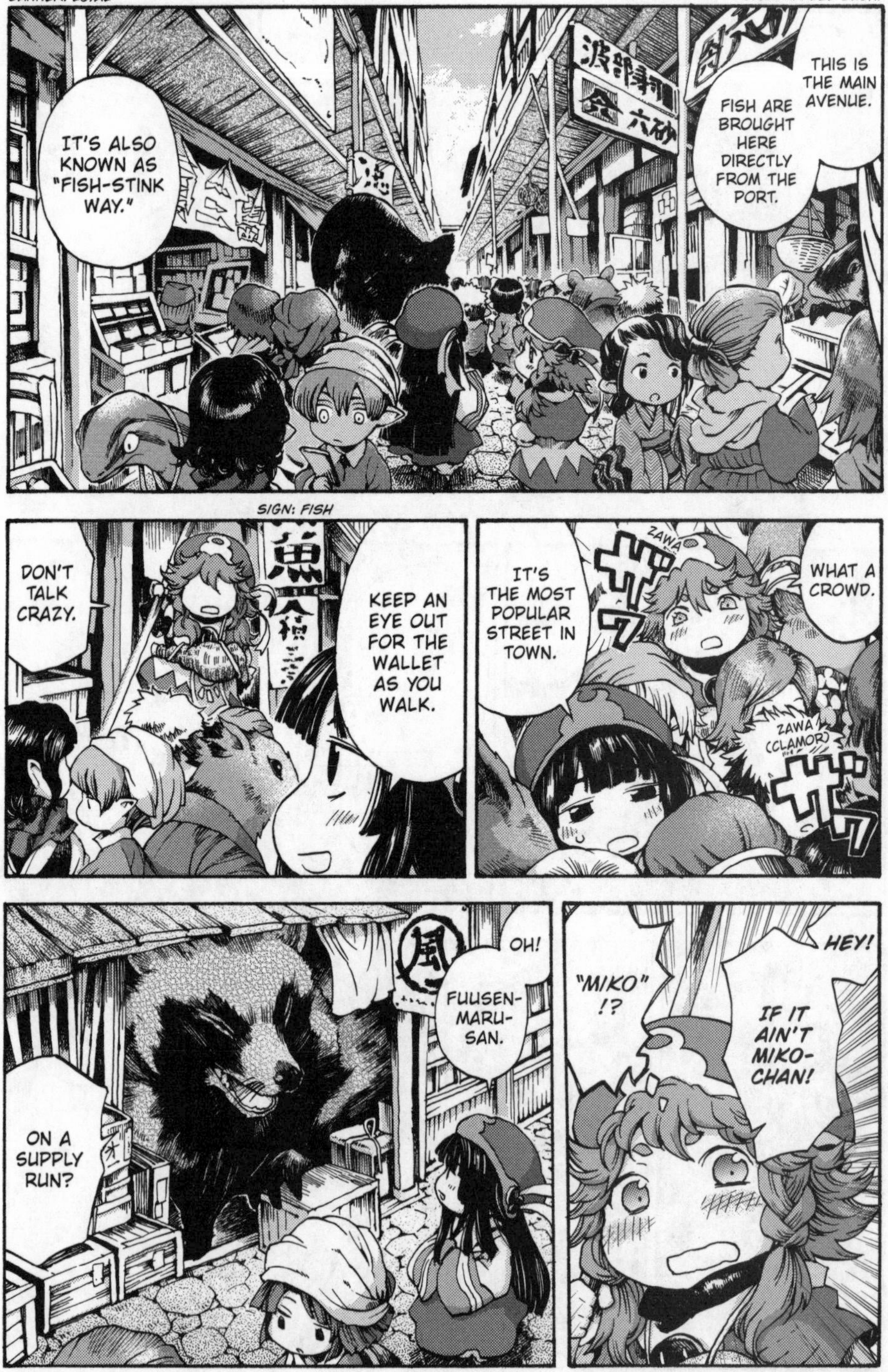
THIS IS THE MAIN AVENUE.
FISH ARE BROUGHT HERE DIRECTLY FROM THE PORT.
IT'S ALSO KNOWN AS "FISH-STINK WAY."
ZAWA
WHAT A CROWD.
IT'S THE MOST POPULAR STREET IN TOWN.
ZAWA (CLAMOR)
KEEP AN EYE OUT FOR THE WALLET AS YOU WALK.
DON'T TALK CRAZY.
HEY!
IF IT AIN'T MIKO-CHAN!
"MIKO" !?
OH!
FUUSEN-MARU-SAN.
ON A SUPPLY RUN?

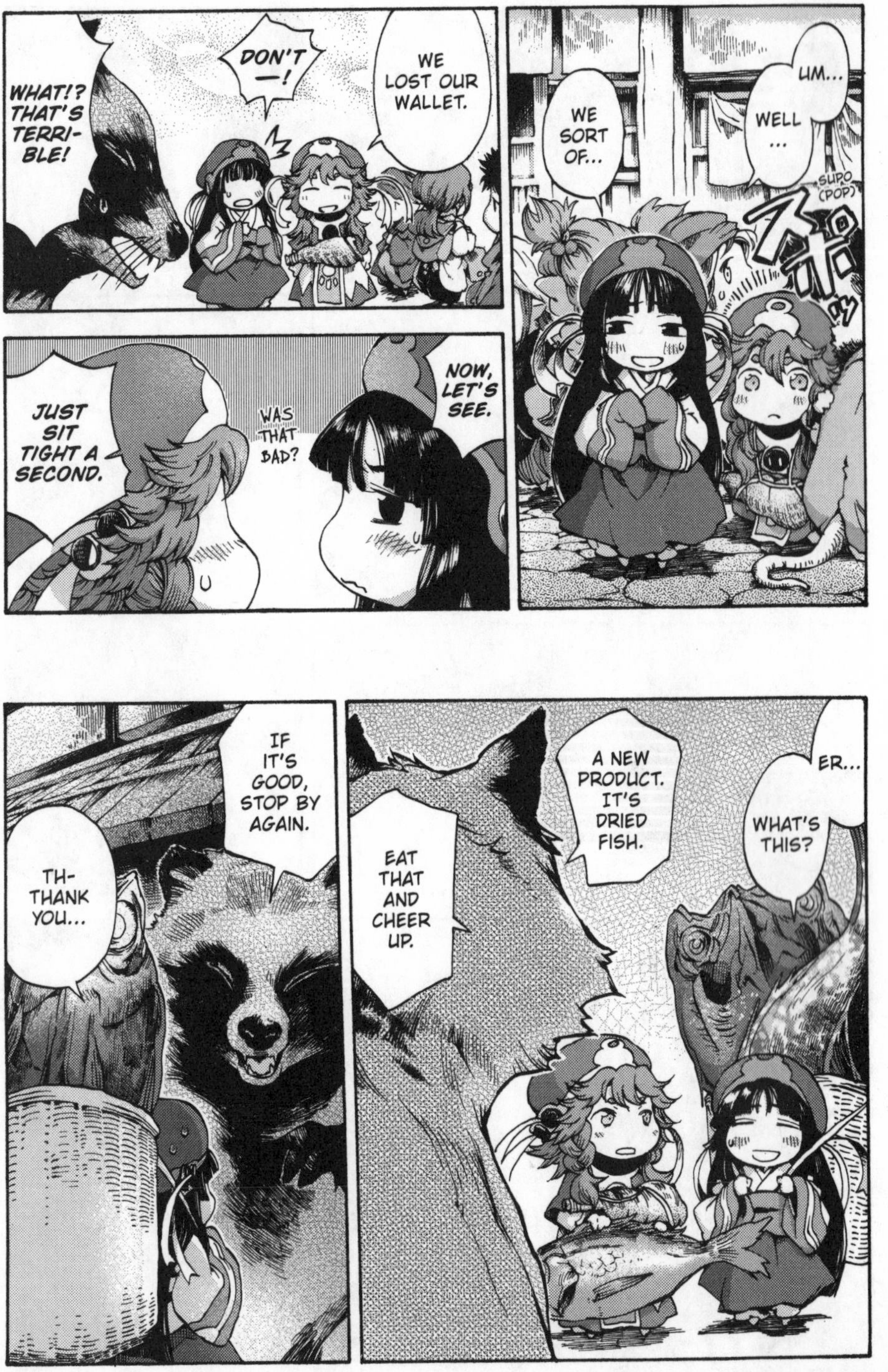
UM... WELL ...
WE SORT OF...
SUPO (POP)
WE LOST OUR WALLET.
DON'T—!
WHAT!? THAT'S TERRIBLE!
NOW, LET'S SEE.
WAS THAT BAD?
JUST SIT TIGHT A SECOND.
ER... WHAT'S THIS?
A NEW PRODUCT. IT'S DRIED FISH.
EAT THAT AND CHEER UP.
IF IT'S GOOD, STOP BY AGAIN.
TH-THANK YOU...

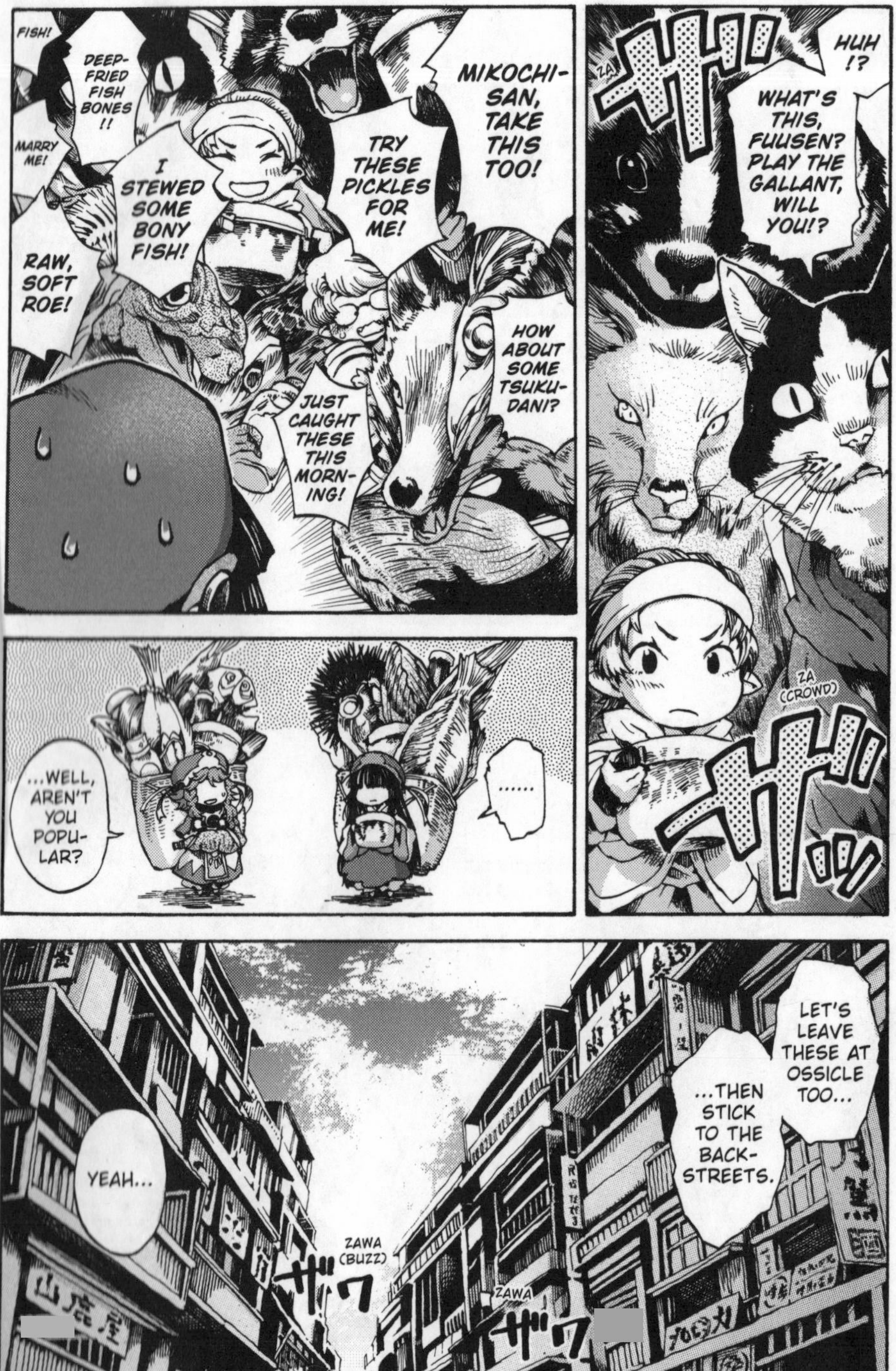
ZA
HUH!?
WHAT'S THIS, FUUSEN? PLAY THE GALLANT, WILL YOU!?
ZA (CROWD)
MIKOCHI-SAN, TAKE THIS TOO!
TRY THESE PICKLES FOR ME!
HOW ABOUT SOME TSUKU-DANI?
JUST CAUGHT THESE THIS MORNING!
I STEWED SOME BONY FISH!
DEEP-FRIED FISH BONES!!
FISH!
MARRY ME!
RAW, SOFT ROE!
......
...WELL, AREN'T YOU POPU-LAR?
LET'S LEAVE THESE AT OSSICLE TOO...
...THEN STICK TO THE BACK-STREETS.
YEAH...
ZAWA (BUZZ)
ZAWA

SIGN: YAMAGA STORE

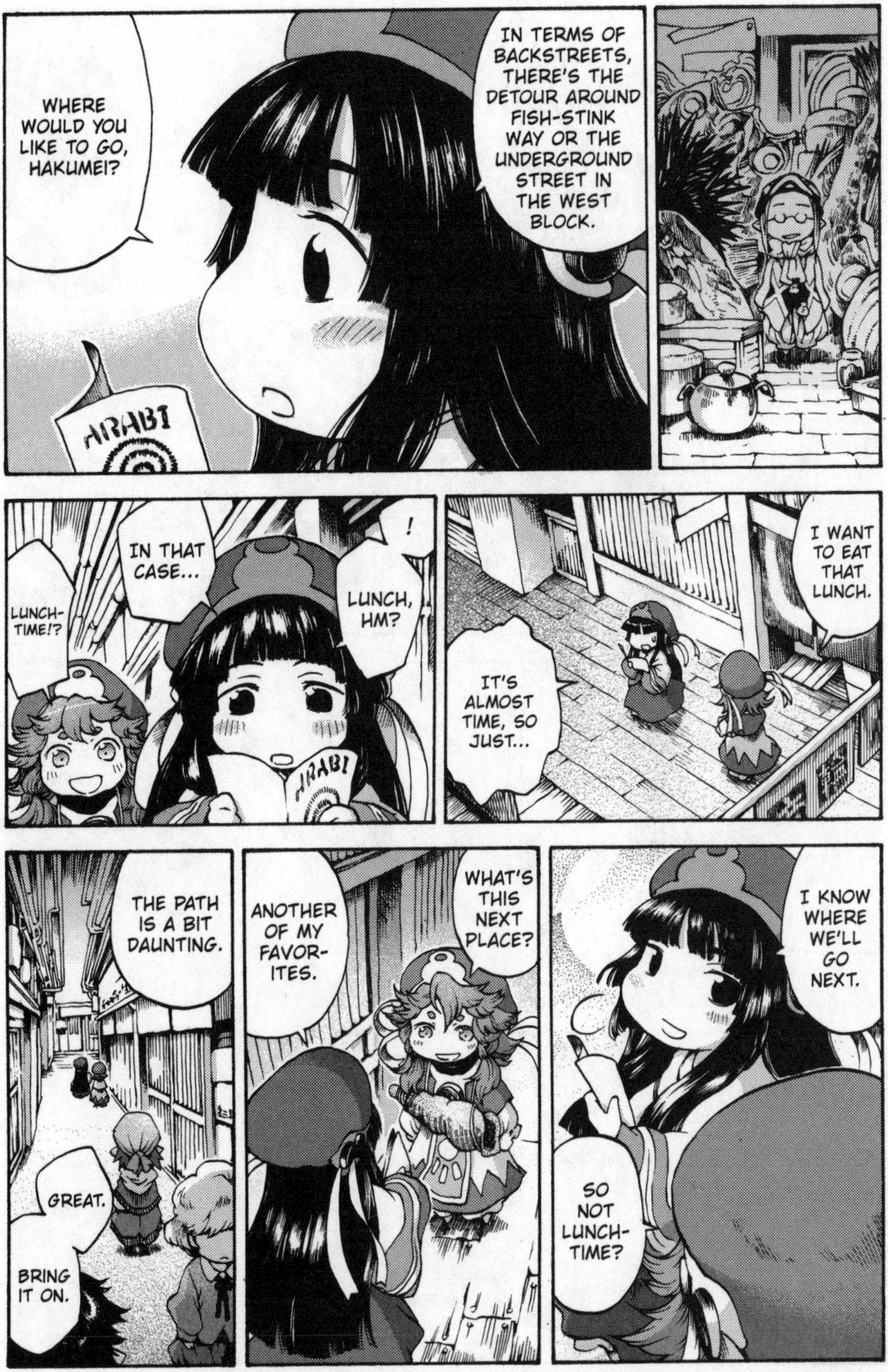
IN TERMS OF BACKSTREETS, THERE'S THE DETOUR AROUND FISH-STINK WAY OR THE UNDERGROUND STREET IN THE WEST BLOCK.
WHERE WOULD YOU LIKE TO GO, HAKUMEI?
ARABI
I WANT TO EAT THAT LUNCH.
IT'S ALMOST TIME, SO JUST...
!
LUNCH, HM?
IN THAT CASE...
LUNCH-TIME!?
ARABI
I KNOW WHERE WE'LL GO NEXT.
SO NOT LUNCH-TIME?
WHAT'S THIS NEXT PLACE?
ANOTHER OF MY FAVOR-ITES.
THE PATH IS A BIT DAUNTING.
GREAT.
BRING IT ON.

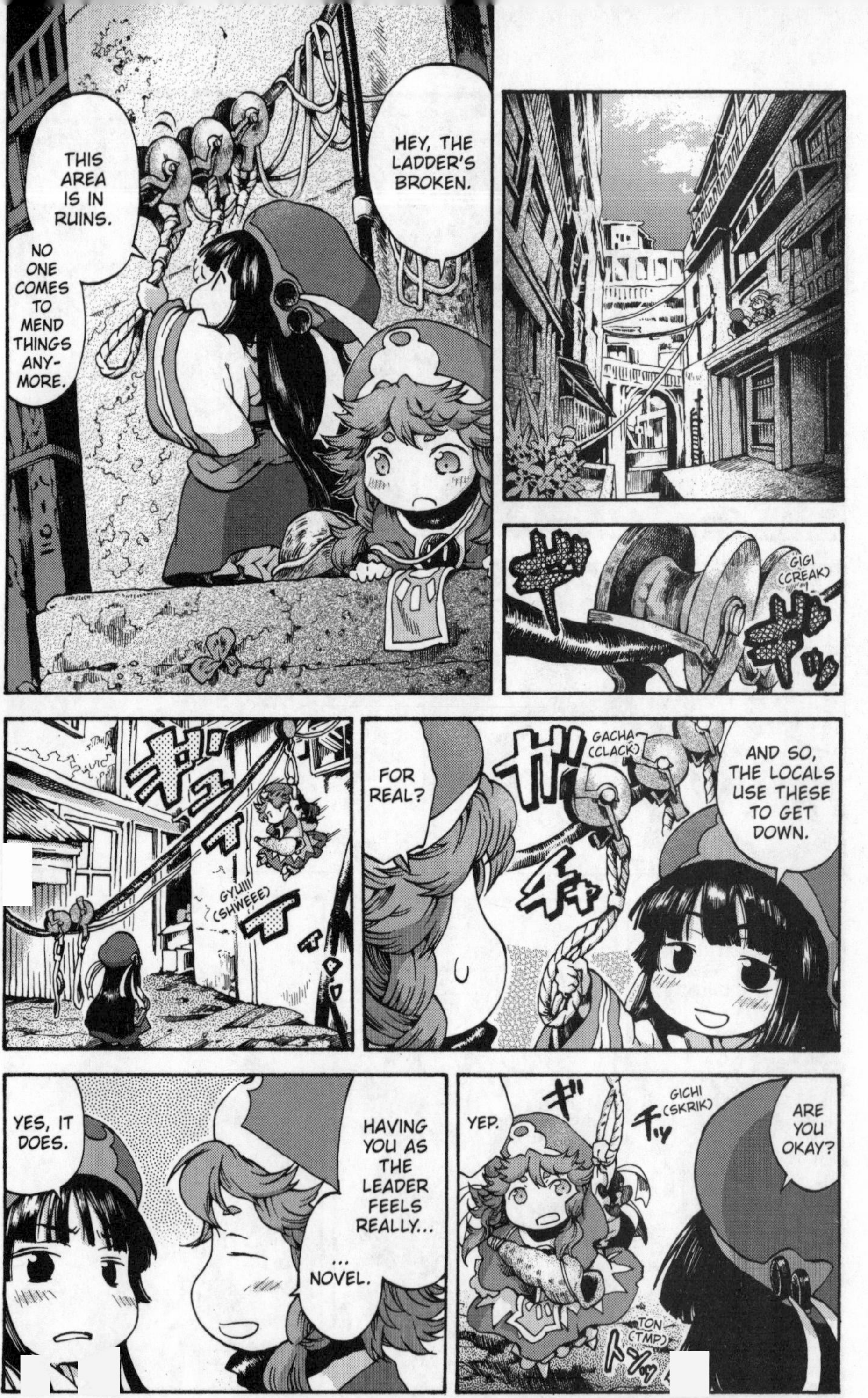
GIGI (CREAK)
HEY, THE LADDER'S BROKEN.
THIS AREA IS IN RUINS.
NO ONE COMES TO MEND THINGS ANY-MORE.
AND SO, THE LOCALS USE THESE TO GET DOWN.
GACHA (CLACK)
FOR REAL?
GYUIIII (SHWEEE)
ARE YOU OKAY?
GICHI (SKRIK)
YEP.
TON (TMP)
HAVING YOU AS THE LEADER FEELS REALLY...
...NOVEL.
YES, IT DOES.

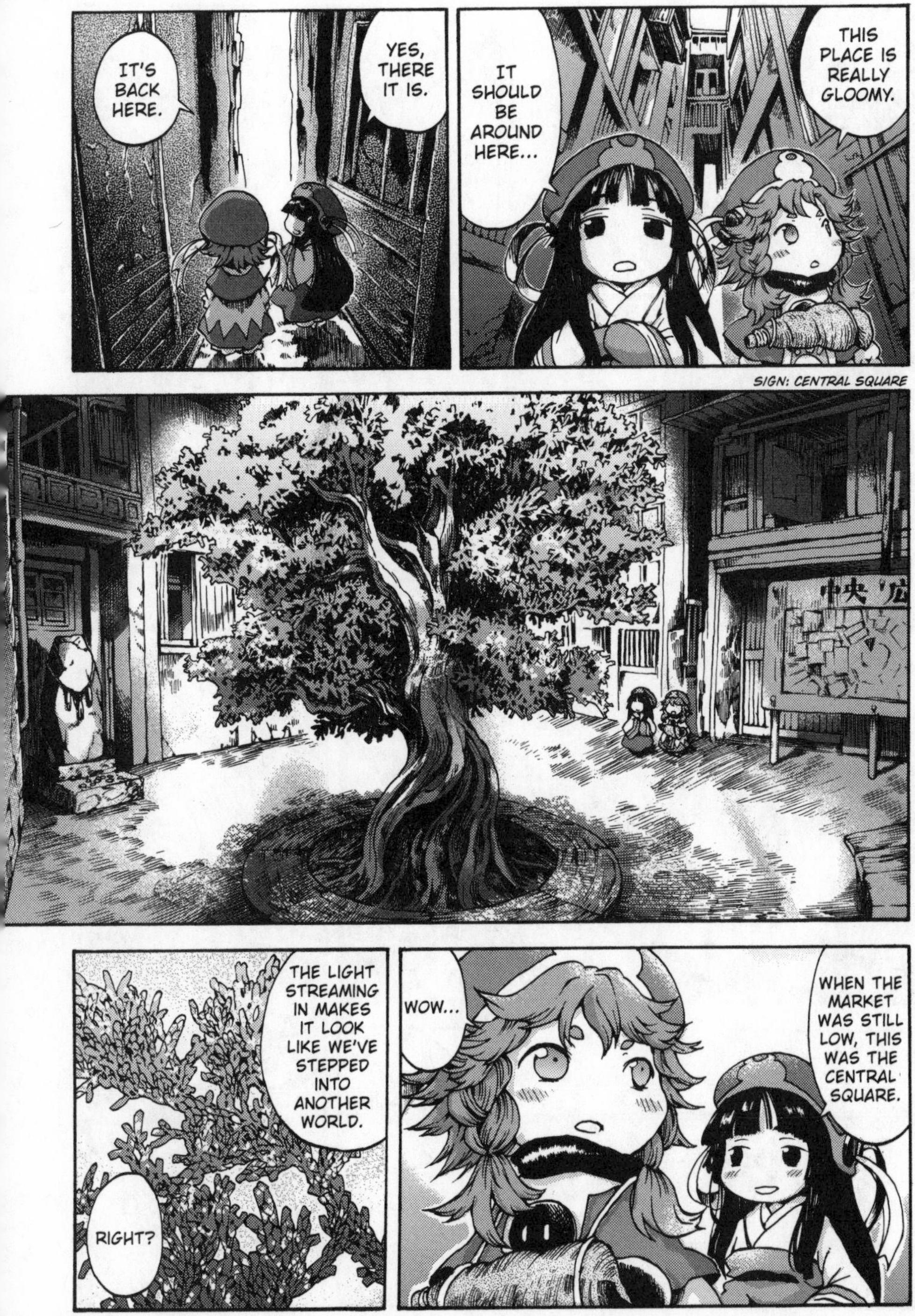
THIS PLACE IS REALLY GLOOMY.
IT SHOULD BE AROUND HERE...
YES, THERE IT IS.
IT'S BACK HERE.
SIGN: CENTRAL SQUARE
WHEN THE MARKET WAS STILL LOW, THIS WAS THE CENTRAL SQUARE.
WOW...
THE LIGHT STREAMING IN MAKES IT LOOK LIKE WE'VE STEPPED INTO ANOTHER WORLD.
RIGHT?

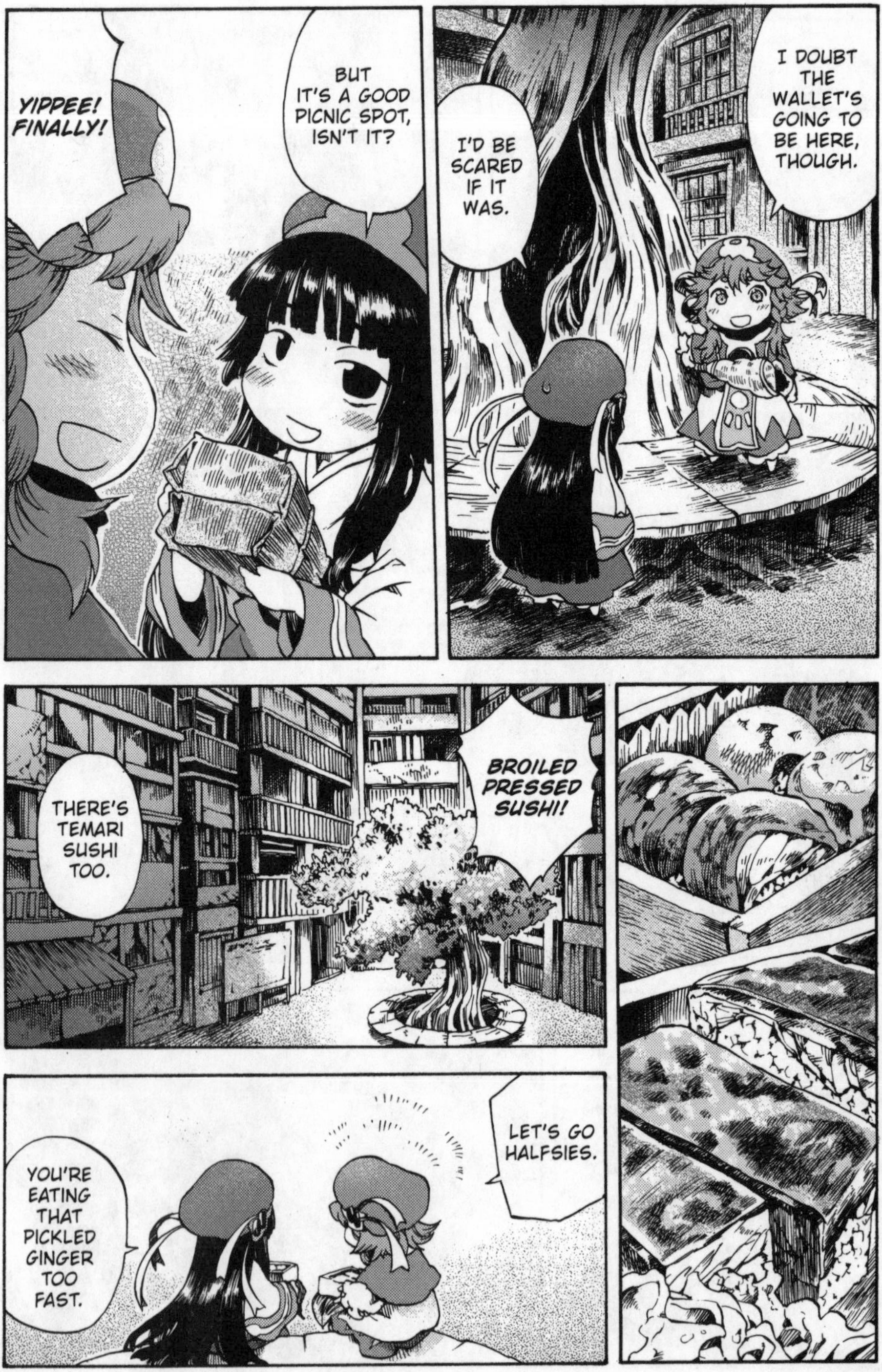
I DOUBT THE WALLET'S GOING TO BE HERE, THOUGH.
I'D BE SCARED IF IT WAS.
BUT IT'S A GOOD PICNIC SPOT, ISN'T IT?
YIPPEE! FINALLY!
BROILED PRESSED SUSHI!
THERE'S TEMARI SUSHI TOO.
LET'S GO HALFSIES.
YOU'RE EATING THAT PICKLED GINGER TOO FAST.

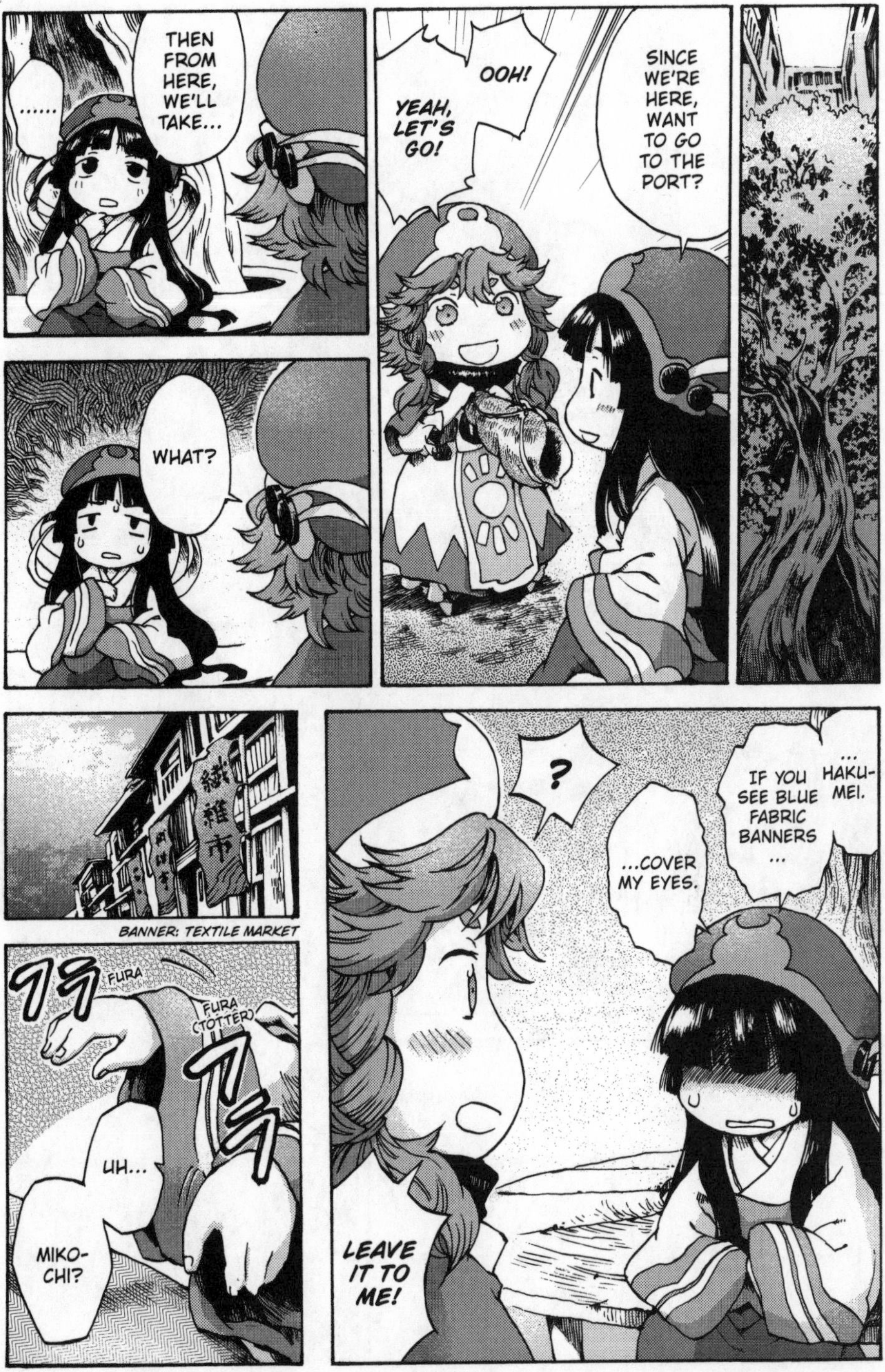
SINCE WE'RE HERE, WANT TO GO TO THE PORT?
OOH!
YEAH, LET'S GO!
THEN FROM HERE, WE'LL TAKE...
......
WHAT?
... HAKU-MEI.
IF YOU SEE BLUE FABRIC BANNERS ...
...COVER MY EYES.
?
LEAVE IT TO ME!
BANNER: TEXTILE MARKET
FURA
FURA (TOTTER)
UH...
MIKO-CHI?

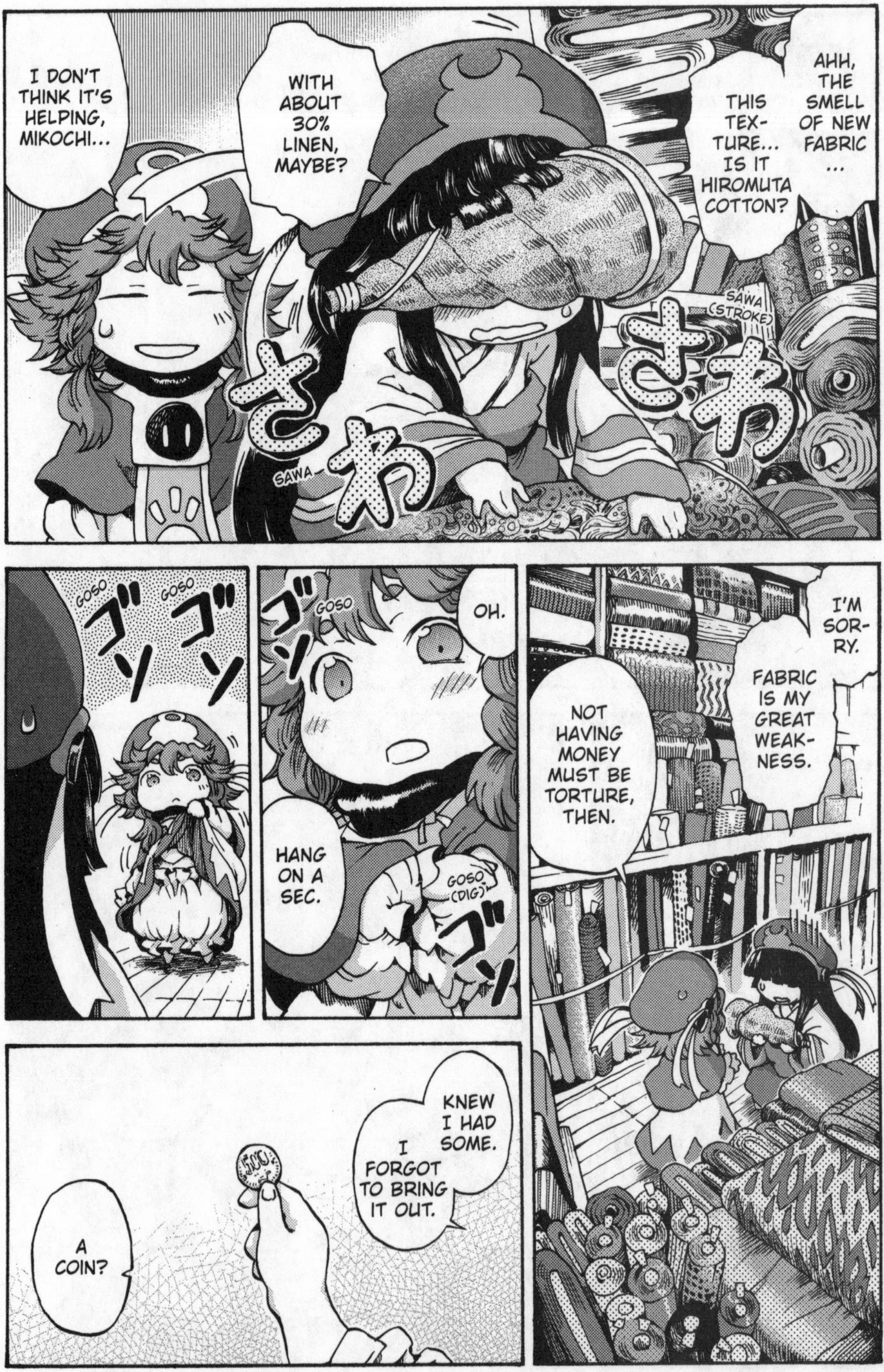
AHH, THE SMELL OF NEW FABRIC ...
THIS TEX-TURE... IS IT HIROMUTA COTTON?
WITH ABOUT 30% LINEN, MAYBE?
I DON'T THINK IT'S HELPING, MIKOCHI...
SAWA (STROKE)
さわ
SAWA
さわ
I'M SOR-RY.
FABRIC IS MY GREAT WEAK-NESS.
NOT HAVING MONEY MUST BE TORTURE, THEN.
OH.
GOSO
ゴソ
HANG ON A SEC.
GOSO (DIG)
ゴソ
GOSO
ゴソ
GOSO
ゴソ
KNEW I HAD SOME.
I FORGOT TO BRING IT OUT.
A COIN?

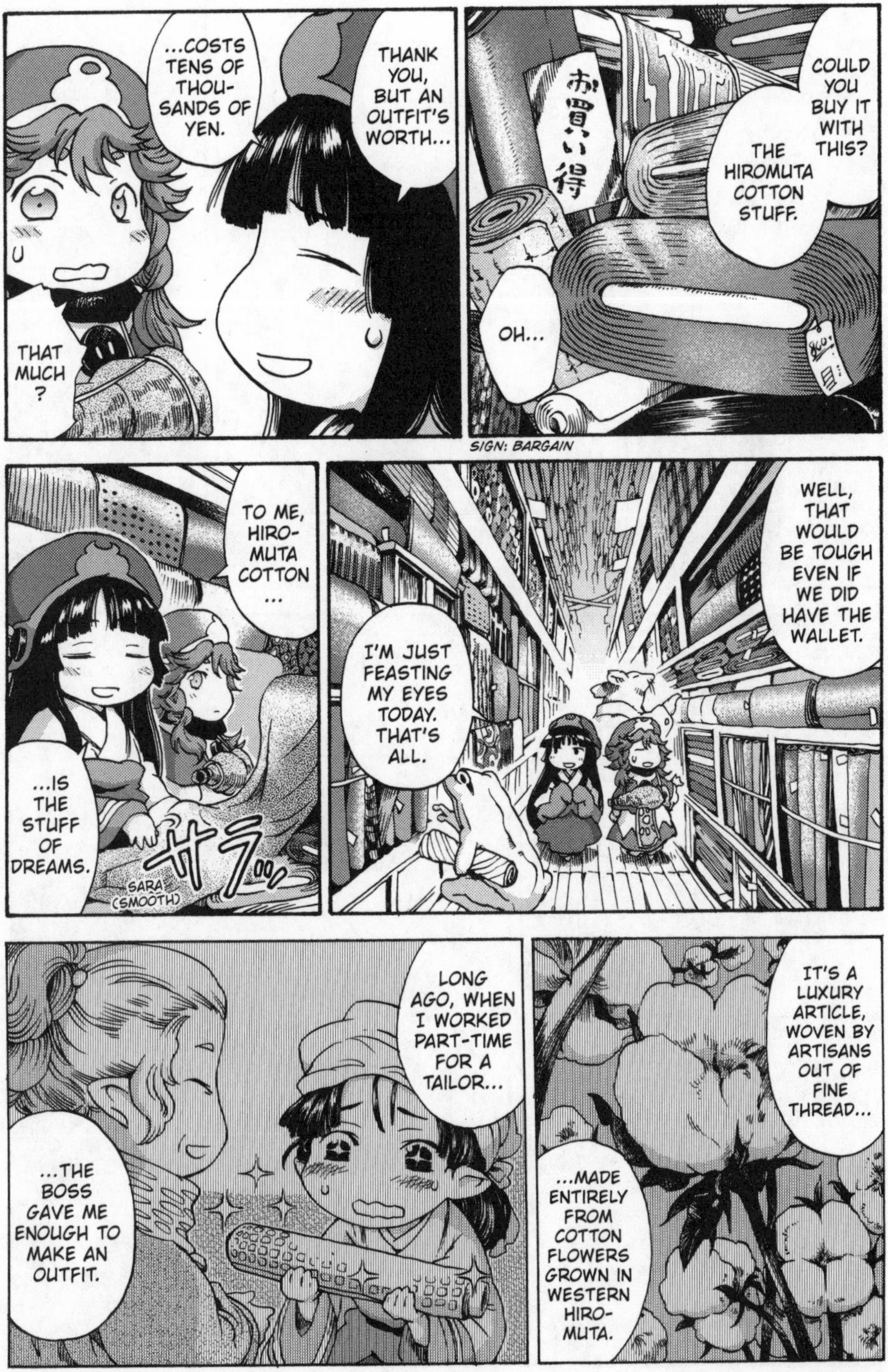
COULD YOU BUY IT WITH THIS?
THE HIROMUTA COTTON STUFF.
お買い得
OH...
SIGN: BARGAIN
THANK YOU, BUT AN OUTFIT'S WORTH...
...COSTS TENS OF THOU-SANDS OF YEN.
THAT MUCH?
WELL, THAT WOULD BE TOUGH EVEN IF WE DID HAVE THE WALLET.
I'M JUST FEASTING MY EYES TODAY. THAT'S ALL.
TO ME, HIRO-MUTA COTTON...
...IS THE STUFF OF DREAMS.
サラ
SARA (SMOOTH)
IT'S A LUXURY ARTICLE, WOVEN BY ARTISANS OUT OF FINE THREAD...
...MADE ENTIRELY FROM COTTON FLOWERS GROWN IN WESTERN HIRO-MUTA.
LONG AGO, WHEN I WORKED PART-TIME FOR A TAILOR...
...THE BOSS GAVE ME ENOUGH TO MAKE AN OUTFIT.

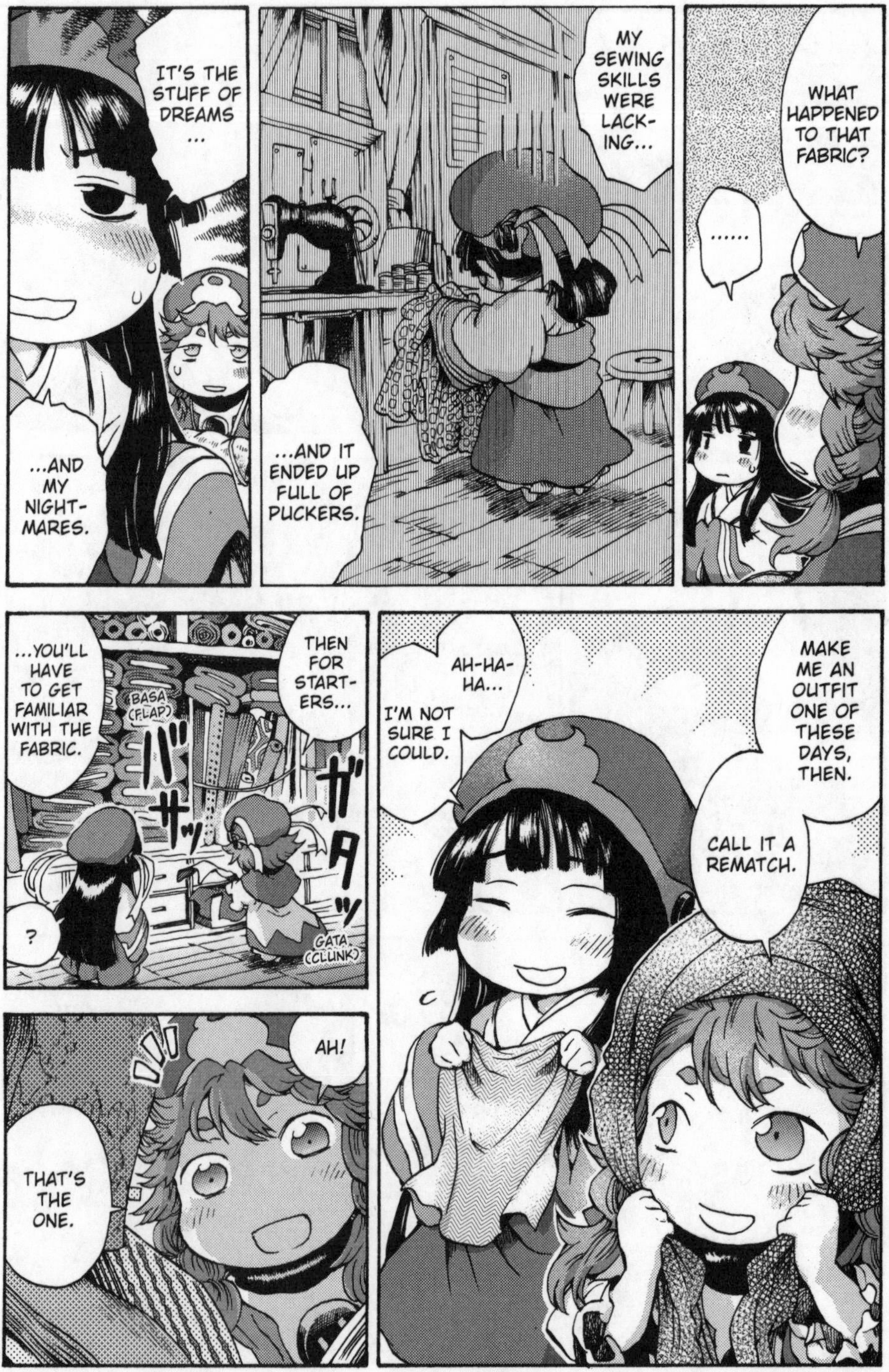
WHAT HAPPENED TO THAT FABRIC?
......
MY SEWING SKILLS WERE LACKING...
...AND IT ENDED UP FULL OF PUCKERS.
IT'S THE STUFF OF DREAMS ...
...AND MY NIGHTMARES.
MAKE ME AN OUTFIT ONE OF THESE DAYS, THEN.
CALL IT A REMATCH.
AH-HA-HA...
I'M NOT SURE I COULD.
THEN FOR STARTERS...
...YOU'LL HAVE TO GET FAMILIAR WITH THE FABRIC.
BASA (FLAP)
バサッ
ガタッ
GATA (CLUNK)
?
AH!
THAT'S THE ONE.

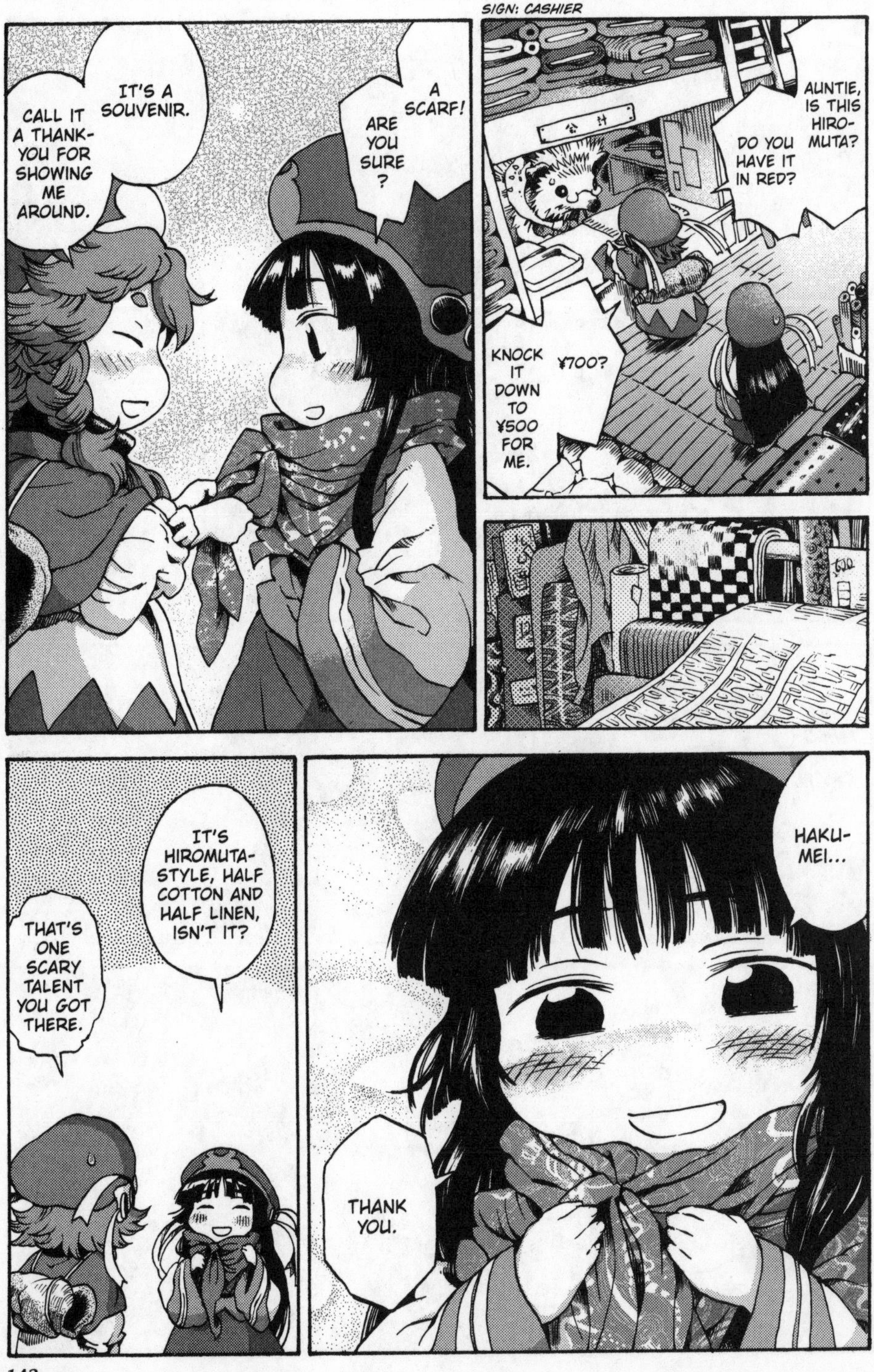
SIGN: CASHIER
AUNTIE, IS THIS HIRO-MUTA?
DO YOU HAVE IT IN RED?
¥700?
KNOCK IT DOWN TO ¥500 FOR ME.
A SCARF! ARE YOU SURE?
IT'S A SOUVENIR.
CALL IT A THANK-YOU FOR SHOWING ME AROUND.
HAKU-MEI...
THANK YOU.
IT'S HIROMUTA-STYLE, HALF COTTON AND HALF LINEN, ISN'T IT?
THAT'S ONE SCARY TALENT YOU GOT THERE.

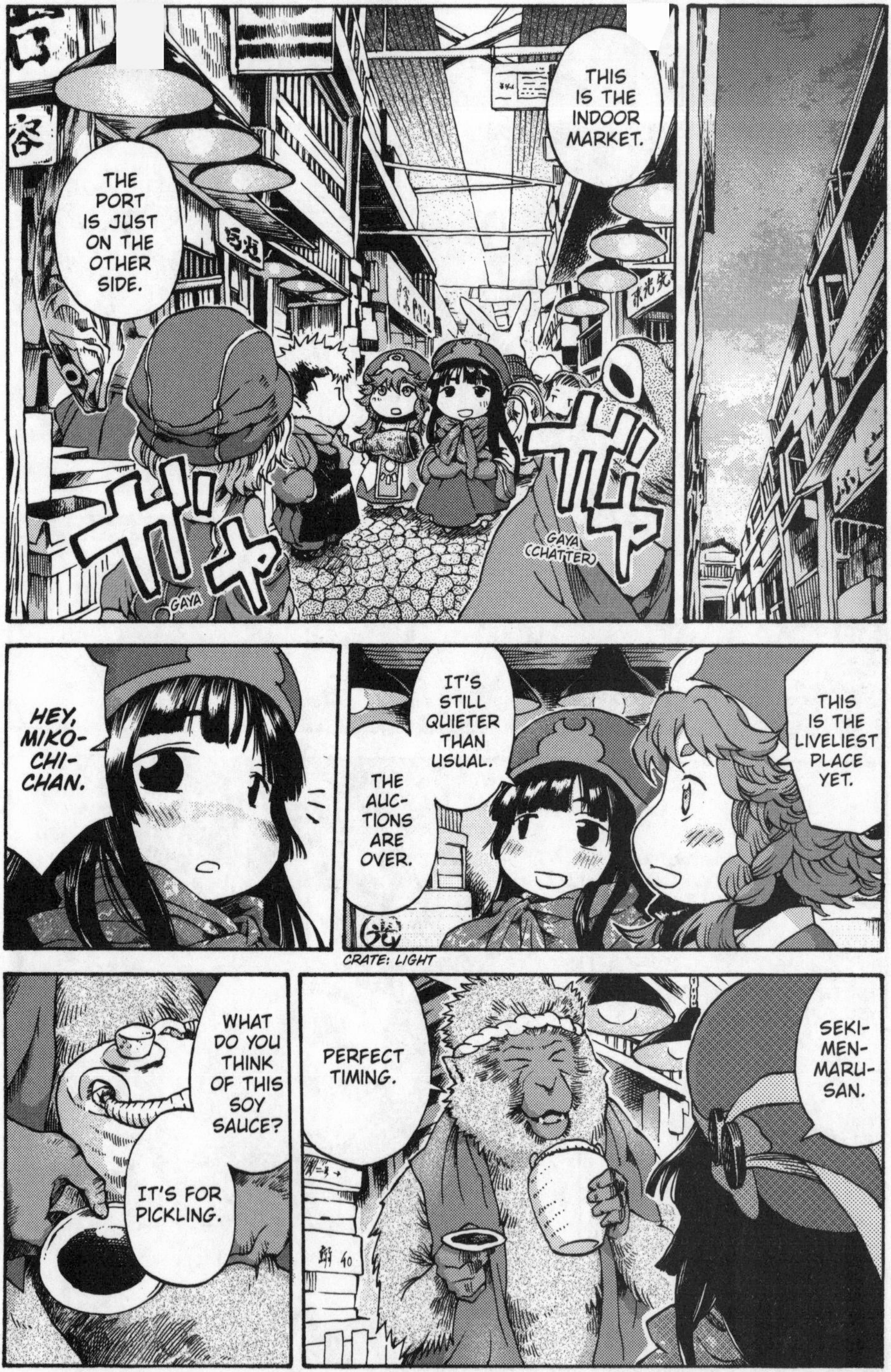
THIS IS THE INDOOR MARKET.
THE PORT IS JUST ON THE OTHER SIDE.
GAYA (CHATTER)
GAYA
THIS IS THE LIVELIEST PLACE YET.
IT'S STILL QUIETER THAN USUAL.
THE AUCTIONS ARE OVER.
CRATE: LIGHT
HEY, MIKO-CHI-CHAN.
SEKI-MEN-MARU-SAN.
PERFECT TIMING.
WHAT DO YOU THINK OF THIS SOY SAUCE?
IT'S FOR PICKLING.

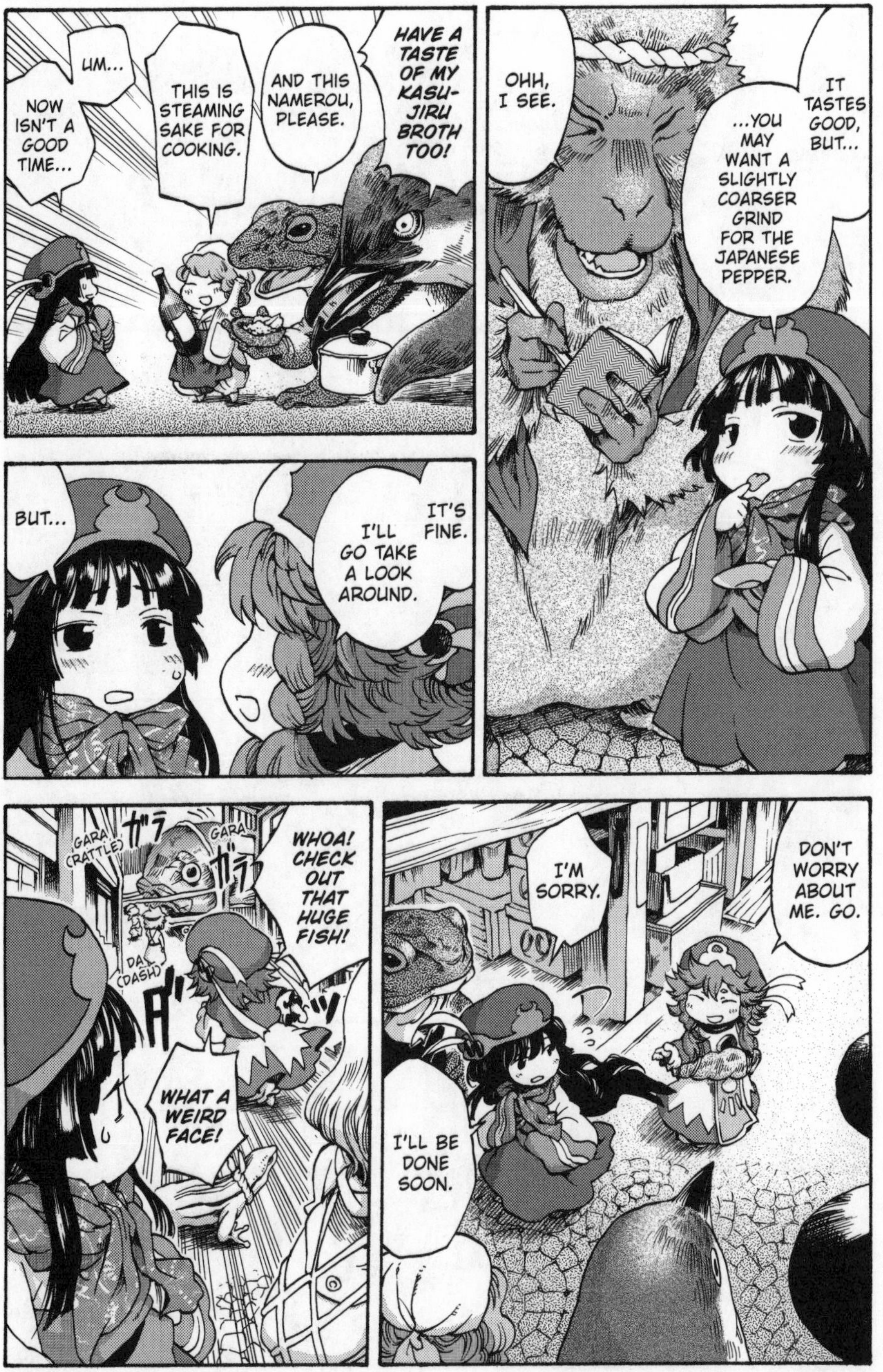
IT TASTES GOOD, BUT...
...YOU MAY WANT A SLIGHTLY COARSER GRIND FOR THE JAPANESE PEPPER.
OHH, I SEE.
HAVE A TASTE OF MY KASU-JIRU BROTH TOO!
AND THIS NAMEROU, PLEASE.
THIS IS STEAMING SAKE FOR COOKING.
UM...
NOW ISN'T A GOOD TIME...
IT'S FINE.
I'LL GO TAKE A LOOK AROUND.
BUT...
DON'T WORRY ABOUT ME. GO.
I'M SORRY.
I'LL BE DONE SOON.
WHOA! CHECK OUT THAT HUGE FISH!
GARA
GARA (RATTLE)
DA (DASH)
WHAT A WEIRD FACE!

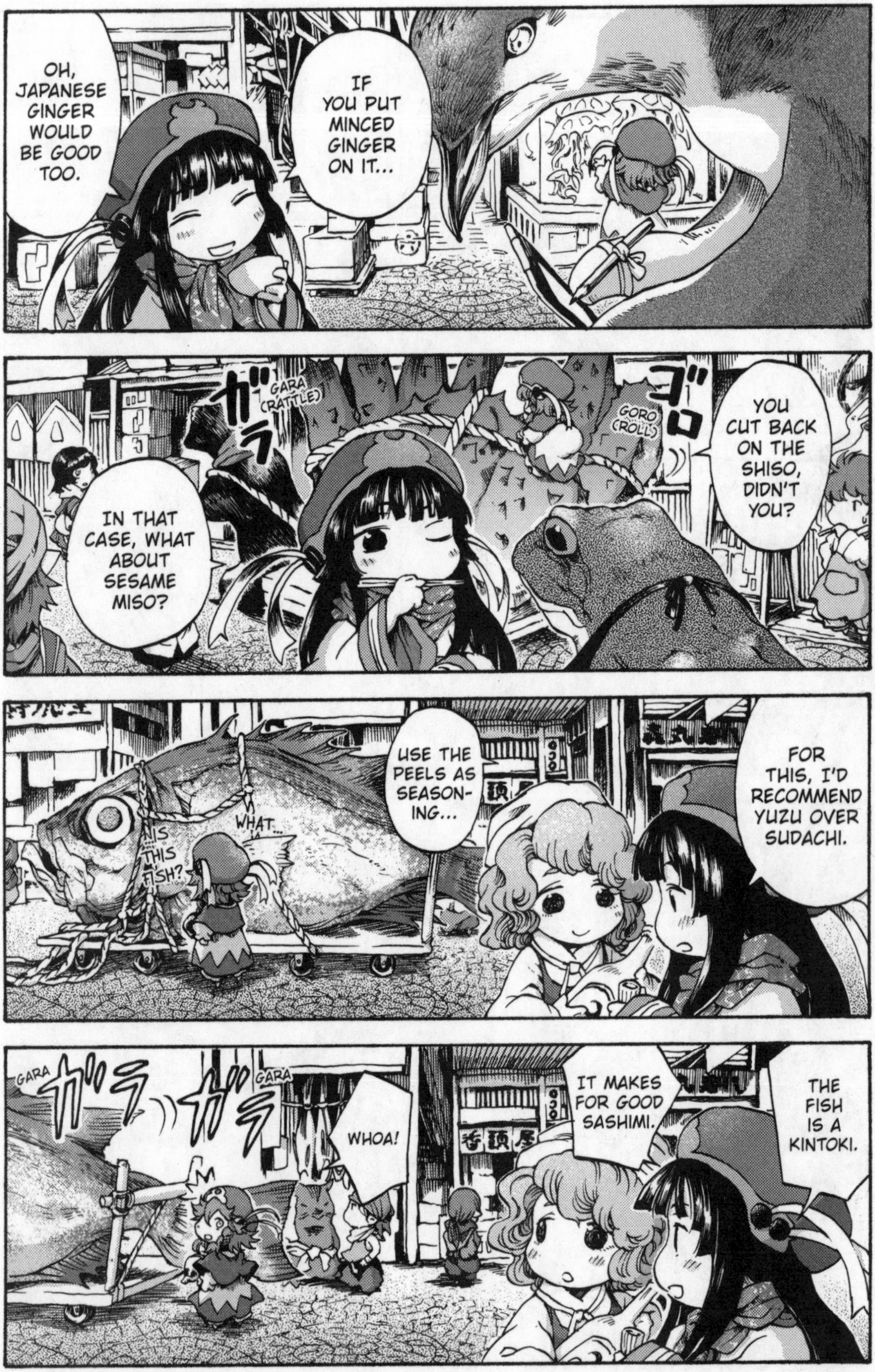
IF YOU PUT MINCED GINGER ON IT...
OH, JAPANESE GINGER WOULD BE GOOD TOO.
YOU CUT BACK ON THE SHISO, DIDN'T YOU?
ゴロ
GORO (ROLL)
ガラ
GARA (RATTLE)
IN THAT CASE, WHAT ABOUT SESAME MISO?
FOR THIS, I'D RECOMMEND YUZU OVER SUDACHI.
USE THE PEELS AS SEASON-ING...
WHAT...
IS THIS FISH?
THE FISH IS A KINTOKI.
IT MAKES FOR GOOD SASHIMI.
WHOA!
ガラ
GARA
ガラ
GARA

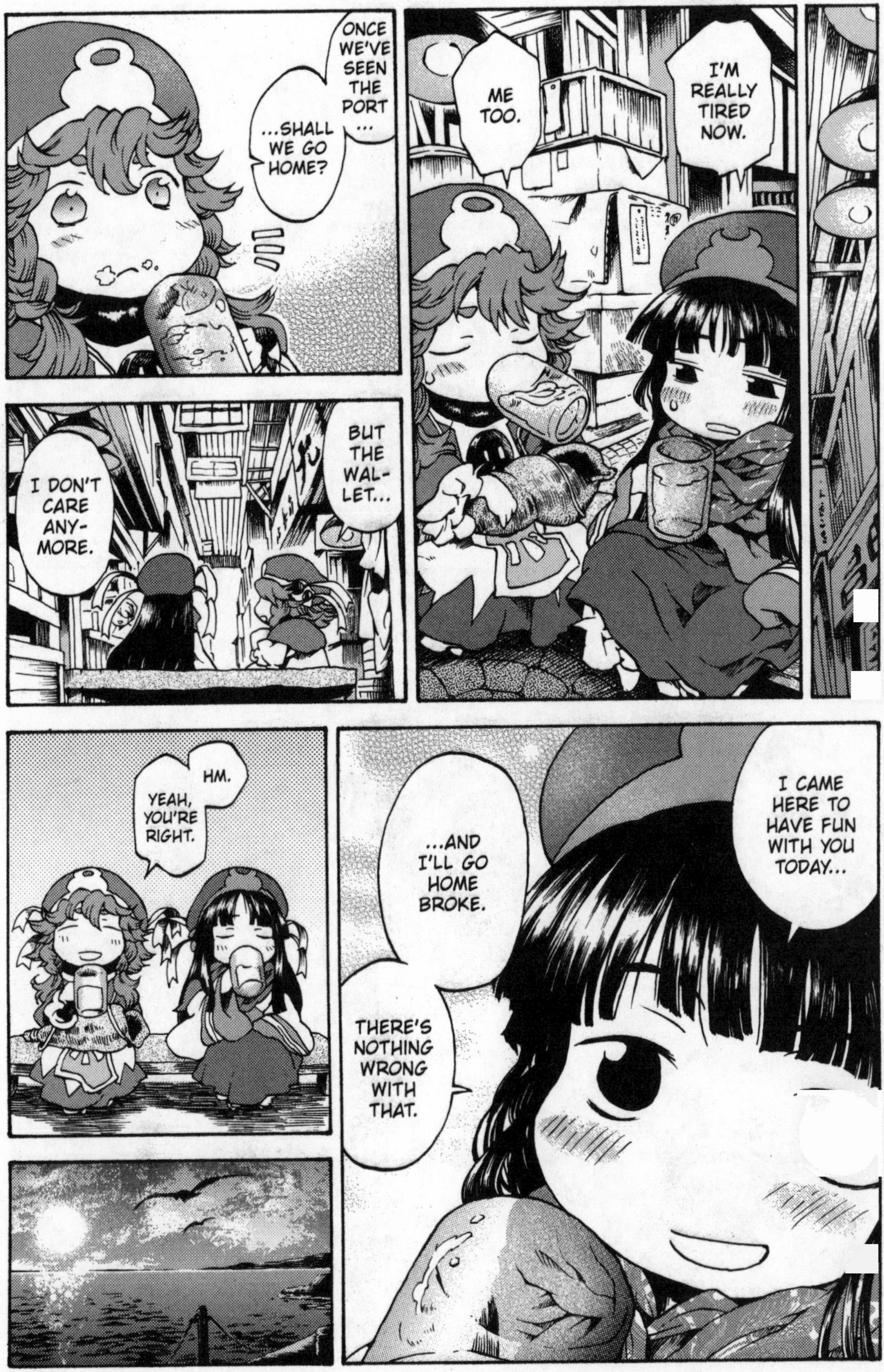
I'M REALLY TIRED NOW.
ME TOO.
ONCE WE'VE SEEN THE PORT...
...SHALL WE GO HOME?
BUT THE WAL-LET...
I DON'T CARE ANY-MORE.
I CAME HERE TO HAVE FUN WITH YOU TODAY...
...AND I'LL GO HOME BROKE.
THERE'S NOTHING WRONG WITH THAT.
HM.
YEAH, YOU'RE RIGHT.

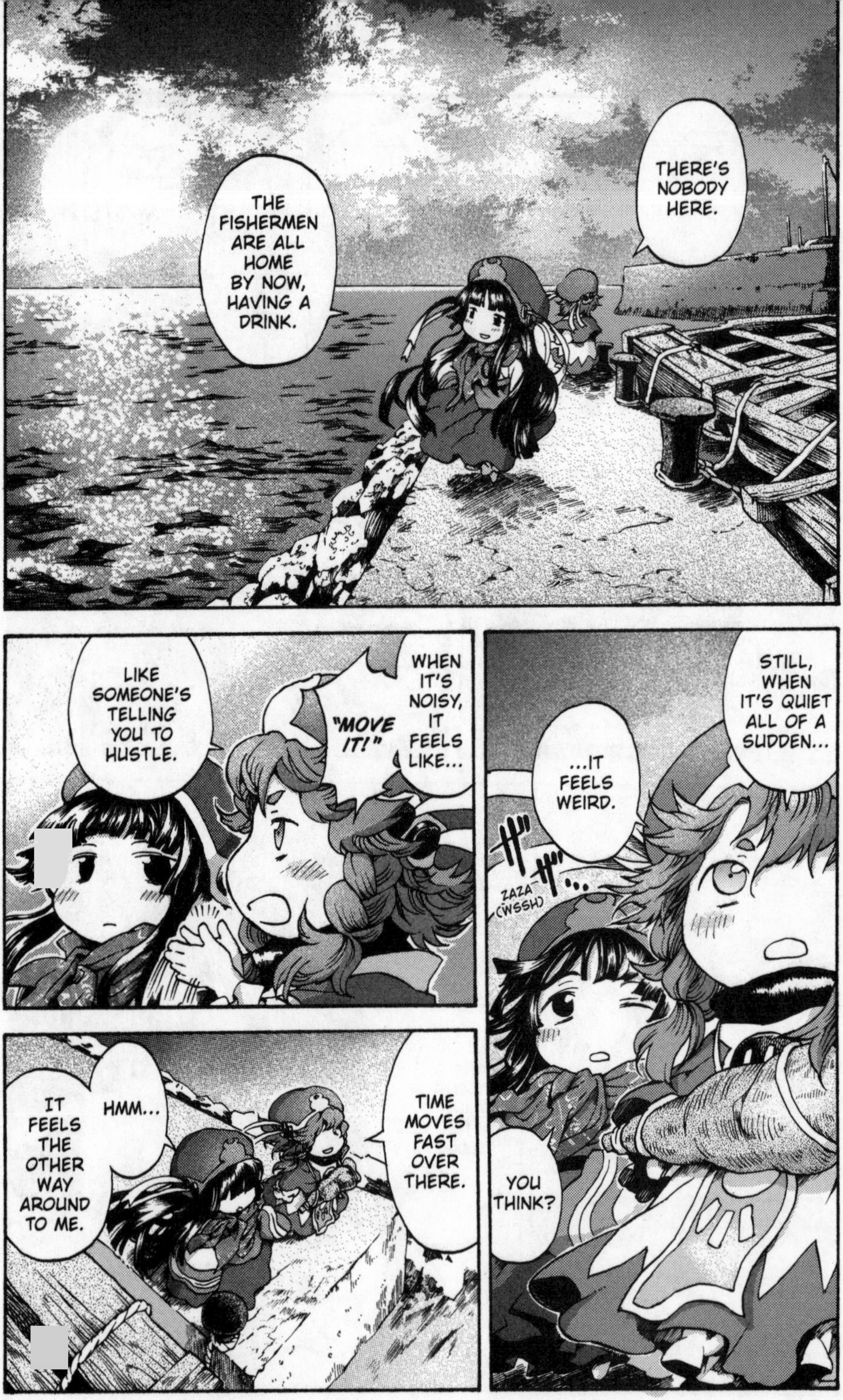
THERE'S NOBODY HERE.
THE FISHERMEN ARE ALL HOME BY NOW, HAVING A DRINK.
STILL, WHEN IT'S QUIET ALL OF A SUDDEN...
...IT FEELS WEIRD.
ZAZA (WSSH)
YOU THINK?
WHEN IT'S NOISY, IT FEELS LIKE...
"MOVE IT!"
LIKE SOMEONE'S TELLING YOU TO HUSTLE.
TIME MOVES FAST OVER THERE.
HMM...
IT FEELS THE OTHER WAY AROUND TO ME.

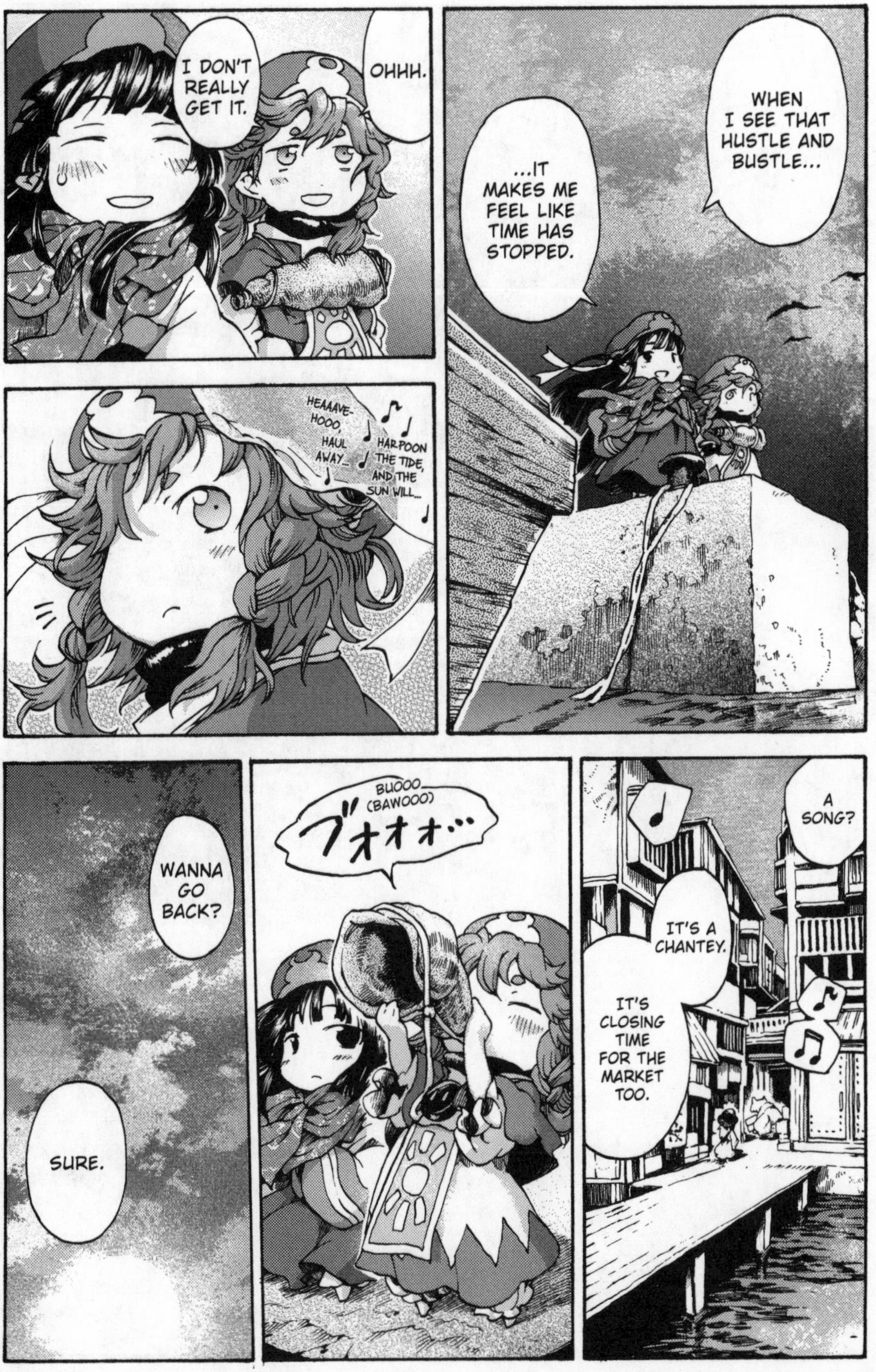
WHEN I SEE THAT HUSTLE AND BUSTLE...
...IT MAKES ME FEEL LIKE TIME HAS STOPPED.
OHHH.
I DON'T REALLY GET IT.
HARPOON THE TIDE, AND THE SUN WILL...
HEAAAVE-HOOO, HAUL AWAY...
A SONG?
IT'S A CHANTEY.
IT'S CLOSING TIME FOR THE MARKET TOO.
BUOOO (BAWOOO)
ブオオオ
WANNA GO BACK?
SURE.

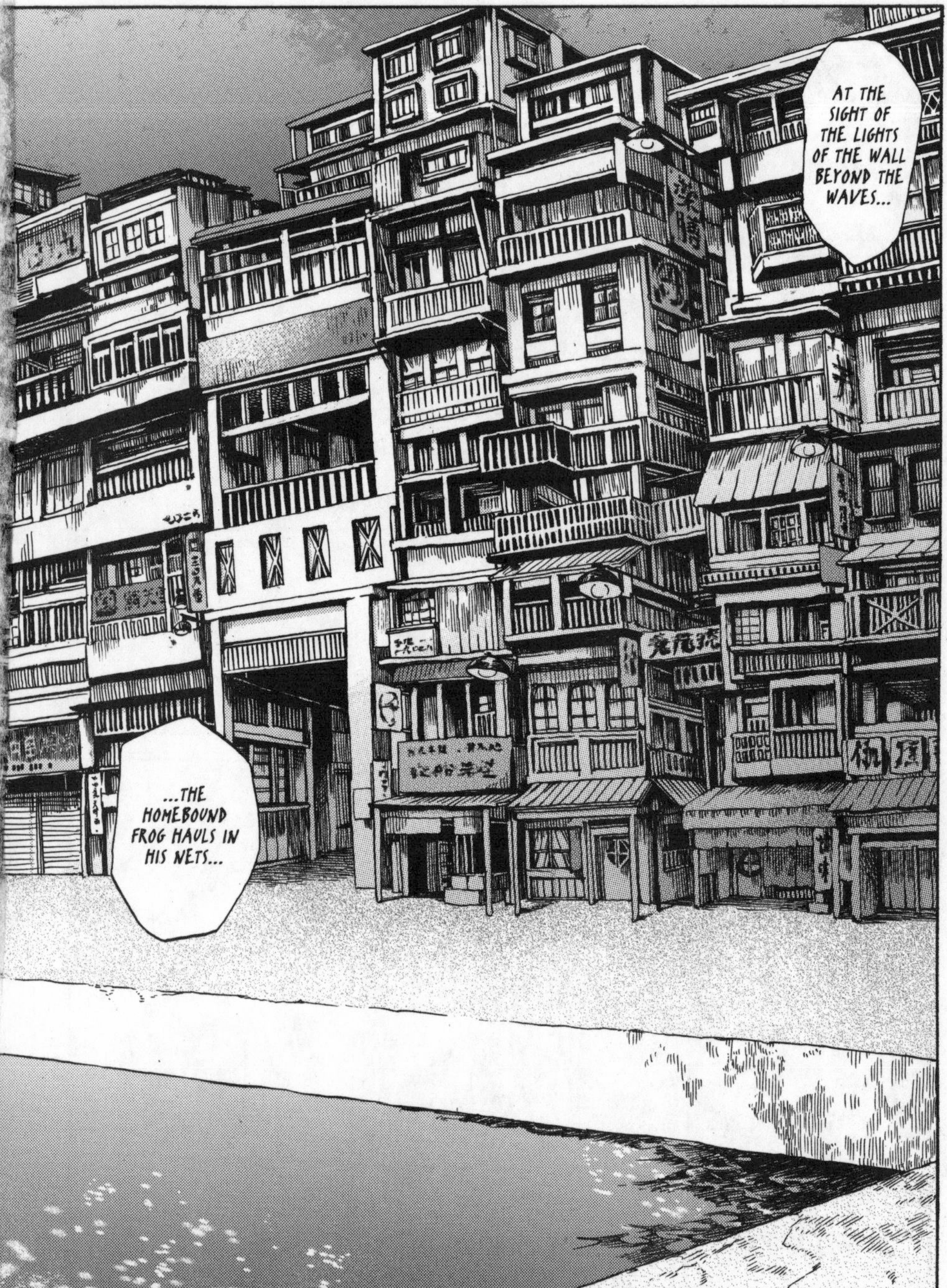
AT THE SIGHT OF THE LIGHTS OF THE WALL BEYOND THE WAVES...
...THE HOMEBOUND FROG HAULS IN HIS NETS...

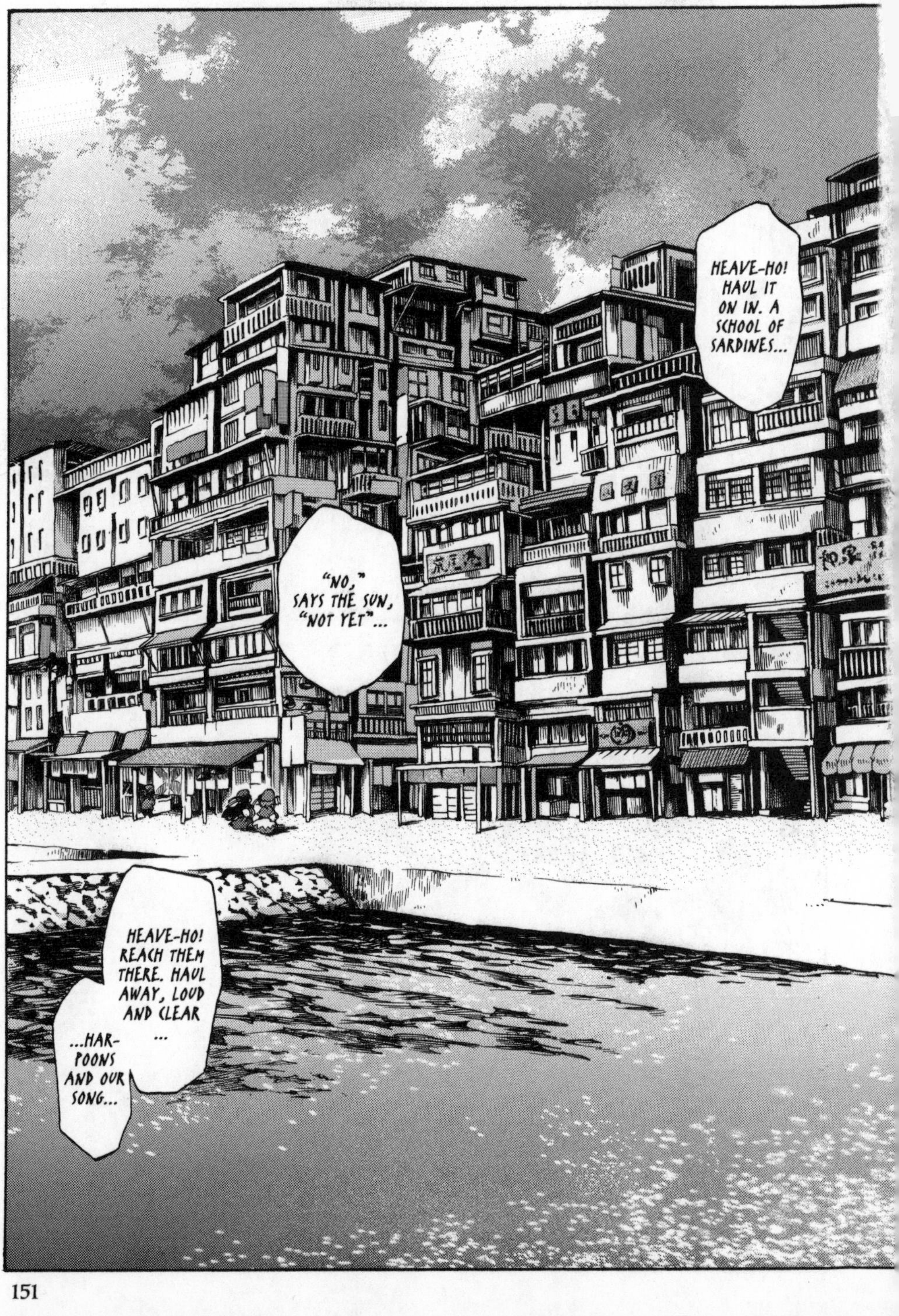
HEAVE-HO! HAUL IT ON IN. A SCHOOL OF SARDINES...
"NO," SAYS THE SUN, "NOT YET"...
HEAVE-HO! REACH THEM THERE. HAUL AWAY, LOUD AND CLEAR ...
...HARPOONS AND OUR SONG...

I'VE BEEN HANGING ON TO IT SINCE I FOUND IT.

I JUST COULDN'T SEEM TO CATCH YOU, MIKOCHI-SAN.

MY WALLET?

......

SIGN: PUB

IF YOU WANT TO SHOP, SOME PLACES ARE STILL OPEN...

UU...

MY LEGS ALREADY FEEL LIKE WOOD.

I'M SORRY FOR ALL THE TROUBLE.

UM...

WELL, I...

OH.

RIGHT.

152

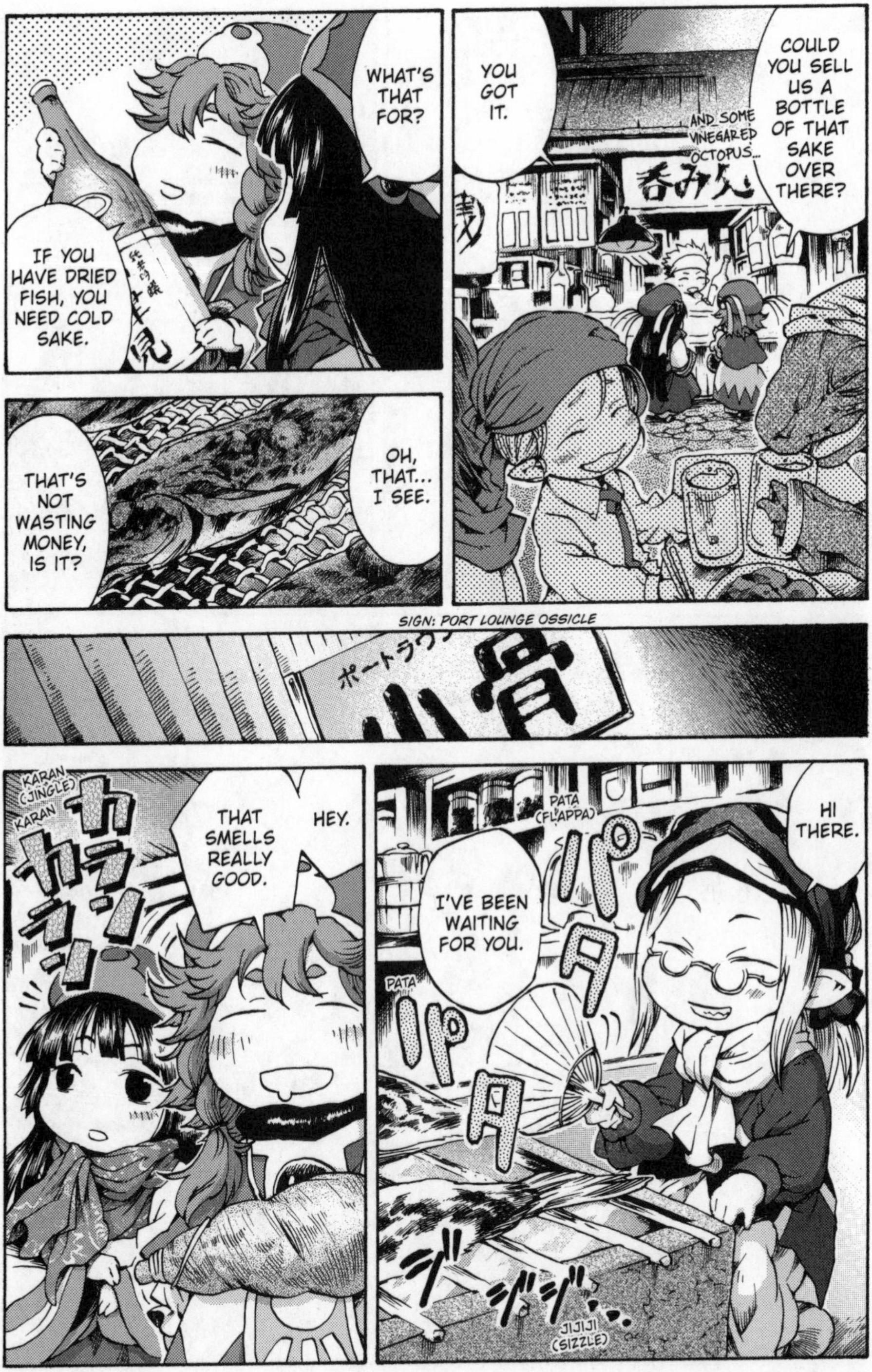
COULD YOU SELL US A BOTTLE OF THAT SAKE OVER THERE?
AND SOME VINEGARED OCTOPUS...
YOU GOT IT.
WHAT'S THAT FOR?
IF YOU HAVE DRIED FISH, YOU NEED COLD SAKE.
OH, THAT... I SEE.
THAT'S NOT WASTING MONEY, IS IT?
SIGN: PORT LOUNGE OSSICLE
HI THERE.
PATA (FLAPPA)
I'VE BEEN WAITING FOR YOU.
PATA
JIJIJI (SIZZLE)
HEY.
THAT SMELLS REALLY GOOD.
KARAN (JINGLE) KARAN

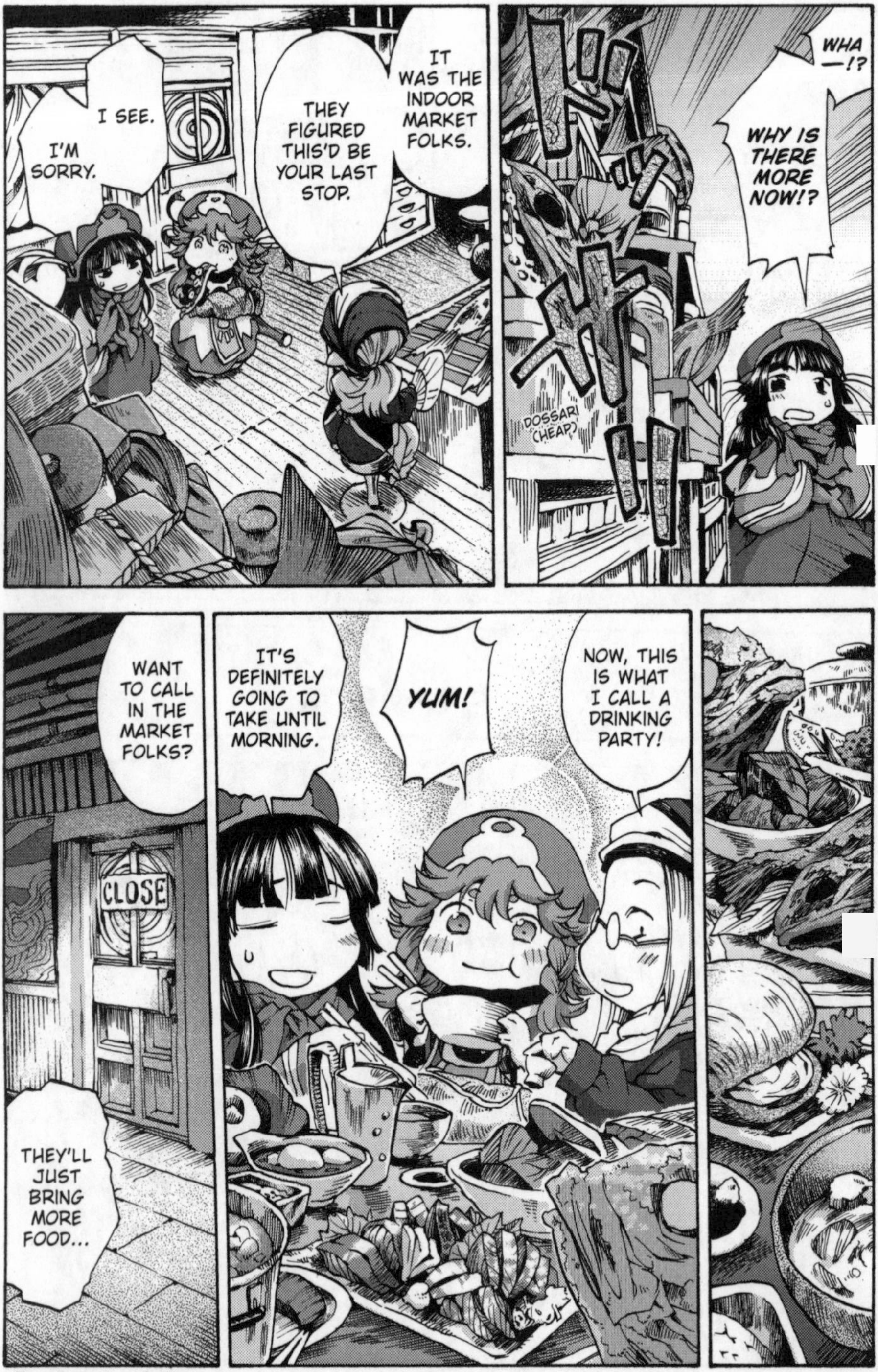
WHA—!?
WHY IS THERE MORE NOW!?
DOSSARI (HEAP)
IT WAS THE INDOOR MARKET FOLKS.
THEY FIGURED THIS'D BE YOUR LAST STOP.
I SEE.
I'M SORRY.
NOW, THIS IS WHAT I CALL A DRINKING PARTY!
YUM!
IT'S DEFINITELY GOING TO TAKE UNTIL MORNING.
WANT TO CALL IN THE MARKET FOLKS?
CLOSE
THEY'LL JUST BRING MORE FOOD...

Chapter 6 • End

They say Arabi's Building Block Market began with shops set up by three prominent figures: the fisherman Kikyuumaru, the wholesale fabric merchant Willie, and Kyuuka the coffee roaster. Each of these three contributed to the town's development. The first harvested a wide variety of marine products that capitalized on the characteristics of the tranquil, shallow Bay of Arabi; the second established a method of cotton cultivation that used the mud of the tidal flats; and the third provided a place where workers could relax.

People gathered and attracted others, building up the original incarnation of present-day Arabi around the now-ruined central square. The square still contains a stone monument engraved with the trio's names today.

The unique, "layered" building method is said to have its roots in a joke the three made one day while drinking together:

"If we piled 'em up, we could build as many stores as we want, couldn't we!?"

—Excerpt from the *Port Town Arabi Tour Guide*

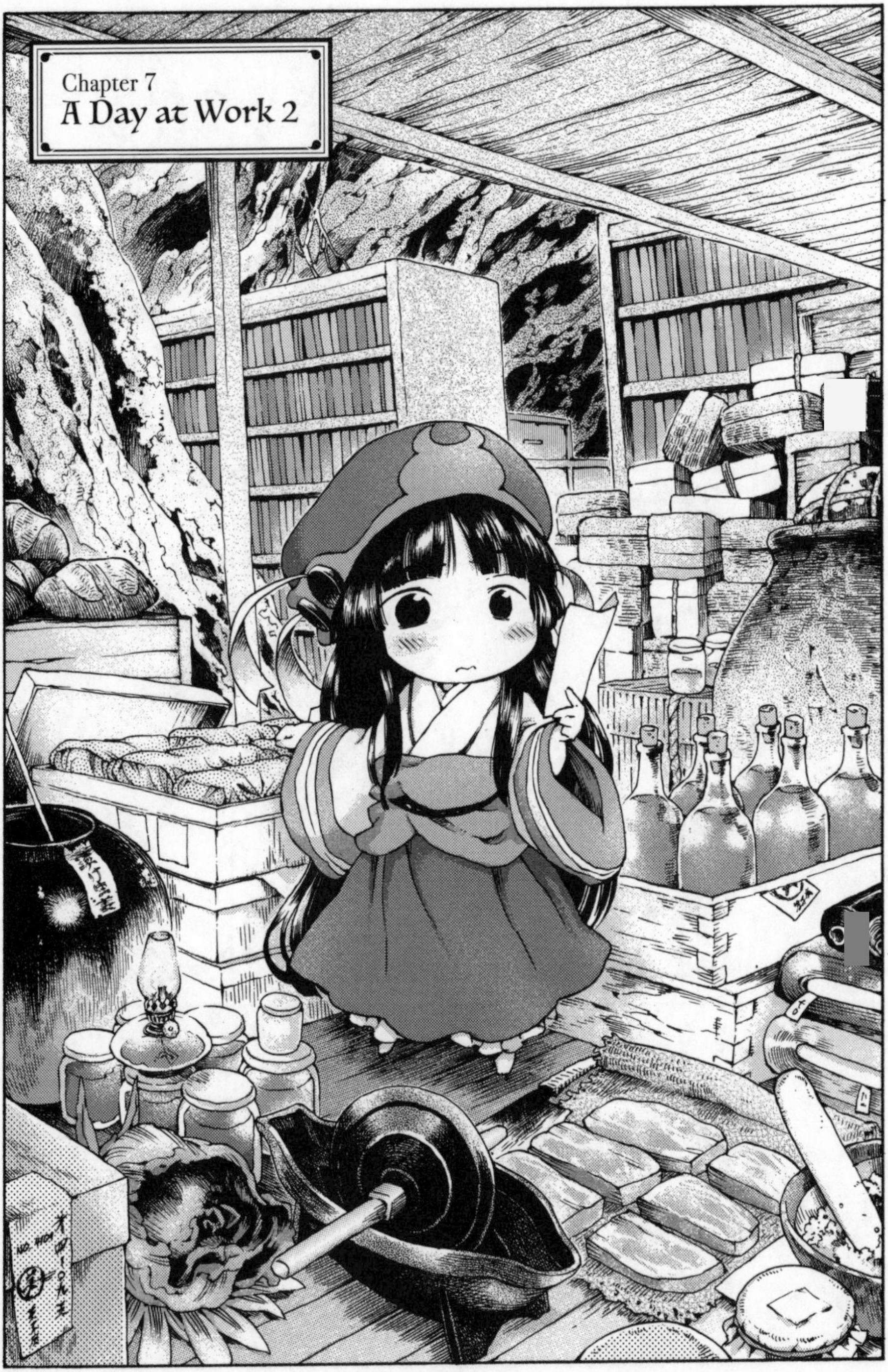
Chapter 7
A Day at Work 2

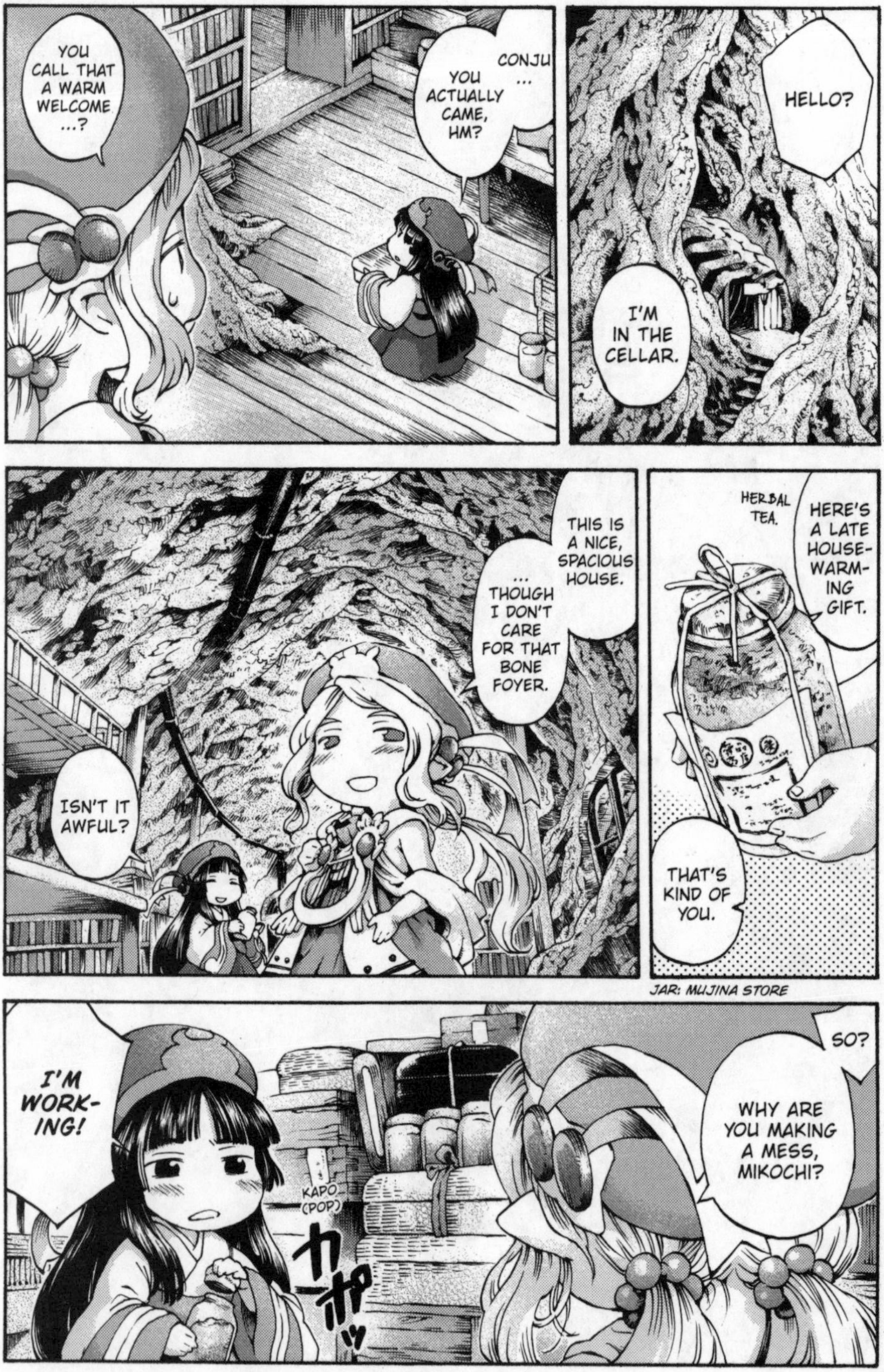
HELLO?
I'M IN THE CELLAR.
CONJU... YOU ACTUALLY CAME, HM?
YOU CALL THAT A WARM WELCOME...?
HERE'S A LATE HOUSE-WARMING GIFT.
HERBAL TEA.
THAT'S KIND OF YOU.
THIS IS A NICE, SPACIOUS HOUSE.
...THOUGH I DON'T CARE FOR THAT BONE FOYER.
ISN'T IT AWFUL?
JAR: MUJINA STORE
SO?
WHY ARE YOU MAKING A MESS, MIKOCHI?
KAPO (POP)
I'M WORKING!

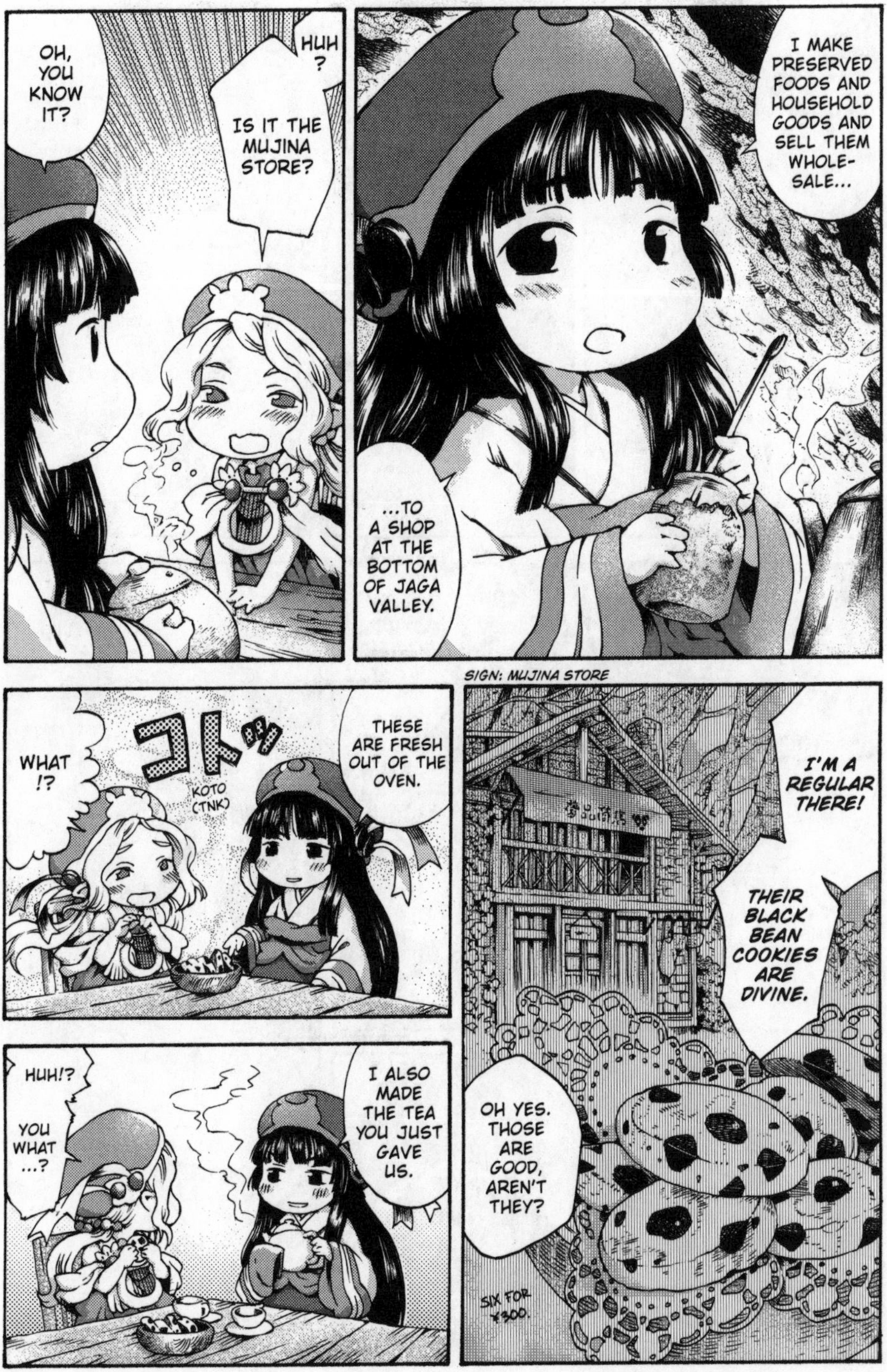
I MAKE PRESERVED FOODS AND HOUSEHOLD GOODS AND SELL THEM WHOLE-SALE...
...TO A SHOP AT THE BOTTOM OF JAGA VALLEY.
HUH? IS IT THE MUJINA STORE?
OH, YOU KNOW IT?
SIGN: MUJINA STORE
I'M A REGULAR THERE!
THEIR BLACK BEAN COOKIES ARE DIVINE.
OH YES. THOSE ARE GOOD, AREN'T THEY?
SIX FOR ¥300.
THESE ARE FRESH OUT OF THE OVEN.
コトッ
KOTO (TNK)
WHAT!?
I ALSO MADE THE TEA YOU JUST GAVE US.
HUH!?
YOU WHAT...?

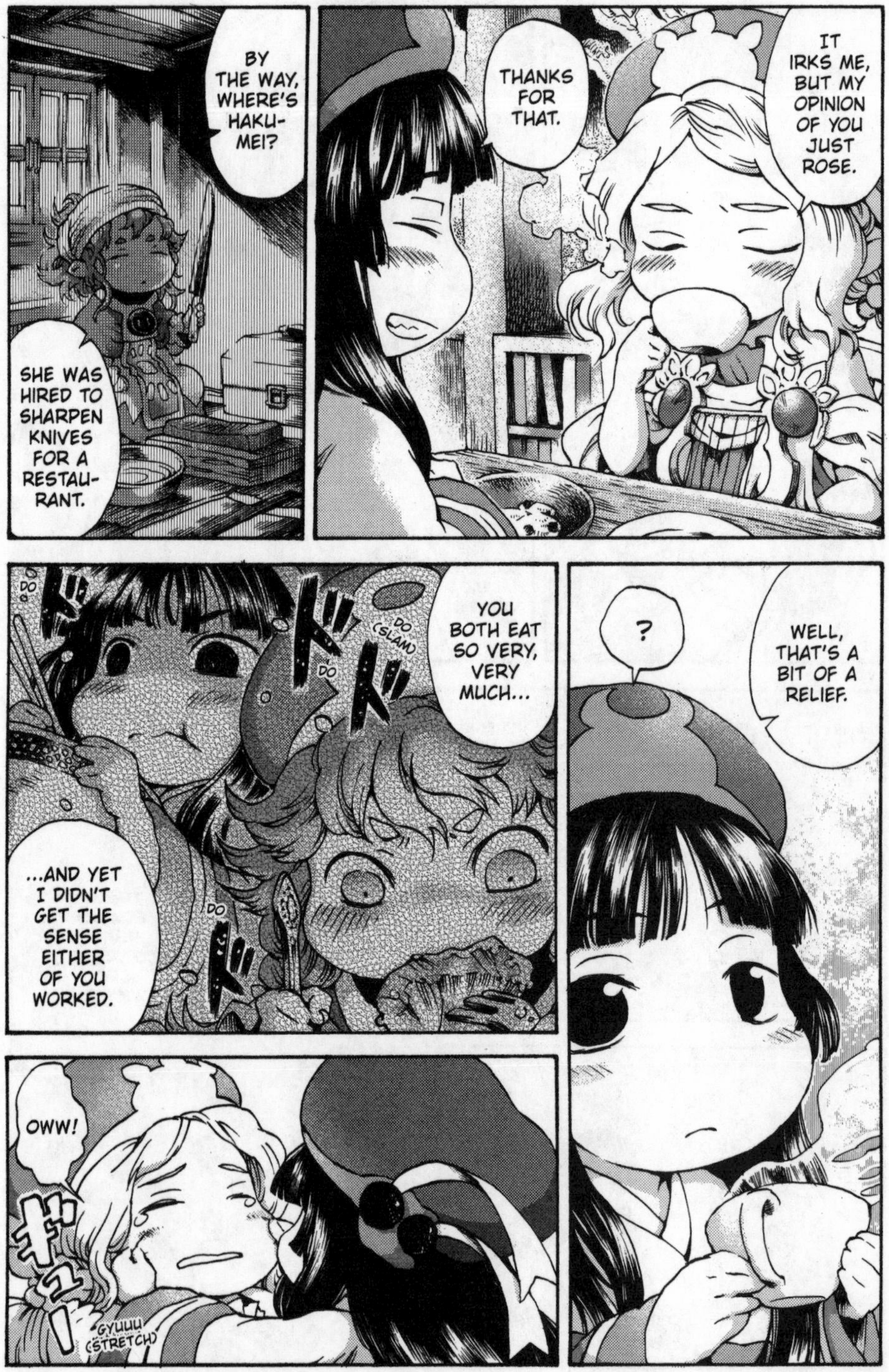
IT IRKS ME, BUT MY OPINION OF YOU JUST ROSE.
THANKS FOR THAT.
BY THE WAY, WHERE'S HAKU-MEI?
SHE WAS HIRED TO SHARPEN KNIVES FOR A RESTAU-RANT.
WELL, THAT'S A BIT OF A RELIEF.
?
YOU BOTH EAT SO VERY, VERY MUCH...
DO (SLAM)
DO
DO
...AND YET I DIDN'T GET THE SENSE EITHER OF YOU WORKED.
DO
OWW!
GYUUU (STRETCH)

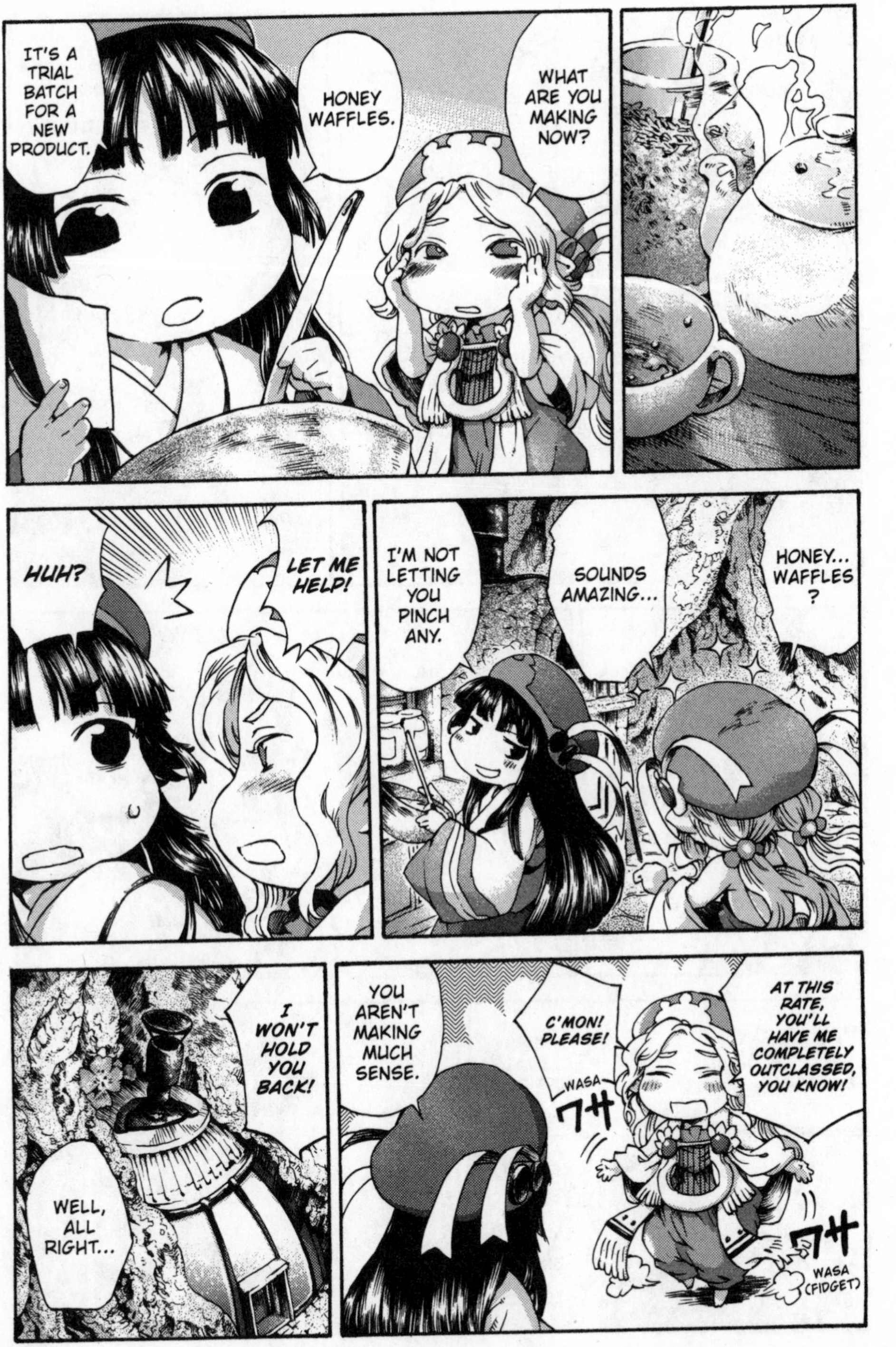
WHAT ARE YOU MAKING NOW?
HONEY WAFFLES.
IT'S A TRIAL BATCH FOR A NEW PRODUCT.
HONEY... WAFFLES?
SOUNDS AMAZING...
I'M NOT LETTING YOU PINCH ANY.
LET ME HELP!
HUH?
AT THIS RATE, YOU'LL HAVE ME COMPLETELY OUTCLASSED, YOU KNOW!
C'MON! PLEASE!
ワサ
WASA
ワサ
WASA (FIDGET)
YOU AREN'T MAKING MUCH SENSE.
I WON'T HOLD YOU BACK!
WELL, ALL RIGHT...

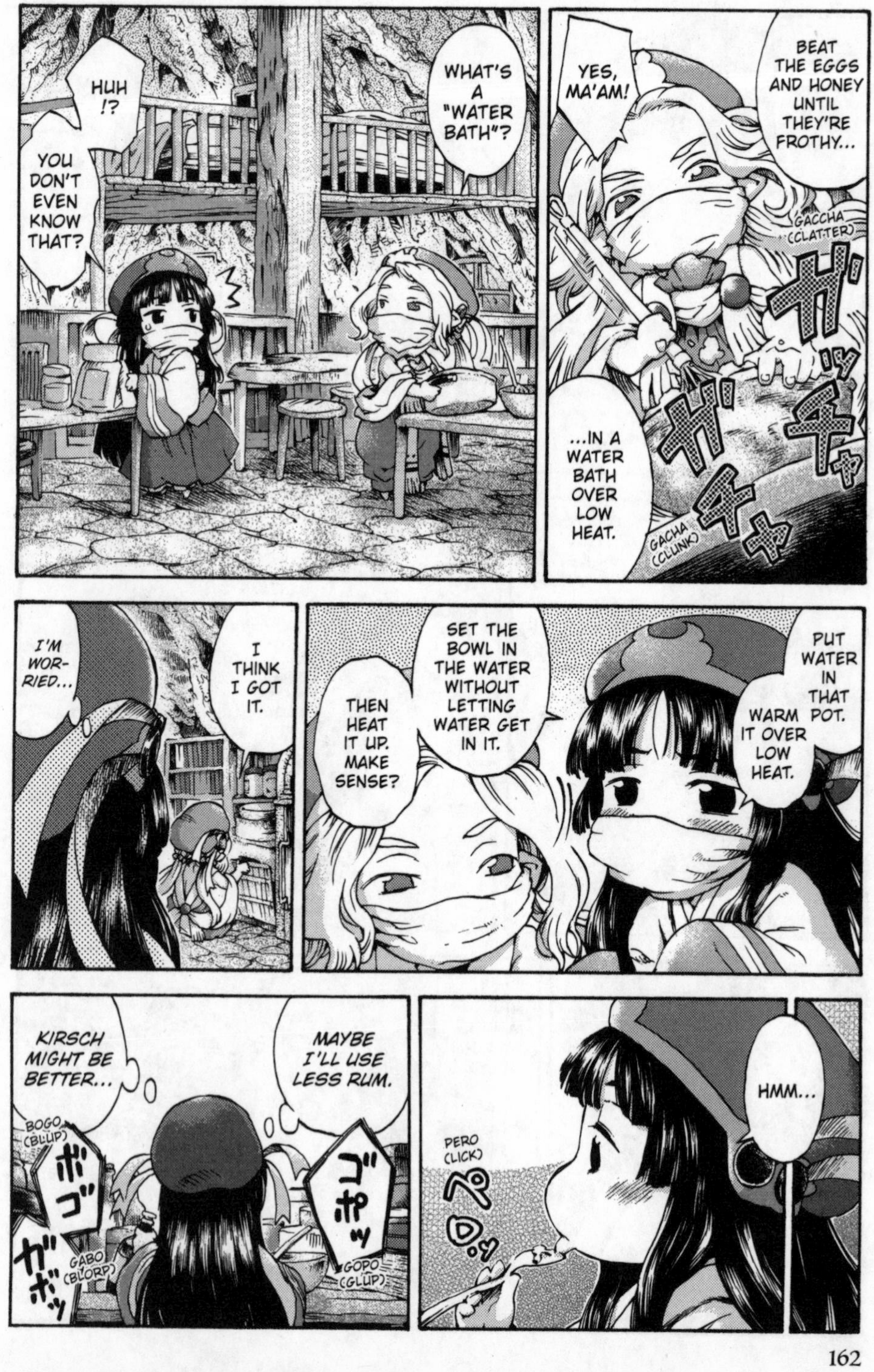
BEAT THE EGGS AND HONEY UNTIL THEY'RE FROTHY...
YES, MA'AM!
GACCHA (CLATTER)
ガッチャ
...IN A WATER BATH OVER LOW HEAT.
GACHA (CLUNK)
ガチャ
WHAT'S A "WATER BATH"?
HUH!?
YOU DON'T EVEN KNOW THAT?
PUT WATER IN THAT POT.
WARM IT OVER LOW HEAT.
SET THE BOWL IN THE WATER WITHOUT LETTING WATER GET IN IT.
THEN HEAT IT UP. MAKE SENSE?
I THINK I GOT IT.
I'M WORRIED...
HMM...
PERO (LICK)
ペロッ
MAYBE I'LL USE LESS RUM.
GOPO (GLUP)
ゴポッ
KIRSCH MIGHT BE BETTER...
BOGO (BLUP)
ボゴ
GABO (BLORP)
ガボッ

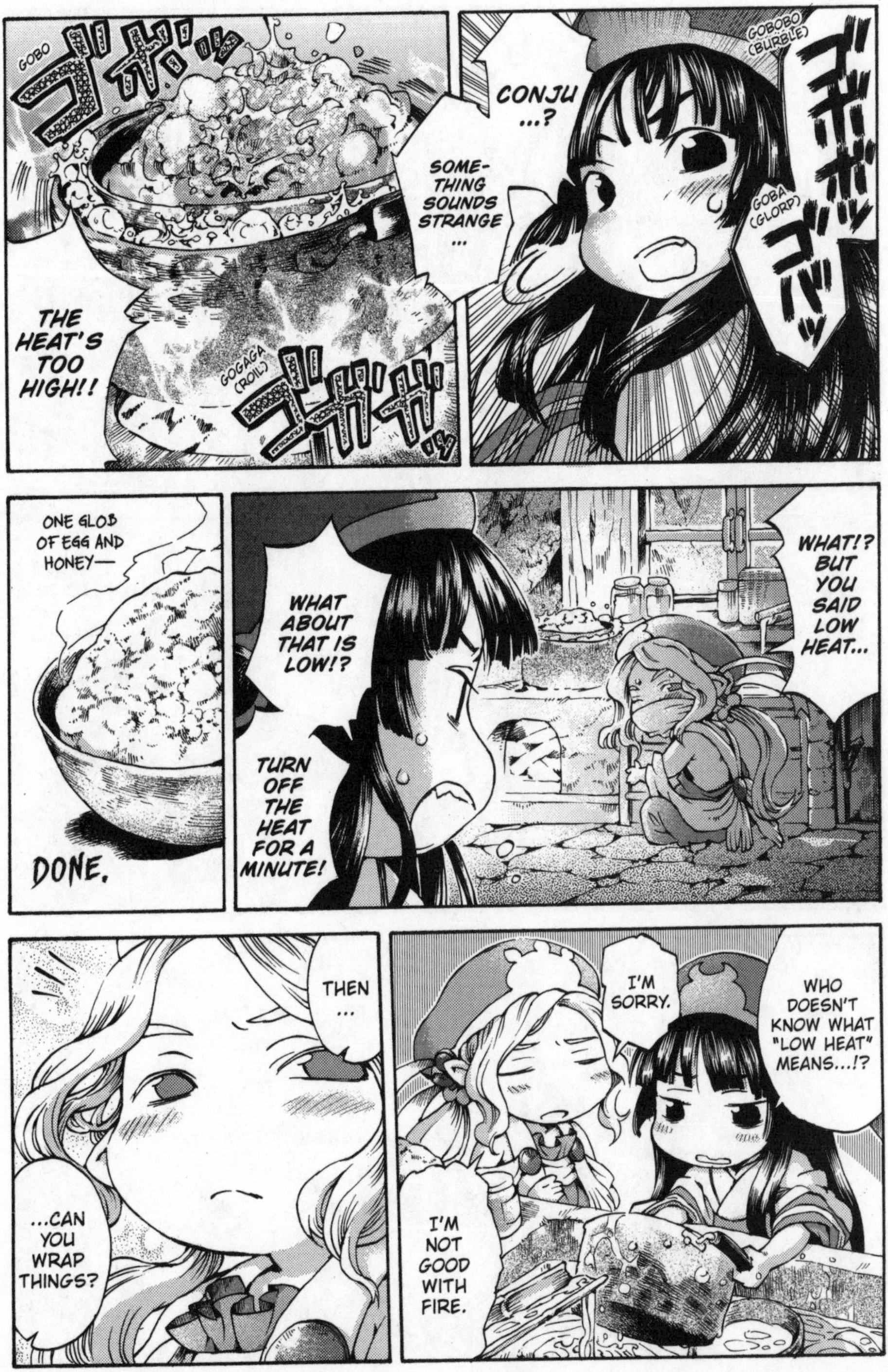
GOBOBO (BURBLE)
CONJU ...?
SOME-THING SOUNDS STRANGE ...
GOBA (GLORP)
GOBO
THE HEAT'S TOO HIGH!!
GOGAGA (ROIL)
WHAT!? BUT YOU SAID LOW HEAT...
WHAT ABOUT THAT IS LOW!?
TURN OFF THE HEAT FOR A MINUTE!
ONE GLOB OF EGG AND HONEY—
DONE.
WHO DOESN'T KNOW WHAT "LOW HEAT" MEANS...!?
I'M SORRY.
I'M NOT GOOD WITH FIRE.
THEN ...
...CAN YOU WRAP THINGS?

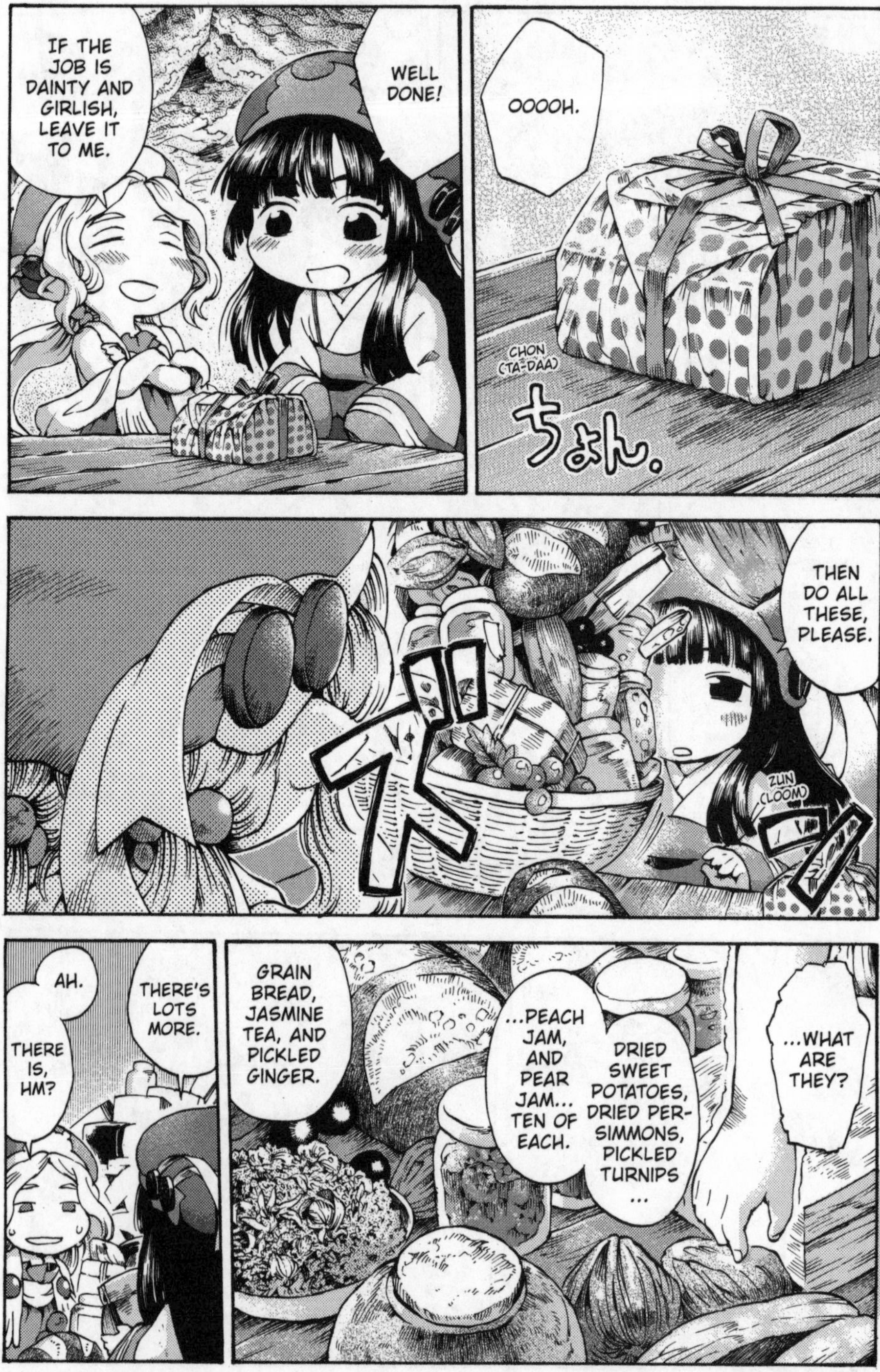
OOOOH.
CHON (TA-DAA)
ちょん。
WELL DONE!
IF THE JOB IS DAINTY AND GIRLISH, LEAVE IT TO ME.
THEN DO ALL THESE, PLEASE.
ZUN (LOOM)
...WHAT ARE THEY?
DRIED SWEET POTATOES, DRIED PER-SIMMONS, PICKLED TURNIPS ...
...PEACH JAM, AND PEAR JAM... TEN OF EACH.
GRAIN BREAD, JASMINE TEA, AND PICKLED GINGER.
THERE'S LOTS MORE.
AH.
THERE IS, HM?

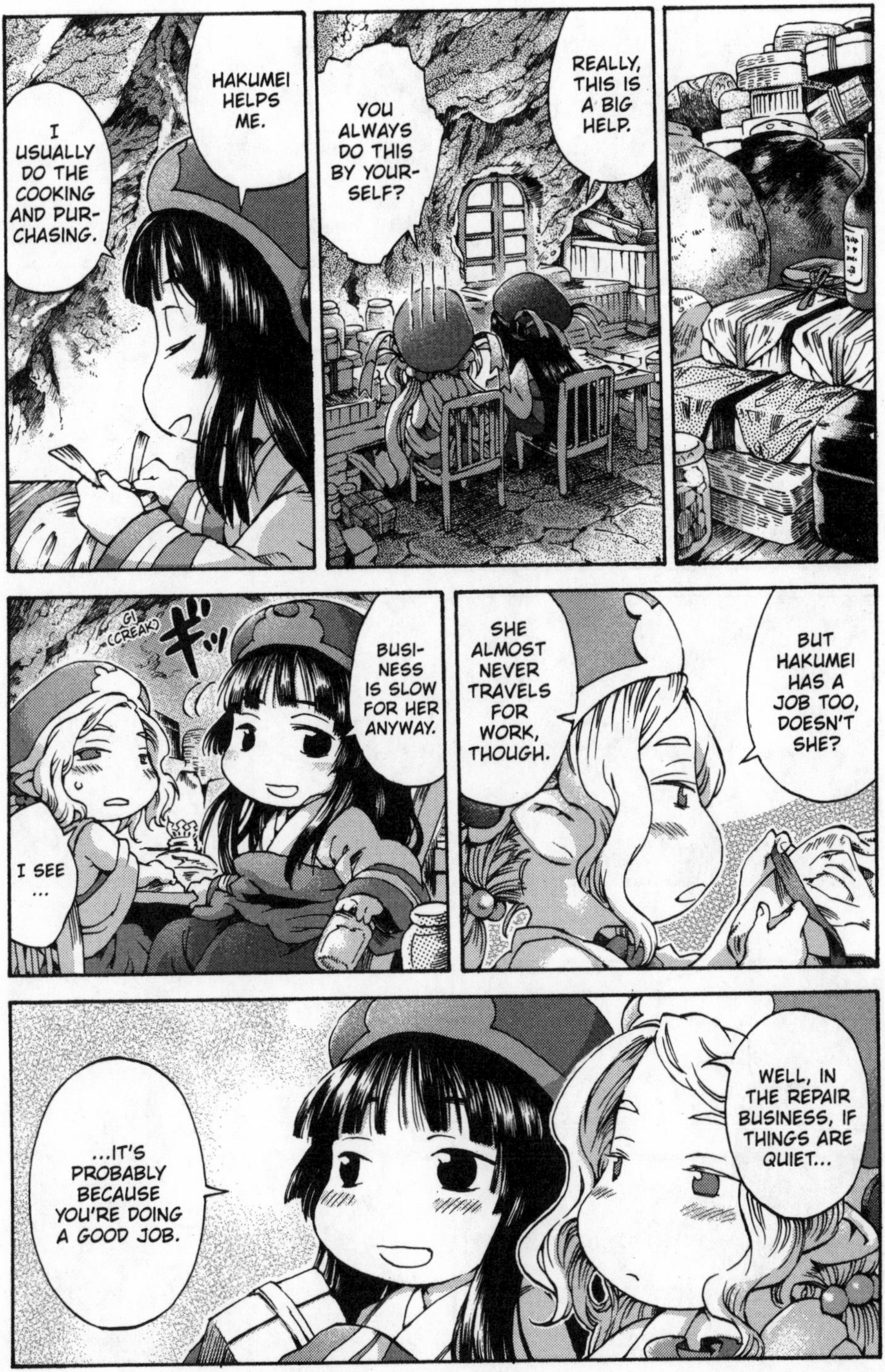
REALLY, THIS IS A BIG HELP.
YOU ALWAYS DO THIS BY YOUR-SELF?
HAKUMEI HELPS ME.
I USUALLY DO THE COOKING AND PUR-CHASING.
BUT HAKUMEI HAS A JOB TOO, DOESN'T SHE?
SHE ALMOST NEVER TRAVELS FOR WORK, THOUGH.
BUSI-NESS IS SLOW FOR HER ANYWAY.
ギッ
GI (CREAK)
I SEE ...
WELL, IN THE REPAIR BUSINESS, IF THINGS ARE QUIET...
...IT'S PROBABLY BECAUSE YOU'RE DOING A GOOD JOB.

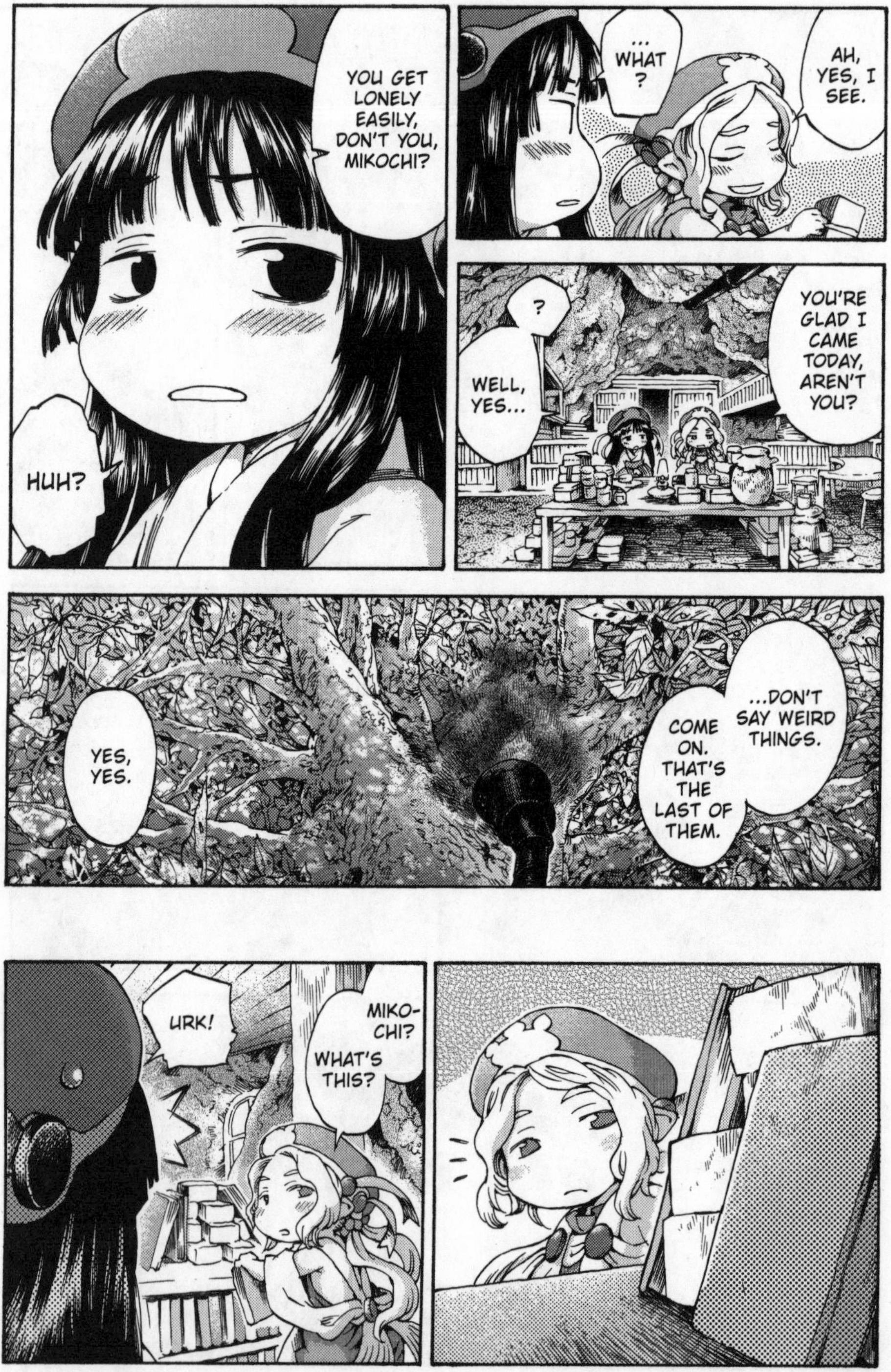
AH, YES, I SEE.
... WHAT ?
YOU'RE GLAD I CAME TODAY, AREN'T YOU?
?
WELL, YES...
YOU GET LONELY EASILY, DON'T YOU, MIKOCHI?
HUH?
...DON'T SAY WEIRD THINGS.
COME ON. THAT'S THE LAST OF THEM.
YES, YES.
MIKO-CHI?
WHAT'S THIS?
URK!

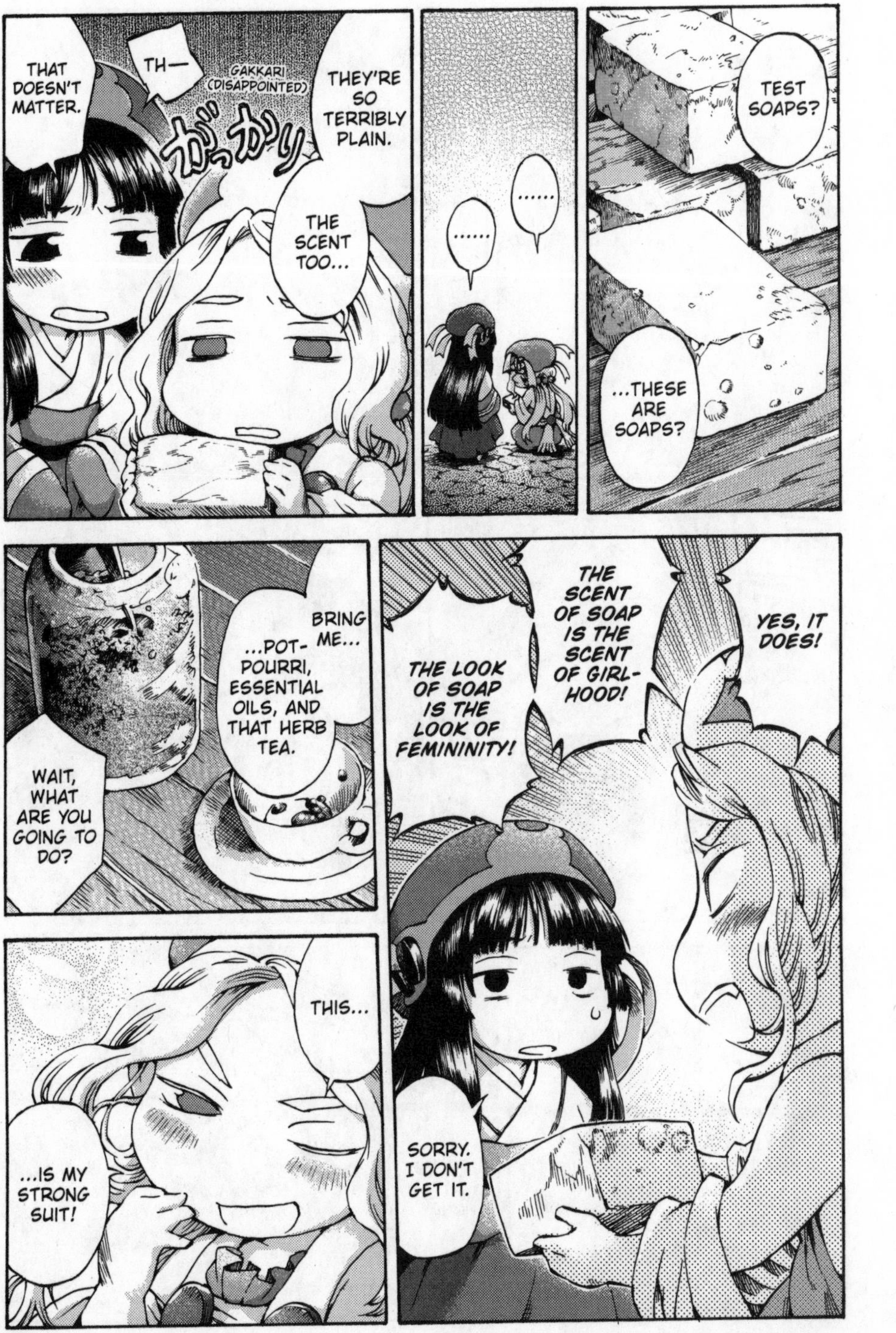
TEST SOAPS?
...THESE ARE SOAPS?
......
......
THEY'RE SO TERRIBLY PLAIN.
THE SCENT TOO...
GAKKARI (DISAPPOINTED)
がっかり
TH—
THAT DOESN'T MATTER.
YES, IT DOES!
THE SCENT OF SOAP IS THE SCENT OF GIRL-HOOD!
THE LOOK OF SOAP IS THE LOOK OF FEMININITY!
SORRY. I DON'T GET IT.
BRING ME...
...POT-POURRI, ESSENTIAL OILS, AND THAT HERB TEA.
WAIT, WHAT ARE YOU GOING TO DO?
THIS...
...IS MY STRONG SUIT!

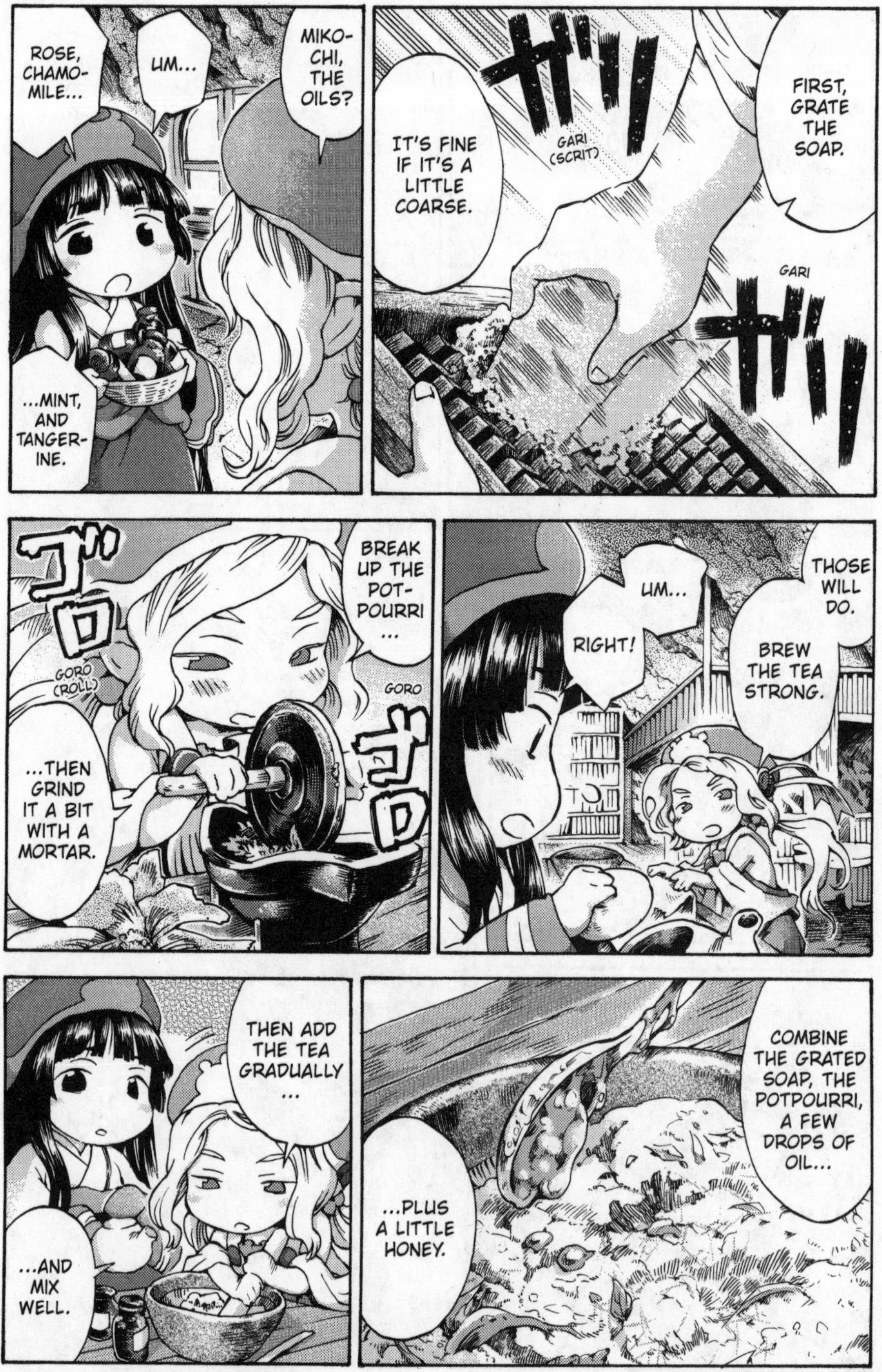
FIRST, GRATE THE SOAP.
GARI (SCRIT)
IT'S FINE IF IT'S A LITTLE COARSE.
GARI
MIKO-CHI, THE OILS?
UM...
ROSE, CHAMO-MILE...
...MINT, AND TANGER-INE.
THOSE WILL DO.
BREW THE TEA STRONG.
UM...
RIGHT!
BREAK UP THE POT-POURRI ...
GORO
GORO (ROLL)
...THEN GRIND IT A BIT WITH A MORTAR.
COMBINE THE GRATED SOAP, THE POTPOURRI, A FEW DROPS OF OIL...
...PLUS A LITTLE HONEY.
THEN ADD THE TEA GRADUALLY ...
...AND MIX WELL.

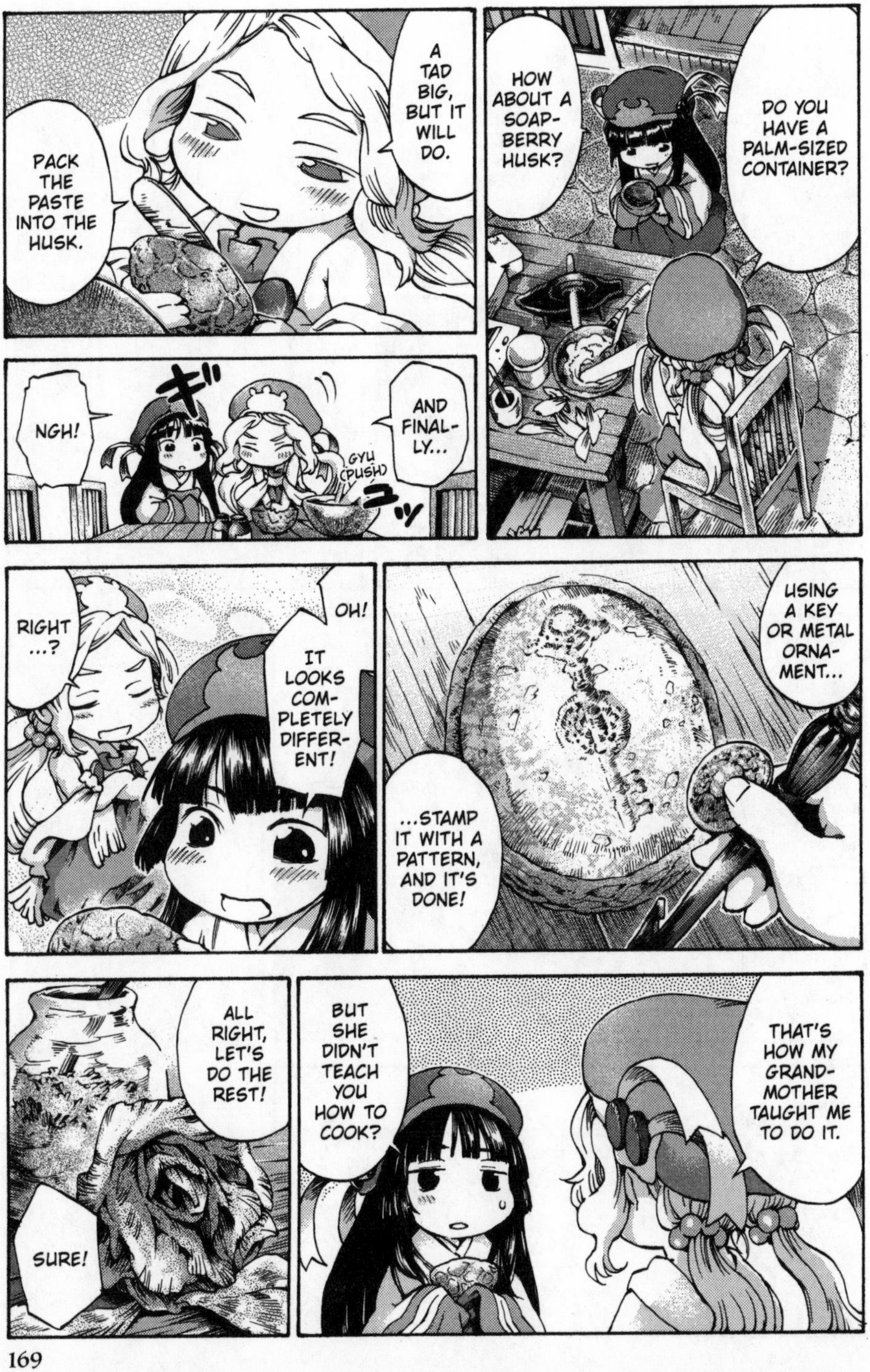
DO YOU HAVE A PALM-SIZED CONTAINER?
HOW ABOUT A SOAP-BERRY HUSK?
A TAD BIG, BUT IT WILL DO.
PACK THE PASTE INTO THE HUSK.
AND FINAL-LY...
GYU (PUSH)
NGH!
USING A KEY OR METAL ORNA-MENT...
...STAMP IT WITH A PATTERN, AND IT'S DONE!
OH!
IT LOOKS COM-PLETELY DIFFER-ENT!
RIGHT ...?
THAT'S HOW MY GRAND-MOTHER TAUGHT ME TO DO IT.
BUT SHE DIDN'T TEACH YOU HOW TO COOK?
ALL RIGHT, LET'S DO THE REST!
SURE!

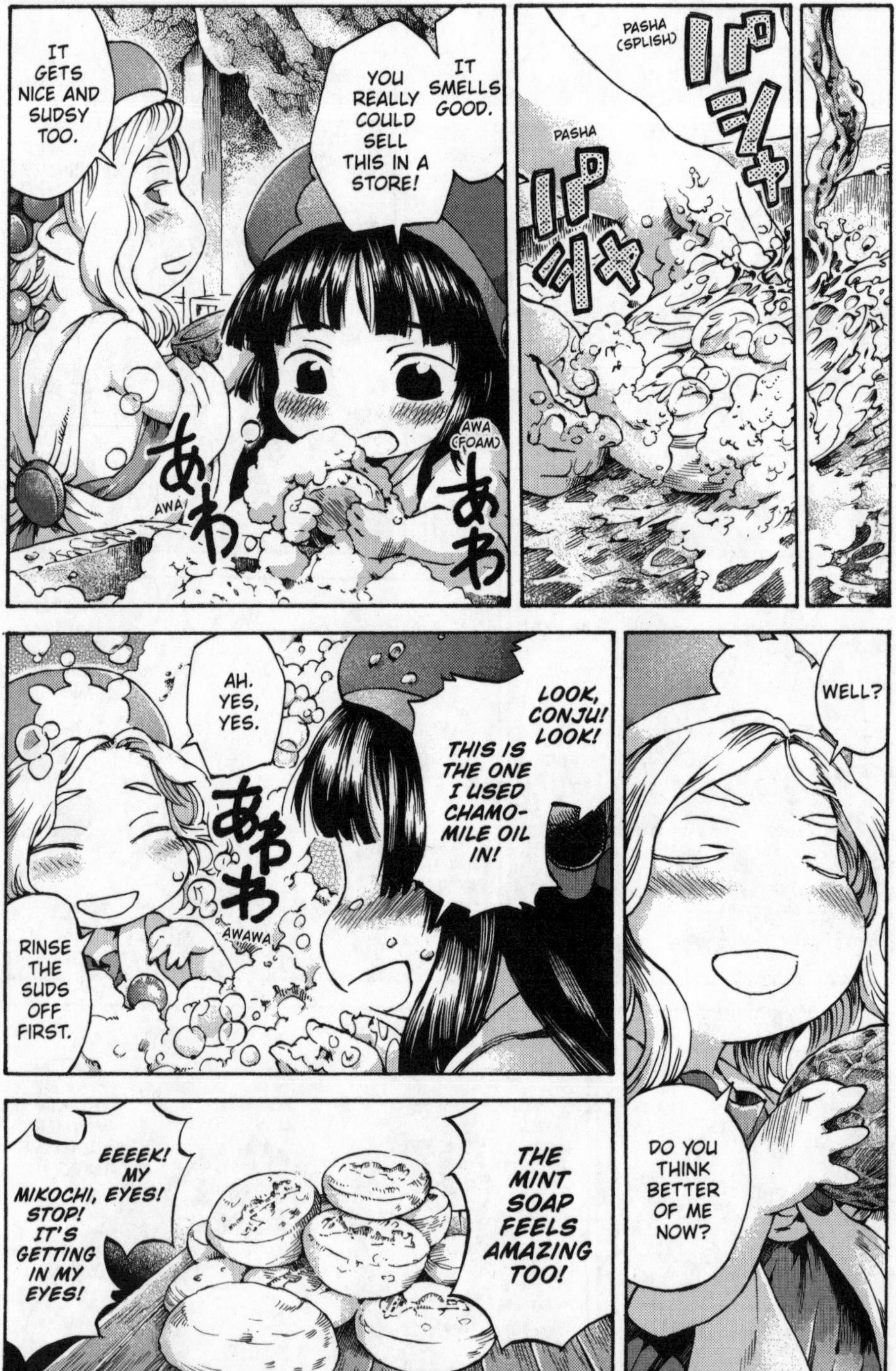
PASHA (SPLISH)
パシャ
PASHA
パシャ
IT SMELLS GOOD.
YOU REALLY COULD SELL THIS IN A STORE!
IT GETS NICE AND SUDSY TOO.
AWA (FOAM)
あわ
AWA
あわ
WELL?
DO YOU THINK BETTER OF ME NOW?
LOOK, CONJU! LOOK!
THIS IS THE ONE I USED CHAMOMILE OIL IN!
AH. YES, YES.
あわわ
AWAWA
RINSE THE SUDS OFF FIRST.
THE MINT SOAP FEELS AMAZING TOO!
EEEEK! MY EYES!
MIKOCHI, STOP! IT'S GETTING IN MY EYES!

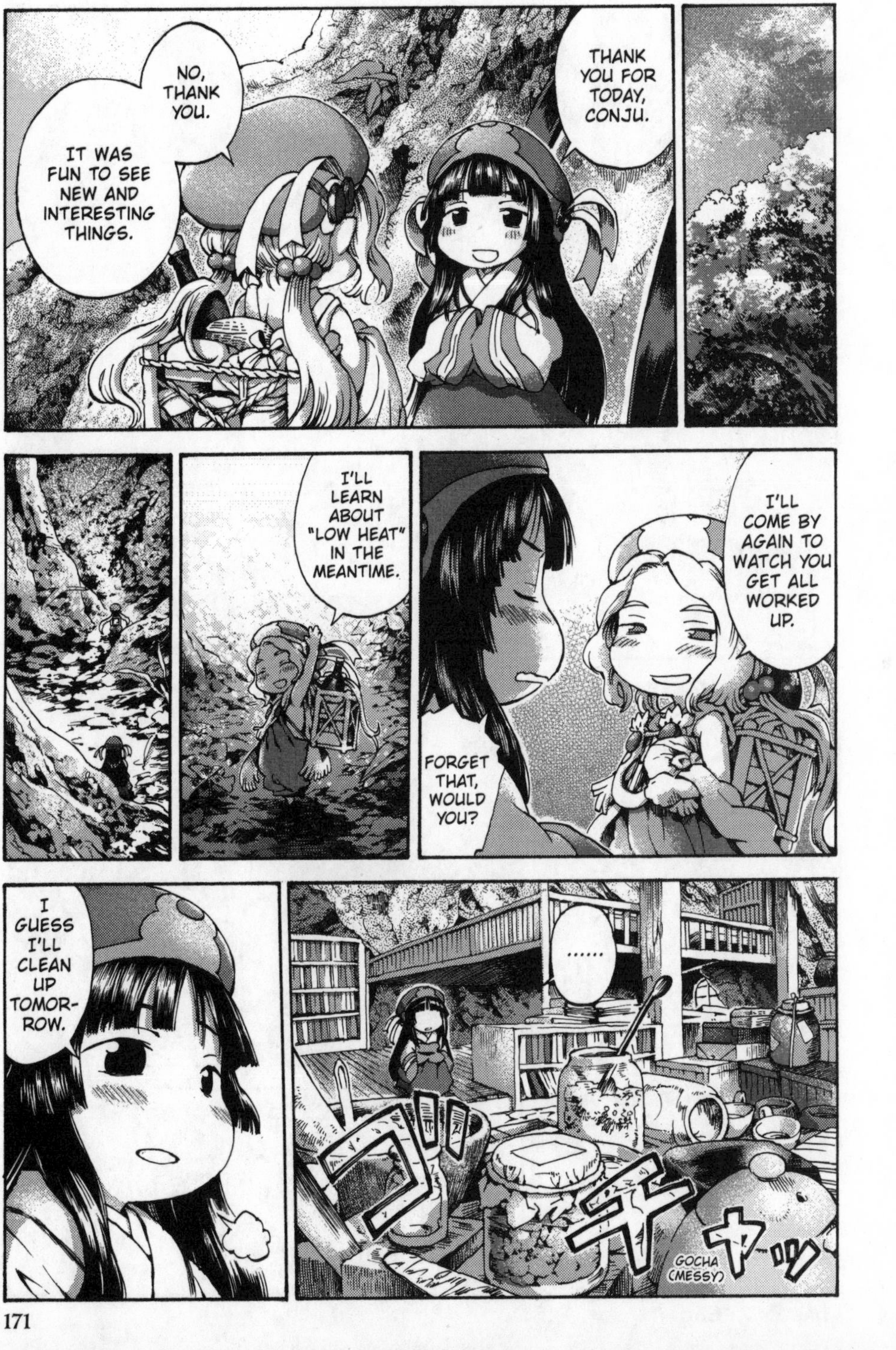
THANK YOU FOR TODAY, CONJU.
NO, THANK YOU.
IT WAS FUN TO SEE NEW AND INTERESTING THINGS.
I'LL COME BY AGAIN TO WATCH YOU GET ALL WORKED UP.
FORGET THAT, WOULD YOU?
I'LL LEARN ABOUT "LOW HEAT" IN THE MEANTIME.
......
GOCHA (MESSY)
I GUESS I'LL CLEAN UP TOMOR-ROW.

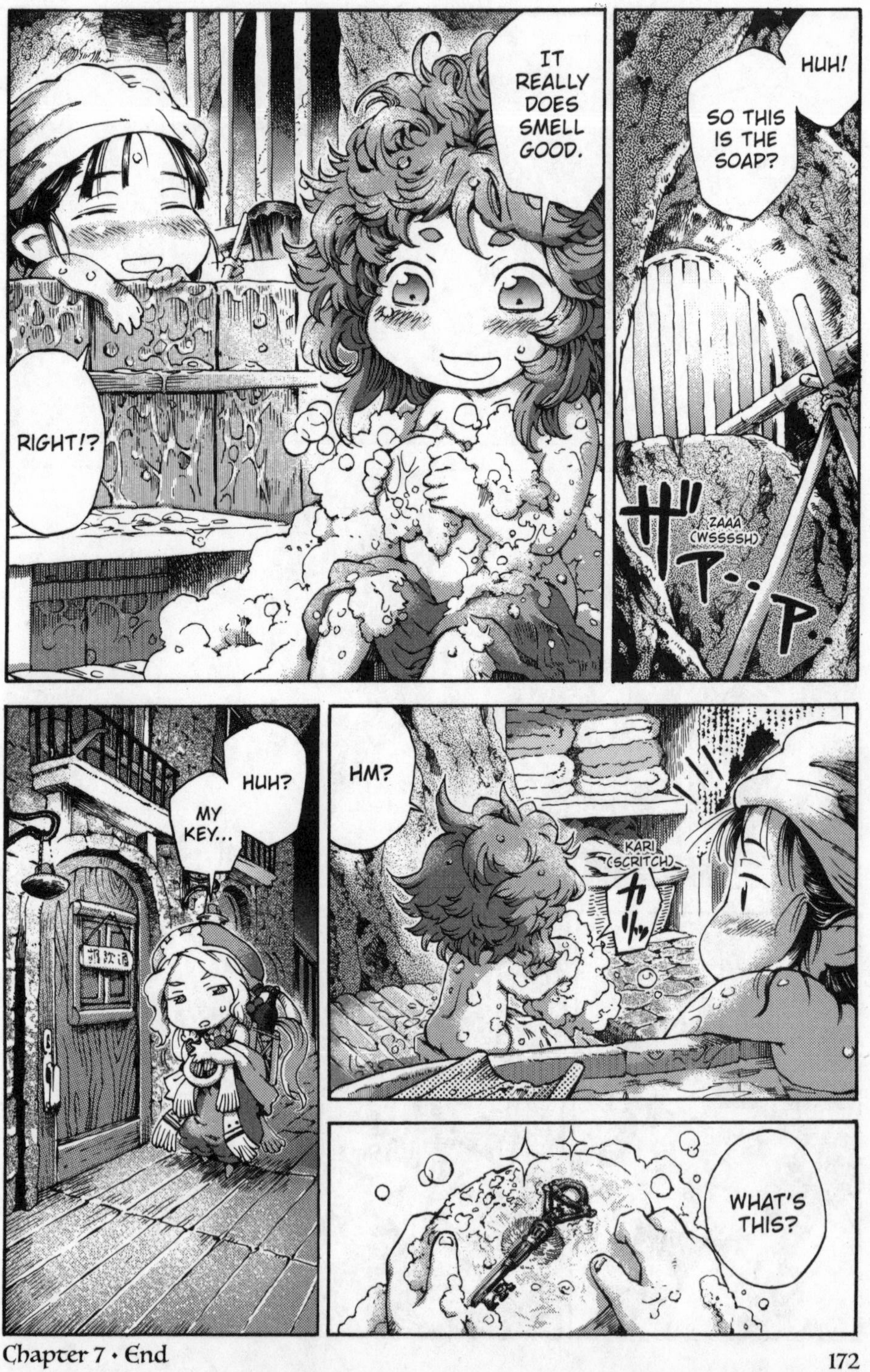
HUH!
SO THIS IS THE SOAP?
ZAAA (WSSSSH)
IT REALLY DOES SMELL GOOD.
RIGHT!?
HM?
KARI (SCRITCH)
WHAT'S THIS?
HUH?
MY KEY...

Chapter 7 • End

SHE SPENT THE NIGHT AT HER NEIGHBOR'S.

"Listen. I don't mind you staying here for the night, but…"

"Hmmmm?"

"Showing up out of the blue to monopolize my bed like this takes some nerve."

"It's an awfully firm bed, isn't it…?"

"Also, sleeping in the nude in someone else's room with no hesitation is really questionable."

"I can't sleep…in my clothes…Zzz…"

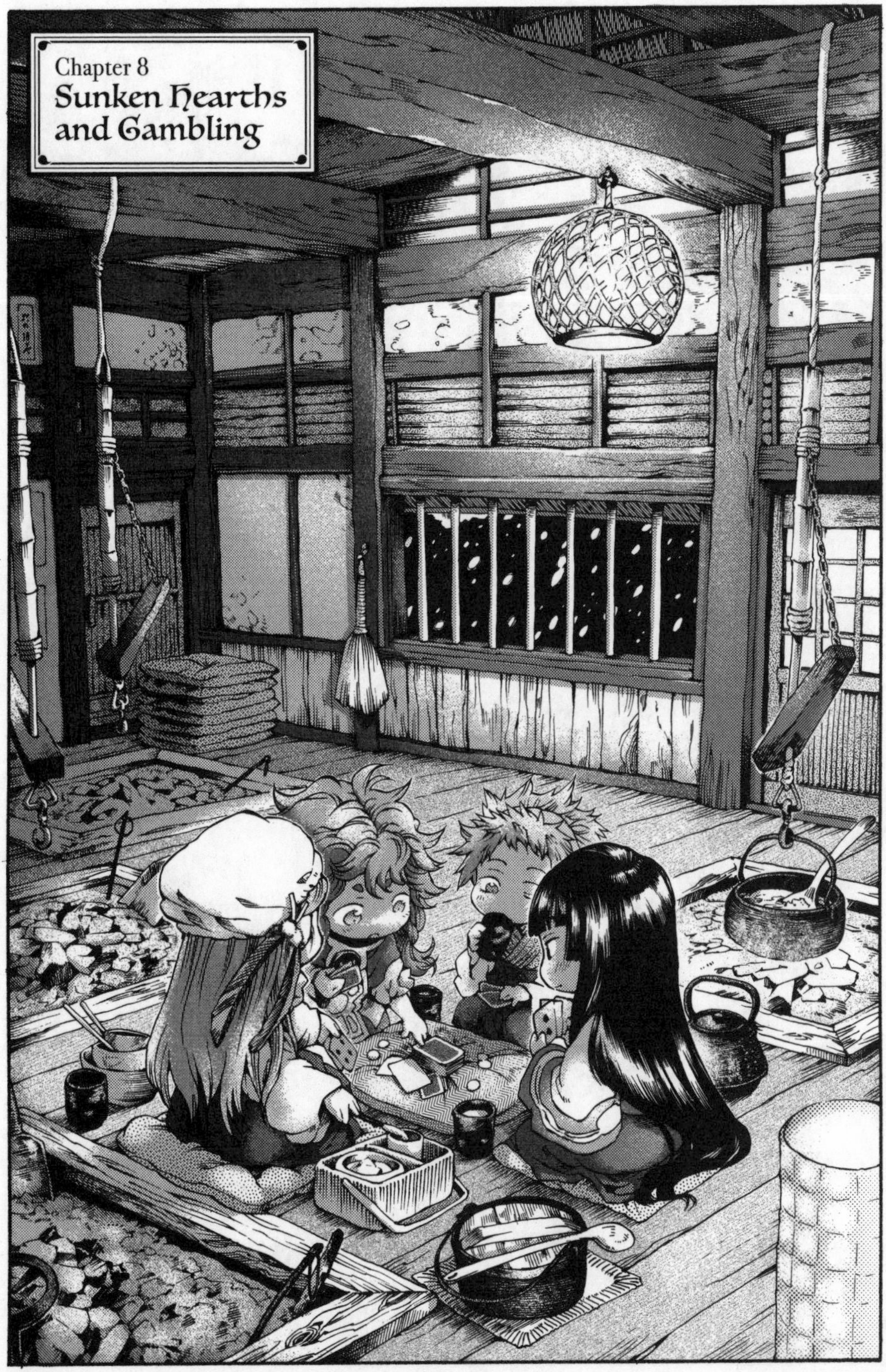
Chapter 8
Sunken Hearths and Gambling

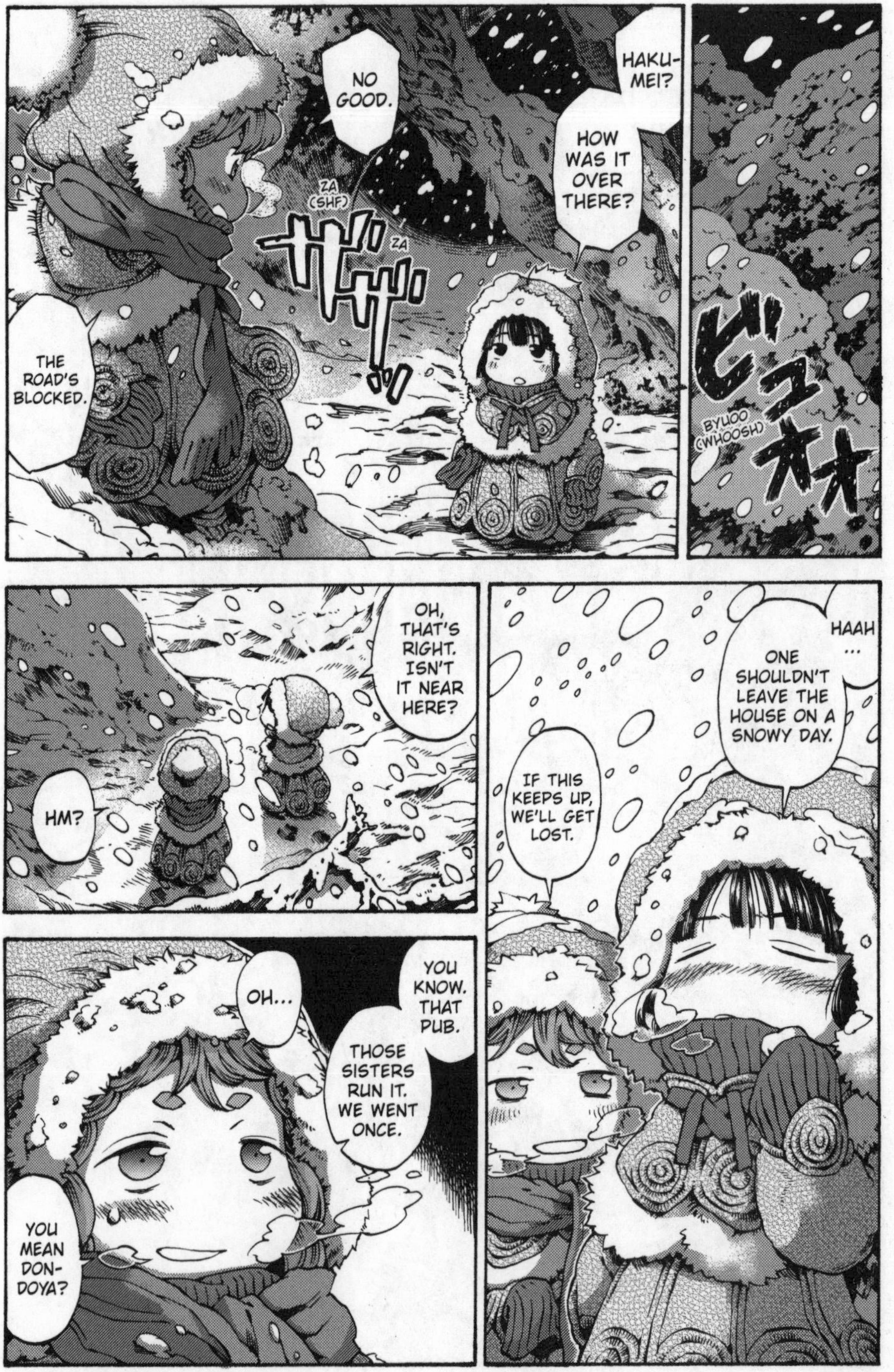
BYUOO (WHOOSH)
HAKU-MEI?
HOW WAS IT OVER THERE?
NO GOOD.
ZA (SHF) ZA
THE ROAD'S BLOCKED.
HAAH...
ONE SHOULDN'T LEAVE THE HOUSE ON A SNOWY DAY.
IF THIS KEEPS UP, WE'LL GET LOST.
OH, THAT'S RIGHT. ISN'T IT NEAR HERE?
HM?
YOU KNOW. THAT PUB.
THOSE SISTERS RUN IT. WE WENT ONCE.
OH...
YOU MEAN DON-DOYA?

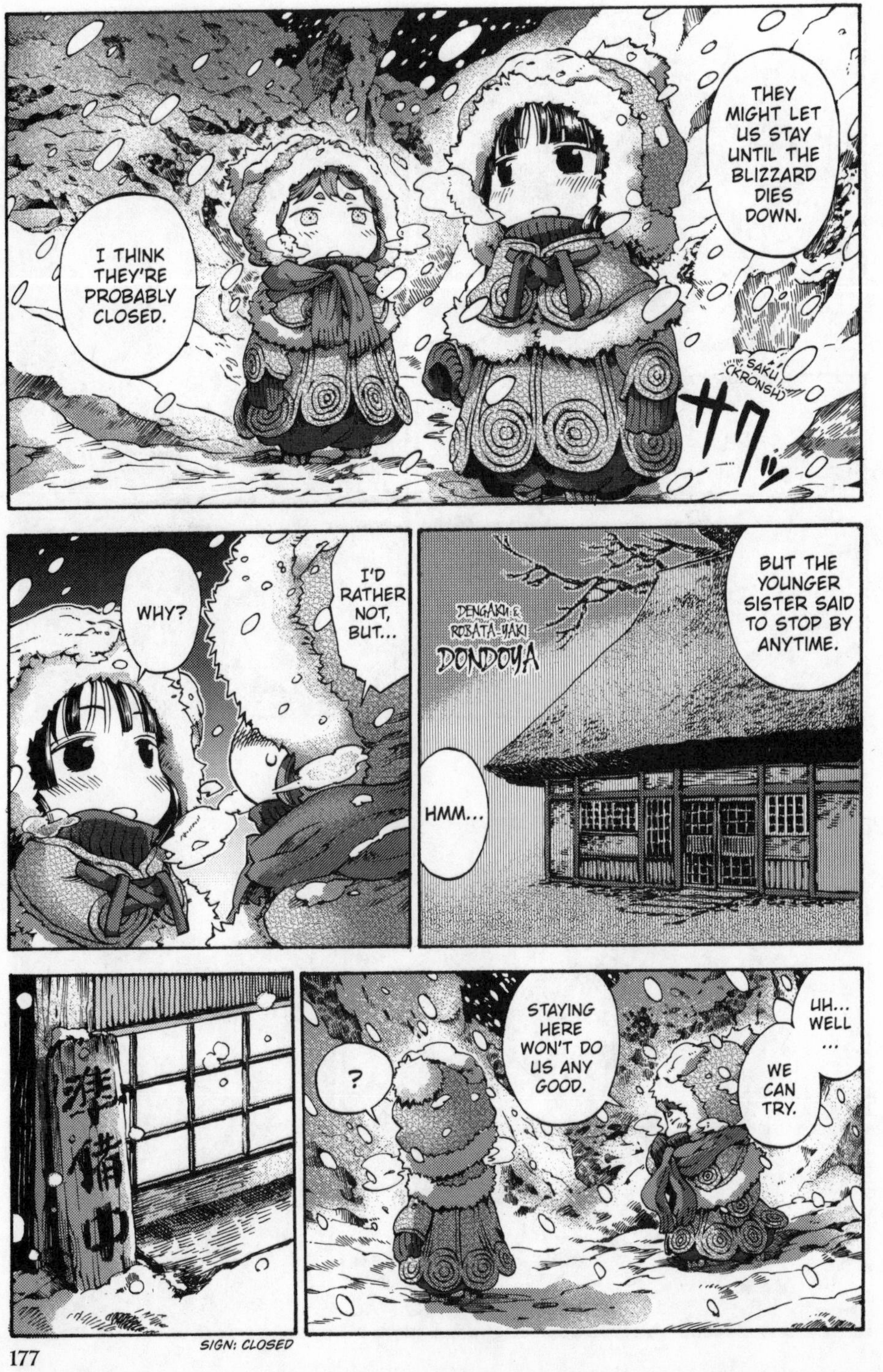
THEY MIGHT LET US STAY UNTIL THE BLIZZARD DIES DOWN.
I THINK THEY'RE PROBABLY CLOSED.
SAKU (KRONSH)
サクッ
BUT THE YOUNGER SISTER SAID TO STOP BY ANYTIME.
DENGAKU & ROBATA-YAKI
DONDOYA
HMM...
I'D RATHER NOT, BUT...
WHY?
UH... WELL ...
WE CAN TRY.
STAYING HERE WON'T DO US ANY GOOD.
?
準備中

SIGN: CLOSED

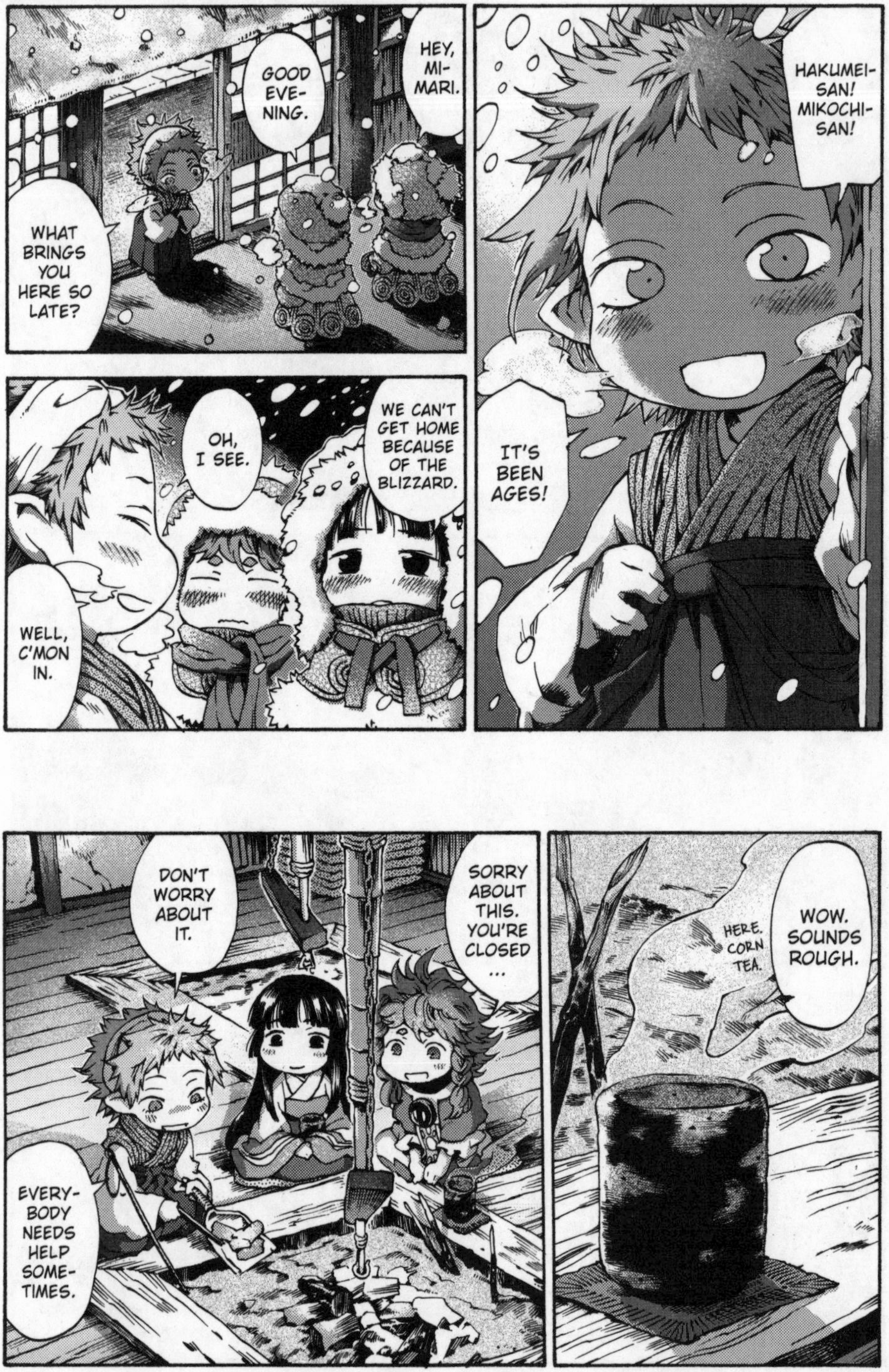
HAKUMEI-SAN! MIKOCHI-SAN!
IT'S BEEN AGES!
HEY, MI-MARI.
GOOD EVE-NING.
WHAT BRINGS YOU HERE SO LATE?
WE CAN'T GET HOME BECAUSE OF THE BLIZZARD.
OH, I SEE.
WELL, C'MON IN.
WOW. SOUNDS ROUGH.
HERE. CORN TEA.
SORRY ABOUT THIS. YOU'RE CLOSED ...
DON'T WORRY ABOUT IT.
EVERY-BODY NEEDS HELP SOME-TIMES.

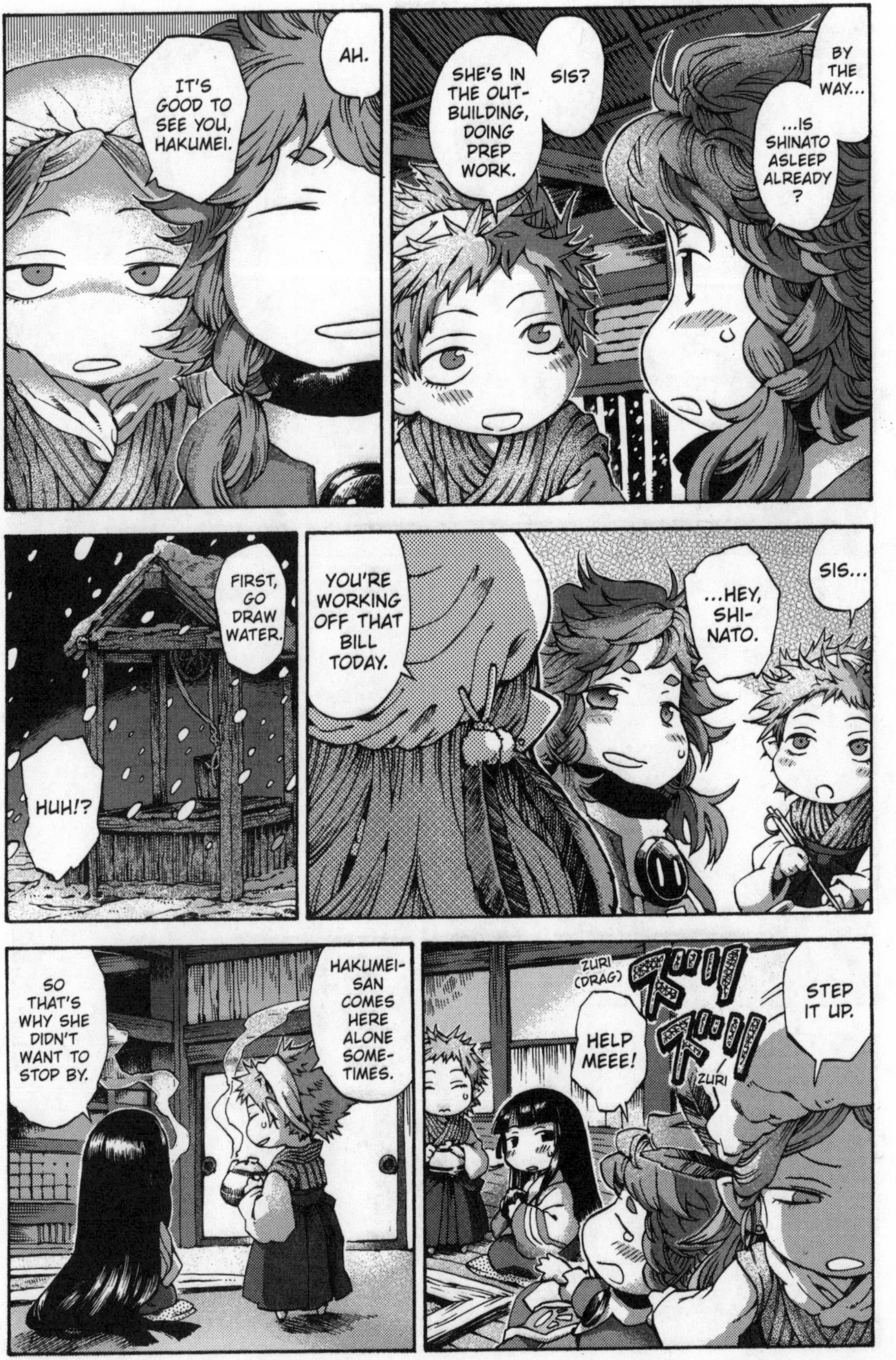
BY THE WAY...
...IS SHINATO ASLEEP ALREADY?
SIS?
SHE'S IN THE OUT-BUILDING, DOING PREP WORK.
AH.
IT'S GOOD TO SEE YOU, HAKUMEI.
SIS...
...HEY, SHINATO.
YOU'RE WORKING OFF THAT BILL TODAY.
FIRST, GO DRAW WATER.
HUH!?
STEP IT UP.
ZURI (DRAG)
ZURI
HELP MEEE!
HAKUMEI-SAN COMES HERE ALONE SOMETIMES.
SO THAT'S WHY SHE DIDN'T WANT TO STOP BY.

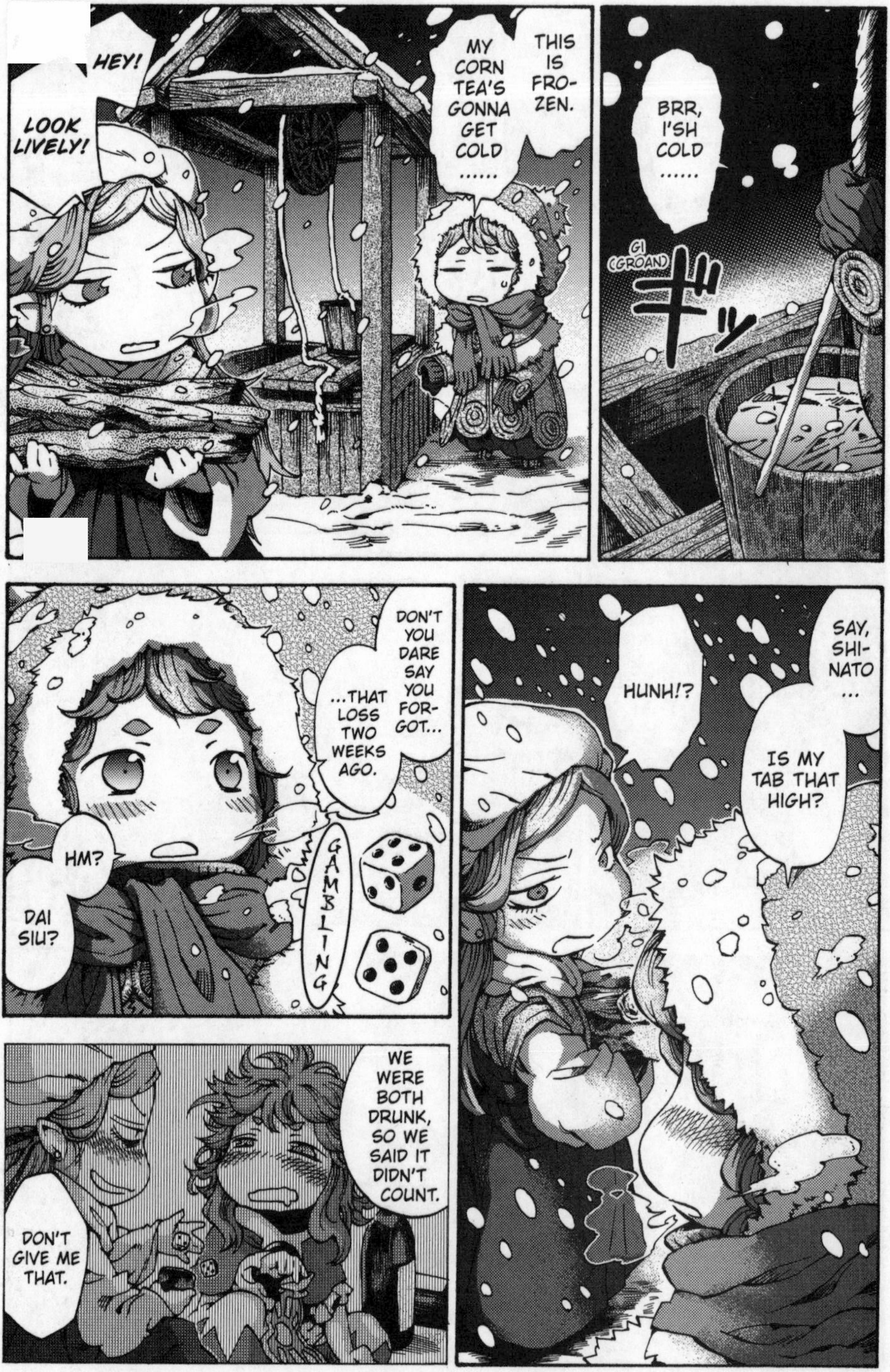
BRR, I'SH COLD ......
GI (GROAN)
ギッ
THIS IS FRO- ZEN.
MY CORN TEA'S GONNA GET COLD ......
HEY!
LOOK LIVELY!
SAY, SHI- NATO ...
IS MY TAB THAT HIGH?
HUNH!?
DON'T YOU DARE SAY YOU FOR- GOT...
...THAT LOSS TWO WEEKS AGO.
GAMBLING
HM?
DAI SIU?
WE WERE BOTH DRUNK, SO WE SAID IT DIDN'T COUNT.
DON'T GIVE ME THAT.

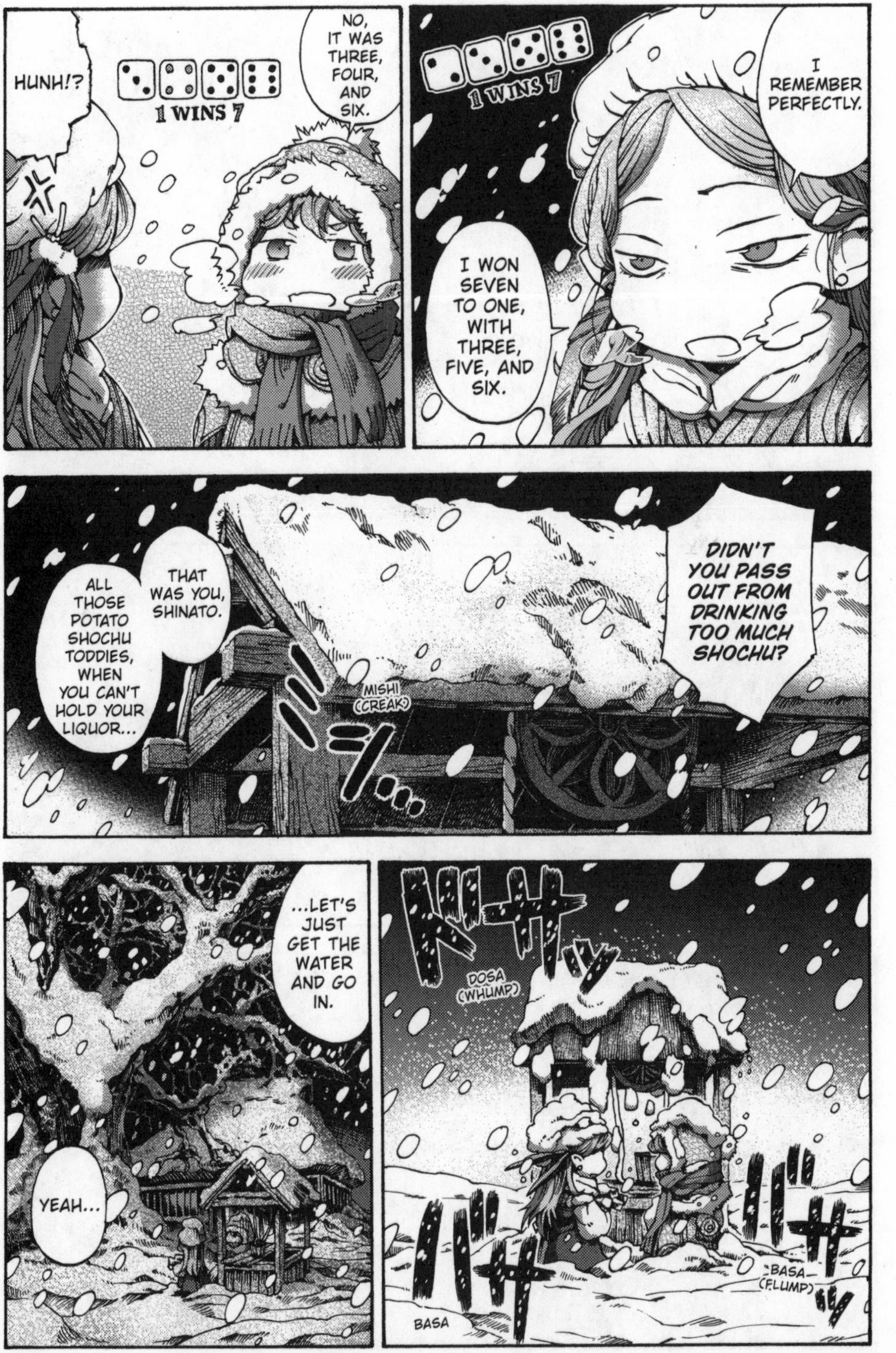
I REMEMBER PERFECTLY.
1 WINS 7
I WON SEVEN TO ONE, WITH THREE, FIVE, AND SIX.
NO, IT WAS THREE, FOUR, AND SIX.
1 WINS 7
HUNH!?
DIDN'T YOU PASS OUT FROM DRINKING TOO MUCH SHOCHU?
THAT WAS YOU, SHINATO.
ALL THOSE POTATO SHOCHU TODDIES, WHEN YOU CAN'T HOLD YOUR LIQUOR...
MISHI (CREAK)
DOSA (WHUMP)
BASA (FLUMP)
BASA
...LET'S JUST GET THE WATER AND GO IN.
YEAH...

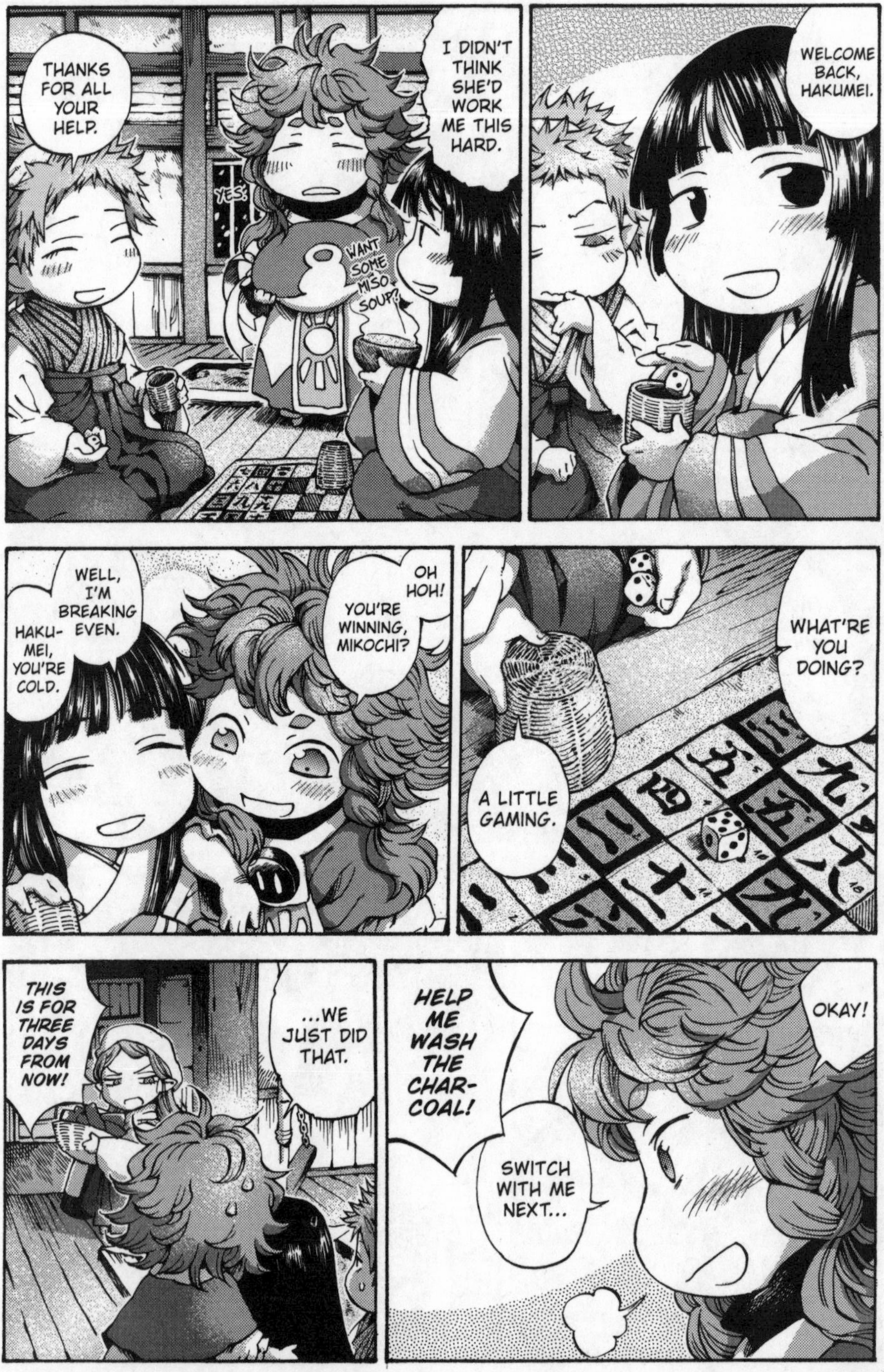
WELCOME BACK, HAKUMEI.
I DIDN'T THINK SHE'D WORK ME THIS HARD.
THANKS FOR ALL YOUR HELP.
YES.
WANT SOME MISO SOUP?
WHAT'RE YOU DOING?
A LITTLE GAMING.
OH HOH! YOU'RE WINNING, MIKOCHI?
WELL, I'M BREAKING EVEN.
HAKUMEI, YOU'RE COLD.
OKAY!
HELP ME WASH THE CHARCOAL!
SWITCH WITH ME NEXT...
...WE JUST DID THAT.
THIS IS FOR THREE DAYS FROM NOW!

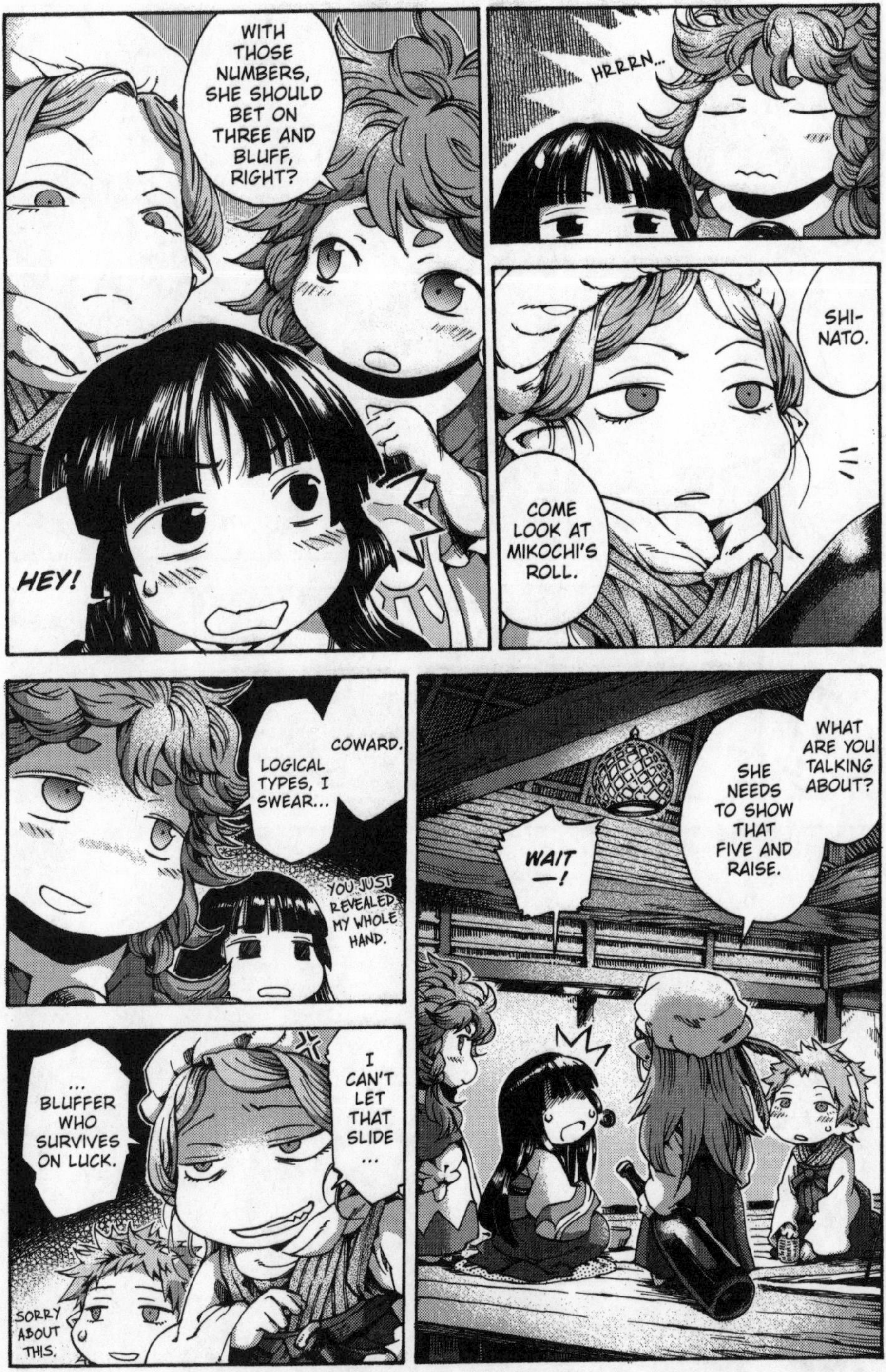
WITH THOSE NUMBERS, SHE SHOULD BET ON THREE AND BLUFF, RIGHT?
HEY!
HRRRN...
SHI-NATO.
COME LOOK AT MIKOCHI'S ROLL.
COWARD.
LOGICAL TYPES, I SWEAR...
YOU JUST REVEALED MY WHOLE HAND.
...BLUFFER WHO SURVIVES ON LUCK.
I CAN'T LET THAT SLIDE...
SORRY ABOUT THIS.
WHAT ARE YOU TALKING ABOUT?
SHE NEEDS TO SHOW THAT FIVE AND RAISE.
WAIT—!

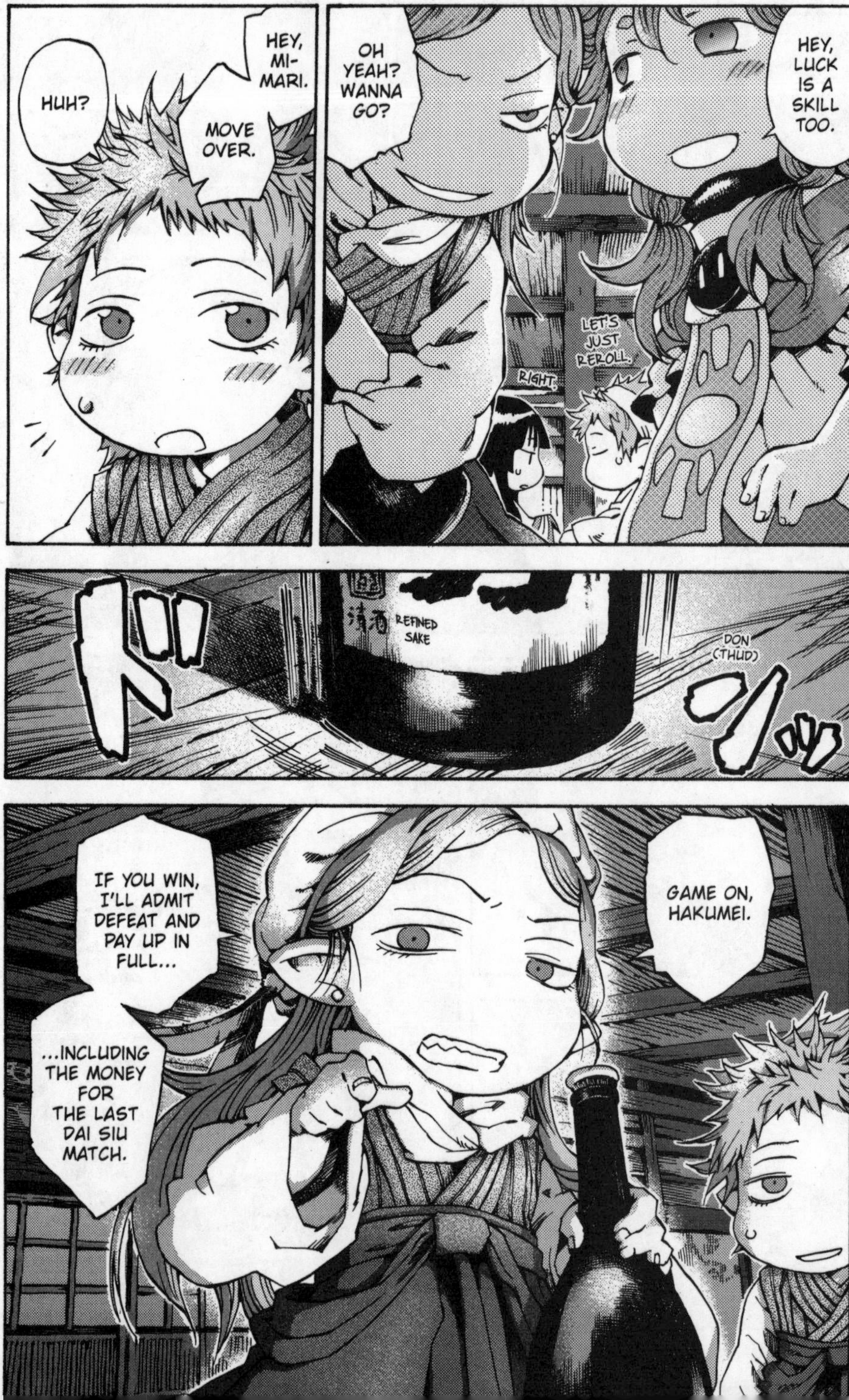
HEY, LUCK IS A SKILL TOO.
OH YEAH? WANNA GO?
LET'S JUST REROLL.
RIGHT.
HEY, MI-MARI.
MOVE OVER.
HUH?
REFINED SAKE
DON (THUD)
GAME ON, HAKUMEI.
IF YOU WIN, I'LL ADMIT DEFEAT AND PAY UP IN FULL...
...INCLUDING THE MONEY FOR THE LAST DAI SIU MATCH.

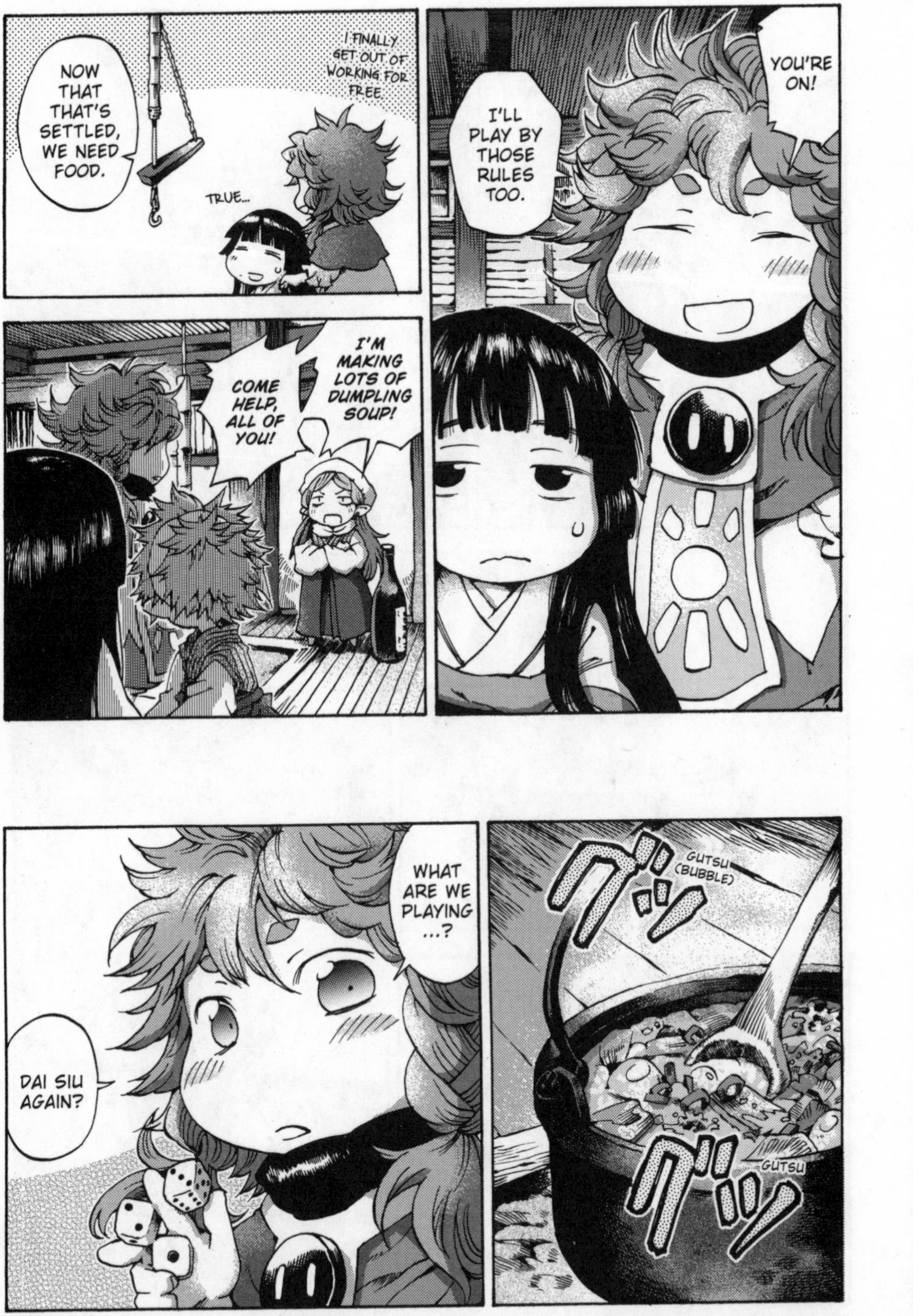
I'LL PLAY BY THOSE RULES TOO.
YOU'RE ON!
NOW THAT THAT'S SETTLED, WE NEED FOOD.
I FINALLY GET OUT OF WORKING FOR FREE.
TRUE...
I'M MAKING LOTS OF DUMPLING SOUP!
COME HELP, ALL OF YOU!
GUTSU (BUBBLE)
GUTSU
WHAT ARE WE PLAYING ...?
DAI SIU AGAIN?

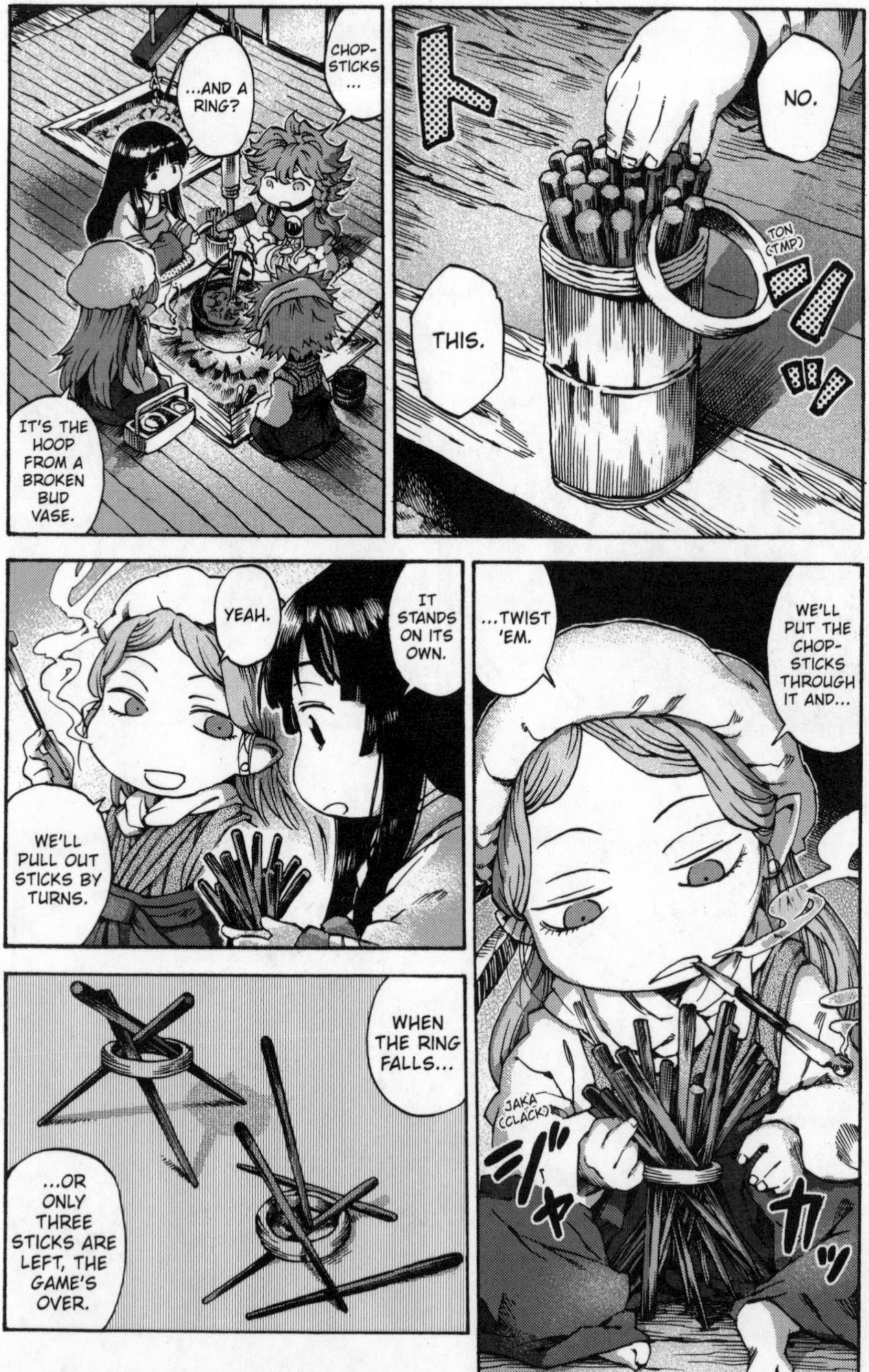
NO.
ト
TON (TMP)
THIS.
CHOP-STICKS...
...AND A RING?
IT'S THE HOOP FROM A BROKEN BUD VASE.
WE'LL PUT THE CHOP-STICKS THROUGH IT AND...
...TWIST 'EM.
JAKA (CLACK)
ジャ
カッ
IT STANDS ON ITS OWN.
YEAH.
WE'LL PULL OUT STICKS BY TURNS.
WHEN THE RING FALLS...
...OR ONLY THREE STICKS ARE LEFT, THE GAME'S OVER.

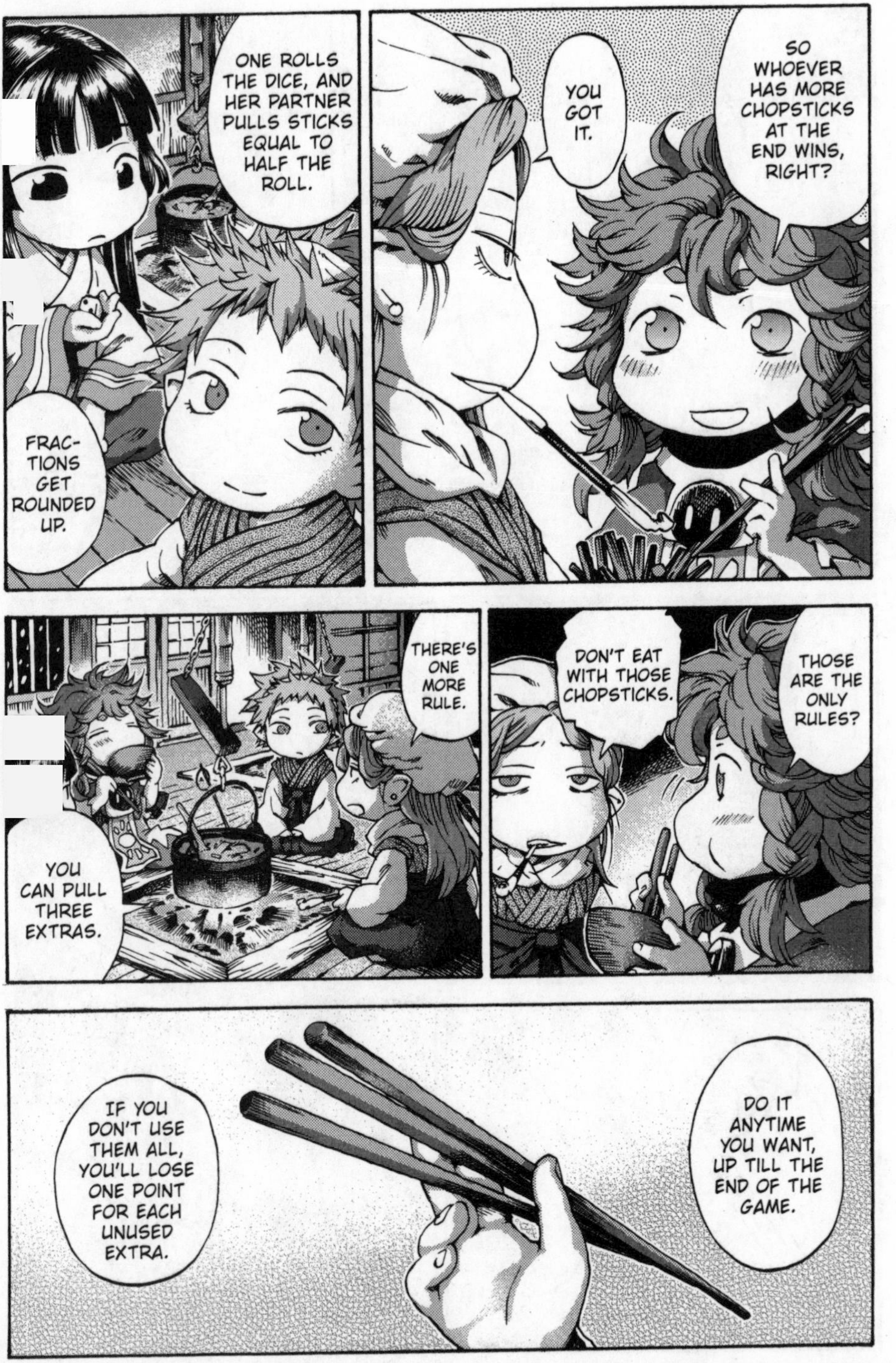
SO WHOEVER HAS MORE CHOPSTICKS AT THE END WINS, RIGHT?
YOU GOT IT.
ONE ROLLS THE DICE, AND HER PARTNER PULLS STICKS EQUAL TO HALF THE ROLL.
FRAC-TIONS GET ROUNDED UP.
THOSE ARE THE ONLY RULES?
DON'T EAT WITH THOSE CHOPSTICKS.
THERE'S ONE MORE RULE.
YOU CAN PULL THREE EXTRAS.
DO IT ANYTIME YOU WANT, UP TILL THE END OF THE GAME.
IF YOU DON'T USE THEM ALL, YOU'LL LOSE ONE POINT FOR EACH UNUSED EXTRA.

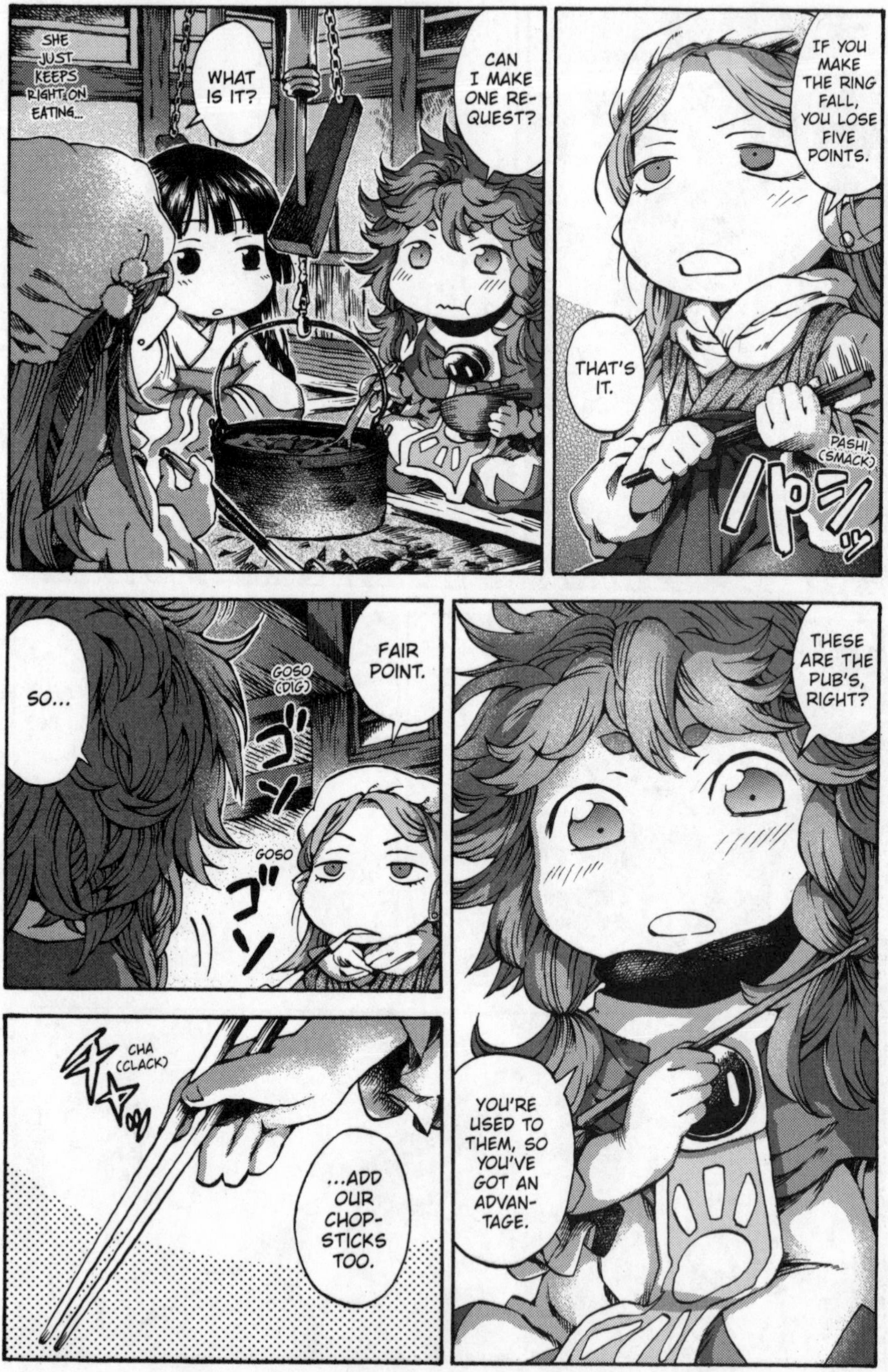
IF YOU MAKE THE RING FALL, YOU LOSE FIVE POINTS.
THAT'S IT.
PASHI (SMACK)
CAN I MAKE ONE RE-QUEST?
WHAT IS IT?
SHE JUST KEEPS RIGHT ON EATING...
THESE ARE THE PUB'S, RIGHT?
YOU'RE USED TO THEM, SO YOU'VE GOT AN ADVAN-TAGE.
FAIR POINT.
GOSO (DIG)
GOSO
SO...
...ADD OUR CHOP-STICKS TOO.
CHA (CLACK)

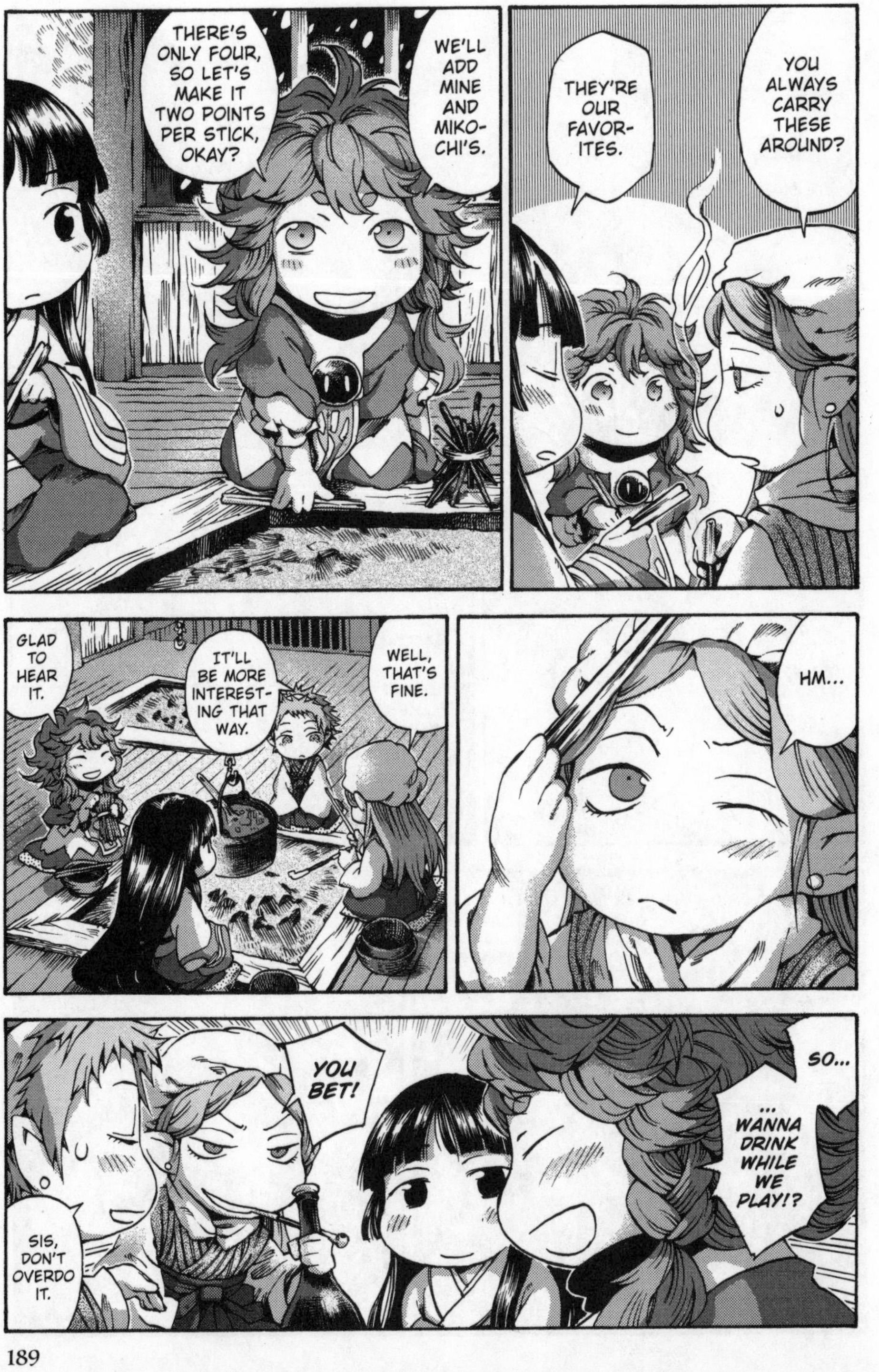
YOU ALWAYS CARRY THESE AROUND?
THEY'RE OUR FAVOR-ITES.
WE'LL ADD MINE AND MIKO-CHI'S.
THERE'S ONLY FOUR, SO LET'S MAKE IT TWO POINTS PER STICK, OKAY?
HM...
WELL, THAT'S FINE.
IT'LL BE MORE INTEREST-ING THAT WAY.
GLAD TO HEAR IT.
SO...
...WANNA DRINK WHILE WE PLAY!?
YOU BET!
SIS, DON'T OVERDO IT.

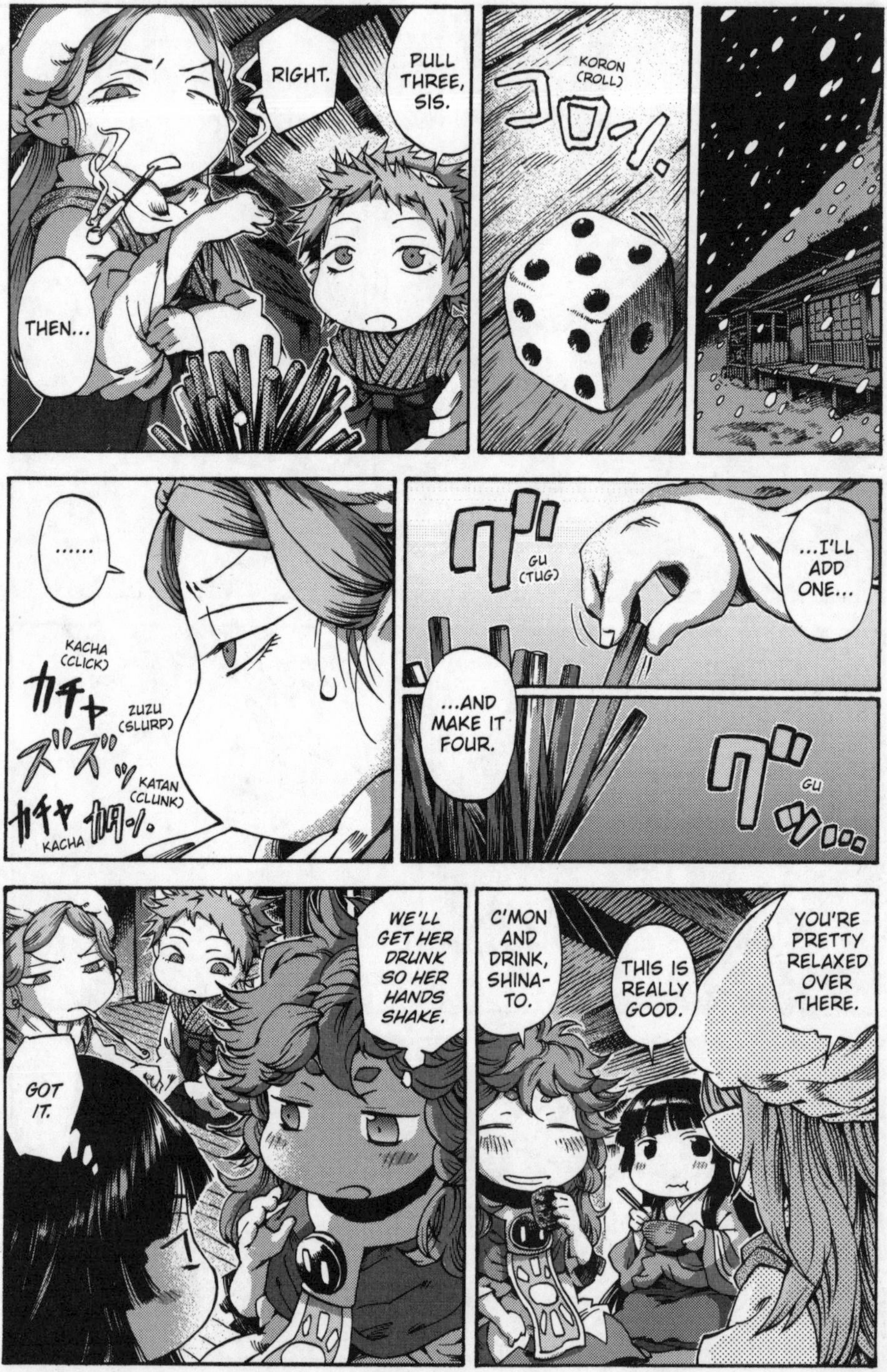
KORON (ROLL)
コロ～ン。
PULL THREE, SIS.
RIGHT.
THEN...
GU (TUG)
グ
...I'LL ADD ONE...
...AND MAKE IT FOUR.
グッ…
GU
......
KACHA (CLICK)
カチャ
ZUZU (SLURP)
ズズッ
KATAN (CLUNK)
カタ～ン。
カチャ
KACHA
YOU'RE PRETTY RELAXED OVER THERE.
THIS IS REALLY GOOD.
C'MON AND DRINK, SHINA-TO.
WE'LL GET HER DRUNK SO HER HANDS SHAKE.
GOT IT.

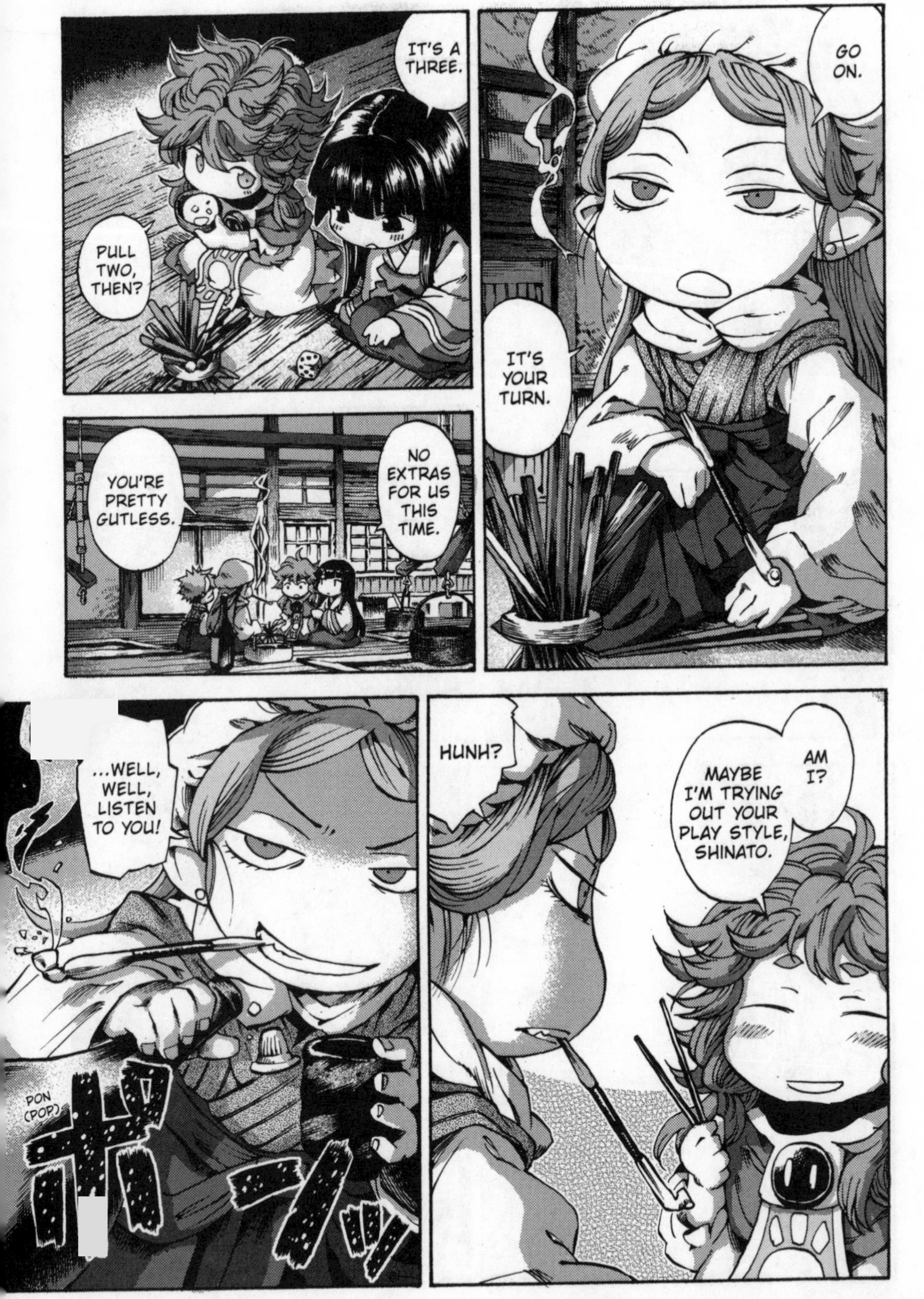
GO ON.
IT'S YOUR TURN.
IT'S A THREE.
PULL TWO, THEN?
NO EXTRAS FOR US THIS TIME.
YOU'RE PRETTY GUTLESS.
AM I?
MAYBE I'M TRYING OUT YOUR PLAY STYLE, SHINATO.
HUNH?
...WELL, WELL, LISTEN TO YOU!
PON (POP)

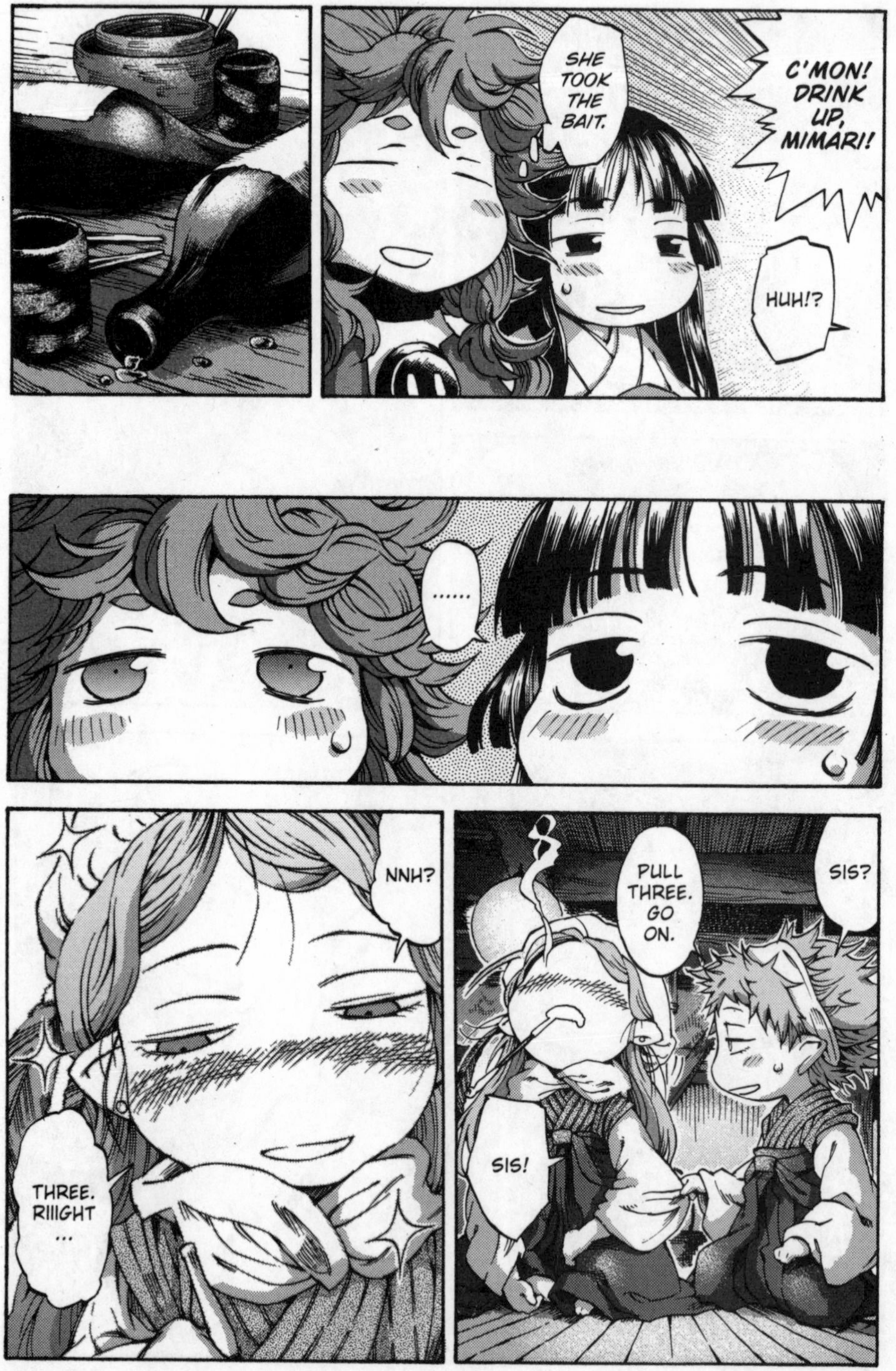
C'MON! DRINK UP, MIMARI!
SHE TOOK THE BAIT.
HUH!?
......
SIS?
PULL THREE. GO ON.
SIS!
NNH?
THREE. RIIIGHT ...

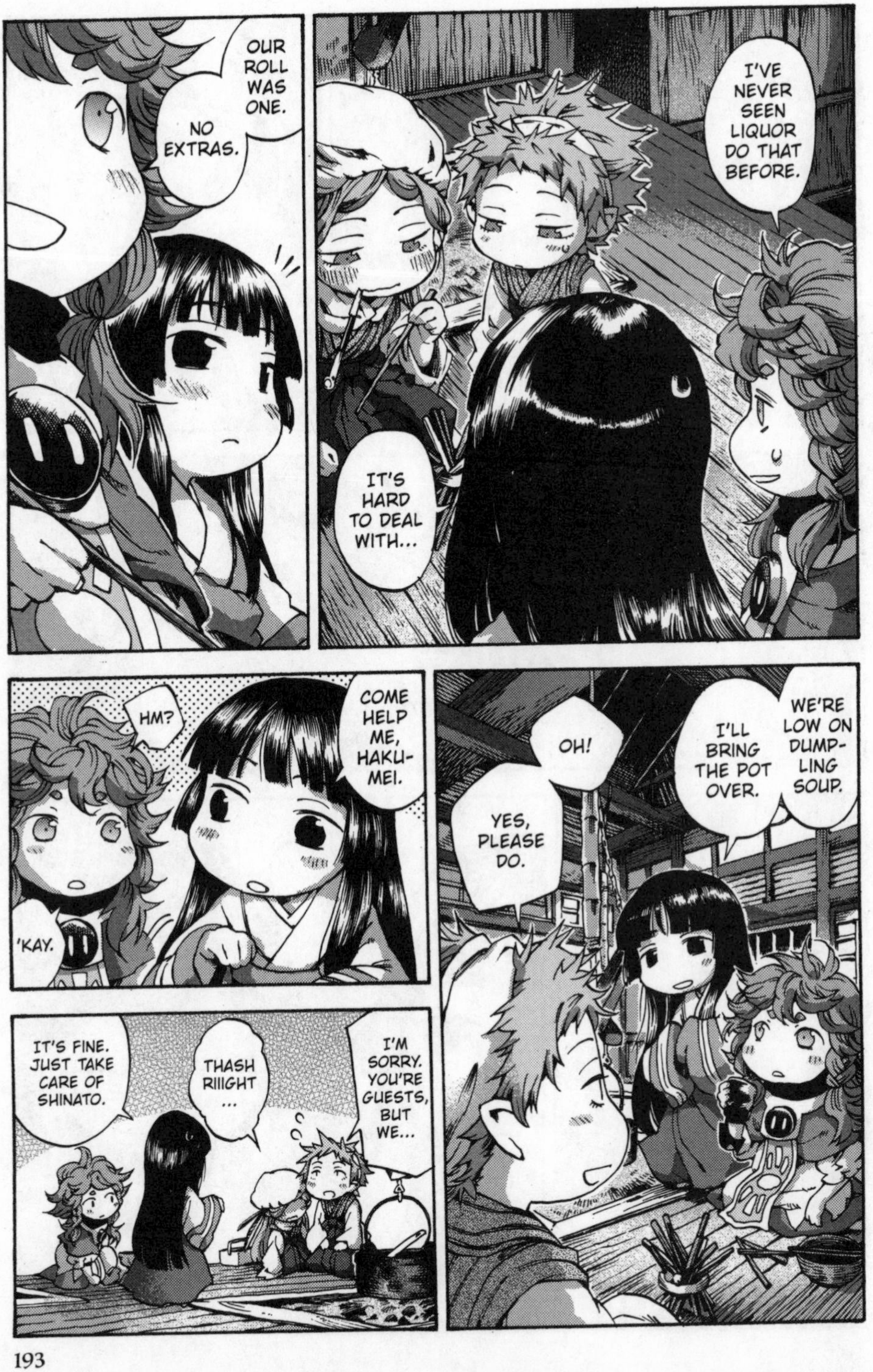
I'VE NEVER SEEN LIQUOR DO THAT BEFORE.
IT'S HARD TO DEAL WITH...
OUR ROLL WAS ONE.
NO EXTRAS.
WE'RE LOW ON DUMP-LING SOUP.
I'LL BRING THE POT OVER.
OH!
YES, PLEASE DO.
COME HELP ME, HAKU-MEI.
HM?
'KAY.
I'M SORRY. YOU'RE GUESTS, BUT WE...
THASH RIIIGHT ...
IT'S FINE. JUST TAKE CARE OF SHINATO.

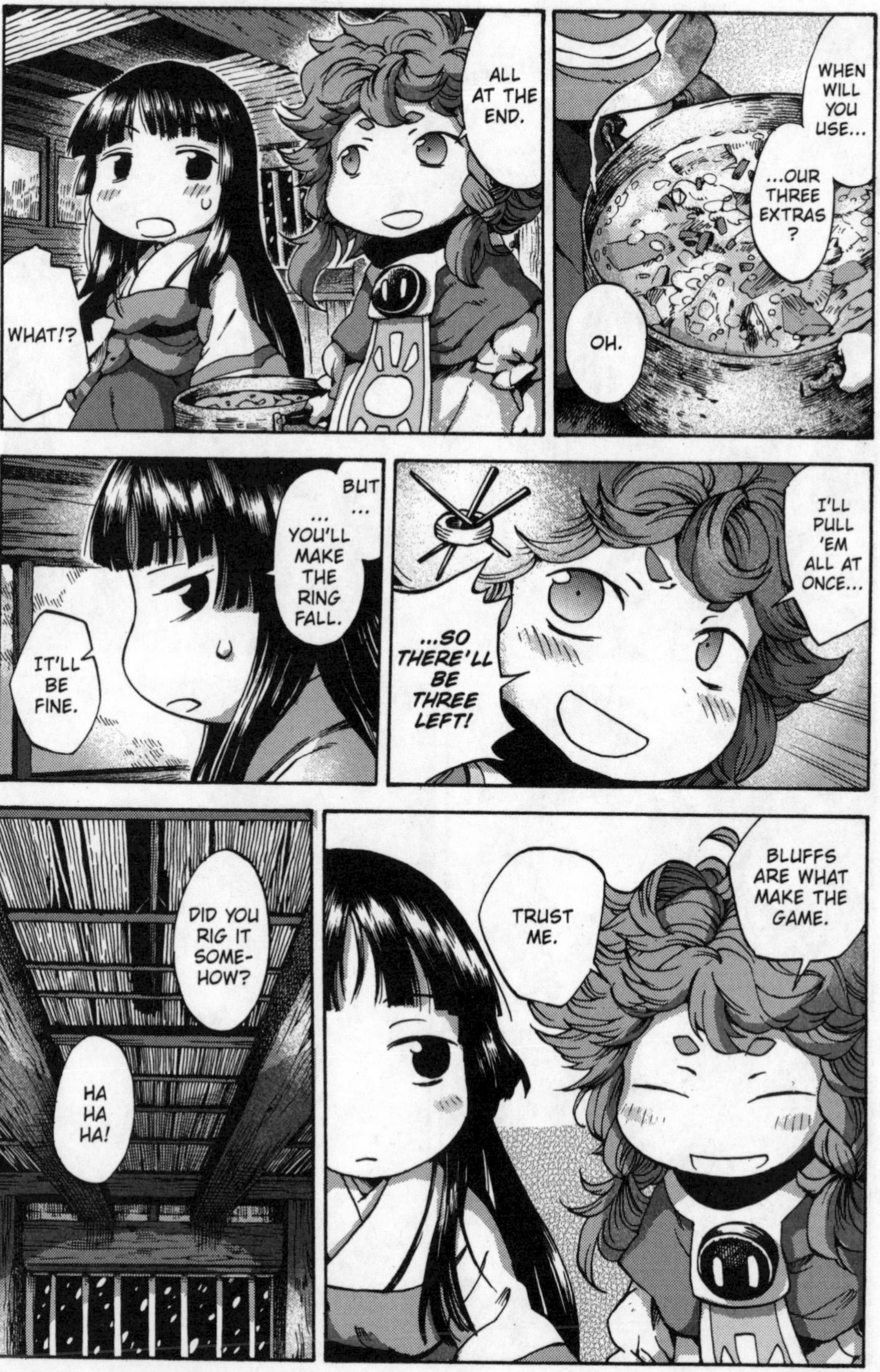
WHEN WILL YOU USE...
...OUR THREE EXTRAS ?
OH.
ALL AT THE END.
WHAT!?
I'LL PULL 'EM ALL AT ONCE...
...SO THERE'LL BE THREE LEFT!
BUT ... YOU'LL MAKE THE RING FALL.
IT'LL BE FINE.
BLUFFS ARE WHAT MAKE THE GAME.
TRUST ME.
DID YOU RIG IT SOME-HOW?
HA HA HA!

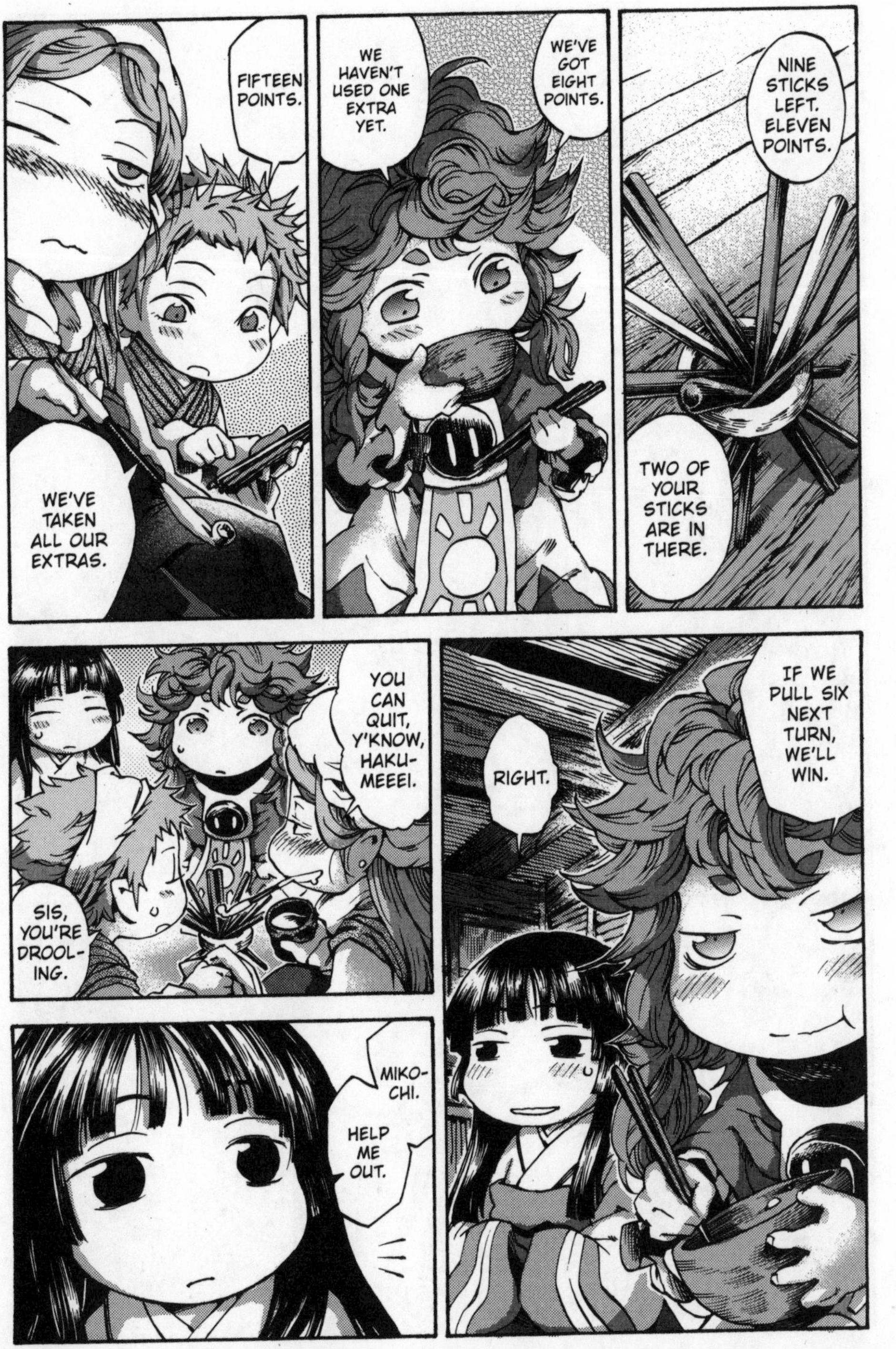
NINE STICKS LEFT. ELEVEN POINTS.
TWO OF YOUR STICKS ARE IN THERE.
WE'VE GOT EIGHT POINTS.
WE HAVEN'T USED ONE EXTRA YET.
FIFTEEN POINTS.
WE'VE TAKEN ALL OUR EXTRAS.
IF WE PULL SIX NEXT TURN, WE'LL WIN.
RIGHT.
YOU CAN QUIT, Y'KNOW, HAKU-MEEEI.
SIS, YOU'RE DROOL-ING.
MIKO-CHI.
HELP ME OUT.

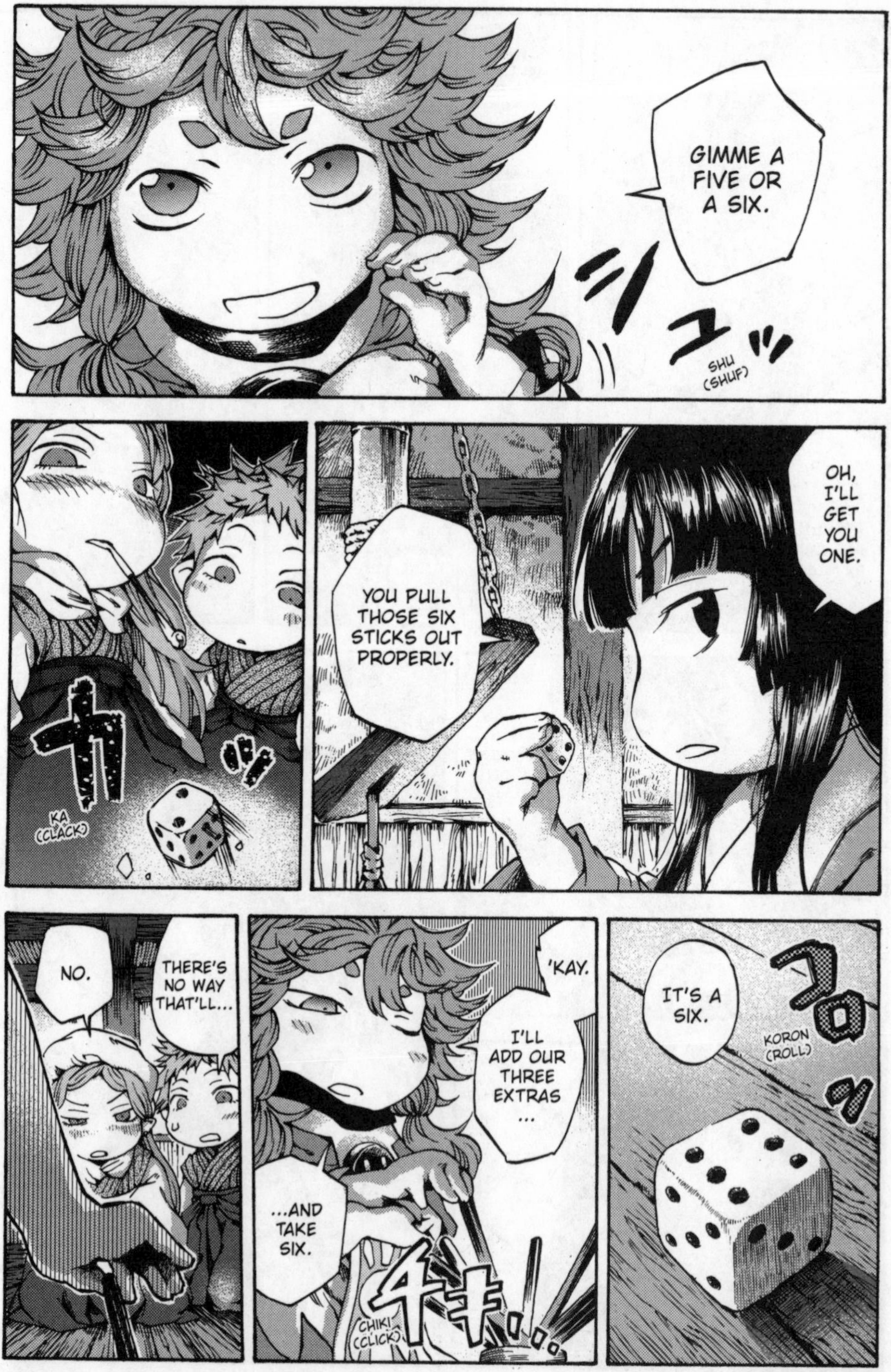
GIMME A FIVE OR A SIX.
SHU (SHUF)
OH, I'LL GET YOU ONE.
YOU PULL THOSE SIX STICKS OUT PROPERLY.
KA (CLACK)
IT'S A SIX.
KORON (ROLL)
'KAY.
I'LL ADD OUR THREE EXTRAS ...
...AND TAKE SIX.
CHIKI (CLICK)
THERE'S NO WAY THAT'LL...
NO.

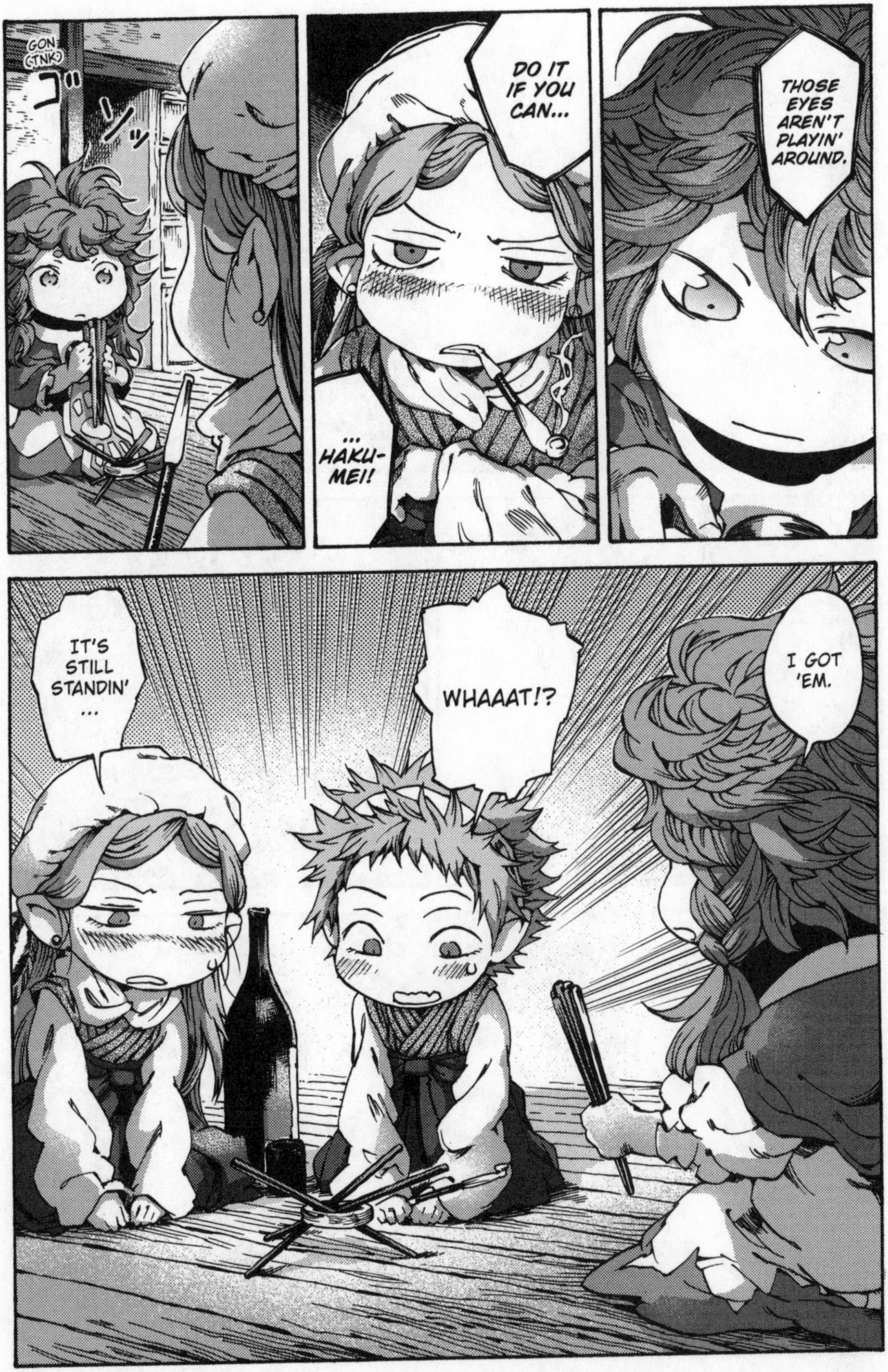
THOSE EYES AREN'T PLAYIN' AROUND.
DO IT IF YOU CAN...
...HAKU-MEI!
GON (TNK)
ゴンッ
I GOT 'EM.
WHAAAT!?
IT'S STILL STANDIN' ...

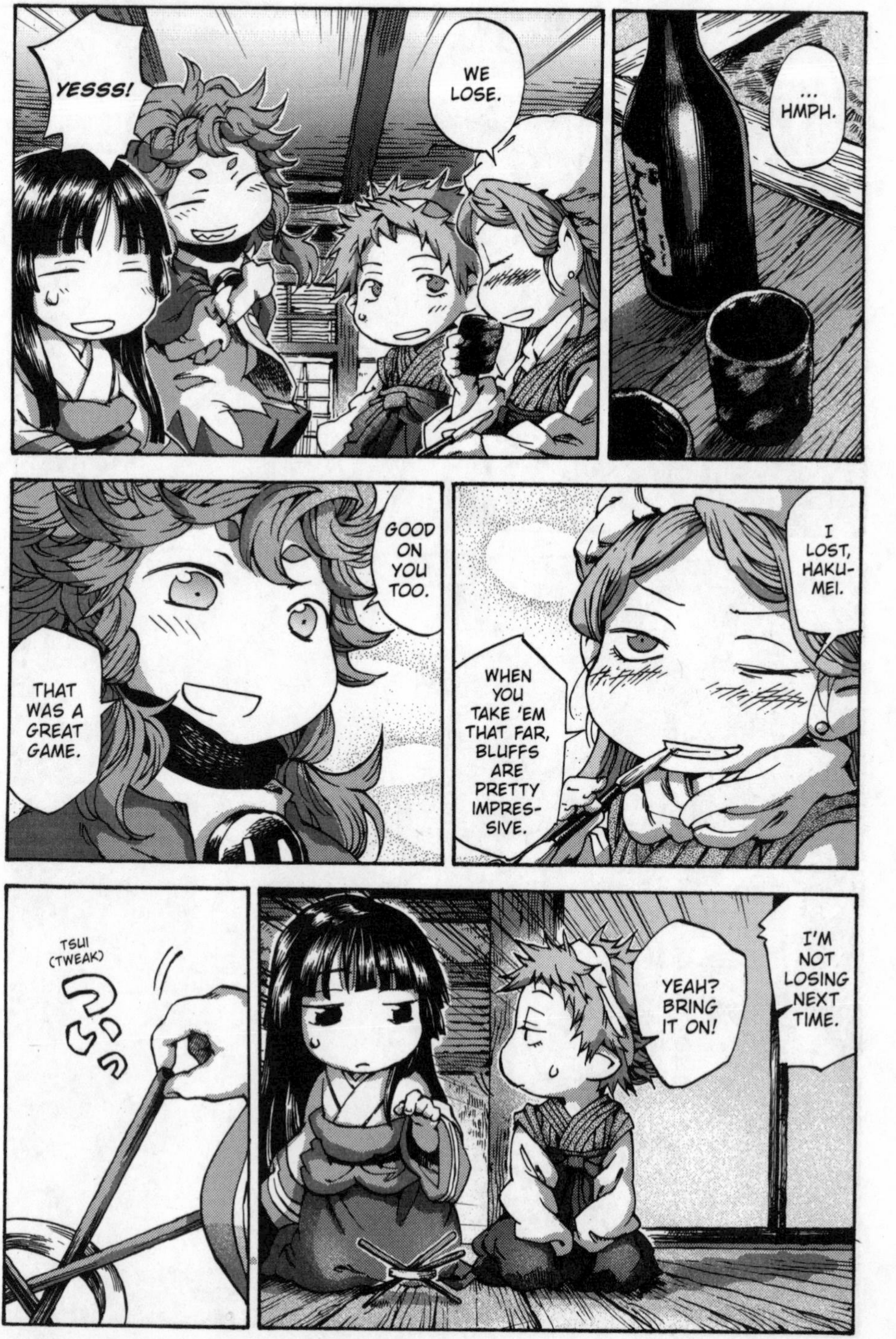
... HMPH.
WE LOSE.
YESSS!
I LOST, HAKU-MEI.
WHEN YOU TAKE 'EM THAT FAR, BLUFFS ARE PRETTY IMPRES-SIVE.
GOOD ON YOU TOO.
THAT WAS A GREAT GAME.
I'M NOT LOSING NEXT TIME.
YEAH? BRING IT ON!
TSUI (TWEAK)

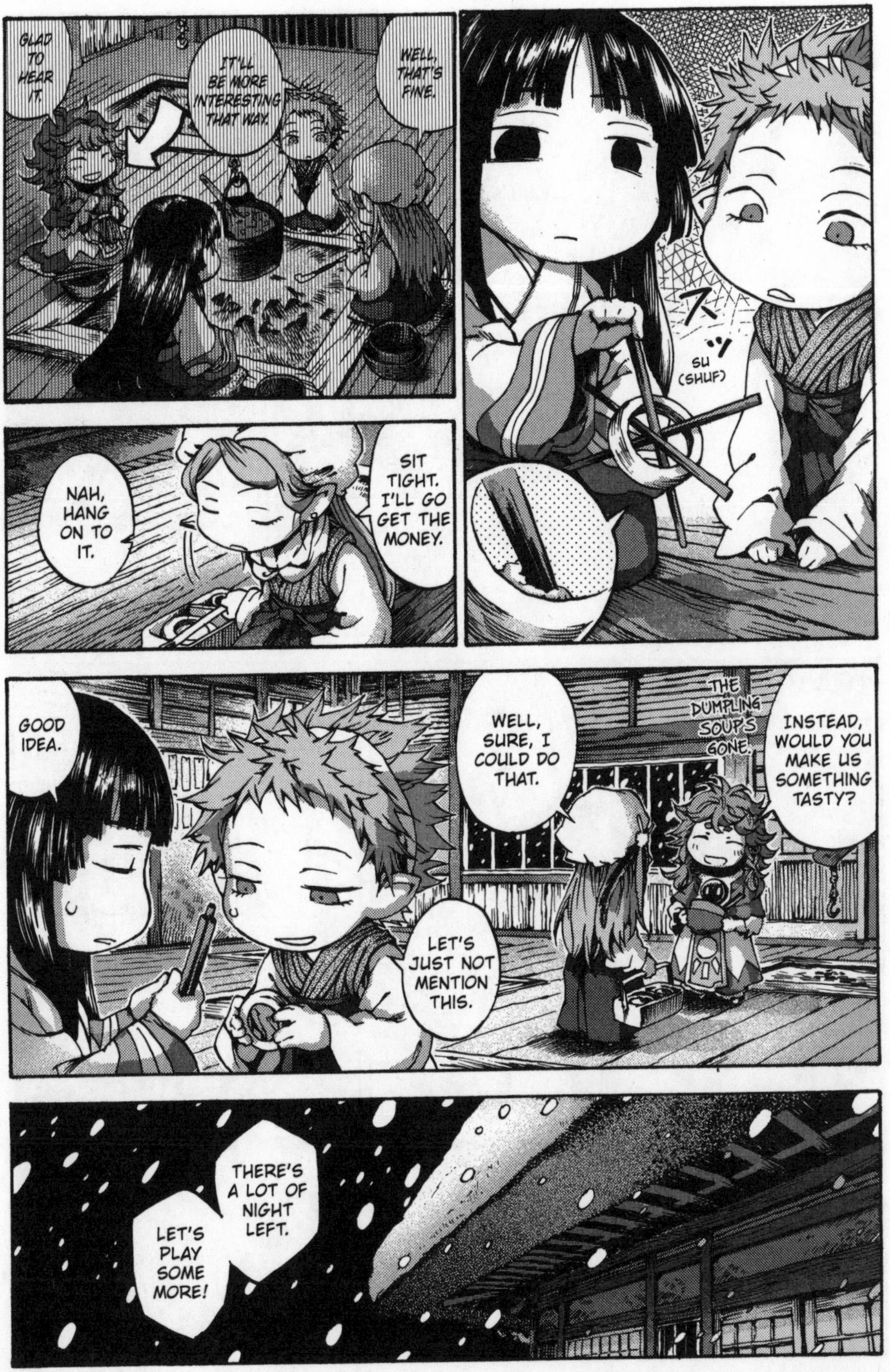
ス
ッ
SU (SHUF)
WELL, THAT'S FINE.
IT'LL BE MORE INTERESTING THAT WAY.
GLAD TO HEAR IT.
SIT TIGHT. I'LL GO GET THE MONEY.
NAH, HANG ON TO IT.
THE DUMPLING SOUP'S GONE.
INSTEAD, WOULD YOU MAKE US SOMETHING TASTY?
WELL, SURE, I COULD DO THAT.
LET'S JUST NOT MENTION THIS.
GOOD IDEA.
THERE'S A LOT OF NIGHT LEFT.
LET'S PLAY SOME MORE!

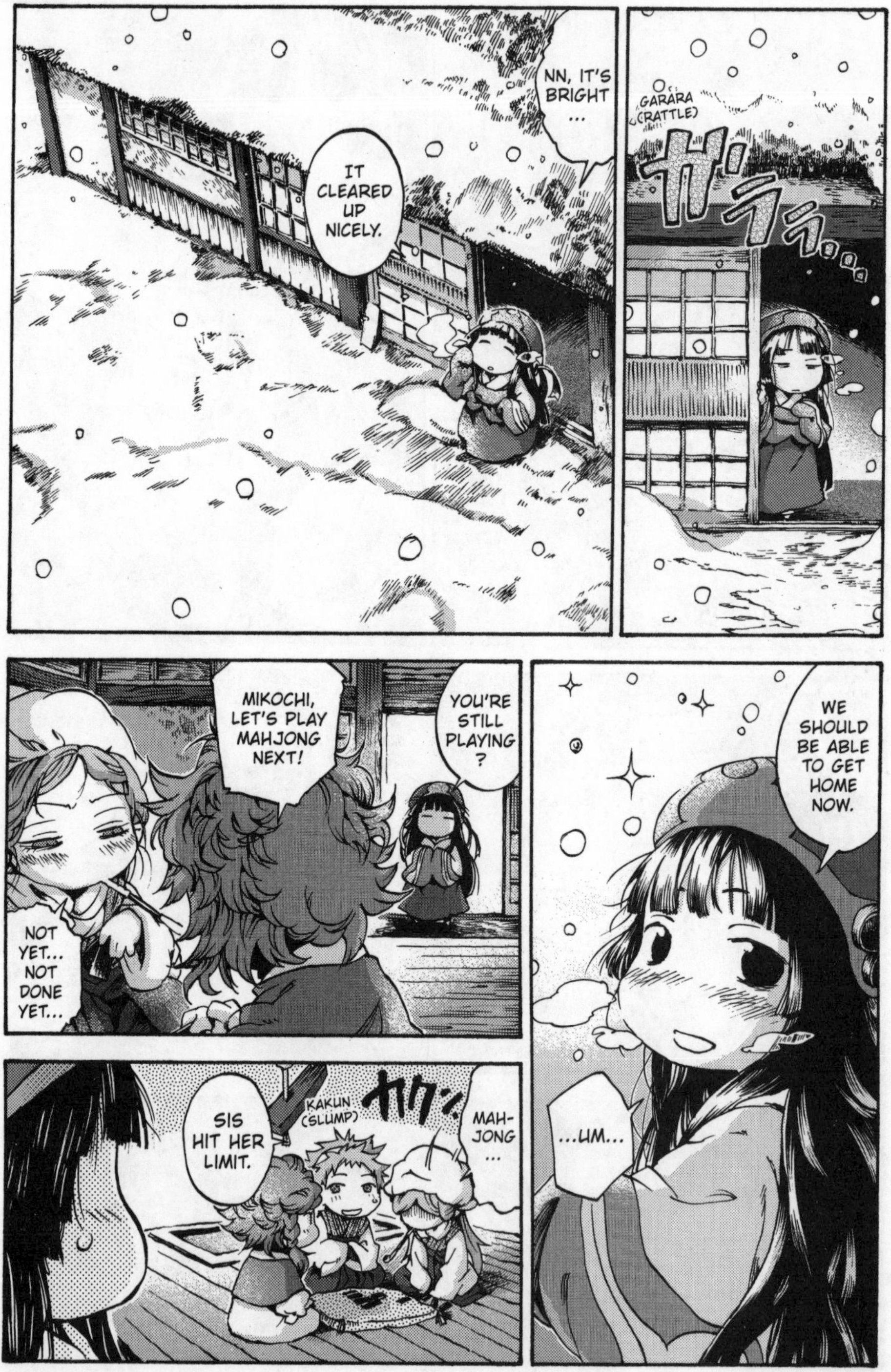
GARARA (RATTLE)
ガラララ...
NN, IT'S BRIGHT...
IT CLEARED UP NICELY.
WE SHOULD BE ABLE TO GET HOME NOW.
...UM...
YOU'RE STILL PLAYING?
MIKOCHI, LET'S PLAY MAHJONG NEXT!
NOT YET... NOT DONE YET...
MAH-JONG...
カクン
KAKUN (SLUMP)
SIS HIT HER LIMIT.

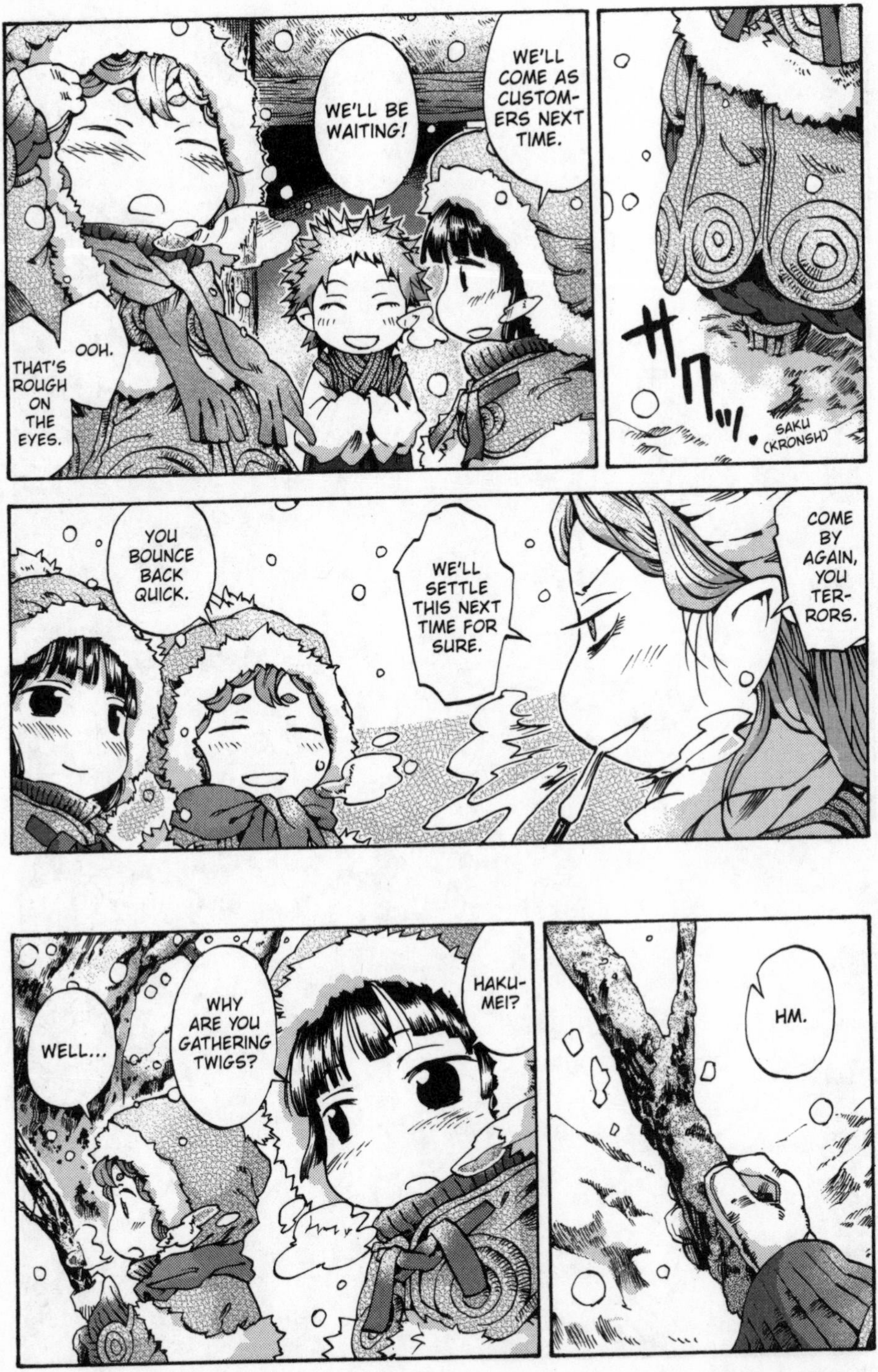
サクッ
SAKU (KRONSH)
WE'LL COME AS CUSTOMERS NEXT TIME.
WE'LL BE WAITING!
OOH. THAT'S ROUGH ON THE EYES.
COME BY AGAIN, YOU TERRORS.
WE'LL SETTLE THIS NEXT TIME FOR SURE.
YOU BOUNCE BACK QUICK.
HM.
HAKUMEI?
WHY ARE YOU GATHERING TWIGS?
WELL...

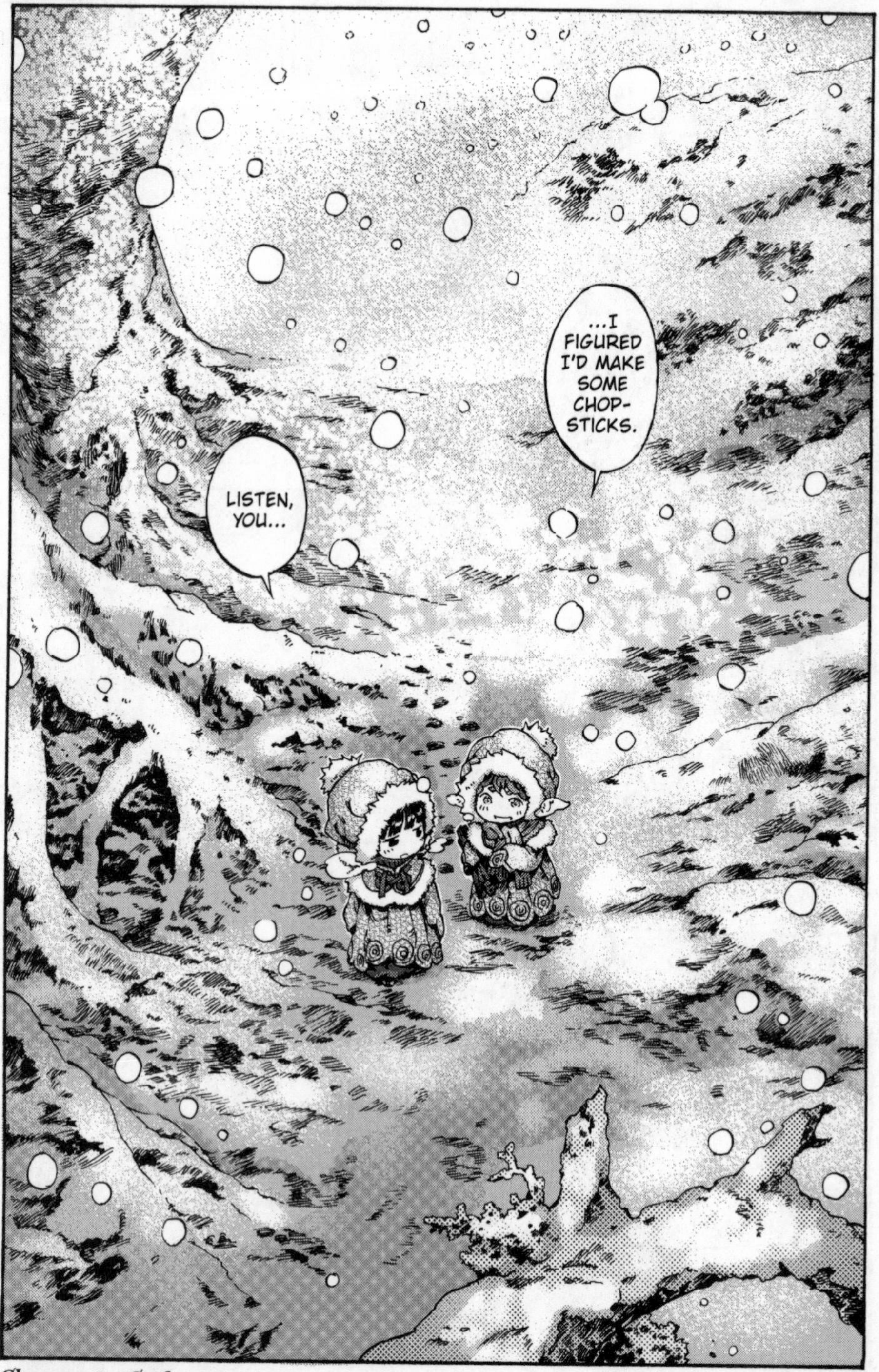
...I FIGURED I'D MAKE SOME CHOP-STICKS.
LISTEN, YOU...

Chapter 8 • End

•*Column*• Underfoot Steps 8 / Octopus Clothes

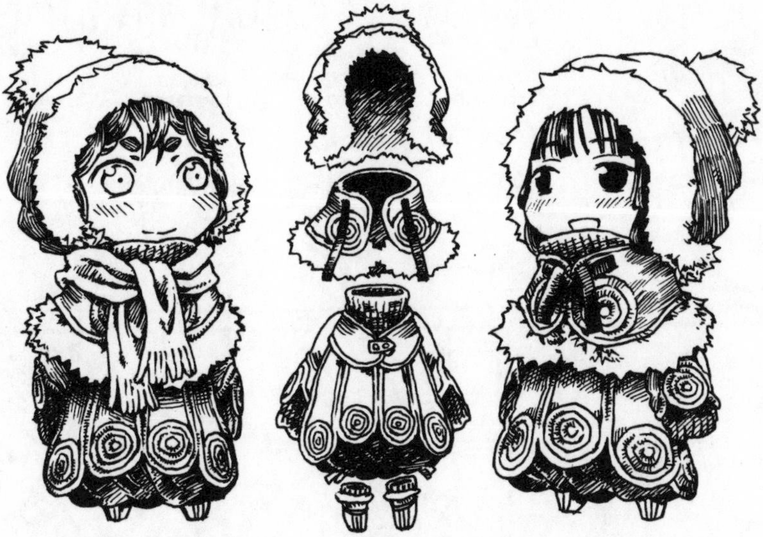

At Port Town Arabi, Hakumei tried octopus for the first time. The flavor made a profound impression on her, and so, she asked Mikochi to make this cold-weather gear. Since Mikochi had never seen a whole octopus before, she got the number of suckers wrong, but that's part of the charm.

The fabric is cotton from Arabi, dyed pink with safflowers. Mikochi sewed on each sucker and the decorative trim by hand, resulting in rather elaborate outfits.

The upper and lower halves are actually one piece (what people call a "coverall"), and apparently, they both wear long underwear beneath.

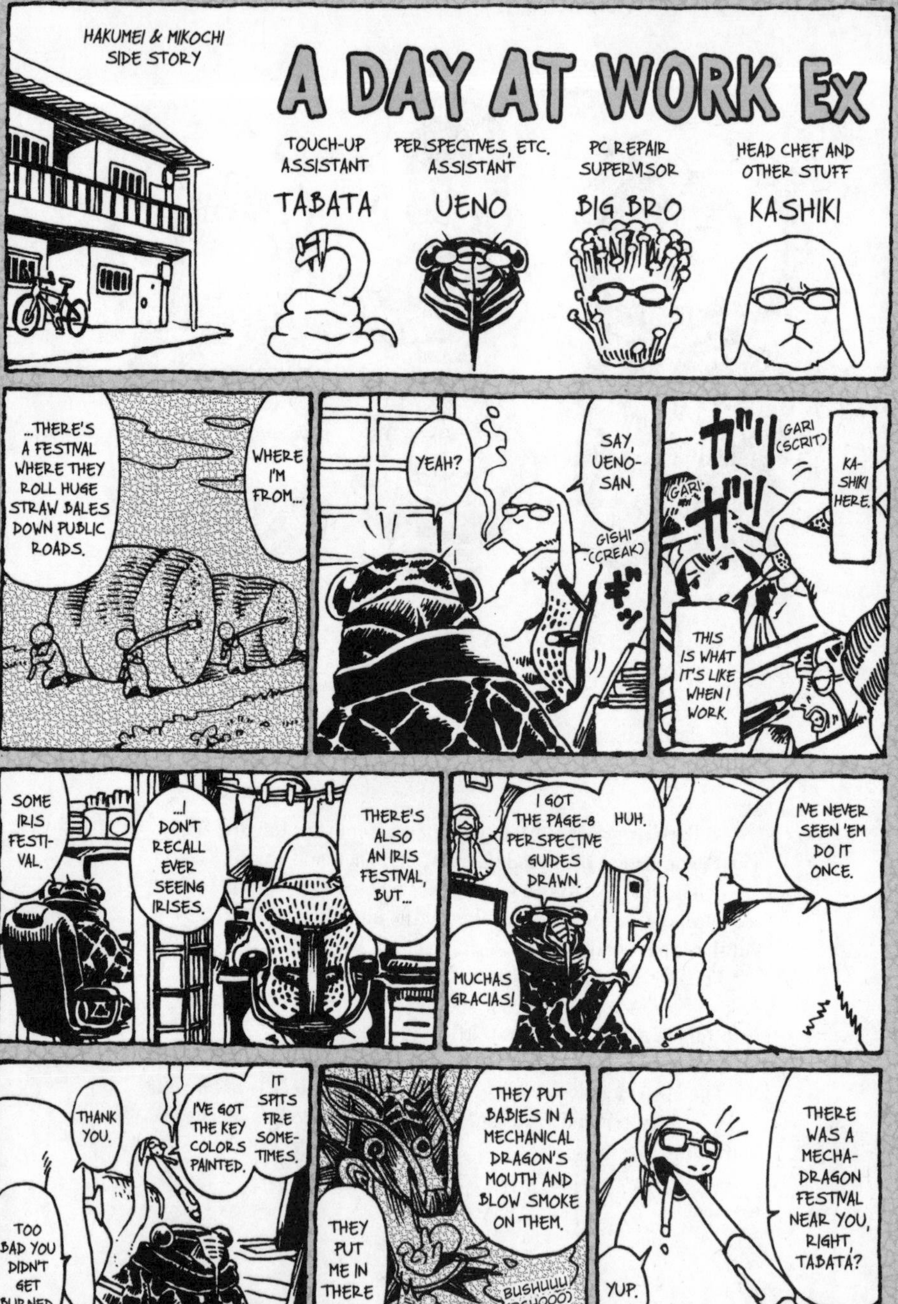
HAKUMEI & MIKOCHI SIDE STORY
A DAY AT WORK Ex
HEAD CHEF AND OTHER STUFF
KASHIKI
PC REPAIR SUPERVISOR
BIG BRO
PERSPECTIVES, ETC. ASSISTANT
UENO
TOUCH-UP ASSISTANT
TABATA
KASHIKI HERE.
GARI (SCRIT)
GARI
THIS IS WHAT IT'S LIKE WHEN I WORK.
SAY, UENO-SAN.
YEAH?
GISHI (CREAK)
WHERE I'M FROM...
...THERE'S A FESTIVAL WHERE THEY ROLL HUGE STRAW BALES DOWN PUBLIC ROADS.
I'VE NEVER SEEN 'EM DO IT ONCE.
HUH.
I GOT THE PAGE-8 PERSPECTIVE GUIDES DRAWN.
MUCHAS GRACIAS!
THERE'S ALSO AN IRIS FESTIVAL, BUT...
...I DON'T RECALL EVER SEEING IRISES.
SOME IRIS FESTIVAL.
THERE WAS A MECHA-DRAGON FESTIVAL NEAR YOU, RIGHT, TABATA?
YUP.
THEY PUT BABIES IN A MECHANICAL DRAGON'S MOUTH AND BLOW SMOKE ON THEM.
THEY PUT ME IN THERE TOO.
BUSHUUU (PSHOOO)
IT SPITS FIRE SOMETIMES.
I'VE GOT THE KEY COLORS PAINTED.
THANK YOU.
TOO BAD YOU DIDN'T GET BURNED.

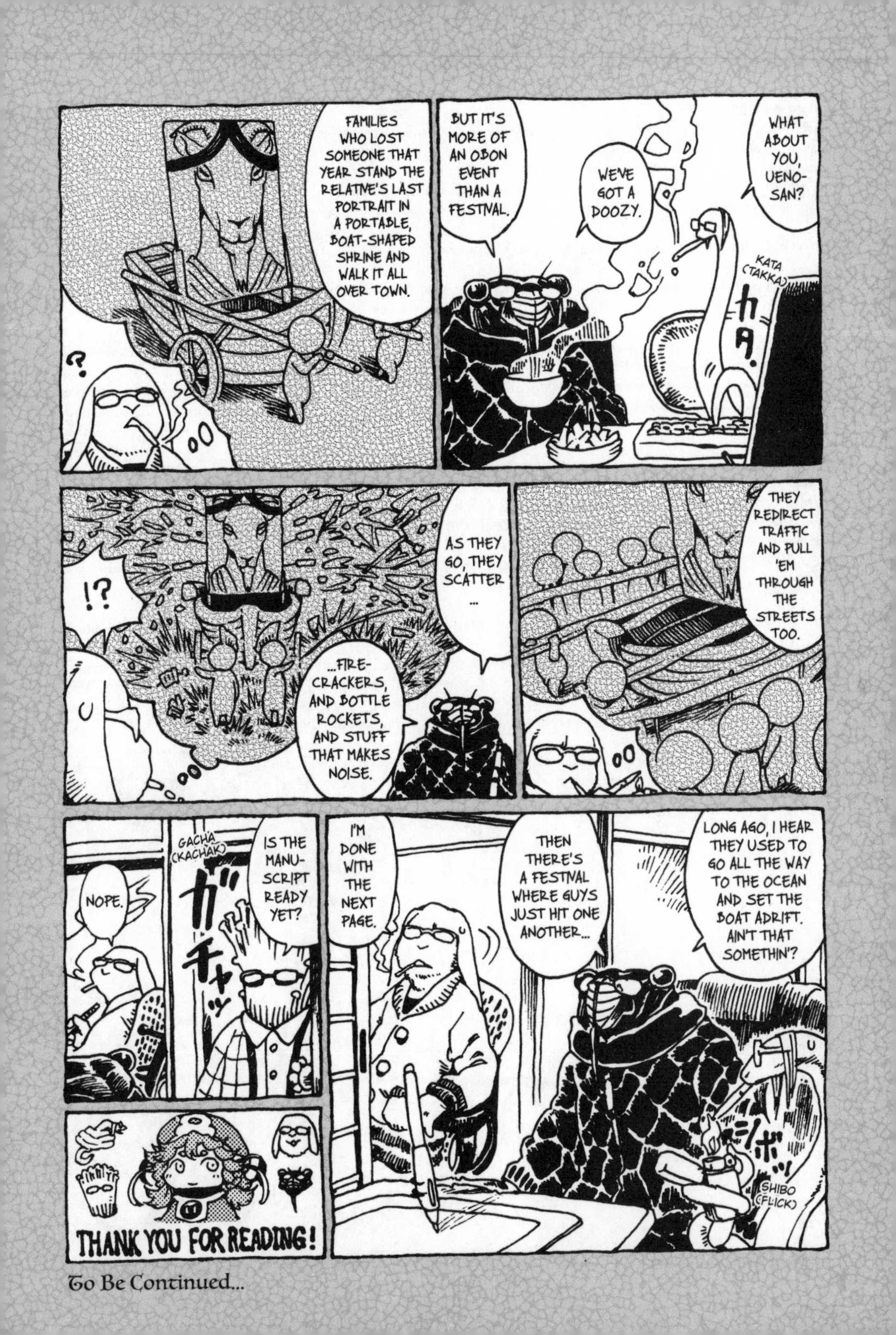
WHAT ABOUT YOU, UENO-SAN?
KATA (TAKKA)
WE'VE GOT A DOOZY.
BUT IT'S MORE OF AN OBON EVENT THAN A FESTIVAL.
FAMILIES WHO LOST SOMEONE THAT YEAR STAND THE RELATIVE'S LAST PORTRAIT IN A PORTABLE, BOAT-SHAPED SHRINE AND WALK IT ALL OVER TOWN.
?
THEY REDIRECT TRAFFIC AND PULL 'EM THROUGH THE STREETS TOO.
AS THEY GO, THEY SCATTER ...
...FIRE-CRACKERS, AND BOTTLE ROCKETS, AND STUFF THAT MAKES NOISE.
!?
LONG AGO, I HEAR THEY USED TO GO ALL THE WAY TO THE OCEAN AND SET THE BOAT ADRIFT. AIN'T THAT SOMETHIN'?
THEN THERE'S A FESTIVAL WHERE GUYS JUST HIT ONE ANOTHER...
SHIBO (FLICK)
I'M DONE WITH THE NEXT PAGE.
IS THE MANU-SCRIPT READY YET?
GACHA (KACHAK)
NOPE.
THANK YOU FOR READING!

To Be Continued...

Translation Notes

Common Honorifics

no honorific: Indicates familiarity or closeness; if used without permission or reason, addressing someone in this manner would constitute an insult.

-san: The Japanese equivalent of Mr./Mrs./Miss. If a situation calls for politeness, this is the fail-safe honorific.

-chan: An affectionate honorific indicating familiarity used mostly in reference to girls; also used in reference to cute persons or animals of either gender.

Currency conversion: Although exchange rates fluctuate daily, a good general estimate is ¥100 to 1USD.

Page 32: Both *anaguma* and *mujina* (the name of the establishment that runs this street stall) mean "badger," though, in this case, *mujina* is written with the characters meaning "dream goods."

Page 40: **Artifact spirits**, or *tsukumo-gami*, are a type of *youkai* ("spirit creature") in Japanese folklore. Household objects and utensils that have been used for a long time (some traditions specify one hundred years) acquire souls and become *youkai*. It is generally believed that any attempt to thwart this outcome by discarding an object before it acquires its soul will only result in angry *youkai*, and some Shinto shrines hold ceremonies to console broken or unusable objects.

Page 59: **Deer scares** are a common feature of traditional gardens in Japan. They're bamboo tubes that are plugged at one end and placed on a pivot; a slow trickle of water flows into the mouth of the tube until the weight of the water tips the tube over, at which point it strikes against a rock, making a clacking sound that's supposed to frighten deer away (to keep them from eating the plants). Since the tube is tipped down, the water flows out, and as it gets lighter, it rights itself. The cycle repeats automatically and regularly, so it would be a good sound source for Sen. However, if it usually runs on evening dew, the cycle will be extremely slow; a rainy day would make it go much, much faster than George is used to, causing him to have "mood swings."

Page 66: In Japan, people often have a small, official **stamp** of their name, which can be used to "sign" documents.

Page 123: The plethora of **signs** on this page and elsewhere in this chapter include (but are not limited to) "Fountain," "Firefly Lamps," "Medicine Wholesaler," "Aureole Restaurant," "Surf Mice," "Swift Mountain Restaurant," "The Great Man," "—sold by weight," "Pentagon Island," "Tsukudani West," "Fortress Shoppe," "Yakuzen" (cooking that incorporates ingredients/elements from traditional Chinese medicine), and "Rice Bowls."

Page 124: The **circled characters** you see on signs throughout the market are the first character in the owner's family name, like an initial.

Page 127: ***Arani*** is the head and other bony parts of a fish boiled in soy sauce.

Page 132: *Fuusen* means "balloon," while *-maru* is a common suffix for male names. As previously noted, the "wind" character on **Fuusenmaru**'s shop sign is the first character in his name.

Page 134: ***Tsukudani*** is a small portion of seafood, meat, or seaweed slowly simmered in soy sauce, mirin, and sugar as a way of preserving it. It keeps for a very long time, and since the flavor is quite strong, a small amount is usually eaten with steamed rice as a condiment.

Page 138: ***Temari*** (or "handball") **sushi** is sushi molded into the shape of a small ball, shown in the top box in the third panel. **Pressed sushi** is made by lining the bottom of a special (usually wooden) box with sushi toppings, covering them with a layer of sushi rice, then pressing down with the lid of the mold, creating a clean-edged "block" of sushi, as pictured at the bottom of the third panel. In pressed sushi, all ingredients are either cooked or cured; no raw fish is used.

Page 144: ***Sekimen*** means "red face."

Page 145: ***Kasujiru*** is a soup made with sake lees, the sediment that is left over from the sake-making process. ***Namerou*** is a dish made of raw, minced fish or meat mixed with spices.

Page 146: ***Shiso***, or perilla, is an aromatic, grassy-flavored plant, the leaves of which are used widely in Japanese cuisine. ***Yuzu*** and ***sudachi*** are both types of citrus fruit. ***Kintoki*** is a type of large-eyed fish called "long-finned bulls'-eyes" in English.

Page 155: The *kikyuu* in fisherman tanuki **Kikyuumaru**'s name means "balloon," just like *fuusen* does in Fuusenmaru.

Page 177: ***Dengaku*** is tofu or fish that's baked, then coated with miso paste. ***Robata-yaki*** is a cooking method where food is grilled out in the open, in front of customers. It evolved from a very old style of cooking that was done over an ***irori***, a sunken hearth like the one shown on the title page of this chapter.

Page 180: ***Dai siu*** is also known as *sic bo* in China, where it originated. It's a game of chance played with three dice, and players place various bets with varying odds based on the total score or a specific number combination. In this case, a bet was made on the outcome of the dice showing three out of four preselected numbers.

Page 181: ***Shochu*** is a distilled liquor that can be made from a variety of base ingredients, including sweet potatoes, barley, rice, buckwheat, and sugarcane. It has a higher alcohol content than sake.

Page 182: If you burn **charcoal** without washing off the surface dust first, the charcoal crackles and pops and puts burn marks on your floor. The charcoal is submerged and agitated in a bucket of water, then allowed to dry completely for at least a day.

Page 205: **Obon** is a Japanese Buddhist custom held to honor families' ancestral spirits. The festival lasts for three days and takes place in late summer (mid-August in most of Japan, mid-July in the Kanto region), with the starting date varying by region. For the three days of the festival, the spirits of a family's ancestors are believed to return to the family's household altar, and people visit and tend to their ancestors' graves.

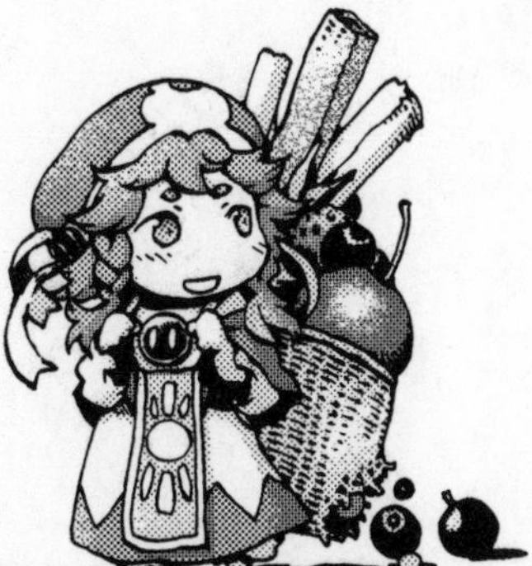

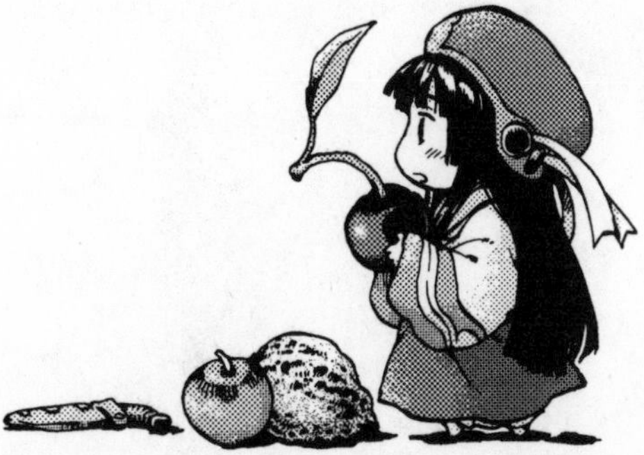

Hakumei & Mikochi 1
Tiny Little Life in the Woods

✄ Takuto Kashiki ✄

Translation: TAYLOR ENGEL   ❧   *Lettering:* ABIGAIL BLACKMAN

HAKUMEI TO MIKOCHI Volume 1
© Takuto Kashiki 2013
First published in Japan in 2013 by KADOKAWA CORPORATION, Tokyo.
English translation rights arranged with KADOKAWA CORPORATION, Tokyo through TUTTLE-MORI AGENCY, Inc., Tokyo.

English translation © 2018 by Yen Press, LLC

Yen Press
1290 Avenue of the Americas
New York, NY 10104

Visit us at yenpress.com
facebook.com/yenpress
twitter.com/yenpress
yenpress.tumblr.com
instagram.com/yenpress

First Yen Press Edition: July 2018

Yen Press is an imprint of Yen Press, LLC.
The Yen Press name and logo are trademarks of Yen Press, LLC.

The publisher is not responsible for websites (or their content) that are not owned by the publisher.

Library of Congress Control Number: 2018941284

ISBN: 978-1-9753-8118-9

10 9 8 7 6 5 4 3 2

WOR

Printed in the United States of America